THE NATURE OF HUMAN SOCIETY

THE THIRD WORLD

THE NATURE OF HUMAN SOCIETY SERIES

Editors: *Julian Pitt-Rivers and Ernest Gellner*

THE THIRD WORLD
Peter Worsley

Second Edition

THE UNIVERSITY OF CHICAGO PRESS

THE UNIVERSITY OF CHICAGO PRESS, CHICAGO 60637

George Weidenfeld and Nicolson Ltd., London W.1

© *1964, 1967 by Peter Worsley. All rights reserved*
Published 1964. Second American edition 1970
Second Impression 1972

International Standard Book Number: 0-226-90751-1 (clothbound)
Library of Congress Catalog Card Number: 74-124639
Printed in the United States of America

CONTENTS

TABLES

ACKNOWLEDGMENTS

VARIOUS FRIENDS and colleagues were kind enough to read the manuscript of the present book: their comments were always useful and encouraging. I thank Ernest Gellner, in particular, for his interest. Edward Thompson's critical inspection was extremely valuable, as were those of Michael Barratt-Brown and John Saville. I am sure they will still find much to criticize. Perry Anderson and his 'équipe', Robert Dowse, Max Gluckman, and Victor Turner all read various versions of the manuscript, and – though they probably do not know it – Tom Bottomore and Ronald Dore helped me a great deal in brief informal discussions.

Special thanks are due to Eileen Lee for typing from an involved original so accurately, even under threat of appendicitis; to Christine Jackson for various kindnesses; to Valerie Gribbin, for her meticulousness in tracking down scores of incomplete references and for preparing the Bibliography; and to the Library Staff of Hull University. Finally, I wish to thank my wife, Sheila Worsley, for her patience in putting up with two years' academic abstractedness during the writing of this book.

The excellent translation of the Senghor poem 'New York' is from *Modern Poetry from Africa* (Penguin African Library, 1962). All other translations are by myself, in consultation with Donald Charlton and Paul Ginestier when things became difficult. Professor G. McT. Kahin kindly allowed me to cite passages from Dr Mohammad Hatta's *Past and Future* and President Soekarno's *Marhaen and Proletarian*.

'Ah,' said the King, and then he began to speak. . . . 'I feel there is a law of human nature in which force is concerned. Man is a creature who cannot stand still under blows. Now take the horse – he never needs a revenge. Nor the ox. But man is a creature of revenges. If he is punished he will contrive to get rid of the punishment. When he cannot get rid of punishment, his heart is liable to rot from it. . . . Brother raises a hand against brother and son against father (how terrible!) and the father also against son. And moreover it is a continuity-matter, for if the father did not strike the son, they would not be alike. It is done to perpetuate similarity. Oh, Henderson, man cannot keep still under the blows. If he must, for the time, he will cast down his eyes and think in silence of the ways to clear himself of them. Those prime-eval blows everybody still feels. The first was supposed to be struck by Cain, but how could that be? In the beginning of time there was a hand raised which struck. So the people are flinching yet. All wish to rid themselves and free themselves and cast the blow upon the others. And this I conceive of as the earthly dominion. But as for the truth content of this force, that is a separate matter.' . . .

I said to him, 'You want to know something, Your Highness, there are some guys who can return good for evil. Even I understand that.' . . . Curiously, I saw that he agreed with me. He was glad I had said this. 'Every brave man will think so,' he told me. 'He will not want to live by passing on the wrath. A hit B? B hit C? – we have not enough alphabet to cover the condition. A brave man will try to make the evil stop with him. He shall keep the blow. No man shall get it from him, and that is a sublime ambition. So, a fellow throws himself in the sea of blows saying he do not believe it is infinite. In this way many courageous people have died. But an even larger number who had more of impatience than bravery. Who have said, "Enough of this burden of wrath. I cannot bear my neck should be unfree. I cannot eat more of this mess of fear-pottage."' . . .

'I also subscribe, but it appears a long way off, for the human species as a whole. Perhaps I am not the one to make a prediction . . . but I think the noble will have its turn in the world.' . . .

I was really sent, and I mean it. The king treated me with classic African dignity, and this is one of the summits of human behaviour. . . .

SAUL BELLOW – *Henderson the Rain King* (Weidenfeld and Nicolson, 1959).

FOREWORD

THE LATE C. WRIGHT MILLS warned us all against the equally unrewarding temptations of 'abstracted empiricism' on the one hand, and 'Grand' or encyclopaedic theories of History and Man on the other. His life's work, instead, concentrated on enhancing our awareness of the way in which the lives of all of us are affected – even in our 'face-to-face' personal relationships – by the major movements of our time. Through such a heightened awareness, he hoped, we could the more effectively resist organized pressures that bear upon us, and more effectively, too, exercise human agency rather than submit to the apparently uncontrolled 'drift' of events.

Analytically, this basic distinction between 'abstracted empiricism' and 'Grand Theory' is as applicable to British sociology as to American. But substantively, another great division of labour appears to have grown up. There are now two main kinds of sociologist in this country: those who think sociology is about affluence in America, and those who think it is about poverty in Britain.

This book is addressed to neither school. Both of them, it is true, are concerned with large and important issues. Yet unless conceived of within a wider framework, these approaches can be no more than parochial obsessions. I am writing, instead, to try and help stimulate a dialogue with those who are becoming increasingly concerned with the central world-fact of the gulf between what, for shorthand, I have called Euro-America (i.e. *North* America) and the rest of the world. The only other problem of this scale of importance is the existence of the Bomb: a subject equally untouched by orthodox sociology.

My 'Third World' excludes the Communist countries, in contradistinction to the use of the term elsewhere, particularly in France, not because I do not recognize that most Communist countries share similar problems to those faced by the countries discussed in this book, but because the latter do constitute a distinctly different set of political cultures. Moreover, the non-Communist 'Third World' is quite enough for one book. For this reason also, I have only touched upon Latin American problems in one or two places. But I recognize that the connections exist.

There is a further reason, however, why I believe that this subject needs opening up – an intellectual reason. Any researcher studying any area of human relationships on whatever scale can set out to raise important problematic issues: few do. Yet we have devoted so little attention to the Third World that the problems lie thickest in those fields.

I have therefore deliberately eschewed writing a work which proves that working-class children have less opportunity to become Cabinet Ministers than children from public schools, or that millions of people in Britain are still poor. Investigations of this kind are very necessary, since the obvious is often denied or neglected. But they are *not* intellectually challenging. They are, rather, demonstrations of what is abundantly evident from everyday experience and from rich documentation. The obvious, however, is often assiduously proved. It is for this reason, largely, that in the United States the sociologist had been described as a man who spends $50,000 to find the way to a whorehouse.

Nor have I refrained from moving beyond analysis to recommendation, particularly in the final chapter, though I believe the sources for the factual documentation underlying both my analysis and my interpretations are adequately indicated. For those who find this a confusion of roles, I can only observe that just as, according to Clemenceau, war is too important a matter to be left to generals, so human survival is far too important a matter to be left to politicians. Those who do not approve of this attitude can always follow the precedent of one whom many (not myself) regard as the 'father' of sociology, Auguste Comte: after Chapter V, they can practise 'cerebral hygiene'.

Hull   PETER WORSLEY

[*29 September, 1963*]

PREFACE TO THE SECOND EDITION

IT has been said that the teacher of today – all too often – is teaching what he learned possibly two generations ago, out of textbooks that were written decades before. Today, the problem is far worse: the rate and volume of production of knowledge, and the rate of change of style of intellectual inquiry, both appear to be increasing exponentially. It was this situation that led the late Robert Oppenheimer to observe that of all the natural scientists who had ever lived, 93 per cent of them were alive at the present moment, and contributing to knowledge; and to quote Casimir's observation that if the *Physical Review* went on increasing at its present rate, it would come to weigh more than the earth during the next century.[1] This statistical fancy enshrines an important truth. In the social sciences, the situation is even worse: not only is there an ever-increasing volume of literary production, but the subject-matter researched into, mainly the contemporary world, itself changes so rapidly. Even the past changes, as new sources, new techniques, new frameworks of analysis, transform historiography.

To bring up to date a work dealing with the 'Third World', involves little short of total re-writing. Indeed, much of the data one uses is *dépassé* by the time a book appears in print, if only because one depends upon publications which themselves normally appear well after the events they describe. More analytical works necessarily involve study over longer time-sequences, and slower processes of digestion, so that the interval before publication is even greater. Further, the writing and publication of a manuscript entails more delay, even for the swiftest of writers and the best-regulated of publishing organizations.

To be 'up to the minute', however, was anything but the aim of this book; rather, to take a look at the general, long-term, and

[1] Robert Oppenheimer, 'On Science and Culture', *Encounter*, Vol. XIX, No. 4, pp. 5.

often secular processes of change that, even in our rapidly-changing world, still take decades to work themselves out.

In this edition, therefore, I have let the original body of the text stand as it was written. The argument would not be enhanced simply by superficial 'up-dating': by replacing the figures for 1962–3 with those for 1967, or by adding in some new facts. It seemed more valuable to essay an overview of recent developments rather than merely 'modernizing' details. Much has become clearer, particularly in countries which had only been independent for two or three years when I wrote. The reader can judge for himself how worthwhile the effort has been, and will be able to evaluate the continuity (or lack of it) between the analysis presented in the new 'Postscript' Chapter, and the argument of the original. This procedure has the virtue of being more honest, and more intellectually illuminating, since, plainly, the new chapter is less sanguine then the original.

But prognostications, extrapolations, or prophecies about the future were not the aim of the original work either. I hoped, rather, that however much the reader might dissent from the conclusions reached, he might have been stimulated to look at his own contemporary society in a global context, with a greater consciousness of time-depth. The pressures of the immediate present are very real and dominating, for all of us. For academics, the pressure towards concentrating on scholarly, detailed and specialized studies are so intense that few resist them. Without detailed studies, of course, generalizing works cannot be written. This is the main trouble with the political sociology of underdeveloped countries today: it is all too commonly 'airport sociology', in which distinguished academics fly from country to country, interviewing leaders in offices and hotels, and never come into contact at all with the life led in the villages. The traditional, tried and true, methodological strength of social anthropology (the narrowness of whose *substantive* concerns I have criticized elsewhere), – the power it derives from 'participant observation', and from grassroots detailed inquiry, in depth and over time – is indeed badly needed in contemporary sociology and political science. Some at least, then, of the shortcomings of this book derive from the inadequacy of the sources one has to use, *faute de mieux*.

I have no desire, therefore, to represent 'intensive' studies as wholly distinct from 'generalizing' research or, indeed, to make this distinction at all. (I have, in fact, spent a year studying a society of only 450 individuals.) The nineteenth-century distinction between 'idiographic' and 'nomothetic' studies, or the modern variant 'descriptive' v. 'theoretical' are not only logically fallacious, but practically-scientifically sterilizing. All description involves selection, classification, generalization. 'Nomothetic' work cannot be generated without empirical raw material in and from which patterns are derived. The ideal scientific desideratum, rather, is to abolish the distinction altogether. In lieu, we should aim at analyses of limited situations – situations which may be very narrow or very large in scale – but *all* carried out, if not *sub specie aeternitas*, at least in the light of general theoretical problems, to which the research is always related and in the light of which it is always designed. Narrowness in time, minuteness of scale, restriction in space, need not mean narrowness of theoretical vision. Equally, our theorising activities should always be anchored to, and located within, empirical inquiry. Lest anyone think theory and detailed close-textured empirical investigation to be incompatible, I urge him to look at the dialectic of scientific procedure used in Jean Piaget's classic study of *The Moral Judgment of the Child*, in which a sophisticated theory of ethics is developed from the study of humble games of marbles in Swiss schoolyards, but this particular strategy of inquiry is itself suggested by prior and sophisticated methodological cogitation. The contrast between this book and the style of Diana and Peter Opie's wonderful and entrancing compendium of *The Language and Lore of School-children* points up the difference between designed scientific, analytical research, and 'collecting' within only implicit categories, on the other.

To see the general in the particular is one aspect of scientific procedure: to move from the face-to-face level and short-term sequences of events to the study of world macro-processes is another aspect of the same needed vision, achieved only very rarely in social science in a few writings such as William Foot Whyte's *Street Corner Society*, which takes us from corner-gangs in a New World Italian city-slum to the national level of Republican and Democratic politics – and even the international level of a world that then included Mussolini – the whole analysis so easily and logically developed that the complexity of the operation is almost unnoticed and intellectually painless.

To turn to 'the particular' we are here concerned with, one major shortcoming of the original edition of this book must be noted. In Chapter 1, I developed the theme of colonial society as an essentially 'administrative' society, in which party 'politics' was seen, by a mandarin elite (who were all-powerful, and therefore all-political), as generated out of sectional self-interest on the part of 'agitators' who appealed to the non-rational in otherwise honest, simple peasants. I quite failed to pick up the importance of this theme later when discussing the evolution of the one-party state. Yet here is one obvious source of the one-party phenomenon: that the politicians who grew to political eminence during the colonial era had no experience, until the eve of independence, of a political order in which competing parties and legitimate opposition, were permitted and institutionalized. They experienced, too, the repression of the parties they did start up.

This very important point had been brought to my attention, in a response to an early 'try-out' of some of the arguments subsequently developed into this book, in the form of a letter from Christopher Fyfe, who (as noted on pages 228 and 292) observed that I had placed inadequate emphasis, in explaining the phenomenon of the one-party state, on the legacy of colonialism. Mr Fyfe was persistent, and returned to repeat this criticism in a review of *Third World* in *New Society*.

To a social scientist, one's own behaviour is a legitimate object of inquiry investigation. Why did I ignore a clear and positive suggestion which I myself had anticipated, but had not developed – to the extent of citing Fyfe's critical and suggestive note, but still omitting to develop its main point?

The sociology of occupations suggest to me that even sociologists who like to think of themselves as more sensitized than most to an historical time-perspective – like myself – are still likely to dwell upon contemporary or recent determinants of behaviour (e.g. in this case, the unifying influence of the independence struggle), or *structural* explanations (e.g. the undifferentiated class-structure) rather than more long-established and deep-rooted *processes*. When one moves to the discussion of the present, it is all too easy to deal with it in terms of quite contemporary relationships, and to forget, to some degree, the results of fifty years of colonialism. Probably, too, there is a tendency to concentrate on the contemporary actors, the successful nationalists (particularly by those whose political sympathies are on the side of the nationalists – as mine are), and to neglect those other actors who were the decisive pre-Independence power-wielders and dominated the culture of that era: the colonial officials. Though there was a strong and ultimately successful movement against the Establishment, it was that Establishment that was dominant, and had to be overthrown, in the first place, and their culture conditioned those they ruled deeply.

I do not wish to imply, with recent writers like Fitch and Oppenheimer, that Nkrumah's CPP was hopelessly compromised and complicit almost ab initio. I am aware, as they appear not to be, that Nkrumah was gaoled, and that real mass struggles did take place. But the extent of these struggles can also be exaggerated: the two martyrs killed in Ghana's struggle for independence, or the two student-heroes of the revolution against the military government in the Sudan, contrast with the million dead of the Algerian Revolution.

That two such different struggles produced one-party, then military, regimes, suggests that the common feature is their subjection to long periods of colonial rule, in which the theory and practice of government-and-opposition never took root.

So sociologists, who so often, and justifiably, preen themselves when they observe the inability of historians to catch what is new and emergent, need to be careful that in concentrating on the recent they do not lose sight of the compulsions of the past.

Their mutual need of each other is apparent from another issue touched upon in this book. Historians are all too often chroniclers of events, descriptive empiricists and theoretically naïve. Sociologists are great over-producers of conceptual schemata, but are not notable for their solid knowledge of substantive societies. The particular varieties of populism cited in this book from the recent history of the world outside Euro-America, are, I now realize, rather special variations of a species of social-movement classically known from nineteenth-century Russia and America. Before we can extend the label 'populism' to describe these contemporary movements, we need to demonstrate the connection more closely than I was able to do here. It was a large enough task, however, to attempt to generalize about the Afro-Asian-Latin American contemporary movements; elsewhere, the discussion will be opened on this wider comparative theme.

Finally, a few details. To this new edition, I append an additional bibliography relating to the new chapter. And I have been able to correct two mis-statements of fact, for whose correction I am indebted to Professor Michael Banton, who showed me that Congo-Brazzaville was not Gabon; and to Mr J. N. Mallik of Calcutta and Dr André Beteille, who drew my attention to the confusion between Aurobindo and Barindra Ghosh (an error which I think I can legitimately blame on my sources!). And I owe a particular debt to Mr Phil Leeson, who guided me, from his wide and sceptical knowledge, through the minefields of the statistics on international aid.

Manchester
June, 1967

PETER WORSLEY

THE CREATION OF THE WORLD

UNTIL our day, human society has never existed. Societies, yes; cultures and empires which extended over large areas and influenced millions of people. Nor could it be otherwise before the growth of civilization. We could expect no world-wide human community in a Palaeolithic Europe only inhabited by a few thousand men. 'In modern terms', the archaeologist tells us, 'the total output of energy in savage Europe at any one time probably never exceeded that of a single four-engined bomber'.[1]

But even when the great civilizations developed, they set their boundaries somewhere. Whatever their claims to universal dominion – and the Chinese Empire had no Foreign Affairs Department, since it *was* civilization, and all else barbarism – they recognized the existence of life beyond the *limes*, but only barbarian life. The line where civilization ended was patrolled by armed men, guarded by Roman and Chinese walls. As to what lay beyond, they were not too interested.

This mutual ignorance was tragi-comic. It could be fatal. Surajah Dowlah, Nawob of Bengal, whom Clive defeated at Plassey, believed that there were only 10,000 people in all Europe.[2] The Chinese too, thought that Europe was short of population.

In 1793, Ch'ien Lung, Emperor of China, addressed a barbarian potentate, George III of England, in response to the mission of Earl Macartney, sent by George to Peking:

'You, O King, live beyond the confines of many seas, nevertheless, impelled by your humble desire to partake of the benefits of our civilization, you have dispatched a mission respectfully bearing your memorial. . . . To show your devotion, you have also sent offerings of your country's produce.

I have perused your memorial: the earnest terms in which it is couched reveal a respectful humility on your part, which is highly praiseworthy. . . .

As to your entreaty to send one of your nationals to be accredited to my Celestial Court and to be in control of your country's trade with China, this request is contrary to all usage of my dynasty and cannot possibly be entertained. . . . It may be suggested that he might imitate the Europeans permanently resident in Peking and adopt the dress and customs of China, but it has never been our dynasty's wish to force people to do things unseemly and inconvenient. . . .

Swaying the wide world, I have but one aim in view, namely to maintain a perfect governance and to fulfil the duties of the State. . . . As your Ambassador can see for himself, we possess all things. I set no value on objects strange and ingenious, and have no use for your country's manufactures. . . .

You, O King, from afar have yearned after the blessings of our civilization. . . . I have already taken note of your respectful spirit of submission. . . .

[Regarding trade] . . . Our Celestial Empire possesses all things in prolific abundance and lacks no product within its borders. There is therefore no need to import the manufactures of outside barbarians in exchange for our own produce. But as the tea, silk, and porcelain which the Celestial Empire produces, are absolute necessities to European nations and to yourselves, we have permitted, as a signal mark of favour, that foreign *hongs* should be established at Canton, so that your wants might be supplied, and your country thus participate in our benificence.

Regarding your nation's worship of the Lord of Heaven [Christianity] . . . Ever since the beginning of history, sage Emperors and wise rulers have bestowed on China a moral system and inculcated a code, which from time immemorial has been religiously observed by the myriads of my subjects. There has been no hankering after heterodox doctrines. . . . The distinction between Chinese and barbarians is most strict, and your Ambassador's request that barbarians shall be given full liberty to disseminate their religion is utterly unreasonable.

It may be, O King, that the above proposals have been wantonly made by your Ambassador on his own responsibility, or peradventure you yourself are ignorant of our dynastic regulations and had no intention of transgressing them when you expressed these wild ideas and hopes. . . .

Do you, O King, display even more energetic loyalty in future and endeavour to deserve for ever Our gracious affection. . . .'[3]

Despite the high tone and universalistic pretensions of the Chinese Emperor, his society was ill-equipped to withstand the incursions of commercial Europe. But for a society that believed that 'as there is one sun in the heavens, so there can be but one great supreme power on earth', it was hard to realize that the sordid opium-dealing foreign devils represented a far greater power than China. Even as late as the Opium War:

'. . . the belief that foreigners, and particularly the English, would die of constipation if deprived of rhubarb was widely held . . . in China. It had its origin, I think, in the practice, so widely spread in early nineteenth-century Europe, of a great purge every spring, rhubarb-root being often an ingredient in the purgatives used. The seasonal purge was thought to be particularly necessary in the case of children, who without it would be sure to develop worms. However . . . later, [the Chinese official responsible for eliminating the opium trade] modified his views about rhubarb, and said that only tea could be considered an absolute necessity.'[4]

The gulf between cultures was too great to be easily bridged, too great at times even for mutual comprehension. When, periodically, men burst through barriers of mountain, speech, ocean, rampart, they gasped with amazement at what they found. How could men lead such animal-like existences? Were these, in fact, 'men' at all? In Cape Colony, the primitive nomads were hunted for sport. In Tasmania, in 1830, settlers combined with soldiers, police, and criminals, in a military battue across the island to wipe out the entire aboriginal population.[5]

In the earliest days of settlement, things had often been different. At the Cape, relations between White and Black had been equitable enough for marriages between Dutch men and Hottentot women to be common. The most famous case was the marriage in 1664, of the explorer, van Meerhof, to Eva, a Hottentot woman, the wedding being celebrated by a bridal feast at Government House.[6]

This brief period of tolerance did not last long. Hottentot and Kaffir Wars, plus large-scale importation of slaves, soon changed things. By 1792, the Church Council of Cape Town declared that there was no longer any secular or religious reason why slaves professing Christianity should be freed.[7]

But elsewhere, Europeans found cultures very different from those of the Hottentots or the Australian Aborigines. When they encountered these civilizations, they asked a very different question. How could such magnificent civilizations have remained unknown to us? In the thirteenth century, when Marco Polo arrived at the city of Hang-chow, then in decline, he found that it was:

'. . . an hundred miles in circuit . . . [with] . . . ten principal squares or market-places, besides innumerable shops along the streets. Each side of these squares is half a mile in length. . . . The streets are all paved with stones and bricks. . . . The whole city must have contained one million six hundred thousand families'.[8]

At this time, life in Europe was insecure, communications primitive, and civilization at a low ebb.[9] Even three centuries later, when European civilization had advanced considerably, non-Europe could still astound the European conquerors of Mexico:

'When we saw so many cities and villages built both in the water and on dry land, and this straight, level causeway, we couldn't restrain our admiration. It was like the enchantments told about in the books of Amadis, because of the high towers, *cués* [temples], and other buildings, all of masonry, which rose from the water. Some of our soldiers asked if what we saw was not a dream. . . .

Then when we entered Iztapalapa, the appearance of the palaces in which they quartered us! They were vast, and well made of cut stone, cedar, and other fragrant woods, with spacious rooms and patios that were wonderful to see, shaded with cotton awnings.

After we had seen all this, we went to the orchard and garden, and walked about. I never tired of looking at the variety of trees and noting the scent each of them had. The walks were lined with flowers, rosebushes of the country, and fruit trees. . . .

Today, all that was there then is in the ground, lost, with nothing left at all. . . .'[10]

A generation after the conquest there was 'nothing left at all': so thoroughly were the high civilizations destroyed or eroded away that they often became completely forgotten, disbelieved in by Whites. Yet the descendants of the conquered remembered.

Man's ignorance of his fellows is not solely a matter of absence

4

of information. It is also conditioned by absence of interest in finding out, and by *a priori* notions and vested interests which determine reactions long in advance of actual contact. 'The facts' were often there, if one chose to look dispassionately. But a South African whose vision of African culture-history is skewed by the distorting lenses of race-superiority cannot see clearly. A recent encyclopaedia, for example, refers to the ancient civilization of Monomatapa as a 'legendary empire believed by early travellers to exist in the interior of Southern Africa', the 'legend' being based on 'distorted accounts of native tribes'[11] – this despite abundant archaeological and documentary material on this empire.[12]

Now myth is not, as the encyclopaedia assumes, merely 'distortion'. Nor is it 'history'. As Malinowski has classically shown, myth acts as a 'charter' for the present-day social order: it 'supplies a retrospective pattern of moral values, sociological order, and magical belief' the 'function' of which is 'to strengthen tradition and endow it with a greater value and prestige by tracing it back to a higher, better, more supernatural reality of initial events.'[13] But it can incorporate, utilize, and elaborate, *for mythopoeic purposes*, actual historical events as well as sheerly mythical 'events'. Difficult as the task may be, it is therefore often possible to distil history out of folk-legend. And it is dangerous to discount the *historical* value of oral tradition totally:

'In 1914, a French district officer, Bonnel de Mezières, dug into a site that was *suggested by tradition*, (although not by any notable projection above the flat savannah). . . .'

and found what is probably Kumbi Saleh, the capital of the former Empire of Ghana.[14] In South Africa, Venda legends of a secret, sacred hill in the Transvaal were the clue to the discovery of the 'golden burials' of Mapungubwe.[15]

Legends such as these may thus contain a kernel of historical truth. Others are entirely 'mythological'. But Europeans, too, have their mythologies. When Cortes and his companions burned their vessels on the shores of Mexico, the high drama of their action was consistent with the engorged imaginations of men who were not only out for loot, but who also saw themselves as crusading champions of Christianity and as heroes of medieval epic and romance, encountering 'the enchantments told about in the books of Amadis'. A Spain which had been reconquered from the infidel, and which was shortly to be rendered totally uninhabitable for knights by Cervantes, could no longer satisfy the imagination of potential conquistadors. These questing spirits therefore turned abroad, looking for new worlds to conquer. They lusted after the gold of El Dorado, to be sure, but also after the eternal life at the Fountain of Youth.[16] The reality they found – the high civilizations of Mexico and Peru – only confirmed the realism of their wild dreams. But chivalry – and Christian charity – quickly withered as a few hundred men, like ruthless machines, fought for an empire of gold and slaves against hundreds of thousands.

It was Bernal Díaz, the rough foot-soldier whom we saw standing open-mouthed in the Mexican capital of Tenochtitlan (where modern Mexico City stands), Díaz and his comrades, who made Europe's first decisive irruption into the world. They established a fateful relationship of superiority and inferiority which was to sustain the White man in his drive to ultimate world-conquest, and was to lead to the creation of the world as a single social system. However impressed the Spaniards might be at the botanical and zoological gardens of Tenochtitlan, Aztec society did crumble before them. Their sense of superiority is therefore understandable. In Peru, Pizzaro, again, conquered an empire of sixteen million people with only 300 men and fifty horses. Despite their great size and their advanced organization, however remarkable their elaborate cultures, the empires of the New World could not withstand the Spanish attack. In Mexico, Cortes had the assistance of hundreds of thousands of Tlaxcalan allies: he was able to exploit internal rivalries also. And he was profoundly aided by the religious belief that the Spaniards were returning gods, a myth which particularly affected the irresolute Emperor Moctezuma. But neither of these factors account for Pizzaro's triumph in Peru – except in so far as the Supreme Inca, Atahualpa, had barely assumed the reins of power, following a civil war. Pizzaro did, of course, have the example of Cortes to inspire and guide him, too.

Clearly, superior equipment was crucial in the Spanish victory: these hairy white monsters, covered in metal, and mounted on their huge 'deer', struck terror into the hearts of peasant foot-soldiers, bravely though they fought the horsemen and their fears. Bernal Díaz, being a practical fighting man, gives full recognition to the importance of the instruments of war in the Spanish victories: the horse, armour, crossbows, cannons, dogs, and 'engines' of war. But it was not their iron weapons, nor their iron exteriors, that gave the gold of the New World to men like Cortes and Pizzaro. It was also their organization, their discipline, their confidence, and the force of their motivating drives, that gave them crucial advantages. The 'ethic' of the Conquistador was crucial; it helped foster an iron spirit to match their iron fighting-equipment: ruthlessness and determination carried the day.

Once Cortes had burned his boats; once Pizzaro's men had crossed the line he drew in the Peruvian earth, there was no turning-back. Death or victory was the simple choice, and in such circumstances men give no quarter. The Spaniards also had divine support. Cortes' men had been sickened at sacrifices of human beings performed in their honour: the mass sacrifices of the Aztecs horrified them. But at Cholula, in Mexico, and at Caxamarca in Peru, the Spaniards themselves did not hesitate to use premediated, treacherous, large-scale massacre of un-suspecting crowds as a terroristic instrument of policy – and the Church blessed their actions.

Over two centuries later, the superiority of the White man's military discipline and organization was to be demonstrated again, at Plassey, when the fall of another great Empire gave Britain the key to a sub-continent. Clive's victory over Surajah Dowlah at Plassey was not due to overwhelming technological superiority – for the Nawob's armies were as well-equipped as his – but primarily to British discipline, training and drill.[17]

Clive's victory at Plassey, unlike the Spanish conquest of America, was the victory of a country which was developing into the major capitalist industrial power. Because of this, the impact of the British conquest of India, however destructive of the indigenous economy, and however exploitative, nevertheless ultimately set Indian society on the path to modernization.

A repressive and authoritarian Spain, politically and culturally dominated by the backward provinces of Old Castile and Aragon,[18] had been unable to utilize the gold of the Indies for the 'take-off' to modern capitalist industrialization. The wealth of the New

World, instead, was used to bolster up an archaic society. Militarism and xenophobia petrified the social order; an inquisitorial Christianity sanctified it, at home and abroad. Christianity abroad, it is true, produced such noble defenders of the Indian as the great Dominican, Bartolomé de Las Casas.[19] But the Saint of the Indies lost. A Portuguese bishop was to sit on his stone seat at Loanda in West Africa 'blessing the slaves as they entered the holds of the slavers, "and through his apostolic blessing guaranteeing them the inexpressible bliss of a future life with which the short period of earthly tribulation could not be compared" '.[20]

The tradition established on Española (the island divided today between Haiti and the Dominican Republic) – where the Indian population was reduced from some two or three hundred thousand in 1492 to two villages by 1570 – proved irresistible. Violence and terror became an entrenched disposition. War became an art, and colonial war could even inspire art:

'... all the Kings, who Géntoo [Hindu] gods adore,
and dare our yoke reject shall rue the wrath
of hard and hardy Arms, with steel and lowe,
till low to Gama or to Death they bow. ...

.   .   .   .   .

Lo! he returns and bursts what dares oppose,
thro' bullet, lance-plump, steel, fire, strongest hold;
breaks with his brand the squadded host of foes,
the serried Moor, the Géntoo manifold. ...'[21]

Other European countries, more favourably placed, and notably England, were able to benefit from Spanish and Portuguese pioneering experience, and from their own expanding adventures in 'primitive accumulation'. They refrained no less from stark exploitation: after Plassey, Clive alone picked up £2,300,000 plus and annual income of £270,000 per year.[22]

But unlike Spain, this wealth was not used to perpetuate 'booty capitalism' or traditional mercantilism, or merely to construct a bureaucratic colonial plantation-system. It was used to establish a new international division of labour, converting the conquered lands into a resource for a dynamic and expanding industrial capitalism. Out of the prosperity of the 'triangular trade' of the Great Circuit: slaves from Africa to America; minerals and foodstuffs from America to Europe; cheap manufactured goods from Europe and America to Africa: came the prosperity of Liverpool, Manchester, Bristol, and a significant contribution to the mounting of Britain's Industrial Revolution. Thereafter Europe's edge over the rest of the world became marked. The terms of trade became reversed, as the high civilizations of the East went under one by one, their industry destroyed to make way for the products of Manchester, Lyons, Amsterdam, and Brussels, their natural resources transported to feed the factories of Europe.

Objectively, of course, the world had always been one, long before world-wide social relations were established, long before the Spaniards seized America or the British India. Even the most primitive hunters and collectors had never been entirely isolated. Culture was passed along from one society to another, changed and added to, or lost, in the process – by war, intermarriage, conversion, discussion. But the contact was a contact of beads on a thread, though – to use an Irishism – without any thread. Sheer contiguity was the main facilitating mechanism. Small or large, where societies remained politically independent of their neighbours, and were not incorporated into more advanced civilizations, their contacts with the outside were intermittent, accidental, or seasonal. Men might acquire a new type of canoe, a new religious cult, a new overlord, from next door – out there – but they never knew what lay beyond, never penetrated 'out there'. The world looked like this to the Nuer in the twentieth century:[23]

Beyond the range of hills, across the other side of the river, they never ventured. That was the territory of enemies, penetrated only for the purposes of trade, war, and marriage – people one needed principally as victims or friends, suppliers or consumers, but who remained essentially separate and marginal to one's own society, and therefore potentially hostile. To trade with them was to venture into a dangerously-charged atmosphere; one needed to perform the elaborate magical rituals of the Trobriand *kula* exchange to protect oneself.[24]

True, in this 'objectively' single world, highly important contacts were made by people whose jobs involved movement: traders notably, conquerors certainly, and sometimes proselytizers. Even with quite limited equipment, extraordinary journeys could be made. 'Exploration', in fact, normally consisted in being passed from hand to hand, guided along well-worn routes. Sometimes, true explorations were undertaken: Marcus Aurelius sent an ambassador to Nanking in AD 166,[25] the Chinese themselves reached Africa and the Caspian,[26] the Northmen voyaged to North America, and the Polynesians explored the Pacific Islands, long before the high era of the European voyages of discovery.

There has, in fact, never been a 'Shangri La', quite isolated. Human culture has been one – but only 'objectively'. Human culture existed 'in itself', but not 'for men'. Human society only came to exist *subjectively*, men only acquired the knowledge that they were part of a single social world, through the midwifery of European imperialism. The opening scene of the last act in the drama begun by Spain came in the eighteenth century, on the field of Plassey in 1757.

But the frontier zones between the sealed worlds were only crossed gradually. Japan was to remain sealed until 1853. Until the previously separate cultures were incorporated into a developing world-order built on the hard facts of commerce and power, man's discovery of man was easily absorbed into an outlook built on illusion rather than reality. The stories of the medieval European voyagers had been dismissed as 'wondrous tales' of anthropophagi and men who carried their heads beneath their shoulders. Marco Polo was scoffed at, his name a fourteenth-century equivalent of Baron von Munchhausen. The great Ming voyages of exploration were an interlude only in a Chinese history that focused on the

Asian land-mass, a source of curiosities for the Imperial Court – 'auspicious giraffes' – but not the beginning of a new international order. Great empires had risen and fallen long before the Europeans broke out of Europe; new religions had changed men's beliefs and lives. A Golden Horde could sweep through the steppes of the Eurasian heartland, destroying and dominating. But more usually, the conqueror had merely erected a more or less elaborate tax-extorting state system on top of an unchanging and stationary agrarian village economy. The Tungus, Mongol, and Manchu invaders of China themselves had become sinized. To the peasant, they represented a new set of overlords to whom the eternal tribute had to be paid. The European was only the latest in the series.

For Europe, too, the future significance of the great voyages of discovery to the New World and the Pacific was difficult to discern. To eighteenth-century Europe, the meaning of non-Europe was dictated predominantly by the state of Europe itself. The newly-discovered cultures of the South Seas were not just external *facts*; they were *answers* to the intellectual and emotional problems of Europe.

A France questioning the whole social order of Church and King looked to other lands and times for inspiration. To Montesquieu and Voltaire, Persia and China, ancient Greece and Rome, were models from which they could draw hope. But the *philosophes* of the Enlightenment drew fresh inspiration, too, from the accounts of Cook, Bougainville, Freycinet, Flinders, and others who – searching for quite other things – had encountered people living in idyllic Polynesia. The hopes and dreams of reformers rebelling against hardened *anciens régimes* were projected onto these new-found societies.

In Lee Boo, prince of the Palau Islands, and Omai, noble savage of Huahine – exotic visitors to England from the South Seas – Augustan polite society found confirmation of their quite differing, but equally rationalistic and optimistic, theories of human nature: on the one hand, the school of 'hard primitivism' which stressed the ascetic, spartan lives of the islanders; on the other, the 'soft primitivists' who saw Tahiti as an erotic Garden of Eden.[27] The artists employed as human cameras on the voyages of discovery sometimes recorded the people they saw as naturalistically as the plants and animals they drew. But even Nature was seen through European eyes at times: the Australian eucalypt bush was often drawn with the soft foliage and outline of European woodland. When they moved from plants to people, distortion was far more common. Europe's spiritual search infused the vision of even the scientific recorders. Bedraped Greeks disported themselves beneath the palm-trees in the 'grottoes' and 'amphitheatres' of the South Pacific. For the islanders represented living 'evidence' that things could be ordered differently, just as the study of Greece and Rome showed that they had once been different in the cradle of European civilization itself. Human nature, clearly, was created in society. Only change the environment, and humanity would change. Only free man from the distorting effects of irrational social institutions, only strangle the last king in the entrails of the last priest, and a free, natural Man would emerge, a rational creature like the unspoiled children of the Friendly Isles.

Men had begun to know one another, and to reflect on themselves. But the reflection became increasingly conditioned by the nature of their actual, direct relationships on the ground, rather than by the categories derived from their own societies. As Whites came more and more often into conflict with the islanders, the idyll became harder to believe in. 'Is it possible', remarked Jean-Jacques Rousseau, on hearing of the massacre by the Maori of a French explorer, 'is it possible that the good Children of Nature can really be so wicked?' The moral significance of the newly-discovered civilizations began to change as their fate and that of Europe became increasingly – and unequally – inter-linked. As the aborigine of Australia became a nuisance to be eliminated in the expansion of Australian sheep-farming, or a sorry remnant of drink-besotted, ragged hangers-on, the picture of the native of Botany Bay changes; the early naturalism of the Port Jackson painter disappears as quickly as the Grecian and Gothic pastoralism of the Romantic artists. By the early nineteenth century, the aborigine has become a figure of fun: 'King Teapot and his Two Gins . . . as he appeared after having a tightner'.[28] Instead of the Garden of Eden, the evangelizing Christian now saw 'an ignoble and degraded brute who might be saved from eternal damnation only by concerted missionary activity'. The heathen's nakedness was no longer natural innocence, but an affront to the vengeful Lord.

The assumption of the 'natural' superiority of Europe was easily enough made when confronted with the hunting-and-gathering Australia nomads. It was more difficult to assume in regions where the superiority of Europe was by no means apparent. Most of the world was quite unlike New Holland, and at first Europe had little to offer. Even as late as the eighteenth century, visitors to Yedo, the capital of Japan, found a flourishing city of a million inhabitants, more highly populated than any contemporary European city. Elsewhere, the richness of Asian culture had long been apparent.

In the 1620s, the economic historian tells us, Dutch shipping in Indonesia only amounted to 24,000 tons, compared to Indonesian shipping of 50,000 tons, Chinese and Siamese shipping of 18,000 tons, Achinese shipping of 3,000, and Coromandel shipping of 10,000 tons.[29]

Europe's significance in this type of international commerce was peripheral, her products relatively unimportant, her needs great, her civilization no more developed. Gold flowed out of Europe to purchase the products of the East.

The civilizations of non-Europe were quite as advanced and cultured, as cruel and as bigoted, as anything Europe could show. As late as 1824, the Ashanti were strong enough to defeat Sir Charles McCarthy's army, and use his skull to adorn the drums of the Asantahene. In 1879, the Zulu could decisively defeat a British army at Isandlhwana, and offer strong resistance to another nomadic pastoral society, that of the Boers, who, as we are reminded, differed in their cultural equipment from the Zulu only in three decisive respects: they possessed the Bible, the wheel, and the gun.[30] Even on the eve of the twentieth century, an Ethiopian army could defeat Italy, at Adowa, and as late as 1921, 7,000 Spanish soldiers were wiped out by Abd-el-Krim's smaller army in Morocco.

But these were the death-struggles of doomed cultures. Resistance there might be, but Europe inexorably strengthened her grip. The last sovereign independent Indian state, the Punjab, was conquered and annexed in 1848–9; the last attempt to re-create the old order in the Indian sub-continent came ten years later with the 'Mutiny'. Soon afterwards, the whole process was to be speeded up.

The really crucial phase, which ended in the triumphant division of the entire globe between a handful of European Powers, came after 1885. The European achievement in this period, therefore, was not merely a repetition of older patterns of 'imperialism'; it marked the dawn of a new era in human history, characterized by an imperialism of a new type, the response to distinctively new economic and financial pressures in Europe itself. It was to result in the unification of the globe as a single social system. If we were to pick a date for the beginning of world history, therefore, we could do worse than follow Lenin's suggestion, for the year of the Congress of Berlin and the partition of Africa marks a watershed. In comparison, 1914 means nothing. In the eyes of an eminent Asian historian, what we presumptuously call the Great World War of 1914-18 was nothing but 'the European Civil War'.[31]

Within three decades of the Berlin Congress, military conquest and *de facto* political control had translated paper, potential spheres of influence into real empires. The major part of the earth's surface was safely under European control: Tunisia and Egypt were finally occupied in the 1880s; the Mahdi defeated at Omdurman in 1894; and Central Africa occupied by 1900. Certain recalcitrant and marginal areas held out: the French occupation of North Africa, begun at Algiers in 1830, was still not completed when a paper agreement of 1912 gave Morocco to France and Tripolitania to Italy. Not until 1933-4, indeed, was France finally to pacify Morocco; Italy did not overcome the Sanusi until 1932,[32] nor Ethiopia until 1936.

But these were the last resistances of independent societies to absorption. The European world-empires which, between them, encompassed the earth, did not create a set of mutually separated, closed empires on the traditional Chinese pattern. France, Britain, Germany, Holland, Italy, even Portugal and Spain, were interconnected in an over-arching framework of trade and power combinations, alliances and oppositions, that an expanding capitalism engendered.

Europe had accomplished a transformation which created the world as a social system. It was a world-order founded on conquest and maintained by force. The new 'world' was no egalitarian 'family of nations': it was essentially asymmetrical. At the one pole stood industrialized Europe; at the other, the disinherited.

Paradoxically, the world had been divided in the process of its unification, divided into spheres of influence, and divided into rich and poor.

In the process, Europe itself was transformed. The new phase was, indeed, to shatter the traditional West European nation-state for good and all. Now, it became the kernel of a wider imperial system. The nation-state of former times, from henceforth, was to be an archaic category which was never to regain its former significance, even with dissolution of the imperialist world-order. The social space of France now included Indo-China and Algeria; that of Britain, South Africa and India. There could be no going back to the parochial entities of the pre-industrial epoch. Her fate, now, inescapably, involved transcending the traditional limits of a home-centred or Western-European or even Atlantic economy. Britain in particular could never again shrink within her borders: she was dependent on the external world for materials and markets.

The heyday of high imperialism, if exceptionally important, was also exceptionally brief. At the close of the nineteenth century, it looked as though the East had gone under for ever. India's traditional industry had been destroyed long since to make way for Lancashire. The culture of the Chinese mandarin had been displaced by the culture of the coolie. But far from consolidating its control, Europe found a new kind of opposition to her rule developing in the cities which the European dynamic had called into existence, and in the villages disturbed from their millennial slumber. The new threat was that compound of nationalism and social revolution which was to be the hallmark of the twentieth century. This new anti-Europeanism was not a final defiance. It was a new challenge which sought to redefine and re-order the world in a totally new way. The old *resistance*, however, and the new *revolution* overlapped: Moroccan tribes fought French encroachment at one end of the Islamic world, while at the other, Indonesia was establishing her own Communist Party. The old and the new struggles could even merge, in very complex ways: revolutionism, conservatism, old national pride and new internationalist consciousness, could interfuse: Japan's modernization took place via a reassertion of the power of the Emperor; a reforming King Amanullah could stand for the modernization of Afghanistan; the Kabaka in Buganda and the Sultanate in Morocco could become rallying-points for traditionalists and reformers alike, their common meeting-point rejection of the foreigner. Normally, the alien rule of the White man was the target of the nationalists, but in the ferment created by the forcible opening of closed societies, nationalism became a force which could turn against any foreign rule. Even the aid of the White man could be accepted in the cause, as new Arab 'kingdoms' were carved out of a dismembered Ottoman Empire.

Among the indigenous populations of the colonized world, there were those who had made their peace with the Europeans, and who found no place in the budding nationalist movements. Traditional authorities were incorporated into the apparatus of colonial rule. Colonial administrations were only too interested in utilizing the prestige and power of such people in order to maintain a semblance of legitimacy and an apparent continuity of institutions which, in fact, by now had become parts of a machinery steered decisively by Europeans. To the nationalists, such participants in foreign rule, direct or indirect, were branded as 'beni oui-oui'. The 'compradore' capitalist, where he existed, was doubly attacked, both as exploiter of his own people and as agent of the foreigner. The 'nationalist' capitalist, however, was to present for the nationalist movement a major and unresolvable problem, as men searching to remove one kind of social inequality – that entailed in the denial of nationhood – found themselves allied with fellow-nationals who nevertheless exploited them as employees. Movements seeking to strengthen the nationalist appeal by infusing the movement with social policies aimed at securing mass support had to juggle delicately to maintain the loyalty of both worker and master.

The lot of indigenous elements – traditional or new – in the administrative apparatus of the colonial power could be fortunate, but it could also expose the incumbent of office to severe social disapprobation. Eventually, they were to be victims of a growing tide of anti-colonial sentiment, or – more commonly – were to be swept into the nationalist movement themselves. Those who threw in their lot with colonialism had frequently made a fatal misappreciation of the nature of European colonialism. They had based their judgment on the accumulated conventional wisdom of agrarian societies. This imperialism, they had assumed, would settle down, like the empires established by other foreigners in bygone centuries. But the Europeans in fact, established no 'millennial' empires. What has been most striking about European world-rule, considering the overwhelming superiority of the technological foundation on which it was built, is the extraordinary brevity of its duration. This brevity derives from the social disturbance it introduced, for its impact was not, as many who experienced it at first assumed, merely the kind of change that a change of dynasty had classically involved in China. The European impact meant, not merely a change somewhere 'above' in the higher nervous centres of power, but a fundamental transformation of the social life of the ordinary peasant and town-dweller.

Unlike Manchu or Mongol invaders of China, or a succession of South American despotic rulers, the European conquerors of Afro-Asia decisively transformed society. Millions of men were driven off the land, some to be turned into plantation- or city-workers, some into semi-unemployed or unemployed 'lumpen-proletarians', others to become bandits. Men of high status were cast down; clerks and teachers given new dignities. Indigenous commerce struggled against powerful foreign competition, usually backed by a well-disposed government. And the conquered all wore the 'uniform of colour', not as some external symbol of domination, like the pig-tail forced upon the Chinese by the Manchu, but as part of the flesh of their body.

This kind of social transformation evoked a drastic response: militant nationalism, the particular character of which differed according to the special character of each country. Some countries, for example, had never been formally incorporated, politically, into the White Empires. Thailand, for example, under the Bangkok dynasty, was able to maintain a precarious independence, as capable rulers played Britain off against France. Others succeeded in saving significant remnants of autonomy as 'protectorates' or semi-colonies. Latin American states maintained their constitutional independence despite alien economic control. But the most brilliant manoeuvre was brought off by Japan, which accomplished an astounding transformation of her total culture, and thereby avoided direct Euro-American political domination. Young Turks made a less thorough revolution which nevertheless involved a deep modernization of everyday custom – trousers and Latin alphabets as well as strictly political change.

The national and social revolutions by now had become intertwined, inevitably so, since what this kind of imperialism involved was not just governmental domination, but a total revolution.

The great turning-point came in 1905, when Japan showed that a modernized Asian country could meet at least an archaic European Power on her own terms. When, at Tsushima, the vessels of the Imperial Russian Navy sank beneath the waves, the myth of Europe's invincibility sank with them. The victorious Japanese were not the only spectators: millions from China to Peru watched with them. The European could be conquered – if you modernized and if you fought. Henceforward, modernization and the development of military and political power-machines were to be an integral part of nationalist thinking. But for most countries, short of arms and equipment, the only source of power was the mass strength of its population. Mass party organizations, not armies, were to be the principal weapon available.

In 1914, the European Civil War had opened great gaps in the ranks of the Powers holding down non-Europe. Promises were made and ideals held out for admiration by both sets of contenders. The colonized peoples were to some extent affected by the appeals of Wilson's Fourteen Points, though they showed little enthusiasm for the issues involved in European Civil War, however. In less idealistic ways, they looked at the War in *realpolitik* terms, and manipulated the divisions amongst their joint rulers to their own advantage. Some did so skilfully: Japan emerged as one of the victorious Allies, and the Arabs received a 'balkanized' independence for their part. But a new factor was introduced into the situation when Russia dropped out of the ranks of the imperialist Powers.

The impact of the Russian Revolution was not very marked outside Europe in the immediate aftermath of 1917. It had its biggest effect on a China *already* in revolutionary turmoil. But the social revolutionaries elsewhere in the East were bound to be interested sooner or later in a European revolution that called not merely for power for the masses, but also for land and bread, for national self-determination and for the destruction of imperialism. Some of these appeals certainly elicited responses at different times and places amongst the disoriented and hungry working classes of the advanced countries in the grim aftermath of World War I, but *all* of these appeals together were highly explosive in countries where mass distress was not the abnormal result of devastating war, but the chronic condition of everyday life, a condition determined by national subjugation.

Europe was sick of war; Asia was ready for struggle. With Europe now weakened and divided, new possibilities of exploiting these weaknesses and divisions opened up. After Turkey, Japan, and Russia, therefore, 'independence' could no longer be envisaged as an end in itself: it could only be a *beginning*. 'Freedom from . . .' was not enough; plain 'freedom' even more devoid of content. Now, rather, total decolonization was on the agenda of the twentieth century.

The colonial revolution of the twentieth century, therefore, has not been just about votes or constitutions. Men have not striven powerfully for the right to have an *élite* of their fellow-national exploiters thrust upon them, or for the privilege of making a choice at the ballot-box every few years which a cynic has compared to a choice between hanging or drowning.[33] But if they have not struggled for the freedom to starve, neither have they struggled for bread alone. They have striven for freedom to create a new social order and to attain a new dignity. They have asserted a determination to be men, not things; not subjects, but objects of respect, to themselves and to their children, as well as to the outsider; and to express their own personalities in the way of their own cultural heritage, necessarily not that of the White man:

'I feel ridiculous
in their shoes, in their dinner-jackets
in their starched shirts, in their stiff collars,
in their monocles and bowler hats
I feel ridiculous
with my toes, never meant
to sweat from morn to night when they are freed
with my limbs, swaddled and weakened,
taking away the beauty of my body in a loin-cloth
I feel ridiculous
with my neck in a factory chimney

with these headaches which never stop
until I greet someone

        . . . . .

I feel ridiculous
one of their accomplices, one of their pimps
a murderer amongst murderers, my hands terrifyingly red
with the blood of their civilizations. . . .'[34]

For some, then, the culture of the White man was ridiculous
in that it was unnatural and anti-human. For others, on the other
hand, the culture of the West represented progress. A great
Indonesian nationalist and socialist, Soetan Sjahrir, could write, as
late as the 1930s, in a letter written from a Dutch prison:

'What the West has taught us . . . [is a] . . . higher form of living and
of striving . . . and this is what I admire in the West despite its brutality
and its coarseness. . . . I would even accept capitalism as an improvement upon the much famed wisdom and religion of the East. . . .
The East must become Western . . . Faust must reveal himself to the
Eastern man and mind. . . .'[35]

Faust or fool, the White man's coming meant that non-Europe
could no longer hope to recreate its past. But neither could its
future lie merely in the reproduction of Europe.

CHAPTER ONE

THE EUROPEAN INTERLUDE

The Colonial Relationship

EUROPEAN control was not established universally merely by military means. The piecemeal accumulation of empire proceeded in ways as diverse as the societies with which the White man came into contact.[1] Stateless societies could offer nothing but a local resistance. To many peoples, moreover, resistance was hardly the issue. The arrival of the Whites at first meant nothing very significant: too late, like the Kikuyu, they found their autonomy – and their land – gone, and either succumbed quietly or rose in desperate frustration. Elsewhere, the company of Europeans was actively sought as a means of gaining access to the White man's wonders.

The process of disengagement has been equally diversified. But if, in both colonization and decolonization, force has always been the *ultimate* sanction, it has not always been used. A few decisive military–political actions have established new balances of power for whole regions. The repercussions of the most decisive revolutions, too, established more than a local or even regional change; they altered the whole field of forces on the world level. In the postwar world, such crucial events were the independence struggle of Indonesia; the Chinese Revolution, when, in Mao's graphic phrase, China 'stood up'; or Cuba, where social revolution, long incubating in Latin America, was placed firmly on the order paper of the century.

The inroads made into colonialism were not achieved easily. In Indonesia, 'Turk' Westerling had 30,000 people killed in the South-West Celebes alone. Chiang Kai-Shek, strengthening his grip on Formosa in 1947, killed 10,000 people in a few weeks.

Nearly a million Algerians died in seven years. But Algeria's struggle, for example, hard on the heels of French defeat in Viet Nam, transformed French colonial policy as a whole. The example of Algeria, on the one hand, stimulated White *colons* in French West Africa in their fight to preserve a 'double college' electoral system in which they had disproportionate representation.[2] On the other hand, the experience of Algeria taught the new Fifth Republic under de Gaulle that unless concessions were made in 'Afrique Noire', France's interests in the rest of the continent would be threatened by other Algerias.[3]

The mere threat of the translation of potential into actual violence often rendered violence unnecessary. Some Powers, too, were basically prepared to see the colonies – ultimately – freed. Far-sighted Powers, notably Britain, desirous of avoiding useless and expensive repetitions of Indonesia or Viet Nam, embarked on instalments of self-government, which, combined with firm repression of, e.g. a Mau Mau or Malayan Communist uprising, enabled them to preserve their reputation and economic and political influence. Where they ran up against a revolutionary nationalism which was more universally supported by a whole population, as in Cyprus, repression blatantly failed.

The classic instance of flexibility, however, was India, where a British Labour Government, faced by a hostile sub-continent, had taken the path of reason: a crucial event not only for India, but for Burma and Ceylon, and ultimately, for the colonized world, where India's non-revolutionary transition to independence inspired other countries to persist in efforts at negotiation and pressure when they might otherwise have taken up arms in despair and anger. Even France, in Syria and the Lebanon, had moved out of more marginal areas where the rewards hardly justified the costs of protracted military suppression. Britain, and later America, with large oil and strategic interests in the area, were to maintain their 'presences' longer, to the extent of military intervention.

In the present era of constitutional progress towards independence for both British and French West African colonies, it remains important, therefore, to understand the complex interaction between violent and non-violent methods in the process of decolonization. The achievement of the peaceful transition to independence in 'Afrique Noire' was largely paid for by citizens of countries like Viet Nam and Algeria, where the battle had been a specifically military one. In those countries, violence of the most extreme kind was resorted to:

'Suddenly, I felt as if a savage beast had torn the flesh from my body. . . . Ja—— had attached the pincer to my penis. The shocks going through me were so strong that the straps holding me to the board came loose. . . .'

The Frenchmen who did this were not some exceptional sadists in the midst of an otherwise civilized society. Every society has its pool of potential torturers. But only certain situations facilitate their emergence, their utilization as a means of 'social control'. Sadists are only used as an everyday instrument of policy by governments pushed to desperate extremes.

One of the 'acceptable' uses of violence is against people who are totally hated or totally despised . . . and feared. Many of the French torturers in Algeria were professionals, but ordinary French conscripts, too, were ultimately to participate or acquiesce in such horrors. They had not been brought up as torturers. But they had matured in a society where, over a long period, hurt pride in cumulative loss of empire, defeat and occupation, induced aggressive responses which were easily directed against available scapegoats. Any society permeated by generations of colonial experience has some scapegoats readily available. Torture was certainly practised by Europeans upon Europeans in their tens of thousands during World War II. But these Europeans, were conceived of as *Untermenschen*, beings without rights or value. 'Torture', Sartre has remarked, 'is required by racial hatred'. What it expresses, therefore, is a hierarchy of contempt and fear, whose visible signs are printed in skin colour or physical features. The colonial heritage, in which rule is based upon superior force and believed superior status, is chronically potentially productive of the ultimate hurts men can inflict upon their fellows. The Bomb would no doubt have been used on Germany had events run differently, but its use at Nagasaki and Hiroshima was more easily accepted in the West because it was used on hated and feared Orientals.

The use of ultimates in violence is easier in societies where hierarchies of contempt had been centuries in the making and were deeply-entrenched. Even when West European countries had become fired by the liberating ideas of the French Revolution, the application of them ceased the other side of the Cape of Good Hope. The Batavian Republic of the Netherlands might preach liberty, equality, and fraternity, but not for its colonial possessions in the Indies.[5]

Colonial relations have been a powerful counteragent to the classic liberal ideals. They have been as much part of the continuing tradition of a France or a Britain as notions of democracy and individualism. The predominance of one tradition or the other has fluctuated from time to time. But there has always been enough of the colonial tradition to make it easy to evoke deepseated responses on the basis of familiar sentiments. French youths had still had to be educated in brutality, but there was a tradition of superiority to draw on. For Holland and Britain, too, the colonial tradition was absorbed into the culture of the metropolitan country. Generations of soldiers and civilians received their education in the streets of Port Said, Aden, and Calcutta. Fear and ignorance on the one hand *and* superiority and contempt on the other are the contradictory constituent elements which make up the peculiar syndrome of this dehumanized relationship. In the face of the myriads of threatening, wheedling beggars, the White man felt sickened, frightened, confused, even defiled:

'Everyday life appears to be a permanent repudiation of the very notion of human relationship. . . . For if you tried to treat the destitute as equals, they would protest against your injustice. They do not want to be equal. . . . But this incessant pressure, this ingenuity, always alert to trick you . . . in the end becomes insupportable, even from human beings. And yet, how does one harden oneself?'[6].

White men did learn to harden themselves: the working-out of guilt and revenge showed itself over many decades, most strikingly, in recent years, in the popularity of Suez in 1956.

The non-White, too, evolved a complex of defence-mechanisms. The 'alienation' of man from man so lamented in the industrialized societies of the West was as nothing compared to the extreme alienation of the colonizer from the colonized. The African evolved his own code for handling the White man:

'(1) The first thing to remember always is that we do not know the hearts of Europeans.

(2) Show respect; if necessary, agree to lies.

(3) Never forget to fear the White, for if you fear him, you will be ready when he deceives you.

(4) Listen carefully to what he says and watch what he does, and you will learn a lot.

(5) Most Europeans and most Natives deceive, but no European can feel the pain of a Native.

(6) Europeans hate us and show us no respect.'[7]

The European, the Swazi King remarked, had to *prove* himself to be an *umuntsu* (person).[8] Europeans believed that the African mentality was 'primitive', 'prelogical', below our comprehension – but also, therefore, because of its incomprehensibility, unpredictable and to be feared. In extreme, Europeans believed that Africans were universally cannibalistic by proclivity, given to the practice of ritual murder; Africans, equally, went in terror of the White man, seeing in autopsies and blood-transfusion services the continuation of the ancient manufacture of *mumiani*, the medicine of 'mummy' made from the blood of murdered men.[9] More often, the conflict is milder, diluted and more oblique: the writer has sat in the huts of 'non-Europeans' in three continents, listening to otherwise quite friendly mothers telling their children crying in fear at the proximity of a White man: 'If you don't shut up, the White man will eat you.' The belief was not, however, always a 'bogey' story told to frighten children, but a real and persistent belief firmly held by adults, too.[10]

Recent research has emphasized that people tend to see members of other unfamiliar groups in terms of stereotypes precisely *because* they only 'know' them externally. They do not interact with them as total personalities, and only meet each other in restricted role-capacities. As a result, they do not observe the other's behaviour intimately enough to see the extent of their individuality or the extent to which, in practice, they deviate, being human, from the 'official' norms of their societies. Consequently, the stranger is seen 'in the flat', only as a member of a category; he lacks the idiosyncratic features of an individual human personality. (Hence the common phenomenon of the over-rigid conformity of the recent convert, who knows the official norms, but lacks experience of 'allowable and patterned departures from the norms which the long-established members of the group ... have acquired ... in the course of their socialization'.)[11]

The social gulf built into the depersonalized official relationship between White ruler and non-White ruled is one which peculiarly facilitates thinking of the Other as insensitive 'submen' by the rulers, and as heartless gods by the ruled. Fanon has remarked that the *colon* is right in his familiar claim to 'know' the colonized people better than others, precisely because he has *created* his personality.[12]

This misattribution of characteristics to the Other was inevitable in a world where mutual ignorance ran so deep that after centuries of mutual confrontation between the Muslim and Christian worlds, a noted Western student of Islam could write in 1957 that

'... Muslims do not at all understand the faith of Christians ... in general, they do not even know that they do not understand'.[13]

Mutual ignorance, however, was not based merely on absence of intimacy. It was grounded in a relationship of power. The domination of Europe over the rest of the world precluded familiarity and fostered hatred as well as illusion.

Political domination made possible not merely the subjection of the non-European, but also a process of reduction and levelling-down. By the late nineteenth century, the rich diversity of cultures and societies in the world outside Europe had been subjected to a process of simplification. The high cultures of the Americas, as we have seen, had long since been wiped out. In India, notably, political dominion paved the way for the destruction of the traditional Indian handicrafts industries, particularly textiles, to make way for Lancashire. But the simplification was also a simplification of human categories.

By the late nineteenth century, the 'natural' superiority of Europe was a standard article of faith. The once-respected and diverse cultures of the East had been ground down to common inferiority. The coolie of Canton had his replica on the Hooghly. Today, reading Needham's epoch-making account of Chinese science and civilization,[14] we wonder that the coolie era could have so effectively wiped out the memory of the preceding centuries; that a Macaulay could ever have been so arrogant as to claim that 'a single shelf of a good European library was worth the whole native literature of India and Arabia'.

Yet the great cultures of Japan and China, India and Southern Asia came to be dismissed with contempt – or, at best, as quaint 'orientalism' – by a Europe confident in the ineluctable evolutionary sweep of history towards its summation: 'the steady material and moral improvement of mankind from crude stone implements and sexual promiscuity to the steam engines and monogamous marriage' of the high nineteenth-century Western world.[15] The relationship of the rest of the world to Europe had become one of inferiority and backwardness. Even European revolutionaries believed in the coming of socialism in the industrial countries of the West. Non-Europe had been left behind in the evolutionary process, its social institutions and cultural heritages now only so many archaic and bizarre survivals.

The superiority of the West was never seen by the West merely as a matter of technology. It was a total superiority. For Livingstone, Manchester and the Bible went hand-in-hand, not out of rationalizing hypocrisy, nor from any double-dealing crude use of religion as a 'justification' for more sordid material interests, but because each was a part of a cultural whole, ethically superior to what it had displaced.

Technological and military superiority went hand in hand with organizational superiority, increasingly – indeed, often from the beginning – infused with an ethico-religious sense of divinely-ordained inevitability. 'Primitive' now become a label applied indiscriminately to the coloured peoples of the world. Social science grew up reflecting the division of the world: anthropologists largely studied non-Europe, apart from peasant folk-traditions in Europe itself. Though a Tylor might in fact study Mexico, a Bastian Burma, or a Rattray the Ashanti, the tendency was to link the study of these complex cultures with the study of the simple Australian aborigines and the Bushmen of South Africa. Sociologists, on the other hand, studied Whites – dockers in the East End, poverty-stricken 'children of the Jago' as primitive in many respects as the nomads at the other end of the earth. The great danger was that the disinherited of Europe might see his image in the dispossessed of Africa or Asia:

'I was in the East End of London yesterday and attended a meeting of the unemployed. I listened to the wild speeches, which were just a cry for "bread", "bread", "bread", and on my way home I pondered over the scene and I became more than ever convinced of the importance of imperialism. . . . My cherished idea is a solution for the social problem, i.e. in order to save the 40,000,000 inhabitants of the United Kingdom from a bloody civil war, we colonial statesmen must acquire new lands to settle the surplus population, to provide new markets for the goods produced in the factories and the mines. The Empire, as I have always said, is a bread and butter question. If you want to avoid civil war, you must become imperialists'.[16]

Rhodes' remedy did not necessarily mean shares in super-profits for all, but it certainly meant a greater degree of personal involvement in imperialism for the masses, via emigration, colonial service, or simply through the acceptance of the belief that their interests depended on the maintenance of the Empire.

Belief in the inevitability and rightness of Empire was not, as commonly supposed, a cardinal article of faith throughout the nineteenth century, even amongst the ruling strata of society, let alone among hungry East Enders. Radicals like Cobden and Bright opposed the closer association of Britain with what we now call the 'white dominions', though they were not against close links with India or Ireland. 'Social imperialist' doctrines only triumphed with difficulty over an entrenched and vocal school which asserted classical liberal doctrines of free trade even within the ranks of the Conservative Party. Not until the turn of the century did Tory, Liberal, and Labour leaders become convinced of the correctness of basing Britain's economic and political strategy on Empire.[17]

Amongst the colonized no less than the colonizer, the doctrine of inevitability of European empire did not always root easily. The colonization of the personality was a lengthy and complex process. The colonized, too, had to learn his role in the new pattern of relationships. China's traditional attitude of superiority towards the outside world, for example, was maintained and even deliberately stimulated. It provided a ready-made seedbed for the imperially-fostered anti-Europeanism of the Boxer Rising. It was also, however, assimilable into the context of a new nationalism which differed markedly from the ancient, self-regarding sentiment of a superior, closed Celestial Empire. Populations of the great 'Asiatic' societies had carried on living in the unchanging patterns enjoined by religions which bade men cease from earthly striving, and where the cycle of reincarnation mirrored the oscillation of village life over the generations and the seasons. In Marx's classic picture of the Indian village, he saw

'. . . the key to the secret of the unchangeableness of Asiatic societies, an unchangeableness in such striking contrast with the constant dissolution and refounding of Asiatic states, and the never-ceasing changes of dynasty. . . . [in] those small and extremely ancient Indian communities, some of which have continued down to this day. . . . based on possession in common of the land, on the blending of agriculture and handicrafts, and on an unalterable division of labour. . . .'[18]

States had disappeared, dynasties crumbled, but the village community had persisted and had grown again after destruction. It had been unnecessary for the ruler to interfere closely in the day-to-day life of the village; enough to collect the taxes each year. In this respect, paradoxically enough, the *laissez faire* liberal dream of a government which would confine itself to the classical minimal functions of keeping the peace and the preservation of society against internal disorder and external threat, was most closely approximated to by the despotisms of the East. Tradition, however, rather than contract, was the basis of organization.

The new European empires were of quite another kind. Neither Chinese claims to superiority, nor the millennial torpor of the peasant, offered adequate protection, even at the psychological level, in the face of the inroads of Western civilization. The Taiping Rebellion for example, reflected the convulsion of an entire society under the impact of Manchu disintegration and European intervention; deaths counted in tens of millions made the first war of mass-slaughter in the West, the American Civil War, look mild in comparison.

If Gatling guns and Lancashire textiles provided the technical means for establishing the dominance of Europe, it was the internalization and acceptance of the total superiority of European culture, not force alone, that was to hold the non-European in lengthy psychological subordination. The villager might remain ideologically unaffected, but the 'new men' educated on Western lines certainly were affected for a time. Self-liberation could hardly be expected in a Burma where the Young Men's Buddhist Association could declare, as late as 1917:

'We speak English and appreciate the Western way of life. We consider it a privilege and an honour to serve our rulers. We are gentlemen'.[19]

The superiority of the West seemed crushingly self-evident to both conquered and conquerors. It induced in the conquered a sense of inferiority and dependence, and its natural correlate, a belief in the inevitability – even the rightness – of White rule. The technological superiority of ships, typewriters, money, and machine-guns, and White organizational superiority, seemed expressive of the overwhelming total superiority of the Western 'rational spirit'.

It was to be some decades before men most severely subject to deprivation under colonial rule were to recover from the traumatic experience of conquest by such superior power sufficiently to draw other conclusions: that one might imitate the White man, absorb his knowledge, discipline, and energy, in order to prepare to drive him out. Such 'social-revolutionary' notions were to develop, later, in the twentieth century, amongst the disturbed masses and the 'new men', rather than amongst Westernizing bourgeois *élites* of the late nineteenth century 'which grew up . . . in the shelter of the foreign exploiters whose agents, intermediaries and dependents they largely were. . . .'[20]

Other less sophisticated societies, interpreting the impact of the West in their own categories, came to the conclusion that the superiority of the White man was so great that it must derive from quite supernatural sources. The White man clearly did not work. His superior command over resources, then, must in the end be based on his possession of some mystical Secret which he was withholding from the non-White. Only discover this Secret, and the 'Cargo' – the White man's goods – would be yours.[21]

The non-White was weighed down by this internalization of the belief in White superiority as surely as by any repressive machinery. The more strongly he believed, the less necessary the use of force. We shall never adequately know, perhaps, the extent of the impact on the psyches of the colonized made by European colonialism. But a psychiatrist-revolutionary like Fanon has analysed for us the gross mental disorders caused by colonial war,[22] and traced the more insidious psychological tensions generated within the individual, within the family, and between the generations, as a result of the 'colonization of the personality'.[23] In more academic and conservative vein, Mannoni for Madagascar,[24] and Elkins for the New World Negro,[25] have emphasized that the 'Sambo' stereotype of the childlike, dependent, passive, Negro is not just a stereotype, but represents a real 'infantilization' of adult men by other men who became their – harsh or mild – 'fathers'.

The Administrative Society

The new territories absorbed by the European Powers were inhabited largely by peoples living in agrarian, traditionalistic polities. These were made up of innumerable villages only linked together, in the case of the more advanced empires, by an over-arching apparatus of political control and tax-collecting, and by such cultural uniformities as common religious beliefs, kinship-, family-, or caste-systems. In India, for example, the importance of Hinduism as a unifying cultural force has been increasingly emphasized in sociological studies of pre-European India.[26] Through a lengthy historical process of 'Sanscritization' – the adoption of Brahmanic customs by non-Hindu groups, and the incorporation of these groups as castes into a general caste-system – the otherwise self-enclosed local caste-communities could be articulated within an overall, religion-wide cultural community. But the pre-European 'all-Hindu' religious community was certainly not equivalent to the modern Indian nation-state, since Indian nationhood is quite different from traditional Hinduism. Hindus in pre-British India constituted a religious community, not a political society. In eighteenth-century terminology, they made up a 'civil society', but not a 'political society'. They were citizens of quite separate polities, as were Christians and Muslims.

Much has been made, from Marx to Wittfogel,[27] of the way in which, in Asia, large-scale irrigation-works brought in their train centralized political institutions. But lately critics of this thesis have pointed out that the elaborate network of canals or water storage 'tanks' required the mobilization and direction of large masses of labour only in their original phase of construction; that the overall systems were not built as a single complex, but were commonly the result of the knitting together of numerous pre-existing local water-systems; and that their regulation and maintenance after construction scarcely necessitated an elaborate central control system, let alone a totalitarian bureaucracy, and was, again, commonly regulated by local rather than central authority.[28]

If 'hydraulic' pressures towards unification seem to have been exaggerated, neither were the religious values and institutions which pervaded Indian society politically unifying. Hinduism, indeed, spread far beyond geographical India even to Indonesia. Within geographical India itself, the great Buddhist and Hindu Empires, the Mauryan Empire, the Gupta Empire, Vijayanagar, at their height certainly dominated huge areas, but they never succeeded in embracing the whole religious community, let alone the whole of the sub-continent. More usually, this was divided into more numerous and smaller states, carved out within the wider area of cultural identity provided by common religion and common social institutions. Political institutions reposed on organized and centralized power, not on the diffuse ties of an uncentralized religion with no 'church' organization. The Muslim conquest, which produced the Mogul Empire, demonstrates how a political system might develop over the major part of geographical India without any foundation in Hinduism at all. The linking of nationhood to Hinduism was to be a post-European development.

Both Islam and Hinduism, as 'world-religions', had nevertheless become so theologically specialized and so closely tied to radically differing social institutions and cultural traditions – Hinduism to caste-society, and Islam to the culture of the conqueror – that they could not become interfused. In China, on the other hand, the dominant religion, Confucianism, was little more than an elaborate, 'this-worldly', social ethic. To the nomadic conquerors – Tungus, Mongol, and Manchu – who periodically swept down from the steppes to conquer China, it was an acceptable, even necessary, code, if they were to maintain effective rule over an unchanged agrarian order. And, in our day, since Confucianism – unlike Islam, Christianity, or Hinduism – offers no elaborate theological world-view, but rather emphasizes man's responsibility to the earthly polity of which he is a part, Communism has been able to take root, unimpeded by the deep resistance which Hinduism or Islam had provided to it.[29]

Strictly, all of these religions, whatever their universalistic claims, are closely bound to particular cultures. So although Islam might be thrust upon the population by force, it never eliminated the deep-rooted religion it found in being, anchored as this was in a whole institutional and cultural complex, and in particular the joint-family and the caste-system. On the other hand, although the culture of the Moguls became modified by Indianization, it was never totally absorbed by the culture of the conquered, as was the culture of the Manchu conquerors of China, whose relatively primitive culture had not the vitality of Islam, and thus virtually disappeared. Islam, however, persisted in India: its unamenability to Hinduization ensured the perpetuation of a culturally-divided population. In the end, when 'India' did emerge out of the European conquest, it was to be co-extensive with Hinduism: the Muslims were expelled, unassimilable, to form Pakistan. A religion like Hinduism, then, if not *absolutely* universalistic, does differ profoundly from particularistic religions focused on ancestor-cults or earth-cults, and therefore, restricted to narrow, separate social groups: the village, the lineage, etc. It therefore provides a potential criterion of identity upon which *national* identity can later arise. Under the conditions of European domination, this potential identity did become transmuted into an actual and new consciousness of 'nation'.

European culture was even less assimilable than that of the Moguls. The European conquest did not mean yet another change of rulers in the centres of power remote from the villages, as even the Mogul and other conquests had done – despite the physical devastation they might have caused – but a profound disturbance of the whole social order. Caste itself was shaken and rendered ambiguous. The European, moreover, was personally a temporary visitor, insulated by distance from his subjects: physical distance, social distance, ideological distance, and by an overwhelming gulf of power and custom. His very transience protected him from absorption. True, to take a parallel situation, the cold Calvinist ethic of Holland might thaw in the warm climate of the Indies, where a new 'Indisch' style of life emerged:

'In contrast to bourgeois Holland, where the tendency was towards a thrifty frugality and simplicity which concealed a certain prosperity, the mode of living in the 'Indian' towns aimed at maintaining colonial prestige in a society predominantly feudal. There was no attempt to create the atmosphere of the cosy Dutch parlour. Instead, Indian social life was a life of balls and receptions. Luxury was not to be found in the confines of interior rooms but in open gardens. No particular attention was paid to furnishing and decorating. When one was transferred, returned home on leave, or retired, the furniture was auctioned off. The rural character of the towns and the close ties uniting them to the countryside contributed to creating a seignorial manner of living. Horse-riding and hunting, both typical recreations for a feudal class, were highly popular. . . .

. . . The minor 'Indo' (Eurasian) officials also tried to copy . . . [this mode of living] . . . as far as his modest means allowed. . . . This life of external display . . . also found its reflection in the furnishing of houses: gardens and galleries full of luxuriant plants, easy chairs, rocking chairs. The interior furnishing was, however, simple to the point of shabbiness. . . .'[30]

The European could thus certainly be affected by the Asian colonial setting. But those 'Asianized' White passengers to the East who are said to have thrown the cutlery overboard once they passed Suez and to have begun eating with their fingers, are surely much rarer than the – probably equally apocryphal – Englishmen who dressed for dinner in the bush. Colonial service, anyhow, was a transitory situation, not a lifetime condition: the customs of Europe were therefore ultimately preserved and re-charged. Any marked 'colonization' of behaviour was eliminated and the conventional norms of polite European society assumed once more as one's ship passed back through the Canal. 'Colonial' customs persisted only as aberrant and exotic tastes among such nostalgic enclaves as the south coast of England. The European was too thoroughly protected by notions of 'election' and 'service' – whether of religious origin or merely as a self-generating ideology of imperial rule – to be deeply transformed by his service abroad. There might, indeed, be continuity of this very tradition for whole social categories: the colonial servant's returning steamer would pass 'the outward bound troop ship, carrying his son eastward to the family duty'.[31] But for each individual, Europe remained the centre of the universe, to which he would return.

The Europeans did not stay; for this, if for no other reason, they could not be assimilated. As a student of the intellectual history of China recently wrote:

'The bases of their power to perpetuate their power . . . remained out of China. They had no need to know Chinese in any degree whatever.'[32]

In so one-sided a relationship of power, the transformatory effects flowed largely one way: the non-European had to make the adjustments; the colonizer was the agent of change, not the object. He, to be sure, was henceforth to be a different person, a 'colonized personality' himself, but he was never absorbed and – literally – 'alienated' by the culture of the colonized.

In establishing colonial control, the creation of a set of political institutions was the crucial first step. The apparatus of power had to be created, and its authority established. In particular, a State had to be brought into being. Where economic control or overwhelming influence had been long-established, state-building was sometimes merely a consolidation and formalization of an existing *de facto* position. But specialized new political institutions, and their authoritative legitimation, did introduce new elements into the relationship between White and Other. The legitimacy of the new political order had to be unambiguously asserted; its rationale defined. Much of the early violence in colonial territories resulted not so much from direct resistance to the incursions of the Europeans – in some kind of heroic 'national' stand against the invader – (for he was often welcomed, or at least accepted, or the attempt was made to manipulate the White man in one's own private interests) but from the frustrations which resulted when the new colonial governments denied any other group or individual the right to use violence in pursuit of its private ends. *Public* violence could now only be used by the colonial authority. *It* embodied the public interest. All other violence, henceforth, was private and illegitimate. The State arrogated to itself a monopoly of legitimate force, to use Weber's classic terminology, and backed up its claims by the very use of force. Now, disputes had to be taken to the District Commissioner or Collector. Feuds and raiding were not permitted, and were put down by the application of the new, solely-legitimate official violence of the new State. It came as a shock to peoples who had sometimes even allied themselves with the White man in military campaigns against their traditional enemies to find that once the White man had conquered – with their aid – they were thereafter not allowed to use arms against their enemies. *Then*, too late, they often rose against the White man. They had mistaken the nature of his goals.

Ancient political groupings and power-structures could be built into the new structure of colonial rule. For 'stateless' societies, however, the State could not build upon any existing specialized and centralized institutions of power. Here, entirely novel structures had to be introduced: traditional leaders might, indeed, be used, but now as mere units in a centralized, bureaucratized, and hierarchical state.

But a political system founded on force alone is an uneasy and fragile arrangement. Nor is mere negative resignation on the part of the ruled a solid enough foundation of rule. The optimum consolidation of power depends upon its transformation into *authority*, the acceptance by the ruled of the legitimacy of the order under which they live. The elaboration of an ideology of rule, and more especially its internalization by the ruled, is thus crucial if one wishes to avoid a permanent fakir-like condition of sitting on bayonets. Such ideologies did indeed exert a hold on the minds of some of the ruled – though on the educated more than on villagers better 'insulated' by tradition and isolation – in that period of consolidated high colonialism between the end of the era of backward-looking revolt and the beginning of the era of forward-looking revolution. The rationale of rule, however, differed for ruler and ruled. A proconsul might pass on some of his mystique of 'service' to those under him; more often, their acceptance of his right to rule depended upon much more prosaic recognition of his superiority – and his 'progressive' function – in material terms rather than any acceptance of his total cultural superiority. The former could be imitated; the latter never recognized. Only in the simpler societies did the White man's world-view sweep the board; in the face of Hinduism or Islam, it made no such headway.

The establishment, and the material and moral consolidation, of power were thus primary tasks. But the relationship between rulers and ruled was inevitably suffused with hidden tensions. The governing of India, Tagore once remarked, resembled tinned food: the people were 'as little touched by human hand as possible'.[33] Yet although the relationship between colonized and colonizer was one in which power preponderated so heavily on one side that no true equality or interchange could exist, and although the social distance between the two was emphasized in a refined etiquette of segregation,[34] nevertheless the 'frontier' situation, in which very few Whites controlled very many Others, did necessitate a certain degree of familiarity and even closeness in restricted areas of social life. Since the colonized laid no serious claim to human equality, he (or she) could even be utilized, without overmuch fear of serious emotional conflict in the colonizer's psyche, even as a personal attendant to the intimate bodily needs of the Whites: as wet-nurse, domestic servant, concubine, cook, or children's companion.

Within the emotionally powerful network of the family, strong interpersonal attachments could grow up. But outside the family, where such sentiments conflicted with the dehumanized requirements of the colonial society, conflicts of loyalty arose for the White man. And the more isolated he was on the 'frontier', the more strongly he needed emotional attachments. Not for nothing is there a 'Cape Coloured' community of one and a half million in the Union of South Africa, very many of them the descendants of lonely White men attracted by non-White women. Many of the leading exponents of South African apartheid, indeed have 'native' blood in their veins, as genealogists in the Republic have found out, to their embarrassment. In the interstices of the colonial relationship, therefore, peculiar sentimental compensations for the alienation intrinsic to the relationship could evolve. The official could feel himself sincerely the 'father' of his people; the colonized could invest him with the attributes of a parent, at times those of a loving and cherished paterfamilias, at other those of a sterner patriarch. But the bulk of his children, inevitably, could not know him so intimately. The social distance between them emphasized remoteness more than intimacy. The ultimate White authority possessed the attributes, not merely of a parent, but even of a God. The African sculptor turning half-length photographs of Queen Victoria into full-length wooden figures, was never 'quite certain whether the Empress was biologically constructed like other women. . . . When he came to portraying the breast of a Queen . . . he was puzzled and helpless. . . . He was not certain whether a Queen had feet at all, but he wished to make sure, and therefore

37

solved his own problem by carving them neatly hidden under the dress.'[35]

'Frontier' situations involving this degree of White remoteness and loneliness still obtain in some colonial areas even today. In most of New Guinea, for example, despite formal 'direct' rule, in fact villagers in most parts rarely see a District Officer more than once or twice a year, when a curious White man's ritual of lavatory-digging and health parades takes place.[36] Such encouragement to hygiene was backed up, at times, by the point of the gun.

Constitutional theorists remote from the field of events they are writing about have not always noticed the frequent irrelevance of the distinction between 'indirect' and 'direct' rule at this level and in this kind of situation. Often, nominally 'indirect' systems, whether used by the French in North Africa, the Dutch in Indonesia, or the British in Tanganyika, involved as much control over, and manipulation of, the 'traditional' authorities, and the appointment to office of quite *un*-traditional figures, as any system of 'direct' rule. Since they did not exist, 'chiefs' had to be invented for peoples like the Kikuyu or the Plateau Tonga of Northern Rhodesia.[37]

It is sometimes suggested that this passion for 'chiefs' arose because the colonial pioneers were so accustomed to thinking in terms of their own hierarchical and differentiated societies that their opening gambit was inevitably 'Take me to your chief'.

In actual fact, whether chiefs existed or had to be invented, the colonial administrator turned to them basically because he was faced with the problem of creating an administrative system where none existed. In order to communicate at all, one had to have some embodiment of the society to communicate with: one could not deal with an 'acephalous' society where authority was distributed among hundreds of petty leaders. Furthermore, the use of traditional authority-figures was far less costly than paying White or indigenous civil servants. Indirect rule had other advantages: it provided a bridge of legitimation, and it enabled an administration to divide and rule: popular resentments and hatreds could be deflected on to the local officials while the ultimate authority could remain remote, unseen and 'above the battle'. Later, new virtues of the 'indirect' system became apparent: potential nationalist unification could be impeded by preserving or fostering innumerable petty centres of power. In Indonesia between the wars, there were no less than 269 'Native states' in the areas governed by 'indirect rule'; and in their very last struggles to maintain their grip after 1945, the Dutch invented no less than six 'States' of Indonesia and nine 'autonomous territories'.[38] 'Indirect rule' also involved the least disturbance of the status quo, the least revolutionizing of social relations between the conquered and the indigenous junior authorities, and was also least likely to provoke opposition from the minor authority-bearers themselves. It has been a device universally adopted by conquerors, not merely by White conquerors. The Zulu, for example, commonly confirmed conquered chiefs in new positions as 'regional' governors of their people, now incorporated into the Zulu Empire, provided that they remain 'loyal'.[39]

The tables could now be turned on critics who accused imperialism of destroying independent cultures and imposing foreign ways. Was not the colonial administration itself preserving indigenous institutions against innovations that had no place in the traditional scheme of things? Were not these critics themselves the real disturbers of a social order that – as functionalist anthropologists showed us – was a nicely articulated scheme in which everything worked smoothly? And who were these self-styled 'nationalists'? An insignificant minority, with insolent pretensions to speak in the name of 'Nigeria' or 'India'. Sir Hugh Clifford, Governor of Nigeria, put the case classically in 1920. They were nothing but

...'a self-selected and self-appointed congregation of educated African gentlemen who collectively style themselves the West Africa National Conference. . . . I will leave Honourable members to imagine what these gentlemen's experience would be if . . . they could be deposited, unsustained by [British] protection among . . . the . . . cannibals of the Mama Hills. . . . and there left to explain their claims to be recognized as the accredited representatives of these, their fellow nationals'.[40]

Indirect rule thus tended to 'freeze' the social order, inhibiting change in the name of conformity with immemorial custom. Hutu serfs in Rwanda were kept in bondage to their Tutsi masters by Belgian colonialism, until independence in 1962 provided the opportunity for the Hutu to throw off their Tutsi overlords together with the Belgians. An administrative-political system of this kind could thus be justified on both 'traditionalist' and 'rational' grounds. The doctrine was, at base, a colonial variant of that great stream of conservative political thought which rejected radicalism, not on grounds of lazy, non-rational cleavage to what is known and familiar, but on the 'rational' grounds of 'realism'. Society, it suggested, constitutes a complex *system*. Change, nevertheless, does take place, but it is handled most rationally, and with least hurt, when it grows out of pre-existing patterns of relationship. Gradual and piecemeal change is therefore preferable to sudden, large-scale change. Those who advocate the latter are unrealistic and utopian at best, wild and deluded at worst, since they cannot foresee the complex repercussions of the changes they seek to introduce. The unintended consequences of revolutionary change are likely to result in worse tensions than those which the innovators seek to eliminate.

In academic circles, 'structural-functionalist' anthropology, spiced with anti-imperialist sentiment and liberal distaste for European domination and interference, encouraged a reluctance to interfere with 'ongoing' indigenous institutions, a reluctance which dominated the thinking of a whole inter-war generation on colonial questions. Liberalism and conservatism could thus fuse, in the colonial situation, to produce stasis. Not until World War II had shattered the (believed) idyllic calm of the South Seas did the popular anthropologist begin to suggest that perhaps, after all, 'rapid change is not only possible, but may actually be very desirable'.[41]

In the context of the inter-war colonial situation, it was unlikely that either governments or liberal critics would draw the other possible conclusion from functionalism: that if society constituted an interconnected whole, change in one area of social life alone might be ineffective or one-sided, or produce unintended consequences in other areas. But the liberal-conservative conclusions from functionalism could easily be married to the classic Popperian castigation of 'holistic' change,[42] particularly since the Soviet Union of the 1930s presented a singularly ominous example of 'total', 'directed' change. True, Popper might acknowledge the propriety of rapid or even large-scale change in appropriate circumstances, but these qualifications scarcely influenced readers who read his message, overall, as both an anti-totalitarian and anti-revolutionary one.[43] That piecemeal change might, in certain situations, be as inadequate and extreme a doctrine, and as socially disastrous a basis for policy, as 'holistic' change, was not appreciated, nor that most social decision-making necessarily falls somewhere in the huge grey area between these two extreme poles. The price of the failure of some governments in the colonies to introduce adequate doses of social change was to be paid for, ultimately, in explosions like Indonesia in 1947 and the Congo in 1960. The practical content of the doctrine of anti-ideology stood revealed in its full danger.

In Europe, the growth of mass democracy in the nineteenth century had effected powerful modifications of conservative theory and practice. Aristocratic exclusiveness, the reactionary methods of a Metternich, a Castlereagh, or the Tsarist 'Black Hundreds', or the more 'popular' alliance of Church, King, peasantry, and urban mob, became increasingly inadequate in the new era. In Britain, a new kind of 'Tory Democracy' emerged, capable of preserving traditional connections with the inner, exclusive centres of power, but also capable of appealing to the 'man in the pub' and the famous 'man on the top of the Clapham omnibus'. Later, in the face of a new threat from the Liberal Party, conservatism had to be remodelled even further.

In the British colonies, however, where the administrator had vastly increased powers, the classic conservative yearning for an ordered polity found a particularly favourable environment and could flourish relatively undisturbed. 'Even under Dutch rule [in Indonesia], thought by Furnivall to represent the purest type of indirect rule', it has been remarked, 'it is the word "rule" which is operative'.[44] But despite this formal power, the 'State' was thin on the ground, and ill-financed. In this setting, the liberal doctrine of minimal government could take root also, and ultimately flower into 'indirect rule'. And if liberal championship of individualism was silenced in the colonies, the tradition of government never became entirely dehumanized, since it took up the conservative doctrine of Government as representative of and trustee for the whole society, particularly its non-vocal elements. In the closed society of the colonial world, where government was by official, not by people or politician, and where political institutions were therefore founded, not on the representation of competing interests, but on the wise, all-powerful regulation of the whole by a mandarin *élite*, the doctrine could flourish luxuriantly.

In this philosophy, the 'real' people are the dumb peasant masses, between whom and the officials there is held to exist a peculiar bond of sympathy and understanding. As Taft said in 1908: 'We are the trustees and guardians of the whole Filipino people, and peculiarly the ignorant masses'.[45] Other 'spokesmen' (e.g. nationalists) are held to be merely representative of partisan interests – especially the powerful and the educated – not of the whole, and least of all of the illiterate. At worst, they merely represent themselves. But the Administration cares for all.

'Good administration', said Lord Lloyd, formerly High Commissioner in Egypt, in 1933: '... is the first requirement to be fulfilled, and ... all other questions are subordinate to it. ... The real problem has been administrative, and we have chosen to regard it as political. ...'[46]

The 'administrative' philosophy may thus be flavoured with paternalism. It can equally well flourish without any such softening, as an assertion of extreme authoritarianism, with both conservative and revolutionary variants. For the extreme conservative, the classic expression of this point of view came from the archetypal symbol of black reaction, Metternich himself:

'Health and equilibrium are identical ideas, like the ideas of *stability* and *order*, for without order, stability is impossible ... the civilized world is divided into two classes: idealists, democrats and people who want to reform everything are opposed to men of understanding ... the one constitutes the positive element and the [other the] negative element, the conservative element and the destructive element ... the masses are and always will be conservative. ...'[47]

The 'true' people had to be defended against the demagogues: the unsettled, rootless, frustrated 'cosmopolitans' – officials, intellectuals, bourgeoisie, civil servants, artists, lawyers. In his analysis of the rebellious categories of the population, as we shall see, he was not far wrong.

Other colonial systems lacked even the tinge of liberalism we discerned in the paternalist declarations above. Analytically, they are to be classed with totalitarian, monocentric systems, as Ossowski has pointed out,[48] and with other 'total institutions',[49] within the wider society: the prison, the hospital, the ship, the army, the mental asylum.

The Spanish colonies in the New World provide a very pure case. Here, the atmosphere of a system of total control is visible in the obsessionally-detailed regulations which governed all aspects of life: the Indians were to live in towns surrounded by fields, and all within 560 yards of the church steeple, 'so that they could learn to order their lives to the tolling of church bells and to the commands of royal officers'. Each Indian was to keep twelve chickens and six turkeys, and sell them for no more than four reales per turkey and one and a half reales per chicken.[50]

Elsewhere, as in eighteenth century Indonesia, political control was equally all-embracing and bureaucratic. It aimed, however, not at the conservation of tradition, but at a dynamic exploitation delegated to a Company:

'The island of Java became a plantation of the Company, and the relations between the sovereign, which the Company now claimed to be, and its subjects were in substance those of planter and coolie, in which the former was not merely the employer of labour, but also the authority invested with the rights of life and death. . . .'[51]

Subsequently, 'indirect' systems of rule were to be introduced in Indonesia, but forced labour and forced cultivation were to continue, in various forms, right to the end of Dutch rule in 1942. The legacy of this deeply-established bureaucratic colonialism can be seen even today in the independent Republic, where, in the villages, monthly enumerations are carried out by the village headmen, not only of people, but also of trees and livestock, even down to dogs, cats and rabbits. 'For pigs and cows, as for humans, they must give monthly figures (with separate categories for natural deaths and slaughter)'.[52]

Rigid as the political framework might be, therefore, it depended on the use made of the political power whether the social order would be preserved or shattered. In the Indies, the Dutch used

43

their total regulatory power to bring about radical innovations in economic and social life:

'Java had become a vast coffee estate. . . . It was a far-reaching revolution that the plantation-system introduced. . . . Previously, the Dutch had only been merchants buying the spices and rice. . . . The change-over into a plantation-economy involved the actual exploitation of labour . . . in fact, "estate management" over a whole country. . . .'[53]

There are thus many variants of colonial system, each conditioned profoundly by the political, economic and cultural traditions of the metropolitan imperialist power,[54] as well as by the nature of the societies it dominates.

And in the end, whatever the political style of the colonial power, government was only one of the forces bearing on the lives of the inhabitants. Missionaries and planters, prospectors and settlers, to one extent or another, ensured that the coming of the White man did not leave the native undisturbed. He might rarely see a White man, but henceforth his life would never be the same again.

In the colonial situation, whether he sought to be authoritarian or paternalist, bureaucratic or permissive, innovatory or resistant to change, the colonial administrator rested his authority, in the end, on a foundation of power, consolidated by culture and race, which cut him off from his subjects. He might be inclined to consult local opinion: traditional authority, or even, daringly, the vocal 'new men'. But he was disinclined to relinquish decision-making itself. In settler societies, the Whites made sure that liberal tendencies on the part of the Administration never got out of hand. In the last analysis, the message of the colonial administrator was the classic message of the party of order: 'What this country needs,' the proto-nationalists were told, 'is good government, not politics.'

The Raison d'Être

Colonial regimes, however, were not established as some exercise in 'pure power'. They were erected in order to permit the will of the conquering society to be asserted for specific ends. The administrator was not merely there in order to *be* there, like

Everest. The political order, that is, had a content. Power was used for definite purposes, and it was these purposes that shaped the institutions of government themselves – always recognizing that administrators develop their own private vested interests. It is no ideological assertion, but a simple generalization rooted in empirical observation, that the prime content of colonial political rule was economic exploitation.

Two qualifications need to be made: some areas were occupied, not because of direct economic interest in their resources but because they were ancillary to a wider system of imperial domination. Such were the strategically-important territories needed for control over lines of communication and defence. Kenya, for example, was originally merely the land lying between the Swahili East Coast of Africa and Buganda. Uganda itself was primarily wrestled over by French and British – as was the desert Sudan in turn – because of its significance for the control of the Nile valley and the Suez Canal–Red Sea Route. (Later, of course, the intrinsic economic potential of these areas came to constitute an additional reason for colonial interest in them.) In addition, popular demands for the elimination of the slave-trade forced world-Powers into occupying economically uninteresting regions.

The second qualification concerns certain phases in the history of those areas which have been described as 'ultra-colonial' territories; colonies 'owned' by backward European countries, which, because of their own, metropolitan backwardness, failed to modernize the colonial territories which they ruled in name only. Their history is a story of primitive and sterile robbery, through successive modes of exploitation. These range from brutal 'booty' capitalism through to latter-day authoritarian colonial systems in which the colonial territory is used as a 'solution' to misery at home, via the export of unskilled and illiterate White peasants as primitive settlers, and by auctioning the resources of the colonial territory to international corporate capitalist enterprise (which then develops an interest in the regime's continuance and 'stability'). Underdevelopment, and the denial of democracy in Portugal, notably, reproduced themselves in chronic viciousness and backwardness in Angola and Mozambique.[55]

Such 'ultra' colonialisms have for long periods commonly allowed their nominal colonial 'possessions' to vegetate (for example throughout most of the nineteenth century). During this phase, at least, economic exploitation has hardly occurred; indeed, nothing occurred. But without a *raison d'être* of exploitation colonialisms of this kind would have eroded away. They revived and became virulent once more because other expanding colonial powers threatened to seize these areas. Then, their retention became a sacred national cause: prestige was threatened.

'Glory' has certainly been an independent variable of major significance in recent colonial history. Nor is the pursuit of specifically *political* aims anything new. In the nineteenth century, from Algiers to Jules Ferry, France used her North African and other colonial adventures as a device to paper over the cracks in the metropolitan social structure, uniting the divided nation in the common pursuit of national glory, and appealing to common solidarity in the face of a manufactured enemy. The exploitation of the colonies was here a 'psychological' exploitation: its major initial product the creation of national pride in the breasts of Frenchmen. But in the new imperialism after 1885, the importance of colonies as outlets for investment, as markets, and as sources of raw materials changed the character of colonial expansion. Finance-imperialism married with 'social' imperialism. 'Glory' was the greater if it could be validated in the name of a civilizing mission, or of the 'development' of backward regions. Italy in Libya, France in North Africa, Germany in South-West Africa, the Cameroons and German East Africa, all pressed vigorously with colonial transformation, often of a bloody kind. Even for those Powers motivated by considerations of prestige, therefore, the financial-industrial requirements of modern imperialism did not permit their colonial adventures to rest at the level of simple political title to a colonial area. Modern imperialism was inherently transformatory.

The major colonial Powers, however – Britain, France, Belgium, the Netherlands, and Germany – were not stagnant and undemocratic societies like Portugal. They were precisely the most advanced and dynamic societies in the world. *Their* impact on the colonies was revolutionary. And in those key territories they really coveted (in India, Indonesia, Malaya, etc.), as distinct from the resourceless areas occupied for strategic reasons (an Aden or a French Somaliland), government was highly aggressive and innovatory, not sleepy, minimal, and permissive. It was inevitably forceful at least, ruthless at worst.

There were several kinds of economic resource which the colonies offered. Accordingly, the politico-administrative systems developed had different characteristics. Before the nineteenth century, the extra-European world supplied Europe, predominantly, with luxuries: gold, spices, tea. But the Industrial Revolution in Europe revolutionized colonial economic policy: now markets for European products, and raw materials for European factories, were the key need. Because the raw materials were cheaply produced, they were particularly attractive. Capital began to flow towards the colonial areas because the colonial relationship permitted high returns on investment. Capital was not 'exported' in the abstract, however. It had to be employed. Natural resources could not be 'valorized' merely by operations in ledger-books. Their valorization entailed the creation of new patterns of relationship in the colonies. *Men* had to be induced to work in new ways for new people and new ends. The exploitation entailed in colonialism, therefore, was not an exploitation of *things*, fetishistically conceived, but an exploitation between classes of *men*. Geographers may speak of the exploitation of resources. But to utilize or valorize resources, colonialism has to exploit men.

One of Europe's primary requirements was minerals. To win them from the earth, two crucial operations in modernization had to be carried out in a crash-programme: the manufacture of a labour-force, and the development of the mines themselves, plus a communications and transport system to get the ore out of the country (and some elementary processing). The cities it created were not centres of industry, but entrepots through which imports and exports passed. A colonial economy built upon extractive industry is, for these reasons, immediately innovatory. In addition, since a developed mining technology inevitably involves a supply of skilled labour which, initially, only Whites can provide (and later, because they have by then become entrenched, are only *allowed* to provide) an influx of Whites and the development of a caste-ridden 'plural society' are highly probable. The modern political history of South-Central Africa, in large measure, is shaped by its early and continued dependence on mining.

But land is another attractive resource. In the colonial context, it may be exploited in diverse ways: for example, via a peasant economy of small-scale 'horticulture', or by large-scale and bureaucratized plantation-systems. Which of these is adopted depends on the concatenation of a number of factors. One set of variables affecting the social organization and culture of the new colonies was thus constituted by the nature of the economic resource to be exploited, and the relationships of production thereby involved. The political traditions of both the colonizing power and of the indigenous societies constitute a further set of variables. In countries like Buganda and Barotseland, relatively advanced states were able to extract concessions in the form of treaties and 'protectorate' status. But where Europeans set out to direct economic development by politico-administrative means, as in settler or plantation economies, even powerful states such as the Zulu were broken up and absorbed within a new and wider colonial structure. But whether government intervened vigorously or kept in the background, whether it was direct or indirect, whether it undertook economic functions or not, other agencies operating under the protective political shield of government, especially foreign economic and missionary enterprise, unleashed further changes.

The formal relationship of government to the economy thus varied. In Uganda, for example, changes in land-tenure systems introduced by the colonial government laid an important basis for the transformation of the economy into one which could begin to supply the markets of Europe. After the initial, political modification of the land-tenure system, however, the rich black cotton soils were exploited not directly via government quotas or forced deliveries – as in Indonesia – but via the operations of the market. More despotic colonial regimes facilitated more rationalized large-scale, usually foreign-run, agricultural enterprise, as with the large plantations of Sumatra.

One last way in which land could be exploited was by the creation of a settler economy. The export of population to the colonies provided one answer to political and social problems internal to the metropolis.

Europe's demand for the raw materials of the colonies could therefore be satisfied by a variety of mechanisms from market-exploitation of an independent peasant horticulture to centralized administrative direction of a foreign-controlled plantation-economy. Most colonial economies were mixtures of both these and other systems. The nature of the *political* institutions and traditions of both rulers and ruled therefore affected the pattern of *economic* relations; the political institutions themselves were not simply shaped by the requirements of the economy in a one-way manner.

Where a labour-force was needed quickly – in settler territories or in mining and plantation economies – it was quick in the making. Normally, political action stimulated its development. Peasants had to be prised out of self-sufficient traditionalistic economies. Classically, the head- and hut-taxes provided the stimulus. In order to earn the cash to pay them, you had to work for the European. Before long, the 'labour-force' in the towns, plantations, mines, and on European farms, developed new wants: for bicycles, shirts, hurricane lamps, hair oil, film shows, medicine. These could only be satisfied by returning to the White man's work, periodically or permanently. At this stage, the labour-force begins to recruit itself. Government stimulus, even active recruiting, can be relaxed.

Underlying this diversity is one unifying characteristic: it is the imperialist power which dominates the situation, and which seeks to solve its internal socio-economic problems – whether of industrial expansion, capital investment, or the need to create a mystique of national solidarity as a counter to class divisions – by exploitation of colonial territories. For the most part, strictly economic exploitation is the predominant element, transforming mere political control into a process which involves nothing short of the revolutionizing of social relations. For however important 'psychological' exploitation, the central *raison d'être* of imperialism is the extraction of profit from the labour of the indigenous people by Whites by virtue of their control over the political machinery of the state. Only in settler-farmer societies, however, is the actual employer face-to-face with his prey: here, no manager mediates, no hostility can be deflected on to distant invisible owners. The confrontation is not only total, it is also peculiarly direct, and the antagonisms fall along the same line of division in every sphere of relationship: between White and colonized. This is the most explosive of all types of colonial situation.

CHAPTER TWO

AFTER THE DELUGE

From Elite Nationalism to Mass Nationalism

COLONIALISMS before the nineteenth century had often been quite as ruthless and far-reaching in their effect on indigenous society as post-1885 imperialism. They had been so, like modern imperialism, primarily in the interests of the conquering society and its economy. Yet we have followed Lenin in reserving the term 'imperialism' to distinguish modern imperialism sharply from earlier imperialisms. Lenin defined modern imperialism as the 'highest' phase of capital development, in which finance–capital had come to dominate the metropolitan capitalist economy, at a time when the rate of profit at home tended to decline. The export of capital to backward areas, by contrast, offered enormous rewards on investment: super-profits. Others have emphasized that modern imperialism differs sharply from pre-nineteenth-century colonial trade in that the latter consisted principally in luxuries: silk, spices, etc.: whereas modern imperialist trade involves the export of raw materials from the underdeveloped countries to the industrialized ones.

Here, however, we are concerned with the results, rather than the aetiology of imperialism. From this point of view, what is important about the era of high imperialism after 1885 is not that it is 'the highest stage of *capitalism*', but that it is *a new phase in human social development altogether. Imperialism brought about the consolidation of the world as a single social system.*

Pre-nineteenth-century mercantile trade had been essentially marginal in the economic life of the overwhelmingly agrarian economies of both West and East. But as the nineteenth century wore on, the rest of the world became increasingly an intrinsic and significant part of the modern capitalist industrialism of Western Europe. It is in this evolution to a new level of organization of human social relations – the emergence of a world system of society in response to the demands of Western capitalist economic development – that the real historic significance of modern imperialism really lies.

The penetration of the White man into the non-'Western' world was thoroughgoing and convulsive in its effect. The transformation wrought by imperialism was not economic, political, administrative, industrial, agricultural, technological, or ideological. It was all of these. Previous essays in empire might have been devastating – 'booty capitalism' – but they had not always *modernized*. Political revolution could be absorbed: Latin America after Bolívar settled down to generations of domination by land-owners who were (and are) primarily interested in maintaining their privileged domination of agrarian societies.

The power of the White man's culture, by contrast, is evident, for example, in the way it transformed society in the Highlands of New Guinea, *even before the White man himself was actually physically present.*

Here, steel axes were traded in from 'uncontrolled' areas. Within twenty years, a technological revolution had been effected; the few remaining stone axes were only retained by old men as keepsakes. In many areas, religious 'Cargo Cults' broke out, expressions of the emotional and intellectual disturbances which the coming of the White man had sparked off.[1] To a great extent, it is true, the societies of the Highlands were able to absorb these changes within the framework of traditional institutions and ideas: a decrease in the amount of labour-time needed for pure subsistence production led to an expansion of the amount of time devoted to luxury trade and to ritual exchanges. This persistence of traditional patterns was possible because the changes were largely of a technological kind: people were only marginally drawn into the European market-economy. Increasingly, however, both groups and individuals are now beginning to produce for the European market.

The European impact, here, has been relatively gentle, however. Where it was more violent, even advanced cultures could offer little resistance. But whether it was gentle or violent, gradual or sudden, certain basic problems had to be solved everywhere. The first was to create a new administrative system. And in order to administer a sub-continent such as India, the new structure would have to be created on a scale commensurate with the greatness of the conquered territory. It is commonly recognized, even by its critics, that the Indian Civil Service was an instrument appropriately imaginative in conception and organizationally elegant in form.

In staffing the new machinery, two principal courses are open: either you use traditional authorities, and thus consolidate your own rule by absorbing some of the legitimacy accredited to traditional rajahs, chiefs, administrative officials, landowners, priests, etc. – what we normally describe as 'indirect' rule – or you create 'new men'. The difficulties – and the conservatism – inherent in indirect rule, we have already seen. Traditional chiefs and aristocrats, absorbed into the colonial administrative machines as paid civil servants *de facto*, found themselves increasingly dependent on the support of the British, French, or Dutch against their own people. Only a few – a Hassan II in Morocco, the Nyasaland chiefs in Central Africa, the Kabaka Mutesa II in Uganda – might ultimately opt to identify themselves with popular anti-colonial sentiment.

At the bottom of the administrative ladder, the village headmen were in a particularly difficult position, torn between their conflicting allegiances to colonial Governments and to the people they lived amongst. Like foremen or, junior NCO's, they were particularly liable to get stomach ulcers. The people looked to them to represent their interests to Government; Government saw them as the ultimate grass-roots instrument for carrying out official policy and for selling it to the people.[2]

The major alternative was Macaulay's: the creation of 'a class who may be interpreters between us and the millions whom we govern – a class of persons Indian in blood and colour, but English in tastes, in opinions, in morals and intellect'. In view of India's decisive weight in the history of East–West relationships, the record of Macaulay's experiment provides an important type-case which merits closer examination. It exemplifies the general relationship between imperialism and the reaction to it: modern colonial nationalism.

The traditional Mogul administrators of India were quite

unsuitable material as administrators of British India. The people who came to fill the ranks of the Indian Civil Service, therefore, were 'new men'. The traditional Muslim rulers, in most parts of the country, found themselves passed over, and rapidly outstripped by Hindus in education, in commerce, and in industry too. This was not merely because the Moguls had been the military enemies of the British, but rather because their traditional culture as autocratic rulers of a predominantly Hindu agrarian society had developed in them a 'trained incapacity', to use Merton's phrase, for easy adaptation to the new order.

Staffing the ICS involved the recruitment, training and organization of thousands of civil servants out of people not accustomed to ruling, but thereby more adaptable. Some of the traditional rulers and their staffs might be incorporated into the new Civil Service, but the spirit of rationalization which had inspired the remoulding of the *British* Civil Service was equally to provide the inspiration for a new instrument of rule in India. It is one of the ironies of history that the Liberal Party, the party of *laissez-faire*, reorganized not only the Civil Service, but the British educational system and the Army too, and gave the world that crucial modern political invention, the caucus-dominated party-machine. Britain was to stamp itself upon India in a way that was to shape the future of that country. The consolidation of geographical India into political India was to be, in large measure, one of the lasting legacies of the great imperial machinery set up by Britain in India. But not exclusively so: British rule alone did not determine the future shape of Indian nationhood. The other major element was Hinduism – part of India's pre-European, not post-European cultural heritage. Out of the interplay between British domination and traditional culture came modern India – geographical India, consolidated into a polity by Britain, but without its Muslims.

The new officials had to be educated to rule, as Macaulay pointed out. But the expansion of Western education for the new Indian middle classes was more than a political device. It was part and parcel of the rationalist philosophy of the middle classes in Victorian Britain, extended to their equivalents in more benighted parts of the globe. Educational philosophies – themselves rooted in conceptions of society – have thus strongly stamped the societies they have been applied to. Today, for example, the Philippines have an extraordinarily large number of institutions of higher education; college graduates are thick on the ground as in the United States, which shaped the educational system of the Philippines.

British educational policy in nineteenth-century India was much more *élitist*, however, than US policy in the Philippines. It was essentially one of downward filtration. The professions were the most numerous of the new class of Anglicized Indians. Lawyers and government officials were the largest groupings, though they were very restricted in numbers before the 'Mutiny'. Industry and commerce were not to produce many recruits for the new middle classes because they were so weak. On top of the legacy of despotic and monopolistic Mogul rule, the plunder of India under the East India Company and the Company's restrictive economic policies left Indian industry and commerce in a very feeble condition. Flourishing industries had been destroyed. The export of cotton piece-goods fell disastrously in the first quarter of the nineteenth century;[3] at the same time, imports of cotton from Britain steadily increased: the import of cotton goods went up sharply in 1859, and doubled in ten years. Indian exports of raw cotton to Lancashire, however, increased. She now supplied raw materials, not finished goods. The imposition of free trade meant that English manufacturers could always undersell local production. During the American Civil War, when cotton supplies from the USA were cut off, India's exports of cotton boomed. But even this trade steadily diminished as the century wore on.[4] The de-industrialization of the economy, and 'the Drain' (the flow of capital from India to Great Britain), inhibited the development of Indian industry until the third quarter of the nineteenth century.

Agriculture too, was made to stand the burden of the Drain. The export of food and other agricultural produce was to lead to periodic and increasingly serious famines. A vigorous indigenous bourgeoisie was absent in India. When it did come, therefore, nationalism was to be led not by the bourgeoisie, but by the Western-educated professionals and civil servants.

Bengal, and in particular its chief city, Calcutta, naturally came most heavily under European influence. Whatever the economic rapacity of the British, they never developed a totally repressive society such as the Spaniards imposed upon the New World. For one thing, they were faced with the administration of hundreds of millions of people spread over a huge country and firmly-committed to much of their persisting traditional culture, principally their religious values and institutions. As early as 1769, the Governor of Bengal had learned from Mogul experience

'that [the Hindus] would suffer Death rather than any Indignity to their Cast . . . the Mahomedans, who have usually carried their Conquests by the Edge of the Sword . . . when they arrived in Indostan, found it absolutely necessary to sheath the Sword, from a thorough Conviction, that they would deluge the Country with Blood before they could convert one Gentoo to their Laws and Religion . . . they therefore wisely became the Guardians and Protectors of the Hindoo Religion. . . .'5

But however deeply-entrenched Hinduism might be, the new middle classes were significantly Anglicized. The early reformers amongst the intelligentsia were, for example, commonly influenced by Christianity. Ram Mohan Roy, the founder of the first modern Hindu reform movement, Brahma Samaj, learnt Hebrew and Greek in order to pursue his researches in Christianity, and in 1820 wrote a book called *The Principles of Jesus: The Guide to Truth and Happiness*. He had also been affected by Islam. Despite its foundations in the Upanishads, therefore, Brahma Samaj was clearly influenced by Christianity: Roy actually opposed the establishment of a Sanskrit College at Calcutta.

Western culture was not universally accepted without question, however; Ram Mohan Roy was succeeded in the leadership of Brahma Samaj by Debendranath Tagore, a convinced Hindu opposed to Christianity. But he was superseded in the 1860s by Keshab Chandra Sen, founder of Veda Samaj in Madras (which later became the Brahma Samaj offshoot in South India), a fervent admirer of Christianity and Western culture who opposed caste and favoured social reforms via state action. 'The Brahma Samaj,' Misra concludes, 'became the religion of the educated class of Bengali Hindus'. Western culture drove deep into the minds of the Indian intelligentsia:

'. . . educated Bengalis prided themselves on the use of wine and champagne, pipes and beefsteak. . . . To English-educated Indians, who in Bengal were for the most part Brahma Samajists, everything Indian looked primitive and barbarous, dirty and odious'.[6]

For Indians, education thus became the key to progress. The educational innovations of the British were therefore received well; the principal criticism was that they were not ambitious enough. Indigenous reformers thereupon sought to fill the gap themselves. Syed Ahmed Khan organized Aligarh University for Muslims; Ram Mohan Roy built up Benares University for Hindus. Similarly, in Egypt, men like Muhammad Abdu poured their energies into religious reform and the spread of Western-style education.

At this phase of its development, then, the new Indian intelligentsia, however much it operated within the framework of received religion, Hindu or Muslim, sought to remould those creeds in the light of the new European knowledge. Ishararchandra Sharma, the Brahmin Principal of the Sanskrit College at Calcutta, was influential in persuading Government to enact the law of 1856 which sanctioned the remarriage of widows. Both Brahma Samaj and the Bombay Prarthana Samaj repudiated caste and invoked Hindu scripture to justify their position.[7] Ram Mohan Roy too, aligned himself with Macaulay and the 'Anglicists' against the 'Orientalizing' school of Warren Hastings, Minto, Munro, Elphinstone and others who believed equally firmly in the superiority of Western culture, but who considered that it would be best communicated to the masses via the various vernaculars. In the battle between 'Anglicists' and 'Orientalists', the 'Anglicists' won out, and not merely because they had the weight of European official support behind them. In other Oriental countries, too, religious reformers attempted to adapt traditional religion in the light of the teachings and the evident success of the West. Sarekat Islam in Indonesia, Wahhabism in the Arab world, the Muhammadyah in Egypt, all displayed similar tendencies, though the relative weight given to Western and traditional Muslim elements varied.[8] Even Khedive Ismail of Egypt could remark that 'Egypt is part of Europe now.'

The appeal of Western culture was twofold: firstly, that of modern scientific and technological knowledge; and secondly, the new understanding of human society which Western learning promised. An Indian Marxist, writing more than a century later, in the era of Stalin, when the culture of the West was under severe attack in the Soviet Union, is still sufficiently moved, in reflecting upon what the coming of Western culture had meant in terms of new concepts of democracy, national freedom, rationalism, universalism, ethical and political theory, that he breaks into a lengthy panegyric on English culture, and denounces the deficiencies of India's ancient heritage:

'The advantages of the knowledge of English as a result of the introduction of modern education in India cannot be overestimated. . . . Neither Chanakya, the ancient author of Arthra Shastra, nor Vyas, the immortal composer of the Mahabharat, could arm [the Indian economist] with theoretical means to solve modern economic problems. . . .'[9]

The Liberal values enshrined in the educational system of Victorian England, exported to India, thus helped to shape a typically liberal intelligentsia among Indians themselves. This Indian intelligentsia, however, never exhibited quite the same single-mindedness as the westernizing pioneers in Japan: a divergence that profoundly affected the subsequent historical development of those countries. Japan, unlike India, of course, was able to preserve much more of her cultural autonomy because she succeeded in retaining her political independence.

The Indian intelligentsia read avidly the writings of Mill, Ruskin, and Spencer. Inevitably, they found contradictions between the recommendations of these thinkers and the actual Western-created institutions under which they lived. They went further, and read the political writings of Cavour, Kossuth, Tolstoy, and Parnell, and began to draw lessons from the experience of European nationalities struggling for cultural and political self-expression. They thus found inspiration, not merely in liberalism or 'Manchestertum', but also in the contemporary, and earlier, ideals of democratizing revolutionaries. The American and French Revolutions, in particular, inspired them with new notions of independence, democracy, equality and brotherhood. 'Ram Mohan Roy . . . when he made his voyage to England in 1830, insisted, at considerable inconvenience, in travelling on a French ship to demonstrate his enthusiasm for the principles of the French Revolution'.[10]

'It was not Cavour, the "careful statesman", nor Garibaldi, the "liberal Romantic", who inspired them, but the 'story of high idealism, of youthful sacrifice, of secret societies and secret oaths', told by Mazzini.'[11] Before long, *The Life of Mazzini* was banned in India as a dangerous book. Disciples of Mill and Spencer began to query the ethical and political implications of Macaulay's statement: 'We know that India cannot have a free government. But she may have the next best thing – a firm and impartial despotism'.

It has recently been remarked that the most revolutionary book circulating in Africa today is not *Capital* or the Bible, but Longman Green's basic English Primer. So, in the great imperial dominions of the nineteenth century, men drew critical inspiration not necessarily directly from political writings, but from all Western writing that promoted a spirit of inquiry and dispassionate analysis, whether of the solar system or of the social system. Today, the sources of their inspiration seem strange at times. We are not surprised to find that Ahmad Lutfi al-Sayyid, the eminent nationalist pioneer in late nineteenth-century Egypt, drew on Voltaire, Locke, or Rousseau, but we hardly think of Aristotle, whom Lutfi thought 'the most penetrating mind ever created by God',[12] as a likely inspirer of Egyptian nationalism.

Europeanized to this extent as they were, the new intelligentsia nevertheless soon found themselves disadvantaged because of their Indian-ness. Their numbers, too, were growing: at the end of 1874, the number of college students of all kinds was one short of 5,000.[13] Twenty years later, there were 18,571 students. These were hardly enormous figures: even at the turn of the century, there were only some 30,000 graduates in a population of nearly 300 millions. But there was a large wastage rate: 55–60 per cent[14] of the candidates failed their examinations. Moreover, the newcomers had to make their way against formal and informal barriers. They were excluded from higher posts in the Civil Service, and Indians could only become members of the Legislative Councils by appointment.

In the early phases of their emergence, the new middle classes were far from radical. They were, after all, a privileged stratum, drawn predominantly from the ranks of high-caste Brahmans. Indian land-holders and lawyers sitting in the Bengal Legislative Council therefore fought vigorously for the preservation of *zamin-*

dari rights: British Government officials alone fought for the peasant tenants. And if the new middle classes were no friends of the peasantry, they had quite as little sympathy for the industrial workers, and opposed factory reforms actively.

The Indian National Congress, which eventually emerged in 1885, did so under the stimulus of A. O. Hume, an Englishman formerly in Government Service, who believed that new means had to be found to counter the drift to violence that simple repression engenders. Initially, it was able to enlist both the traditional landed interests and the new educated Indian leadership. Dissatisfaction among the educated was beginning to grow by this time, suffering as they did from discrimination in Government Service, and from inequitable taxation. Traditional landowners also resented government measures which undermined their authority. Indian industry, too, laboured under severe competition from a British industry which was aided by the British Raj. When in 1882, the Imperial Government removed all duties on cotton imports into India, in response to the demands of Lancashire manufacturers, Indian industrialists inevitably found themselves in opposition to Government also.

By the time of the Poona session of Congress in 1895, no less than 437 of the 1584 delegates were members of the commercial classes. The crucial issues on which they fought were the extension of political representation – from which they would benefit most directly – and opposition to imperial economic and military policies.

Modern Indian industry had begun to develop in the 1850s, when the first jute mills and coal mines were opened up. By 1880, there were no less than fifty-six coal mines. Much of this new industry was not merely *in* India; it was Indian-owned. The traditional rich began to invest rapidly in the modern sector of the economy, so that by the 1880s, India had its own millionaires in tea and jute. In 1887, the first Indian Chamber of Commerce was founded. The new capitalist class, at this stage, then, was to render important aid to the budding nationalist movement. Later, of course, it was to develop into a pressure-group whose interests were quite distinct from those of the workers they employed.

Politically aggressive it might be, but at the outset of its career Congress was far from being a socially-radical organization. At the conclusion of its opening session, cheers were raised for Queen Victoria. But the commercial interests which were now so strongly represented in Congress had called into being more than a political instrument through which they could press their interests. They had also called into being a new working-class, and an expanded middle class which was finding life increasingly unsatisfactory.

The westernizing religious *reform* movements of the mid-century began to give way to more militant Hindu *revival* movements by the 1870s. Arya Samaj, founded in Bombay in 1875 by Swami Dayanand Saraswati, took as its watchword 'Back to the Vedas'. The four-caste division of society was advocated, and Islam and Christianity rejected. One year before his death, Pandit Dayanand formed an association for the protection of cows. 'Indian religion for the Indians, and Indian sovereignty for the Indians' gave the new nationalism an infusion of intransigent religious exclusivism. One of the responses to it was to be an upsurge of Muslim religious–nationalist revivalism in reaction to the Hindu revival.

The religious revivalist movements, appealing to centuries-old traditional values, were able to build up a powerful following amongst the less-modernized masses where Congress could not. Increasing anti-British feeling came to a head in the 1890s, when the new activist and politically-conscious educated strata began to turn to terrorism as a solution. As in Tsarist Russia, the educated intelligentsia, in their struggle against despotism, began to move from liberal, indeed romantic, idealism, to the gun and the bomb.[15]

The period of violence began with the murder of a European officer, Mr Rand, in 1897. By this time, militant Hindu revivalism had become more than a creed; it was a large-scale movement. At its head was Bal Ganghadhar Tilak, whose irruption on to the political scene heralded the end of the liberal era and the beginning of the modern period of mass nationalism.

Organized terrorism had been first advocated by Aurobindo Ghosh, a First in Classics at Cambridge who had been rejected for the Indian Civil Service, though he had already passed the *examination*, because of his inability to *ride*![16] Before very long, the new mood was sufficiently widespread for Government to shed its original benevolence towards Congress. By 1900, Lord Curzon could even persuade himself that what he wanted to see was actually happening:

'The Congress is tottering to its fall, and one of my great ambitions whilst in India is to assist it to a peaceful demise.'

Ghosh and his brother Barindra, by merging religion with politics, sparked off a wave of terrorism, mainly by middle-class individuals. Tilak, however, concentrated on the development of parallel *mass* movements, and did not hesitate to appeal to explosive 'communal' religious sentiments in order to achieve his aim. He defended child-marriage and organized the 'Cow Protection Society'. In 1893, he began to use the worship of the elephant-god Ganpati as a means of stimulating mass participation. In 1895, he introduced religious festivals in honour of the Mahratta leader Shivaji, who had revolted against Muslim rule. Street processions and para-military 'training' were now the order of the day, and their targets were twofold: Government *and* the Muslims.

Unlike some extremist Hindu revivalists, Tilak was not unwilling to use English education as a weapon against the British. But he was no compromiser: to him, violence was a logical inevitability in Imperial India. Charged with sedition after the Rand murder, he was committed to jail, though later released. In other areas also, the temperature began to rise.

If unwilling to support terrorism, Indian capitalist interests were only too ready to try out forms of action that would advance their interests at the expense of British industry. The boycott of British goods begun in 1906 was much more to their liking than mass violence, and could be linked with the new social philosophy of Swadeshi, the movement for the revival of traditional crafts and manufactures.

The new militancy was expressed in various ways to differing audiences. But it was all urgent and emphatic, for now the intelligentsia were speaking not to themselves, but to the peasants and city-dwellers. Their task was not easy: to lift a whole people weighed down by a past of millennial bureaucratic empires and a present of alien bureaucratic imperialism. To do so, they had to stand on their own feet. To awaken people, the message had to be loud and simple; to move them into action, it had to be urgent and energetic. 'Strength, strength, is what the Upanishads speak to me from every page', cried Swami Vivekananda. 'Youth,' he called, 'be strong. . . . You will be nearer to Heaven through football than through the study of [the] Gita. . . . You will understand [the] Gita better with biceps, your muscle, a little stronger'.[17] Similarly, in Egypt, Lutfi, in his newspaper *al-Jaridah* attacked the self-abasement of the Egyptian people, the treatment of other people and even oneself as helpless 'animals' – and the other side of the coin: the worship of the strong and the spectacular. Away with passivity and abasement, he counselled; away with submissive adoration of heroes like Napoleon. The people themselves must stand up.

When Tilak was arrested once more in 1908, a general strike of Bombay textile workers broke out. With this event, we enter the new phase of Indian *mass* nationalism that was to dominate the Indian political scene until the British withdrawal. True, the new mood did not affect everybody. As late as 1915, a young Indian from South Africa named Gandhi made a recruiting speech in which he declared: 'I discovered that the British Empire had certain ideals with which I have fallen in love'.[18]

The replacement of the '*élite* nationalism' of the westernized minority by mass nationalism inevitably changed the content of the nationalist ideology. To win the allegiance of the masses it was necessary, on the one hand, to appeal to traditional values and symbols eminently available in Hinduism and Islam, and on the other, to offer solutions to the new problems which peasant and urban-dweller alike found crowding in upon them. The problem for the nationalist movement, at this stage, becomes one of keeping the various classes under the same umbrella.

Signs of strain soon appeared: in 1916, the Aga Khan resigned from the Muslim League, which he felt had become too radical. In 1918–20, there was a big wave of strikes. The leaders of nationalism now became convinced that their major weapon was the power of the masses. But it was often difficult to enlist the masses in the struggle for national independence, a goal so distant that it seemed unconnected with the problems staring them in the face here and now. The new nationalism, therefore, had to adopt a *social* policy, too, if it was to generate enthusiasm amongst the poor and the illiterate for Swaraj. Increasingly, Congress introduced such planks into its policies. The militants amongst the Congress leadership found the situation ideal for the propagation of more revolutionary tactics and more revolutionary social objectives. Civil Disobedience on a mass scale was first used in 1920–1, though it was called off by Gandhi when peasant violence threatened to become widespread. But the power of Congress lay essentially in its mass following, and in the ebb and flow of political struggle it was inevitable from time to time that trials of strength between Government and Congress would take place. When Congress was proscribed in 1930, no less than 90,000 people were committed to jail by the following year. Despite this, radical actions such as the campaign against the salt-tax, or the mass Civil Disobedience of 1932–4, brought new accessions of strength and a new militancy in the leadership. The socialist wing under Nehru emerged as the Congress Socialist Party – within Congress – in the 1930s.

India had become a significantly class-differentiated society by this time. In 1921, there were 12·7 million landless agricultural labourers; by 1931, 65·6 millions. The peasantry had shrunk from 74·6 millions to 65·5, and the urban working-class numbered 15·3 millions.

But though the nationalist movement could often successfully harness these class discontents, it was also split down the middle by them. To keep millionaire industrialists and militant trade unionists in harmony was not easy. But no organization can withstand violence on the scale applied by the British in the 1930s. The era of repression seriously affected Congress morale and organization. With many thousands in jail, membership declined to half a million by late 1936, and the anti-British super-militancy which repression produced among a minority was a reaction not so much of strength as of weakness and desperation. When Subhas Chandra Bose became President of Congress in 1939, it was to be only a short time before he turned to the Japanese as the only hope in a black situation.[19]

And then the world changed once more, irrevocably. World War I might have been largely a 'European Civil War' (albeit one which helped hasten the break-up of China and the rise of Japan), but World War II, emphatically, was not. To the colonial world, it was a supreme opportunity. White masters were turned into White coolies. Asians – Japanese and nationalists – came into power all over Asia. On the Allied side, Indian troops bore the brunt of the Burma campaigns. And the war introduced the more backward peoples of Africa to the world, just as World War I had introduced Ho Chi Minh to Europe, along with hundreds of thousands of other conscripted labourers from Indo-China and soldiers from West Africa. World War II opened up the final phase in the disintegration of imperialism. While the older nations fought against each other, the would-be nations used their opportunity, skilfully combining both legal and underground methods, ostensible 'collaboration' and actual armed violence. Society was turned upside down; millions of people passed through forced-draft cataclysmic experiences: a 'higher education' of killing, deportation, conscription, forced deliveries. They were wheedled, bribed, forced, cajoled; promised dignity, self-rule, pie in the sky.

By 1945, the re-establishment of the old order was clearly impossible. The Dutch tried in Indonesia, the French in Indo-China. The crucial step, however, was taken in India. By 1946, the British realized that the game was up. The Indian National Army officers who had fought alongside the Japanese in Burma were national heroes whom the British might try in court, but dared not punish. The Royal Indian Navy mutinied in Bombay harbour. British troops were war-weary and impatient for de-mobilization, even to the extent of going on strike. Many of them, caught up in the wartime democratic mood, found no pleasure in eternal practice at 'riot drill' (warn them first, then shoot), and even less at the prospect that the skills learnt might have to be used. Neither the Labour Government nor the British people *wanted* to take on the suppression of a sub-continent of 400 million people, even though Britain had more forces under arms than ever before in history.

India received her independence peacefully. In her wake, Syria, the Lebanon, Burma, Ceylon, got theirs. Indonesia and Indo-China had to wrest theirs in bitter war.

Though we have examined the Indian case in detail because of its actual importance, we have also used it to illustrate the general process of the displacement of liberal nationalism by mass nationalism. Though the nationalist movements of every country each have their own specific features, it would not be dfficult to demonstrate at length, for, say, Indonesia, the parallel intertwining of early nationalism with movements of Westernization and religious revivalism, or the early co-operation between the new educated intelligentsia and the wealthy upper classes, old and new, and the subsequent bid for mass support by the radical intelligentsia.

At different rates and times in different countries, but usually in the same direction, modern mass nationalism took root, and drove out the older liberal nationalism. In some pioneer countries, such as India, the phase of 'liberal nationalism', as we have seen, might be spun out over decades. In others, notably in contemporary Africa, similar phases have been compressed into the fervid turmoil of a few years. But liberal nationalism scarcely outlived the heyday of Europe's own *laissez-faire* era. New models – the Turkish Revolution, the rise of Japan, the Russian Revolution – increasingly affected the 'internal' nationalist movements. None of these successful experiments in modernization were liberal models. In the twentieth century, therefore, when nationalists in the colonial countries drew inspiration from outside, they drew it from militant, modernizing, mass nationalism, and from socialism or communism, not from Spencer or Mill. But it would be an entirely Europocentric way of approaching modern nationalism in the Third World to look at it as if it were composed of imitations of Western prototypes – liberalism, socialism, and communism. Nationalism in the colonized countries increasingly took on characteristics of its own. Indeed, 'the nation' was a quite different phenomenon in Asia and Africa. It grew out of African and Asian culture-histories that date back much further than the era of colonization. Nationalism in the Third World, therefore, has to be understood in terms of itself, not merely in terms of those European-derived elements that have been incorporated into it, or in terms of the legacy of European rule. The European conquerors did not build their empires in a cultural vacuum; instead, they found themselves dealing with cultural traditions of great antiquity and diversity which rarely resembled the cultures of Europe.

The Definition of the Nation

The countries that remained colonies after 1945, and whose

liberation was not to come until the 1950s were markedly different, in important ways, from an India or an Indonesia. 'Indonesia is no mere geographical expression', remarks a noted American writer on that country. Culturally, it is 90 per cent Muslim; it inherits an historical legacy going back to the Shrivijaya and Majapahit empires; centuries of trade have given it a *lingua franca*.

But one searches the literature of cultural history in vain for the predecessors of Transjordan, Nigeria or Kenya, countries which *were*, more than Italy, originally mere 'geographical expressions', lines drawn on the map by White men. We must not exaggerate, however:

'Nobody will claim that these frontiers, determined by distant and ill-informed negotiators, were well-adapted to African needs. It is true that their arbitrary nature is often over-emphasized; relatively few were settled by ruler and compasses alone. Since European claims were often based upon treaties with African rulers, these were in many cases where the new frontiers coincided with traditional ones; other things being equal, the colonial powers preferred to follow chiefdom boundaries, where these were known. But even these boundaries might still divide Africans of the same language and culture; and once they came under effective European occupation, they became harder to cross than would have been the case in the past. And in addition there were numerous cases where European political requirements, such as the desire to have frontiers convenient for the collection of customs duties led to the deliberate partition of an African state. Neighbouring Africans with virtually identical cultural traditions now found themselves subject to different laws, learning different languages and different doctrines in school, using new transport routes which carried them toward different ports and capital cities. . . . Distant places without schools or roads often preserved old relationships with their neighbours across the frontier, sometimes to the confusion of colonial officers. Yet even in such places the new colonial frontiers would in the long run shape the political future.'[20]

The modern political structure even of independent Nigeria is the outcome of this transformation by the colonial Power of ancient cultural zones into modern political divisions: the Muslim North, the predominantly-Yoruba Western Region, and the Ibo-majority Eastern Region. Yet it was an unintended development dictated by administrative convenience, not a conscious encouragement to wider political identification.

In 1920, Sir Hugh Clifford had made clear what he considered to be the basic 'national' groupings in Nigeria:

'It is the consistent policy of the Government of Nigeria to maintain and to support the local tribal institutions and the indigenous forms of Government. . . . I am entirely convinced of the right, for example, of the people of Egbaland . . . or any of the great Emirates of the North . . . to maintain that each one of them is, in a very real sense, a nation.
. . . National self-government in Nigeria . . . secures to each separate people the rights to maintain its identity, its individuality and its nationality, its own chosen form of government; and the peculiar political and social institutions which have been evolved for it by the wisdom and by the accumulated experience of generations of its forebearers. . . .'[21]

Even more foolish, he believed, was the suggestion that there is, or could be in the visible future, such a thing as a 'West African Nation' – a 'manifest absurdity', since 'the peoples of West Africa do not belong to the same stock and are not of common descent.' These 'ridiculous claims and pretensions' were 'mischievous'; they were 'incompatible with that natural development of real national self-government which all true patriots in Nigeria . . . should combine to secure and maintain. . . .'

Nigerian nationalism was an absurdity; West Africanism ridiculous. The 'natural' national unit was the traditional 'tribe' or Emirate.

Sir Hugh's outburst is an excellent example of the paternalist administrator's point of view. It did not deny African institutions – it sought to reaffirm them. It did not impose Europe upon Africa – it sought to outflank that 'self-selected and self-appointed congregation of educated African gentlemen who collectively style themselves the West African National Conference', 'from the Left', as it were: from a pro-*African* standpoint. They, not the Whites, were seeking to '. . . impose . . . political theories evolved by Europeans to fit on a wholly different set of circumstances. . . .' The argument is familiar: administrators have always preferred the martial Pathan to the Hindu peasant; the backward Masai to the upstart Kikuyu; the villager to the town-dweller; the illiterate to the 'half-educated'; men who respected 'tribal' obligations and 'the duties to their Natural Ruler which immemorial

custom should impose on them'[22] to men who listened to the
seductive words of 'agitators', if for no other reason than that 'it
is always easier to handle people who do not ask questions'.[23]
Here we find a peculiar fusion of a T. E. Lawrence-type romantic
mystique of the 'noble savage' with the administrative view of
society. All monocentric and bureaucratic societies, from Stalinist
Russia to colonial Nigeria, prefer 'administrative' to 'political'
methods. The open expression of conflict, they (wrongly) believe,
constitutes a weakness; it destroys solidarity internally, and ex-
poses the society to external attack and subversion. Administrative
ideologies are developed to justify the political order: in the USSR,
for theological reasons, Marxists could hardly deny the existence
of classes, or the inevitability of conflict, but these tenets had to be
modified as revolutionary movements became transformed into
state machines. The final ideological stabilization was to come
from Mao Tse-Tung, who asserted that relationships between the
classes in Communist China, though 'contradictory', were 'non-
antagonistic'.[24] Colonialist ideology, too, asserted that society was
'naturally' free from conflict: those who asserted otherwise were
political 'agitators', irrational and destructive forces in a rationally-
ordered polity.

In reality, the conflict-free society does not exist. Men play
numerous roles: they have different interests. Politics is the clash
of these interests. To the administrator, these matters are best
decided by Platonic guardians, who – unlike the self-appointed
leader or the ignorant peasant – *know*. That is their job. Once the
decisions have been taken at the top, the rest of 'normal' political
life becomes devalued to mere administration: the carrying out of
decisions.

Sir Hugh Clifford, therefore, like Mao, eschewed internal
politics – conflict, discussion, factions, the application of force
and pressure by interest-groups. The colonies were given tem-
perate and wise government, order and security. Communist
China, more pressed, was given revolutionary and hard-bitten
government, but also – order and security.

But Sir Hugh did, of course, raise one very real problem.
He was drawing attention to the existence of utterly different
conceptions of what constituted 'nationality': a major problem
for the social sciences, so neglected that nearly all the serious

research on the subject has been contributed by one scholar – Hans Kohn.[25]

The word 'nationalism' is used in at least three distinct and major senses. It is used to refer to: (1) Movements which seek to build, or consolidate, State systems on the basis of pre-existing cultural ties – of religion, language, 'race', etc. – by fostering enhanced consciousness of these ties. The nationalisms of nineteenth-century Europe were classically of this type. Here, the cultural bases of nationalism have existed for centuries. The Polish or Czech language, for example, provided a cultural rallying-point for national sentiment and organization. It was essentially a *unitary* kind of nationalism. *The* nationality was to become co-extensive with *the* State. (2) Movements which establish, or seek to establish, independent States on the basis of common citizenship of entirely novel political and cultural entities – especially those created by foreign colonial powers (e.g. practically all Africa south of the Sahara.) Here the 'nationals' do not necessarily inhabit the same traditional cultural universe: they only share their colonial fate in common. (3) 'Pan' movements – for which, significantly, we have not as yet a special term, since we rarely think clearly enough about them to see that they are quite distinct from (1) and (2). 'Pan' movements transcend established state boundaries: they are built upon much wider cultural affiliations: religious (Pan-Islamism); linguistic and 'cultural' (Slavophilism, Pan-Arabism); physical (*négritude*, Garveyism); even continental (Pan-Africanism).

Both 'Pan' movements and 'orthodox' national movements of type (1) seek to bring new political entities into being, of course. The distinction, therefore, might be considered invalid. The 'Pan' movement, however, is distinguishable in terms of two factors: scale and degree of political innovation. Orthodox nationalism of type (1) base themselves upon some existing State, (English nationalism from Henry VIII to Elizabeth), or portion of a State (nineteenth-century Czech nationalism), or former State (Polish nationalism under Partition). 'Pan' movements seek to combine conventional States to form a much wider super-State – the whole Arab world, the united African continent, etc.

These, of course, are 'ideal' emphases upon key aspects of movements, none of which relies solely upon one type of appeal. They are thus models. We use terms like 'democracy' or 'capitalism' in common speech, even though no one country may actually exhibit all the features which we posit as characteristics of 'democracy'. Similarly, no nationalist movement – no 'historical individual', to use Weber's terminology – is, in actuality, 'purely' religious, 'purely' an appeal to linguistic community, etc. They are all, more or less, multiplex.

Normally, in discussing nationalism, two separate issues are involved, though rarely separated. The first concerns the boundaries of the nation; the second, the kind of social arrangements within those boundaries which the nationalist movement wishes to establish. For the moment, let us examine the first issue.

In Western Europe, the unitary nation-state was triumphant by the nineteenth century. It was normally created out of a fairly culturally-homogeneous population, sharing common language and common religion. Where significant ethnic minorities existed – as in Wales or Brittany – they had uniformity imposed on them by the dominant people inhibiting the 'heartland' – in England, the South-East Midlands; in France, the Ile de France – either by force of arms, or by 'cultural' domination, or both.[26] Unification, centralization, and cultural standardization were imposed and consolidated by war and religion.

Here we are not concerned to examine the causes of the triumph and pre-eminence of the specific 'heartland' areas. For the early European nation-states, they would centre around the growth of centralized markets, and the subsequent elaboration of a whole 'standard' national culture based on the culture of the dominant core-area. The pre-eminence of London and Paris, due to the superiority of their location in economic and geographical terms, facilitated the emergence of the South-East Midlands and Parisian dialects as 'standard' English and 'standard' French respectively. Chaucer's works symbolize this victory: from thenceforth, the major rival English dialects were condemned to the cultural museum of the Chester and Wakefield miracle plays. Elsewhere, backward, not advanced areas, became the core of the new state under an Absolute Monarchy – Spain came to life as a modern state under the leadership of the backward provinces of Old Castile and Aragon, with effects which are still visible in the archaism of Spanish society today.

In Western Europe, the consolidation of the state normally

preceded the serious emergence of nationalism. People who lived in states that became increasingly consolidated as political and economic entities became ever more conscious of their common situation, and developed a common overall culture. The nationalism that emerged was that of the nation-state: more precisely, the unitary nation-state. In countries where the consolidation of the state had been delayed, the nationalist movements of the nineteenth century also sought to develop a single-nation Italy, a single-nation Poland, and so on.

Certain new emphases were visible in nineteenth-century nationalism, however. A new note of universalism, set vibrating by the Enlightenment and by the revolutions of the eighteenth century, rang disharmonically with the older unitary state-nationalism. Rationalistic theories concerning the common elements in human nature had important implications for political theory and for political practice.[27] Men inspired by universalistic concepts and ideals such as allegiance to Reason and Humanity dictated, stretched their mental horizons beyond the limits imposed by their ascribed condition as Frenchmen or Englishmen, and strove to escape from the particularistic bounds set by traditional culture. Freemasonry crossed national frontiers. A Paine, or a Lafayette, showed in their lives that an Englishman could struggle for the rights of Frenchmen to overthrow the past; a Frenchman offer his life for American independence. *Inter*nationalism was injected into the modern liberal and working-class movements by men such as these. The revolutions which emerged were therefore of a more complex character. In Latin America, Bolívar the Liberator dreamed of an 'Amphycthyonic League' which would unite all the liberated Spanish provinces. Mazzini in Europe not only built up a 'Young Italy' movement, but saw it as part of 'Young Europe'.[28]

New ideological currents thus linked specific nationalisms to wider appeals. But there were other reasons why internationalism and nationalism were to develop as complementary rather than antagonistic creeds. In particular, the ethnic situation in the great ramshackle empires of Central and Eastern Europe differed from that of Western Europe. Tsarist Russia was indeed 'the prison-house of nationalities', not merely of one major oppressed nationality. Struggling for their own self-determination, the separate nationalisms of Eastern Europe found themselves aligned against a common enemy. 'Private' nationalism was a poor weapon: it could be too easily turned against equally oppressed brethren of different nationality. No government ever exploited inter-ethnic hostilities with greater skill and assiduity than the Tsarist: the pogrom has stamped itself into the history of that part of the world with effects that are visible today. Despite this vicious 'nationalist' tradition, and the Tsarist use of 'Slavophilism' as an ideology by which internationalist sentiment might be transmuted into a 'supra-nationalist', imperialistic ideology, the mere life-situation of these nationalities did stimulate a new sense of 'international nationalism'. True, this kind of sentiment might be largely confined to the intelligentsia: at peasant level, chauvinistic nationalism and ethnic prejudice were more normal. But the ideas of the intelligentsia were crucial since they provided the leadership.

The history of the new nations which emerged out of the disintegration of Austria–Hungary held quite different lessons for nationalists in Africa and Asia from those which the history of earlier European nationalisms suggested. Some smaller unitary nation-states were still established in Europe even at this time: Sweden, Norway and Finland, for example. But others were quite explicitly *multi*-national, notably Czechoslovakia and Yugoslavia. The nationalities inhabiting Tsarist Russia, again, after a brief independence, for some, during the transition to Soviet rule, thereafter received a formal autonomy (with whatever limitations) within a wider *federal* system.

The new 'potential' nations of Africa and Asia thus found the experience of these multi-national states highly relevant for their own situation, since the colonial entities out of which they had developed were of very recent growth: the Gold Coast came into being as a single unit only in 1901; Nigeria in 1914. In extreme, a capital had to be invented for a backward country like Mauritania, on the attainment of independence.[29] The Upper Volta, to take another case, was detached from the Ivory Coast in 1919 to become a separate colony, only to be dismembered again in 1932, when its administrative buildings and new factories were dismantled, its printing press and public works equipment given to the Ivory Coast, work on its water supply halted, and the municipal council dissolved.[30]

Such recent, often chopped-and-changed, political entities, frequently embracing hundreds of formerly separated peoples, hardly evoked in their citizens the same sense of deep-rooted community that a China, a France, an Egypt, or even a Poland could do. It was tempting, therefore, to dismiss the nationalisms that did emerge among such populations as absurd or irrational pretensions, and to assume that the fanaticism fanned by 'agitators' would soon be dissipated. Borders between these countries were accordingly called 'inter-territorial boundaries', not 'international frontiers'.

To the governors, the irrelevance of nationalism was a deep-rooted article of faith. Because nationalism was irrelevant it was not dangerous: it could even be used to counter *more* dangerous movements. Tribal loyalty, loyalty to a religion, any identification other than nationalism was real and valid and therefore more dangerous. In Indonesia, the Islamic scholar, Snouck Hurgronje, was so convinced that Pan-Islamism, under the spur of Muhammad Abdul's modernism, was the sole great danger, that he advocated a thorough-going programme of fostering Indonesian *national* consciousness – from Indonesianization of the Civil Service to 'national' education – as a counter to Islam.[31]

Underlying some of these attitudes were Western-imperialist assumptions. The Empires of Western Europe, Dutch, French, British, Belgian, represented the high peaks of social evolution: their benefits were now 'offered' to their non-European subjects. But no sooner had the British Empire, for example, become consolidated than it was faced by new challenges: the White Dominions refused to be dominated; nationalist Ireland revolted, and ultra-Conservative proponents of English rule rebelled in the North against their own Government. Indian nationalism was rapidly becoming a dangerous force. By 1936, forward-looking Conservatives like Harold Macmillan were arguing that Britain should base her strategy on co-operation between large industrial states and on the development of international finance corporations, rather than on a protective Commonwealth-colonial economic community.

But ideas die hard, especially when buttressed by hard interests and by appeals to flags, blood, and 'dominion'. The consolidation of Empire coincided with the beginning of its disintegration:

Churchill's celebrated remark about not presiding over the liquidation of the British Empire was already anachronistic when it was made in 1942. This paradox underlies the obscure frustrations and vehemence of a Beaverbrook in the face of nascent nationalism. The most beneficent regime in history was being ungratefully, ignorantly, and wilfully rejected. Nehru, Nkrumah and Nasser were the objects of special hatred and virulent attack, and Suez was to show that Lord Beaverbrook's views were shared by a majority in the country. But whereas the British had learned something from the experience of attempting to contain revolution in Ireland, France and Holland were to carry their 'ultra' nostalgia to the battlefields of Indo-China, Algeria, and Indonesia.

Irish nationalism was relatively 'understandable'. These were people with a distinct and ancient European culture. But it was preposterous to speak of the Nigerian or Congolese 'nation'. Because the colony was commonly an arbitrary creation in the beginning, the denial of legitimacy to the new nationalisms of the colonies was an understandable imperialist reflex. But it was not *merely* an imperialist reflex, for many of these new territories were clearly novel entities with no real pre-European cultural or political unity. The colonizers, however, were not loath to develop artificial 'national' entities when 'Pan' nationalism was the major danger. The extreme in artificiality was reached in the Middle East, where Pan-Arabism was fobbed off by perching alien dynasties from Southern Arabia on top of new 'kingdoms', carved out of existing congeries of sheikhdoms from a dismembered Ottoman Empire. The new despotic rulers of these oil-rich lands were then backed by powerful military support.

Afro-Asian nationalism is thus normally either *narrower* than classical European nationalism, or *wider*. On the one hand, people retain loyalties to their village, clan, or tribe; on the other, they belong to other pre-European political and cultural entities of different ranges of inclusiveness and intensity of meaning: they speak common or related languages. Systems of descent and inheritance; agricultural systems; common historical origins; trade, religious ties, and other cultural bonds link people across modern political divisions, and divide them within the new boundaries. For the simpler societies, in particular, no traditional 'borders' can be discerned with any precision. These complex overlapping fields of cultural community persist even today; in appropriate situations, they are invoked and activated. A broad term like 'traditionalism' scarcely does justice to their complexity, particularly for stateless societies like the Kikuyu, which, though acephalously organized into hundreds of separate territorial units, nevertheless shared common religious beliefs and practices, e.g. common initiation-cults, which gave a measure of integration to the hundreds of thousands of Kikuyu.

But even at their widest – even if half the population of pre-European Africa did live in State societies, and the bulk of them in a few great empires at that – hundreds of pre-White ethnic groups and political communities may still be recognized today in a country like Kenya. Now, however, their 'tribalism' has changed: It is a 'tribalism' of post-colonialism, not the bounded tribalism we saw graphically depicted for the Nuer on p. 9. The meaning of 'tribe' changes, because the world in which the tribe exists, towards which it has to define its identity, has changed. Today, the old tribal divisions have been invested with a new content: the boundary they exist within is the Kenyan state, not the contiguous world of their traditional immediate neighbours. 'Tribal' rivalries are now jostlings for position within the total framework of the State and ultimately of the world: this kind of tribalism is, therefore, quite novel; it brings together coalitions of minor tribelets into political entities which never existed previously. Its modern expression, therefore, is – naturally – the 'ethnic' political *party*.

Contemporary political developments show the importance of these ancient but novel divisions: Nigeria's three Regions, and India's 'linguistic provinces', are modern federal structures grafted on to ancient cultural divisions. In large territories like the Congo or Nigeria, where traditional cultural diversity has been reinforced by unbalanced economic development in different parts of the country, the new nationalism is more often decentralized, multiplex, and federal, than centralized, standardized and unitary. These countries usually have no national language other than that provided by the White conqueror. National unity, then, is something that has to be developed and *worked at*, *after* independence; unification, consolidation and centralization are at a premium. With the attack on the Action Group, and the rapid decline of KADU, Nigeria and Kenya, for instance, seem to be moving towards the elimination of the multi-party system. Ethnic divisions threaten to destroy the scarcely-won unity of the new state: the pioneer independent Black African state of modern times, Ghana, showed the way: the Congo, the ultimate danger. Nkrumah fought his first internal battle against the regionalism of the Ashanti, a people whose proud independence over centuries was reinforced by modern prosperity as the centre of the cocoa-growing industry, and threatened to give rise to two centres of power in the country. Ashanti regionalism took the modern form of the political party: firstly, the National Liberation Movement, and later the United Party. The lessons of Nkrumah's success, and of Lumumba's failure, have not been lost on the new countries: 'tribalism' is a heresy. Even in more advanced countries, severe cultural imbalance brings political regionalism in its train: the Communist uprising in Telengana, or the less violent crisis in Kerala, show how ideological antagonisms can emerge out of modern regional inequality superimposed on ancient cultural divisions.

The consolidation of the new state does not eliminate the fact of ethnic diversity. Where it is very marked, a unitary state is impossible initially: a federal structure has to be adopted, as in Nigeria, the Congo, or Kenya, or ethnic pluralism diverted into the relatively harmless channels of lower-level (district or provincial) administrative divisions.

But the state itself is not an isolate. Because of the newness of the 'nation' allegiances go far beyond boundaries drawn by White men with rulers and survey-instruments. The Ovambo divided by the Angola/South-West Africa interterritorial boundary are no less Ovambo for all that. People are united across borders by economy, ecology, religion, history, and a dozen other factors. The appeal of Pan-Africanism in contemporary Africa thus reflects much more than some inexplicable mystical penchant for romantic grandeur in the new Africa. It springs from three major sources, the first two of which we have already examined:

(1) The persistence into our time of pre-European cultural traditions which do not necessarily coincide with European-created boundaries at all

(2) The recency of these ex-colonial units as integrated 'societies'

and their consequent weakness as consolidated political entities

(3) The attainment of statehood by a quite different route from that travelled by the Old World nation-states, to wit, via struggle against imperialism.

The new states of this century have emerged primarily as a result of the mutual rivalry and competition for world-domination by a handful of advanced Western-European countries. Because they have been subjected to a common life-fate, the peoples of the emerging countries, then, have begun to become aware not only of themselves, but also of their common interests with *other* peoples. The common life-situation they have shared has not been subjection to an Oriental despot, or to a mercantilist European power; it has been, specifically, subjection to modern capitalist imperialism. Colonialism and capitalism, therefore, have been rejected the one with the other, normally. The peoples dominated by imperialist regimes have become bound together because the governments of the imperialist powers have imposed common pressures upon them: the arbitrary drawing of interterritorial boundaries; the denial of their existing social and cultural heritage; the repression of their languages; the disruption of traditional society and economy.

As George Herbert Mead has put it (and his analysis is valid for social groups as well as for individuals), the Self is a social product. The individual can only become conscious of himself when he is forced to think *of* himself, to stand outside his own skin-boundary and see himself as others see him. Then he becomes an 'object to himself', a Me as well as an I.[32] This happens when he encounters an Other. Just as the baby begins to distinguish its body from the rest of the world outside himself, because external forces constrain him, make him feed or urinate at prescribed times in prescribed ways, the colonized become aware of themselves as one, only in contradistinction of their White overlords. Consciousness of self thus arises out of this process of opposition and distinction. The *kinds* of opposition, however, are constantly shifting; new ranges of consciousness and belongingness emerge, and old identifications lose their significance.

President Nasser has put the matter well in *The Philosophy of the Revolution*. For an Egyptian, he says, the world consists of three 'circles': the circle of the Arab world, the circle of the

77

Muslim world, and the circle of the African continent. One might extend this mode of analysis further, for every man belongs to a series of groups and categories, beginning with his family. In Africa the village, 'tribe', linguistic stock, district, province, colony, constitute some of the principal circles of attachment. But the circles are also arranged in various hierarchies. Some allegiances prove stronger than others in different situations. In the last resort, blood may prove thicker than membership of rival parties – or brother may kill brother in guerilla war.

At all levels of allegiance, there are conflicting claims on loyalty. At the highest level, an Egyptian may be moved by feeling for his fellow-Muslims. He may, at other times, burn for the wrongs suffered by fellow-Arabs. (These two circles normally overlap.) He may yearn to be united with fellow-Africans or with the Bandung peoples. Which of these will eventually prove to be the strongest will depend on the overall world situation, constantly changing. It is this competition of allegiance, amongst other things, that has frustrated 'Pan' movements in the past. Despite torrents of Pan-Arabist rhetoric, for example, appealed to by Right and Left alike, by conservatives and modernizers, the Arab Near East after World War I was parcelled up into a number of new polities, some roughly coincident, it is true, with former Ottoman divisions, others merely pseudo-states: Transjordan, Palestine, Syria, Saudi Arabia, Iraq, suddenly appeared on the map. 'Pan-Arabism' (or Pan-Islamism) seemed to be merely an idealistic and illusory dream, a lost cause: the reality was a congeries of client-statelets propped up and controlled by Britain and France. Indeed, one wonders why the world archaically went on using the term 'balkanization', when the more relevant 'arabization' only awaited the coining.

But external frustration of 'Pan' ideals was not the only cause of the failure of Pan-Arabism, any more than it was the cause of the failure of Bolívar's Amphycthyonic League in liberated Latin America. One other set of causes stems from internal class, regional, and ethnic divisions in the new countries, producing a struggle for power between rival *élites*, from the persistence of ancient cultural adherences and the rise of new ones. In general terms, 'the society' is imperfectly integrated, internally and externally.

For all these reasons, the definition of the national unit is not a simple matter. Men are pulled in various directions. They belong to no *single* cultural community: in a sense, indeed, all societies are 'plural'. And this is increasingly the case, since the spread of relationships across the world constantly creates new ranges of connection. To some extent, this has always been so: some form of maximal identification, often linked to language, religion, race, or culture, has no doubt always existed. If we use 'nationalism' to refer to this kind of allegiance and identification, then, we can say that it is as old as human society, and it is merely European ethnocentrism to assert that the nation only emerges in the epoch of 'developing capitalism'.[33] Once the local community ceases to be the principal focus of social organization, people find their lives shaped by membership of ever-wider entities, political and cultural, which give them interests in common. But since men's social and cultural memberships are always multiple, since they belong to more than one 'circle', nationalisms which claim *total* allegiance – and, historically, most nationalisms have done this – can easily be shown to be logically at fault, consequently, to be merely 'ideological' assertions of a spurious unity rather than scientific statements. If we take 'ideological' nationalism at its face value, then, as Kedourie does, and define it in terms of conformity with some single unambiguous criterion such as 'language, race, or religion',[34] it can easily be shown: (*a*) that no population is decisively homogeneous in all respects; (*b*) that all existing 'national' states contain more or less sizeable minorities, whatever criterion one uses; and (*c*) that many 'nationalisms' (e.g. British or American) do not fit these patterns at all, and are not, therefore, properly 'nationalisms'. Nationalism, it is held, is therefore an exclusivist, intolerant, rather silly, even unnecessary or irrelevant set of ideas, for no people is ever 'homogeneous' or 'pure'. The search for total 'logical' purity is a delusion. Are there not, for example, always distinctions of dialect within a language? There is no 'pure' English tongue; only a dialect that became conventionally standardized as the norm. And who can absolutely define what is a dialect and what a language? Physically, too, the peoples of the world are incredibly mixed: even within such recognizably distinct stocks as the Australian aborigines, there are many sub-varieties of hair-colour, height, skin-colour, etc. The demand for absolute purity is spurious, and may well lead, as Hannah Arendt has argued and the Nazis proved, to totalitarianism and to the gas-chamber: the logical end-point of the 'pure' nation-state taken to its ultimate.[35]

The objections to this 'intellectualist' approach to nationalism are twofold. Firstly, 'single-criterion' nationalism is not the only type: all nationalisms themselves, indeed, have postulated something markedly different: the *coincidence* of *numerous* cultural criteria, all of which are asserted to be common attributes of the 'national' group in question. To take a European case, Polish nationalism appealed to common language *and* common religion; among the newer nationalisms, Nasser refers most explicitly to *three* ranges of belongingness.

Secondly, and more importantly, the nation is a *sociological*, and not a *logical* category. Ideological assertions of national solidarity can easily be shown to be at variance with reality – Polish nationalism was shot through with cross-cutting class-divisions, just as the modern Arab national state is subject to the pulls of Pan-Arabism. But nationalism does reflect one important dimension of 'belongingness', and one which has become increasingly decisive in the modern world. Deflation of nationalist claims in terms of their internal inconsistency does not prove their absurdity. They would be absurd only if men operated with totally consistent philosophies. Modern political theory which rejects the claims of nationalism has done so to its own cost – from Metternich to Marx. It usually postulates some overwhelmingly prior focus of attachment – the traditional village or other 'primordial' focus,[36] or the working-class. Other ties are assumed to be insignificant. But the appeals of nationalism lie much deeper: they do not merely satisfy a need for intellectual order in the minds of individuals. (Nor need we swing to the other pole and assume that nationalism is merely an emotional or irrational creed. It is no more nor less irrational than most social and political creeds.)

The needs it serves are social needs: how to realize aspirations, how to overthrow a rejected order, how to live together. In satisfying these needs, nationalism also provides relief and satisfaction for the *individual*, within whose psyche all these cross-pulling forces are in tension. But nationalism is not just a solution at the level of the psyche; it is a set of demands upon society, too – and upon particular societies at particular times. To tell us, then, as the ultimate truth, that nationalism satisfies 'the need to belong together in a coherent and stable community',[37] if unexceptionable, is scarcely illuminating. But it is not even analytically adequate: nationalism also satisfies the need *not* to belong to some communities! This kind of analysis, anyhow, reduces the problem to one of generalized human needs. It de-historicizes Man. *All* people need relationships, need to belong, as Erich Fromm has shown us.[38] But why does *this* kind of 'belongingness' emerge in such powerful form at this point in the historical record? Merely to refer us to general needs ('the need to belong') does not explain why nationalism does this rather than, say, identification with football teams, or why, as Shaw points out in *Saint Joan*, the idea of nationalism is a new and heretical one which is not eternal, but *emerges* at particular times in history:

The Chaplain: He is only a Frenchman, my lord.
The Nobleman: A Frenchman! Where did you pick up that expression? Are these Burgundians and Bretons and Picards and Gascons beginning to call themselves Frenchmen, just as our fellows are beginning to call themselves Englishmen? They actually talk of France and England as their countries. . . . (Scene 4).

Nationalist sentiment is far more than cosy attachment to a reference-group, or a father-substitute. Why does the *nation* become the dominant circle of attachment? Why did people begin to want to belong to a French *nation*, rather than to a province, or to Europe? To ask these questions is to begin analysis where it should begin, rather than bypass the issue by appealing to innate and behaviouristically-conceived generalized 'needs'.

The appeals of nationalism, therefore, are hardly to be adequately analysed at this level of formal logic, for this is an a-social kind of analysis. At best, it will only tells us, in Merton's terms,[39] about the 'manifest' level of social action, not about the 'latent' functions served by the ideology of nationalism – about one important enough aspect of nationalism, but not about the multiplex forces sustaining it. In particular, the logical critique of single-nation nationalism is particularly irrelevant in the era of nationalisms which *are* multiplex, involving, as they commonly do, allegiance to the new state (Nigeria or Indonesia), allegiance to persisting 'sub-nationalisms' (the Muslim North *within* Nigeria, or Sumatran or Javanese culture *within* Indonesia), and allegiance to 'circles' wider than any of these.

It is true that, so far, the 'Pan' movements have been singularly unsuccessful. We have no reason, then, to assume *a priori*, that Pan-Africanism or Pan-Arabism will, in their turn, be anything more than dreams.

'Unitary' nationalisms, too, have often been unsuccessful in the past. 'Potential' nationalities have failed to become self-assertive nations within their private state boundaries: the Catalans in Spain; the Sicilians in Italy; or the earlier 'failed' nation-states of Burgundy, Brittany, or Wales. Because of these cases, some historians have swung to an ultra-relativistic position. Not only are 'Pan' movements, they believe, doomed to remain in the domain of rhetoric, but the nation itself, we are told, is nothing more than

'. . . whatever can get away with establishing its claim to be one . . . the largest community, which, when the chips are down, effectively commands men's loyalty. . . . The simplest statement that can be made about a nation is that it is . . . a body of people who feel that they are a nation, and it may well be that when all the fine-spun argument is concluded, that will be the ultimate statement as well'.[40]

The voice of American pragmatism. In different accents, Fichte once expressed similar views when he declared that 'national self-determination is, in the final analysis, a determination of will.' Whereas the liberal-pragmatic view, however, tends to produce a relativistic and tolerant attitude towards nationalist claims, the Fichtean view easily breeds a respect for achievement and force. When German nationalists met at Frankfurt in 1848 to discuss their own self-determination, Czech and Polish representatives were told that 'mere existence does not entitle a people to political independence: only the force to assert itself as a state among the others'.[41]

Writers on nationalism from Renan onwards have emphasized that:

'races, languages, political traditions and loyalties are so inextricably intermixed that there can be no clear convincing reason why people who speak the same language, but whose history and circumstances otherwise widely diverge, should form one state, or why people who speak two different languages and whom circumstances have thrown together should not form one state. On nationalist logic, the separate existence of Britain and America, and the union of English and French Canada with the Canadian state, are both monstrosities of Nature....'[42]

Whilst French Canadians commonly *do* feel that Canada is a 'monstrous' union, it is true that there is no 'nationalism' calling for the re-unification of Britain and the United States.

The study of failed nationalisms would presumably have to examine the lower level of social development and the marginal, unintegrated position of 'subnationalities' like Wales, Brittany, or Catalonia, rather than fall back on hidden assumptions of historical accident. (Conversely, the reasons for the *success* of the United States of America needs evaluating, too, for the cultural gap between Georgia and Massachusetts in the late eighteenth century was in many ways as large as any between the separate Spanish provinces to the South.)

The ideology of much modern nationalism often runs counter to older nationalist ideology which it appeals to; it can therefore only be brought into line with the older thinking awkwardly and inconsistently. Islam, for example, recognizes no basis for Muslim society other than the true faith. Iqbal, the great Muslim nationalist, rejected the conception of the territorially-based nation as being a Western notion, incompatible with Islam.[43] Yet Islam has tried to reconcile this doctrine with the existence of many separate Islamic 'nation-states', some of which, like Pakistan or Libya, formally and explicitly base themselves upon Islam in their Constitutions, others of which, like Indonesia, have no established state-religion.

The emergence of the nation is thus a social process, not a self-enclosed logical operation. Logicians have 'demolished' the presuppositions of nationalism with relative ease; traditionalists, too, have rejected them. The traditionalist rejection of nationalism reflects an archaic social consciousness, the response of societies in which the rise and fall of political dynasties and movements scarcely affected day-to-day existence in the villages. As we saw for India, early liberal nationalism itself *was* precisely of this character: it was an activity of the urban, Western-educated intelligentsia. Where the villager heard of it at all, he was either uninterested or resistant, just as the liberal nationalism of the nineteenth-century European city intelligentsia failed to enlist the enthusiasm of the Polish peasant, bound as he was by his loyalties to Church and tradition.

But nationalism has expanded, and ultimately penetrated into present consciousness. It has been sustained, has persisted and grown, despite temporary failures, because it seemed to answer real needs of the mass of the population: sometimes separate though parallel needs, sometimes needs common to all. The needs satisfied by contemporary Afro-Asian nationalism can be simply stated. They are:

1. Independence.
2. Decolonization.
3. Development.

The people interested in achieving these things do not inhabit Iraq, Algeria, Burma, or Angola. They inhabit a distinct social segment of the globe: the regions colonized by Euro-America. They share a common past; they have become aware of themselves as having common present interests as a result of confronting a common Other. The analysis of modern nationalism outside Euro-America, then, must begin by distilling the experience of modern imperialism. For despite competing circles of allegiance, the new nationalisms of the twentieth century share one common central point of reference. The person who constitutes the Other, who has been common to all situations and societies, and who has thereby provoked awareness of self, is not the non-Muslim, not the non-Arab, the non-African or non-Asian, but one who is all of these things at once – the White man. Africans have been governed by Frenchmen, by Britons, by Belgians, by Germans, by Portuguese. But they have all shared the experience of White, capitalist, domination. Reduced to infantile dependence, reduced to uniformity, a sense of common fate united peoples divided by older social barriers of ethnicity, class, rank, culture, religion. People drew together, and were *forced* together. Their experiences, it is true, were not absolutely common or uniform. Because they have been governed by the laws of Kenya Colony, or the Protectorate of Uganda, or the Colony of Southern Rhodesia, men's lives have been sensibly different. Laws, economic arrangements, political systems, rules of land tenure, labour regulations, religions, all differed from territory to territory. Yet they were all laws of White men for Africans to obey. Colour identified the basic social compartments.

Territorial boundaries were meaningful. They could mean the difference between paying tax and not paying tax; between being induced to go to work, and being flogged to work. But Africans from Angola, Northern Rhodesia, Southern Rhodesia, Nyasaland, Mozambique, Tanganyika, the Congo, Basutoland, Swaziland, and Bechuanaland, intermingle in the mine-compounds of Ndola, Johannesburg, and Elisabethville.[44] The White man's government and the White man's economy transcended the frontiers of particular colonies, and generated a wider consciousness in response. The United Africa Company operated in the British territories of Nigeria and the Gold Coast as well as the French territories of the Ivory Coast and Niger. It also operated in the Solomon Islands, away on the other side of the world. People who had never seen each other were to be brought into a brotherhood wider than particular nationalisms, precisely in reaction to these giant internationalisms of the Whites.

The common experience of a colonized world was thus crucial in the forcible expansion of horizons. One major factor was the revolution in communications which accompanied White rule. For if it laid the basis for the closer interconnection of governmental systems, it also brought the subjects of those governments closer together. They came into contact with other peoples of whom they had no previous knowledge. They acquired the rudiments of the White man's knowledge from mission schools; via the mission, too, they became part of worldwide churches. They learned that men were equal in the sight of God, but they found themselves equally inferior in the sight of the White man.

Roads, telegraphs, mission publications in indigenous tongues as well as in English and other world-languages; later, radio, newspapers, and letter-post, were decisive agencies in the transformation of Africans-for-the-White-man into Africans-for-themselves.[45] They were to render Marx's characterization of rural life completely out of date, but to make his analysis of the emergence of consciousness eminently relevant. Henceforth, even peasants in the backwoods could be in touch with world events, and with each other. No longer were they isolated from each other, only connected mechanically, in Marx's classic phrase, 'much as potatoes in a sack form a sack of potatoes'. Their contact was now mediated by consciousness, and this consciousness could be translated into social action.

Because of this crucial shift, not only the literate, but even the peasants of the world could become an organizable force: more importantly, the two became linked. What had been the *least* revolutionary social mass was transformed: it was torn from traditional controls, and placed directly in contact with urban influences. This, in fact, has been the crucial social change of the twentieth century. Imperialism had thus brought into being its own 'grave-digger', not merely by revolutionizing production and creating new social classes, but by transforming the total conditions of life even of the peasantry, that mass which ultimately might otherwise have remained an outside spectator. Out of the ranks of the peasantry came the raw material for the formation of new classes, new people, brought into being by being wrenched from the land and restructured into new social systems. Traditional systems of land tenure were shattered; peasants became wage-workers; others became simply work-less. Under these conditions, the peasantry and ex-peasantry became revolutionized. Because of the revolution in communications, their discontent could be co-ordinated and focused: they could be canalized into political revolution.

This dissolution of traditional bonds did not stop at colonial frontiers, or even at continental limits. From the beginning, African nationalism was always more than Africa-wide. Pan-Africanism was first promoted by 'marginal men' who did not even live in Africa, but whose lives had been profoundly shaped by their African heritage. The new Africanist 'Zionism' was born in the 'Diaspora' of the New World, not in Africa.

The first phase in the emergence of nationalism, then, is a negative one – common resistance. In confronting the common Other – the White – the Black man, the African, emerged. He was both African and Black man; for him, two 'circles' of identification existed. For Africans transported to the New World never completely lost the cultural ties with the motherland. In the cults of

Haiti and Jamaica, in the Negro rebel-slave states of Brazil and Guiana, African culture lived on, though not unchanged: the rebel republics and kingdoms often set up slave-owning societies themselves, modelled on the White pattern, with Indians as their victims. In the New World, the old culture had been transformed and hybridized; the synthesis was a *new* Negro. 'To serve the *loa*, [spirits of the dead], you have to be a Catholic', declared a Haitian peasant.[46] African culture did not persist merely as a collection of Negro 'traits', as some American scholars imply,[47] but became transmuted.

The heritage of slavery linked old African and new American Negro. Because of the continued domination of the White – in the New World and in Africa – Pan-Negroism and Pan-Africanism came into the world joined as Siamese twins. At the turn of the nineteenth century, when Africa had been finally pinned-down and divided, 'African' America was beginning to stand up. The National Association for the Advancement of Coloured Peoples was founded in 1908. Straight away, American Negroes moved to contact their African brothers, reviving a link that had never been entirely absent throughout the nineteenth century, but which only became important after 1900.

The career of John Chilembwe[48] illustrates the importance and dynamism of this connection between Africa and the American Diaspora, the source of a disturbing new notion which spread with extraordinary speed in Africa itself: Africa for the Africans. Chilembwe was a Nyasaland Tonga, a people for whom the advent of the Whites had been a boon, since it meant freedom from Ngoni attacks. The Tonga, therefore, cleaved to the new European order: they migrated to the mines, developed their own independent Christian churches, and were eager for education. One independent church leader, John Chilembwe, came under the influence of Joseph Booth, a White evangelist from the United States who was nevertheless a key dispenser of the new American Negro-Zionist religions and of African 'advancement' schemes.

There had been rebellion against the recently-established British rule in Nyasaland before, but these had been rebellions to re-establish the past, by peoples like the Ngoni, who had been trying to restore their former dominance. Though European planters and missionaries hated the upstart teachers who flocked into the new independent churches run by African ministers (and their wives dressed in fine European rig) they had little expected these, of all people, to become violent rebels.

They did so because they came under the influence of a subversive new creed, Christianity. The message the missionaries brought: do not covet thy neighbour's goods; love thine enemy: was so *disinterested* and *hard*, said the Mang'anja, that it could not be a partisan ideology of mere men, even god-like White men. It *must* be the true Word of a God who transcended earthly limitations. So, they concluded,

'. . . [let] the chief white men of Government . . . give up the use of guns and the way of killing those who did not understand their ways of taxing.'

From the beginning, Africans thus learned to interpret the new message in their own way. Christian doctrine became an African weapon, sharper than any spear, since it changed men's minds, not merely compelled their bodies. But it did lead men like Chilembwe – 'the least savage men in the country' – to take up the spear, and die, defeated, in the Nyasaland Rising of 1917.

The New World Negro had learned the White man's culture much more thoroughly, and had learned to *use* it, defensively and offensively. Now he helped Africans – ready and responsive – to stand up for themselves against the White man, as he had learned to do – and to justify their actions by the White man's Book.

The phase of primitive proto-nationalism in independent churches and messianic cults soon gave way to secular action, for, after all, the millennium never arrived. Except in places like the Congo and to some extent in South Africa, where repression closed other doors and generated a desperate need to hope and believe,[49] the African Zionist Churches gave way to 'advancement' movements (educational and 'improvement' associations, etc.), analogous in content to the much more sophisticated Indian 'liberal' reform movements we have already looked at.[50]

Politics in Africa between the wars preserved this Pan-African tradition. Forged as it was by the educated, successful Africans of the New World, it was at first liberal in character, the creation of men who were far from being alienated from their society:

Sylvester Williams, the Trinidad lawyer; in the USA, Dr William
Du Bois, the Heidelberg graduate; Dr Jean Price-Mars, the diplo-
mat, ethnologist and humanist, in Haiti; these were the men who
furnished the ideas that were to take root in a land they had never
seen but which dominated their lives. Their ideas were transmitted
via people like the 'Brazilians' in Lagos – people of African (slave)
descent from Brazil, who returned to Lagos, often reached high
rank in the Civil Service there, and who 'led' Lagos African
society.[51] More militant Africans, less educated and privileged
themselves, like the West Indian Marcus Garvey, the messiah
of the black masses in the 1920s, or George Padmore, Nkrumah's
comrade – now buried in the walls of Christiansborg Castle – began
to take a much more militant Pan-Africanism to wider audiences,
and injected a new note of social revolt and mass militancy that
was to overwhelm and bypass those who, like Danquah in Ghana,
stuck to a more socially conservative nationalism. The latter soon
went under, submerged by the high tides of mass militancy
which the 'new men', the Nkrumahs and the Kenyattas, easily
navigated.

But in the 1920s, the days when Marcus Garvey's Black Star
would adorn the flag of the new independent state of Ghana seemed
remote indeed – except to the believing millions of his fanatical
supporters. In Paris in 1919, in London in 1921 and 1923, in
New York in 1927, insignificant handfuls of 'Africans' from
Martinique, and Louisiana, Senegal and Mississippi, met at Pan-
African Congresses.[52] As yet, therefore, not too many Africans
from Africa itself. Just as Lloyd George assisted an insignificant
knot of Russian revolutionaries to find a hall where they could
hold their Bolshevik Party Congress in 1903, so Clemenceau,
in anti-Anglo-Saxon mood, helped Du Bois bring together fifty-
seven Negroes from French and British African territories, the
USA, and the Antilles, despite Anglo-American governmental
objections. In 1921, there were still only forty-one from Africa
as against thirty-five from the USA. By 1923, Du Bois was dis-
piritedly lamenting that 'Pan-Africanism is only an idea, rather
than a fact'; but four years later, the arrival of 208 delegates from
twelve different countries showed the growing appeal of the Pan-
African dream.

It was World War II which changed everything. Non-violence

– learned from the great teacher of colonial peoples, India[53] – was the chosen method, of necessity, to people who lacked arms and money, but who were nevertheless militant. Under Kenyatta's inspiration, it was preached as a mass technique to frustrate the workings of civil government. It was put into practice so successfully by Nkrumah that by 1957 the great breakthrough, for Africa, was made. The Gold Coast became Ghana after Kwame Nkrumah, son of a goldsmith and graduate of United States Universities and British gaols, was voted out of James Fort Prison and into power by 22,780 votes out of 23,122 in Accra Central constituency. As Minister in Charge of Government Business, he set out immediately to consolidate the power of the Convention People's Party internally, in the face of Ashanti regionalism and chiefly opposition. But, equally quickly, he started to translate into action the dreams of African unity.

Manchester had been the unlikely setting for the drawing-up of the post-war order of battle. The Pan-African Congress in that city in 1945 brought together the militants whose careers bridged the pre- and post-war eras: Padmore, Kenyatta, Nkrumah, Du Bois. From then on, Pan-African nationalism was to spurt forward with such speed that the first comprehensive statement of its tenets, George Padmore's *Pan-Africanism or Communism?* only appeared a year before Ghana's independence.

But Europe would see no more Pan-African Congresses. Henceforth they were to be held in the mother-continent itself. As early as December 1953, Nkrumah had called a small Congress at Kumasi. By 1958, there were enough independent African countries to make possible the calling of the first Conference of Independent African States at Accra. Then followed a flood of Conferences and Congresses: at Cotonou, Accra, Casablanca, Addis Ababa ... conferences of trade unionists, and – still in Europe – conferences of Black African Writers and Artists in Paris and Rome.

The latter were particularly important in building up among the new *élite* a total *African* alternative to the cultural domination of Europe and the West. Politicians might attack the institutional mechanisms of alien control; artists struggled to free men from the spiritual domination of non-African ideas and values. The elaboration of *négritude*, the delineation and celebration of a distinctively Black-African culture with a rich past, was the especial task of a brilliant team of writers focused around the journal *Présence Africaine*. In literary terms, the richest products were the poetry of Léopold Sédar-Senghor and Aimé Césaire. A new view of African history also began to emerge. Ghana and Mali, the symbolic names for new African states, were the names of great medieval African empires. Monomotapa, Kongo, Axum, Kitara, Swahili East Africa, were re-introduced into world-history centuries after they had disappeared, though they have still to reach the school history-books of the West.

In striking back against the contempt of the West, resistance to centuries-old suppression naturally produced extreme reactions among some writers. Inevitably a great deal of the literary output of the embittered and frustrated early Pan-Africanists was as viciously racist as anything dreamed of in Dr Verwoerd's philosophy.[54] History and ideology intertwined: Cheikh Anta Diop supplied badly-needed correctives to European historiography of Africa, but also under-emphasized the differences between pre-European African cultures, and the fact that not all 'Africans' were Negroes.[55]

The assumption of White superiority was bound to produce its opposite. But basic assumptions were sadly in need of questioning. One of the basic divisions in past writing on Africa, for example has been the (reasonable) distinction between Arab-Mediterranean North Africa and Africa 'South of the Sahara' (Afrique Noire). Today, Africa in revolt has completely changed the picture – and has raised questions about its validity for earlier epochs of African history. The contacts between Negro Africa and the North across the Sudan are now being re-examined. These revaluations of the past involve more than the mere straightening out of the historical record for the sake of intellectual clarity. They also bear importantly upon the social problems of the present. Only a few intellectuals have developed a mystical preoccupation with blackness, and even they rarely take the doctrines of *négritude* seriously as the basis of policy: a Senghor may refer, *en passant*, to his black brothers in the Caribbean or Melanesia, as at Cotonou in 1958, but Africans are not terribly interested.

Négritude, in fact, does not, as Colin Legum suggests, rest, 'deep at its quivering, sensitive centre . . . on colour consciousness

. . .';[56] rather, colour consciousness is itself an expression of the colonial experience, and of the common fate of the Black man under imperialism. Today, certainly, political Pan-Africanism, or just plain African nationalism, is not concerned merely with the *fact* of blackness, but with the *consequences* of blackness, the *content* of being Black. Modern Pan-Africanism starts from quite new, intra-African, bases, different from those on which the older *négritude* reposed, though the latter did contribute importantly to the building up of a self-awareness and self-confidence that had been lost.

So far, we have considered modern nationalisms principally insofar as they seek to redefine the wider units of belongingness. The accent has been upon the boundaries of the variously-conceived 'national' units, rather than on their social content. And, historically, this is the way the older, intellectualist nationalist and 'Pan' movements themselves approached the question. But as more and more formerly colonized states achieve or approach independence, and are faced with the practical problems of development; as they find themselves, too, forced to define their positions in the world Cold War; as the problems of development become increasingly bound up with those of establishing larger political units than the 'dwarf states' left behind by the retreating glaciers of imperialism, issues of social policy and of the consolidation of the state become much more closely intertwined.

CHAPTER THREE

THE VARIETIES OF REVOLUTIONARY EXPERIENCE

Nationalism and Communism

WE are so accustomed to looking at the rest of the world in terms of Western-European historical experience that we might feel tempted to consider the impact of social-democracy on Asia and Africa before examining the impact of Communism. Yet to do so would be to invert the historical record, for in Asia at least Communist parties commonly developed *before* social-democratic parties.[1]

It was the Russian Revolution of 1917 that made Communism a 'material force' in the colonized world, not so much because its theory 'gripped the masses', but because its practice – the achievement of revolution and the construction of a new kind of society – inspired the hope that others might learn how to achieve their revolution from the peoples of Russia. It was the 'institutionalized Marxism' of the Soviet state, therefore, that inspired men, rather than the intellectual coherence of historical materialism.

But the new nationalisms were stimulated by the Soviet experience into an awareness that there was not only a problem of, revolution, but also of revolution for – what? In Africa, before World War II, the attainment of independence seemed such a remote possibility that nationalists rarely devoted much serious thought to outlining the kind of society they hoped to see after White men had gone. Though the elements of an independent nationalist ideology were present, the synthesis of these elements was hardly achieved until the 1950s.

In Asia, where the nationalist movements were much older,

in more advanced and longer-colonized countries, varieties of nationalism were developed long before 1917, and became entrenched. Ultimately they were to become exhausted and discredited. But this took a long time, and the striking fact about Communism in Asia before World War II is its extraordinary inability to become a serious rival to nationalism – with one vitally important exception, China. In Europe, too, Communism was easily contained, despite the chronic revolutionary situation in many countries after 1918.[2]

Communism in China succeeded for four key reasons. Firstly, as we have seen, it was not opposed by any coherent traditional other-worldly religion, such as Hinduism or Islam. Confucianism was a conservative and largely secular *ethic*, tied to an order of society which had disintegrated. Moreover, some habits of mind derived from it, notably traditional habituation to an integrated and bureaucratized social order, could be adapted to new ends. The Chinese Revolution, however, did also involve a radically-new activation of the latent energies of ordinary people. Secondly, China had been undergoing political and armed revolution for decades, notably, the vast violence of the Taiping Rebellion and later, the Boxer Rising and the Revolution of 1911. A half-century of Western intrusion had seriously unbalanced the traditional rural order, and had brought into being a new revolutionary working-class in the major cities, particularly Canton, Hong Kong, and Shanghai, but the Western Powers had not successfully established an overall colonial political system, nor modernized the economy. This huge country, then, was in a chronically revolutionary condition.

Thirdly, Chinese Communists evolved a new revolutionary strategy appropriate to this situation. Initially, they had based themselves on the cities. The result was bloody defeat at the hands of Chiang Kai Shek who butchered tens of thousands in the 1926 Canton Commune. It took many years before the Chinese Communists recovered from Canton and from the disastrous advice of foreign Comintern agents such as Roy, Sneevliet, and Borodin, who circulated easily, especially across the adjoining Soviet border. In the end, they did the unprecedented: they built their revolutionary base where the majority of the poor lived – in the country-side. The peasant, not the worker, was to be the backbone of the revolution. Theoretical dogma was swept aside in revolutionary practice. After the celebrated 'Long March' to Yenan, Chinese Communism consolidated itself in a remote rural area, not in exposed positions in the cities.

Finally, orthodox nationalism, culminating in Chiang, had, by this time, shot its bolt: it had led the country into economic disaster; into the political and social chaos of decades of civil war and near-defeat by Japan; it had imposed a vicious police regime; and finally, had led China into a new political dependence upon the major capitalist power.

The absence of ideological barriers: the chronic revolutionary situation; the *dépassement* of orthodox nationalism; the peasant strategy; all these formed a unique constellation of circumstances favourable to the triumph of Communism which have not – yet – been paralleled elsewhere in the newer Asian countries. Here, nationalism still retains its dynamic, and social revolution has barely begun. Nationalism and Communism have therefore been able to work together; quite often, however, they have come into conflict, sometimes violently, particularly since 'domestic' Communism was largely 'international' (Moscow-controlled) Communism, anyhow.

In India in 1931, for example, we find the Communists denouncing Gandhi as a 'Judas'. A decade later, R. Palme Dutt, the English Communist leader and authority on India who profoundly influenced the policy of the Indian Communist Party, could still refer to Gandhi as the 'pacifist evil genius of Indian politics'. The intensity of the denunciation of Gandhi and Congress shifted, of course, with the changing international party line. But conflict with nationalism was recurrent. During World War II, for example, at a time when Congress leaders were in gaol or underground, the Communists were collaborating with the British. Their cadres trained as a volunteer force under British officers, and the Party Secretary denounced strikes, even if the conditions of the workers were 'hellish' and 'intolerable'.[3] After Independence, in Telengana in 1947, Communists led armed peasant revolt against the Government of the newly-independent country, and in 1948, the Nizam of Hyderabad was pleased to lift the ban on the Communist Party in order to use it as a counter-force to Congress.[4]

95

In Indonesia, the 'anti-fascist' line which had damped down the anti-Dutch struggle since 1938[5] was still in operation in 1945, so that the leaders of the Indonesian Communist Party who had been interned in the Netherlands were flown out to Indonesia, like Lenin in his sealed train, to undermine the nationalist struggle.[6] This line was rapidly changed, but in 1948 came another *volte-face*, dictated from Moscow in response to the challenge of the Marshall Plan. This was the new 'hard line' that also produced Telengana. An exiled Indonesian Communist, Muso, was flown out from Moscow to head the Madiun Revolt against Soekarno's government at the very height of Dutch military operations against the hard-pressed Republic. Soekarno and Hatta were denounced as 'Fascist Japanese quislings'.

Despite this recurrent conflict between nationalism and Communism, the striking feature of the post-Stalin era has been the extraordinary popular amnesia concerning these extremely serious anti-nationalist actions. Unlike the socialists, the Communists have been able to gather a new access of strength after every one of these serious reverses. There are several key reasons for this extraordinary resilience of Communism.

Firstly, the fortunes of local Communist Parties have been importantly affected by changing attitudes towards the Soviet Union, with which, until very recently, all Communist Parties were unquestioningly identified, both by themselves and by others. In the underdeveloped world, whatever political mistakes the Soviet Union may have made, she was nevertheless not one of the Powers which actually governed the lives of the colonial peoples. Britain and France, Belgium and Portugal, not the Soviet Union, have been the rulers of Africa. Today, the United States, not the Soviet Union, props up dictatorial 'client' regimes in South Korea, Pakistan, and South Vietnam. The Soviet Union, on the other hand, came into being in struggle against imperialism and had to fight for her very existence against the armies of fourteen capitalist powers. The offences committed by the USSR against its own national minorities, from the initial suppression of Central Asian and Caucasian independence movements after 1917 to the deportation of the Chechen-Ingush, the Volga Germans, and the South Ossetians, and the endemic anti-Semitism,[7] easily escaped the attention of peoples intimately familiar and far more directly preoccupied with capitalist imperialism. For these things happened in the remote Eurasian heartland. To the South African, however, Dr Verwoerd is someone present in his own country, visibly dictating how he shall live, here and now. In India, neighbour of the newer Communism of China, a serious unified national opposition to Chinese Communism only emerged with the actual large-scale military invasion of India. Previously, there was concern over the fate of Tibet, some worry about the Chinese presence in Ladakh and the North-East Frontier District, but even so, the tendency was to regard the Khampa resistance to the Chinese in Tibet as merely a reactionary 'tribalist–feudalist' rising against a modernizing government; the Communist experiment excited much admiration.[8] Communist repression in Europe caused even less perturbation. The Hungarian Revolution was easily dismissed with a shrug by many people in the backward countries. This was not the 'classic' imperialism of capitalist powers in Asia or Africa. It was a private 'ideological' quarrel between rich European super-Powers, who displayed their customary sensitive concern with European matters in their passionate battles over Hungary in the UN, but continued to do nothing about Algeria or South Africa, and were content to allow the rest of the world to starve on. To internationalists these attitudes may seem alarmingly parochial – and morally insensitive. They were nevertheless widespread, and were classically expressed in the *tu quoque* comment of the Lebanese delegate to the UN in November 1956, who asked why they should be expected to show special concern over the suppression of freedom in one European country when the same thing was happening all over the colonial world.

The USSR, then, has always been able to harness a good deal of this anti-imperialist sentiment. Imperialism and capitalism are regarded as interrelated; the former, indeed, is normally seen in Leninist terms by the intelligentsia of the new states, as merely a phase in the development of capitalism. Independence and socialism went together.

Recently, the USSR has been able to appeal much more directly to the peoples of the emergent world, by radio, printed matter, cultural delegations, aid schemes, etc. etc. But sympathy with the USSR, and actual organizational connections, had been developed over many decades. More normally, however, pro-Soviet sentiment was promoted, not from the Soviet Union direct, but indirectly via local Communist Parties, which, despite the vacillations of Comintern policy dictated from Moscow, threw themselves vigorously into the anti-imperialist struggle.

The connection with organized Communism, however, was merely part of the wider appeal of a whole range of militant Left-wing ideologies. Over many decades, colonial liberation movements had established links with the European revolutionary Left. Communists and other militant left-wingers like Tom Mann in South Africa, and Ben Bradley and Lester Hutchinson at the Meerut Conspiracy Trial in India, had actually fought shoulder-to-shoulder with their brothers in the colonized territories themselves. R. Palme Dutt was the most important voice of international Communism, apart from Moscow itself, directing operations in the sub-continent. In England itself, the first Communist MP was an Indian, Shapurji Saklatvala.

In settler territories like South Africa, English militants brought their socialist ideas with them.[9] White Communists, not only through political work, but also through such activities as the African night-school movement, which began in South Africa in 1925 and reached its height in the 1930s and 1940s,[10] built up a tradition of mutual respect which has insulated South African liberals from joining in the usual denunciation of Communism – especially since they have all suffered together under the Suppression of Communism Act. And Africans did not hesitate to elect Communists to the few Bantu/Coloured seats where they could stand until the Suppression of Communism Act closed this channel of protest.

Wartime brought Left-wing British soldiers into very close contact and personal friendship with African and Asian revolutionaries.[11] Close contacts between the European Left wing and the nationalist militants were also developed in Europe itself. Between the wars, men like Krishna Menon, Nkrumah, Nehru, Kenyatta, and George Padmore established political and personal friendships with the Labour Party, the Communist Party, and the ILP. After 1945, the connection with the militant Left was strengthened, largely owing to the efforts of Fenner Brockway, the moving spirit behind the Movement for Colonial Freedom (and a score of more specialized 'anti-colonial' campaigns and movements), whose role in this period is best described by his title, 'MP for Africa'.

In France, the course of political developments was different. The contact with the French Left had been important for men like Ho Chi Minh. But after World War II, armed revolutions had to be fought in Viet Nam and Algeria, often against 'socialists' like Mollet. The French Communist Party, too, failed to reproduce its struggle against the Viet Nam war. When the battle shifted to Algeria the liberalism of the Mendès-France period was over. The French African territories eventually obtained their independence not from the French Left but from de Gaulle.

Nevertheless, in the French territories today, the intellectual influence of Marxism – albeit 'Africanized' – is profound. It is the only serious political ideology, debated, modified, re-interpreted, seriously and pragmatically used by leaders as far apart as Sékou Touré on the Left and Senghor on the Right. In comparison, Catholic, and certainly existentialist, influences are negligible.

The major reason for the continuing appeal of militant Communism, then, has been the success of the Soviet Union. The very *fact* of the Soviet Union is impressive to the under-developed countries. Africans are largely unmoved by academic hypothecation which postulates that Russia would have achieved levels of technological development near those she has actually arrived at, and at far less social cost in human misery, whether she had had a revolution or not. What they do know, empirically and not hypothetically, is that a country of peasants, equipped, in 1917, only with wooden ploughs, was able to challenge the richest country in the world for world leadership within forty years – and to put the first man into space. The Soviet Union and the Communist world, with whatever fluctuations and setbacks, and at whatever grim cost, have done the job they want to do – and fast. And whatever the failure of the theoreticians of the USSR to develop a political theory which locates the revolutionary peasantry at its centre, the Soviet state has in practice certainly revolutionized its peasants.

The USSR provided an organizational model, not merely of economic development, but of overall organization. To new countries who were faced with the creation of total organizational machinery: political machinery; administrative machinery; educational machinery; trade union machinery: the USSR has provided recent experience, France or Britain has not. A strong, centralized State, governed by a single party dedicated to the planned modernization of a backward, agrarian society, seemed a relevant model for the new Africa.

The USSR is also a multi-national state. It has succeeded in forcibly modernizing not merely the Russian Federated Soviet Republic but also Central Asian territories like Uzbekistan, Caucasian republics like Georgia, and even the backward nomadic hunting societies of Siberia. Whatever the deficiencies of Soviet policy towards its minority nationalities, the structure of the Soviet state has been based upon a multiplicity of Union Republics, Autonomous Soviet Socialist Republics, Autonomous Regions, and National Districts, within which national languages are used, and some degree of 'national' cultural expression is encouraged. The Soviet Union has combined high centralization with explicit, if limited, recognition of national autonomy. This dual allegiance to a newly-created state, combined with persisting allegiance to a lower level of 'nationality', seems a possible model to new countries similarly concerned to foster a sense of, say, 'Nigerian' identity, concurrently with traditional membership of lower-level, 'narrower', ethnic affiliation.

With the disintegration of Soviet-centred Communism into a 'polycentric' grouping, following the Yugoslav defection and the subsequent loosening of the Stalinist machinery for inducing world Communist conformity, and in particular since the emergence of China as the major contender for leadership of the Communist world, the appeals of Communism have become more powerful, not less. An increasingly wealthy Soviet Union has been able to offer aid without political conditions and at lower rates of interest than those normally entailed in loans from the West: Egypt got her loan for the financing of the Aswan High Dam, notably, at the customarily-low Soviet rate of under 2 per cent.

The patent dismantling and disintegration of the 'monocentric' apparatus of Communist world-politics has, in fact, removed many of the fears of the new nations who are naturally highly sensitive to any threatened inroads upon their newfound independence. The emergence of China, particularly, though it has frightened the more moderate and especially those who border upon China, has also special attractions for others, in so far as China's revolution was a revolution in a peasant country. For a while, too, it appeared to be solving the problem of the 'Great Leap Forward' to a modernized economy very rapidly.

China's experience even seemed more relevant than that of the USSR, for the Chinese Communists had achieved their revolution in a *contemporary* under-developed semi-colonial state, in the teeth of modern imperialism, despite the Cold War, and in a country even more backward and agrarian than Tsarist Russia. The victory of Communism in China has therefore been strikingly influential, too, in assisting the spread of Communism to two of her neighbours, Viet Nam and Korea (though Russia's Red Army was initially the agent of Communist victory in the latter country, and in Viet Nam, Ho Chi Minh also used Kuomintang and American support skilfully.) Moreover, China's victory broke more than a material structure of power: it also broke an intellectual stranglehold which had impeded many revolutionaries and socialists from achieving a correct appraisal of the balance of social forces in their own countries and which had therefore led them to misdirect their political and organizational steps. Just as Lenin, brilliant opportunist in practice, rationalizer in theory, had made the first world-historic inroads on deterministic Marxism, not merely in his writings, but in his actions, by creating a revolution in an underdeveloped country instead of in an advanced industrial bourgeois democracy, so Mao, a generation later, consolidated this change by consciously and explicitly basing his revolution on the theoretically least revolutionary social class in his underdeveloped and semi-colonized country. Following Lenin's lead, he stood Marx on his head. For even if Chinese Communism still paid theoretical lip-service to the 'leading role of the proletariat',[12] in practice it rid Marxist theory of its Europocentric assumptions once and for all: no longer were the proletarians *the* revolutionary force; no longer did revolution *in the West* claim theoretical and practical priority. Nineteenth-century Marxism was thus turned into a tool more adequate to the demands of the twentieth century, and revitalized as a revolutionary force.

But the promise of the Chinese Revolution was slow in being

realized, and unsuspected difficulties came to the fore. Now, as China – like the Soviet – still grapples unsuccessfully with her agricultural problems, the new countries are less certain about the relevance of the Chinese model. In typically pragmatic vein, Sékou Touré remarked, before he had ever been to China, that 'the success of the Chinese Revolution was evidence of the correctness of the principles which have been the motor force in the actions of the Chinese people'. But, he insisted, in other countries quite other principles might be indicated. *Results* were the proof of the adequacy of the principles.[13]

After visiting China, he was more emphatic:

'Why should we [take China as a model]? I have just been over China. It is a very different country from ours. I found nothing in China's experience that could interest us.'[14]

The results achieved in China are still ambiguous. The problems the Chinese face differ importantly from those facing Africa. But Communism still commands great respect and attention in the new states. It commands respect among the political *élites* because the achievements of the Communist states offer them a model for advance, and a source of practical aid with which to achieve that advance. But, above all, Communism appeals to the masses, because the Communist Parties have been increasingly successful in establishing themselves as the parties of radical agrarian reform and militant trade unionism. Communists are willing to fight; they *achieve* their leadership; it is not somehow, mysteriously handed to them from Moscow, for Moscow has no power to hand leadership in Indonesia to anyone. Leadership has to be won in the countryside and the towns of that country. It is this self-sacrificing militancy that regenerates the Communist position after defeats, not merely Soviet sputniks (which the peasant knows little, if anything, about).

The results are visible in the growth of the Communist vote in the recent Indian elections, and in the absence of elections in Indonesia, where the Communist Party would probably register a significant advance, at least in Java, if elections were held. The Communists have established themselves as the major alternative, as the party of social revolution, in countries where nationalism has lost its dynamic and failed to make the economic breakthrough.[15] In Asia, there is a growing market for social revolution; in Africa the time has yet to come.

Nationalism and Social Democracy

When the first socialist parties emerged in the East, they found themselves up against well-entrenched, older and much more dynamic Communist parties. In Asia – apart from Japan (hardly an 'under-developed' country) – only in Burma and Indonesia has Social Democracy made serious headway. The reasons for this failure will become clearer as we examine the Indonesian case in more detail. For Africa, we will also examine the similar failure of a favourably-placed Social Democratic movement, that of Senegal.

In Indonesia, the Socialist Party had, in the person of Soetan Sjahrir, an outstanding leader, world-renowned as spokesman for his nation and twice Premier in early Governments of the revolutionary regime. His Party, moreover, played a peculiarly important role in helping to shape the political thinking of the new Indonesia,[16] particularly amongst the youth, the city-dwellers, the intellectuals, and the Army. Yet it never succeeded in turning itself into a really mass party. After the consolidation of the young Republic, it failed to grow. In electoral terms, it obtained only 3 per cent of the votes at the 1955 election, as against over 20 per cent for the nationalist party, PNI.

The reasons for this striking failure lie in the Europe-centred nature of this kind of social-democracy, in its theory, in its practice, in its organizational structure, and in the social composition of its membership. Soetan Sjahrir himself, with his intellectual brilliance and ultimate political impotence, embodies the whole tragedy of social-democracy in Asia.

Like the liberal nationalists, their precursors, the apostles of orthodox social-democracy in Asia remained spiritually closely tied to the concepts of the West. No matter how revolutionary they were – and the sincerity, the dedication, the intellectual honesty, and passion of a man like Sjahrir is beyond question – they were basically operating within a European framework of thought. For the most part, the pioneering Asian socialists were westernized, urban intellectuals who rejected their own culture.

Sjahrir himself has left us a vivid picture of his own feelings. A cultured Hollandophile, he had no time for the nationalist celebration of the indigenous heritage:

'Here there has been no spiritual or cultural life and no internal progress for centuries. There are the much-praised Eastern art-forms, but what are these except bare rudiments from a feudal culture that cannot possibly provide a dynamic fulcrum for people of the twentieth century? . . . For our spiritual needs we are in general dependent on the West, not only scientifically but culturally.'[17]

For him, a socialist, the clash was not fundamentally one between East and West, but between feudal and bourgeois culture. The basic task was to develop an *élite* socialist party of trained cadres. These politically and formally highly-educated men, equipped with a scientific-socialist understanding of the laws of social development, would therefore be able to judge the moment when social revolution was imminent. Inevitably, Westernized intellectuals were bound to predominate in such a party; inevitably, there was hardly a place for illiterate, ignorant peasants, with whom the intelligentsia had nothing in common. More importantly, a positivistic determinism tended to inhibit this political leadership from action, for the 'productive forces' in Asian society had, it appeared, scarcely developed to the point where a social revolution was possible. It was necessary to wait until they were. In the meantime, the more 'utopian', less 'scientific', nationalists jumped into action. They imposed human agency on the situation, and made a revolution.

Technically, of course, socialists were committed to mobilization of the workers and the peasantry, and did recognize that a national-bourgeois revolution for independence could precede a socialist one. Emotionally and socially, however, the intelligentsia was sharply cut off from the peasant rooted in his traditional village-culture. Because of this conflict between ideology and practice, a good deal of rationalization had to be produced to fill the gap. In reality, the party was dominated by a 'cadre', 'vanguard' conception of the party. A sectarian party of this kind was effectively disbarred from making an effective union with the most revolutionary force in Indonesian society – the peasantry.

The gulf between sectarians like Sjahrir or Hatta, and popular nationalists like Soekarno, was to be one of the continuing threads running through the history of the Indonesian revolution. The sectarianism might be a sectarianism of the Left, like Sjahrir's, or a traditionalist sectarianism, like the Muslim variety preached by Hatta. Both these men were to be central figures in the establishment of independence; both were to be eclipsed. For socialist or Muslim, their sectarianism cut them off from the less intellectually-schematic masses whom a Soekarno could easily reach. Both Sjahrir and Hatta early showed signs of the habits that were to bring them into eminence – and to failure – as leaders of mass parties. Soekarno, equally, showed early signs of those gifts which were to enable him to outshine both. As early as 1927, Sjahrir and Hatta both refrained from direct association with Soekarno when the latter formed the first serious nationalist party, the Partai Nasional Indonesia. Instead, they formed a small, close group of conscious, dedicated, trained nationalists. Soekarno's movement, in contrast, reached a membership of 100,000 in two years: it earned him exile, and a permanent place in the leadership of Indonesian nationalism.

The same divergence was exhibited at the very birth of the Indonesian Republic. When the Declaration of Independence was read at the house of the Japanese Admiral, Mayeda, Sjahrir was not present, despite his eminent role in the wartime underground movement, for he refused to sponsor the Declaration, declaring it insufficiently revolutionary and anti-Japanese. Later, Sjahrir's Socialist Party became a disciplined cadre party, demanding high self-discipline and training of its members, who retained a 'lofty' attitude towards mass work, and even approached elections with some reluctance.[18] Partly, too, this 'closed' party system was dictated by fear of communist infiltration.[19]

The socialists were not simply cut off from the peasant by their physical separation in the towns. They were cut off much more seriously by self-imposed ideological barriers, for they accepted the orthodox Western socialist view that the working-class was the prime bearer of socialism. True, the more perceptive, like Sjahrir, might point out that in Asia, where 'poverty is evenly distributed and the well-to-do only a very small group, the ideals of socialism are not only the hope of a single group, but they represent the hopes of the whole people',[20] but they were still reluctant to come out decisively and identify the peasant as the key to the revolutionary situation. The man who did so in practice (with whatever jesuitical glances in the direction of orthodox Marxist theory on the 'leading role' of the proletariat) was Mao Tse Tung. In consequence, he led Asia's most successful and important social revolution.

The socialists, if sectarian, were by no means inactive. After all, Sjahrir *was* a key figure in the independence struggle. Credit for keeping the socialists in touch with the mass movement should probably go to the Dutch, whose blanket repression of nationalism created a new brotherhood amongst prison graduates, whether socialist, Muslim, or communist. In prison, they discovered that they were all Indonesians, and they discovered, too, that peasant and intellectual shared the same life-situation in one overwhelmingly crucial respect: they were both subjects of an imperialist Power.

The Dutch helped alter Sjahrir. When he heard that he had been sentenced to exile in Digoel in remote New Guinea for his mild nationalist-educated activities, he wrote:

'. . . it was as though I was recalled to my people . . . to my people and to everything that ties me to the destiny and suffering of these millions. My personal grief is finally only a small part of that greater, general suffering, and it is just this that is my deepest and strongest bond. And now, perhaps, just when I have to renounce what I love best in the world, now I find myself more firmly and indissolubly bound to my people than ever before! We have so often misunderstood one another, that people and I. I have been too abstract for my people, too far removed from the framework of their concepts, too 'Western'. They have often made me despair at their lack of will and their misconceptions; angry and impatient at their petty faults. They filled me sometimes with bitterness, but now I know that their destiny and the goal of my life are one; we were and we still are mutually bound to each other. Now that my people require from me the dissolution and the destruction of my personal happiness, the separation from my loved ones, now all my sorrow disappears, and there remains only my deep feeling of belongingness and alliance to this down-trodden people of mine'.[21]

Colonialist repression thus created that combination of forces which was to be the explosive charge which would demolish the whole structure: the combination of revolutionary intelligentsia, land-hungry peasant, and semi-unemployed town-dweller. Nationalism was now no longer confined to Westernized officials, teachers, clerks, or lawyers. These men now took their knowledge to the peasantry, just as the Narodniks had done in nineteenth-century Russia. Where they did not, they remained politically limited, like the socialists.

The men who did harness the new discontents more effectively were men like Soekarno. As early as 1927, he had built the Partai Nasional Indonesia around a doctrine that drew upon an eclectic mixture of both Western and Asian thought. But running through it was a set of ideas that was internally consistent and which was to be reproduced in the ideologies of later colonial nationalisms. Infinitely less systematic than Sjahrir's thinking, less rooted in scholarship, he nevertheless produced a syncretic ideology couched in language accessible to the peasant, flavoured with overtones from Islam, Hinduism, Buddhism, and Javanese mysticism, as well as elements from Western Marxism and liberal humanism, the whole being seasoned with homely pithy sayings and examples. But the real basis of his appeal was that he actually did call for revolution. If we want to hear what Danton's advice – 'de l'audace, encore de l'audace, et toujours de l'audace' – sounds like in the accents of revolutionary Indonesia, here it is:

'Gentlemen: why do we, leaders of the people, who well know history, grow ponderous, become wavering, whilst it is not only today that we've used the slogan of "Indonesia Merdeka"? . . . there are two millions of youths, whose single slogan is A Free Indonesia, Now: if, for instance, the Japanese Army today were to surrender affairs of state to you, would you decline it, saying: Just a moment, wait a while, we ask this and that be finished first, and only then we will dare accept the affairs of state of Free Indonesia? (Cries of No! No!)

. . . If our people . . . are already prepared to die, to defend our country Indonesia, though it be with bamboo spears, then at that moment the people of Indonesia are ripe for freedom. (Loud applause.)

Think of this matter and try to compare it with human beings. Human beings are like that, gentlemen! As an example, I'll compare freedom with marriage. There is he who dares marry, he who quickly dares marry, there is he who is afraid to marry. There is he who says: "Ah, I do not dare marry, wait until I earn Rp. 500. . . . When I already own a stone house, when there are already carpets, already electric lamps, when I already own feather beds, already own a complete set of furniture, already own a casket of silver spoons and forks, already own this and that, yes, when I already own even baby's layette, then only do I dare marry. . . .

There is a person more daring than that: the man-in-the-street! If he has but a shack, with one mat, with one cooking-pot: he will marry. . . . It is pluckiness of heart which is necessary. . . .

Gentlemen, the question is this: – do we dare to be free, or do we not?'[22]

As Borkenau once remarked, 'On the fields of history the prize does not go to the man who holds the soundest theory about racing but to the man who runs best.' Practical politicians rarely produce polished, integrated philosophical systems. Even the more coherent world-views of a Touré or a Senghor contain a strong dash of empiricism and pragmatism, and are readily adapted to the flux of events.

Most nationalist ideologies have not attempted even this degree of systematization: they accept dualism, inconsistency, even make virtues of them. Here, for example, is Ba Swe, President of the TUC (Burma):

'Marxist philosophy rejects the theory of creation; but it does not oppose religion. In point of fact, Marxist theory is not antithetical to Buddhist philosophy. The two are, frankly speaking, not merely similar. In fact, they are the same in concept. But if we want to have the two distinguished from each other, we can safely assume that Marxist theory occupies the lower plane, while Buddhist philosophy occupies the higher. Marxist theory deals with mundane affairs and seeks to satisfy material needs in life. Buddhist philosophy, however, deals with the solution of spiritual matters with a view to seek spiritual satisfaction in life and liberation from this mundane world. . . . I declare that I have implicit faith in Marxism, but at the same time I boldly assert that I am a true Buddhist. In the beginning, I was Buddhist only by tradition. The more I study Marxism, however, the more I feel convinced in Buddhism. . . . I now believe that for any man there should be no obstacle to become a Marxist . . . Marxism cannot provide an answer for spiritual liberation. Neither can Science do so. Only Buddhist philosophy can. . . .'[23]

Internal consistency, then, however important to the logician, is not the consideration which determines whether a philosophy becomes adopted by a mass movement or not. In saying this, we need not lapse into irrationalism. It is *not* the case that *any* philosophy will do. Above all, the ideology must provide *answers* as well as *interpretations*; it must tell people how to cope with felt problems and wants, in language and style accessible and compelling to the ordinary person.

*   *   *

Our second, and briefer, case-study in the failure of socialism concerns Senegal, in particular its capital Dakar, the great city of former French West Africa. The citizens of the four communes of Gorée, Dakar, Rufisque, and Saint-Louis, had had the privilege of electing their own deputies to the French National Assembly in Paris and electing their own municipal governments since the late nineteenth century.[24] These constitutional privileges made it possible for the French Socialist Party (SFIO) to establish branches in Senegal between the wars. Socialism, therefore, was well ensconced when the Liberation of France in 1945 opened up new opportunities for African political self-expression.

In 1946, the leader of Senegalese social-democracy was Lamine Guèye, deputy for Dakar. Because of his pre-war experience, he was, however, more than merely deputy for Dakar: he at once became the *doyen* of all the deputies sent to Paris for the first time by the overseas territories as a result of the 1946 constitutional innovations. Guèye himself played a central role in achieving new civic rights for Africans at this time. The law which bears his name, passed on 30 April, 1946, in the first fine flush of liberation under Socialist and Communist pressure, brought the salaries and family allowances, and to some extent even the housing standards, of African civil servants into line with metropolitan conditions. This was the high-watermark of Guèye's career: he stood at the head of the team of 'new men' from the overseas territories: Senghor from Senegal; Houphouët-Boigny from the Ivory Coast; Apithy from Dahomey; Yacine Diallo from Guinea; Fili Dabo Sissako from Soudan/Niger; Gabriel D'Arboussier from Afrique Equatoriale Française; and Mangabel from Caméroun: thus entrenched, he took the new deputies into alliance with the French Socialist Party.

Participation in French metropolitan politics enabled African

deputies, leagued firstly with the French Socialist Party, and supported by the then powerful Communist Party, to abolish forced
labour; to establish rights to freedom of assembly and association;
to force the abolition of discriminatory penal codes; and to gain
French citizenship rights. But the alliance did not last long. The
first polarization occurred between the militants and the more
conservative. Soon, only Guèye, Senghor, and Diallo remained
with the SFIO. The more militant rapidly established a relationship with the Communist Party; the more conservative with the
Catholic MRP. Before long, these *apparentements* proved equally
unsatisfactory. Dissatisfaction with 'satellite' status grew; so did
consciousness of common interests cutting across the metropolitan
party-lines. By 1950, African deputies had formed a parliamentary
bloc of their own, unconnected with any of the major parties, but
trading votes for favours. Prehistory, in one student's words, had
ended, and history begun.

Guèye, the great socialist figure, was submerged in the rising
tide of nationalism. In 1951, he lost his seat. Eventually, after many
shifts and strategems, he was obliged to make his peace with
Senghor, who had emerged as the leader of mass nationalism in
Senegal. In 1958, Guèye joined Senghor's party, and thus fully
rehabilitated himself in political life, though now – whatever his
persisting influence in Dakar itself – as part of an African-nationalist
mass party under the leadership of another man, not as the unquestioned voice of French-style socialism in Africa. Western-
derived social democracy had failed in Africa, too.

In country after country, the record is the same. Rose remarks
of Sjahrir that his socialism is a Western socialism delivered by an
Asian. The reason for this divorce from the sentiments of the
peasant masses, he suggests, lies in the social composition of the
socialist parties, and in particular of their leaderships. In India,
the Socialist Party was 'overwhelmingly made up of middle class
or educated former peasants and workers'.[25] In Asia generally, the
parties had an urban and industrial base in a sea of peasants.
Sjahrir candidly admits that the Indonesian Party was characterized by exclusivism.[26]

Imperfectly linked with the masses in the East, the intelligentsia
were also overly-identified with the culture of the West.

Direct personal and organizational connections between Whites and African socialists, played some part in establishing an image of the latter, in the eyes of Africans themselves, as friends of the West. Guèye's failure was a harbinger of a growing sentiment: the feeling that the affiliation of African political movements to metro-politan parties or international movements was an acceptance of an inferior, ancillary status, and that the casting off of these ties meant casting off ideological dependence too, including Western-type socialism and communism. Socialism and communism, *redefined to meet Afro-Asian conditions*, naturally, remained as important as before. The more visible favour shown to African allies of the SFIO and the PCF by Governors appointed by the early Liberation governments (e.g. MM. Barthes and Béchard, Governors-General of French West Africa; Governor Latrille and his Communist *chef de cabinet*, Lambert, in the Ivory Coast[27]), now recoiled on the heads of Communist and Socialist sympa-thizers, who were accused of placing their international 'class' loyalties before their Pan-African and nationalist ones.

But the existence of personal connections between Africans and White politicians hardly explains the failure of the socialists: the Indonesian Communist Party, equally, was largely formed by Dutchmen like Sneevliet living in the Indies, and Indonesia was represented by him on the Comintern for many years.[28]

And in actual fact, the organizational connections between Western and Asian Social-Democracy were quite slender. The close control which Moscow attempted to establish over other Communist Parties was not paralleled in the case of the world socialist movement. The Socialist International, for example, never controlled Asian socialist parties, since the latter set up their own 'Asian Socialist Conference' after World War II.

Asian socialism became identified with foreign influence not because of obvious direct foreign control over policy and action, then, but because the *ideas* for which it stood were foreign ideas, inappropriate to hungry countries. European gradualism was inadequate in situations demanding revolutionary action. Follow-ing Guy Mollet's surrender to the demands of White settlers in Algeria for a 'tough' policy, after the 'socialist' Governor Lacoste had been jeered through the streets of Algiers, one of the most articulate spokesmen of revolutionary Algerian nationalism commented bitterly:

'. . . one can say of the European democrats in Algeria what one has had to say repeatedly of the French parties of the Left: for a long time now history has been made without them. . . . The Left has done nothing for a long time. But . . . it has prevented some things happening.'[29]

A fair comment if applied to the activities of the Left over Algeria, where the impotence and inactivity of the Communist and Socialist parties was only relieved by the stand of Jeanson and by the mass desertions of young conscripts. Unfair, however, as a general judgment: in Viet Nam, for example, at certain times, no less than 40 per cent of the material supplied to French troops showed signs of sabotage,[30] for which the French Communist Party can take the major credit. But too often, to Africans and Asians in revolt, even European socialists and communists, whatever their internationalist protestations, seemed to place the needs of Europe's working classes before the needs of the masses of Africa and Asia. And it was difficult for unsophisticated peasants not to condemn all the works of the alien dominating nationality, including their ideologies, Left or Right.

Yet Communism in Asia has been able to overcome these damning associations; Social-Democracy has not. All sorts of special explanations have been introduced to explain this failure; Sjahrir stresses the absence of a democratic and liberal heritage in Asia. Its traditional societies were 'walled-in and incarcerated'. Its capitalist classes had never had to fight their way into legitimate society, as the bourgeoisie, 'pariahs of the feudal world', had had to do in Europe – and thereby extended general human rights. Instead, the Asian bourgeoisie had grown out of the ranks of the 'feudalists' themselves; they had never gone through the 'heroic', democratic phase. In addition, they had generally developed in close partnership with colonialism. Only the working-class and the middle class upheld democratic freedoms in Asia, he believed. The historic task of socialism, therefore, would be to represent and canalize the aspirations of the mass of the people. (Again, characteristically, his scheme has no explicit place for the peasantry.)

But this is precisely what socialism did not do. It failed because it did not translate into action the difference between a liberal critique of colonialism and a socialist one. For the socialists failed to create a solid institutional underpinning for a socialist *expansion* of the formal rights which would have generated enthusiasm for those ideals, and were often so concerned to distinguish themselves from the communists that they became indistinguishable from the liberals. They were extremely active in asserting democratic rights, in resisting bureaucratization and concentration of power, in working for decentralization. They were much less effective in actual land-redistribution, in consolidating independent societies, in achieving the greater economic equality without which the peasant would tend to regard parliamentary democracy and legal personal freedoms as poor protection against starvation. Although socialists can hardly be held wholly responsible, in so far as many factors over which they had little control were involved, when they *were* in power or in positions of influence, they did not achieve what was achieved – at the expense of democracy – in the Communist countries. Critics point to the continuing instability of Indonesia, to its loose federal structure, its failures to achieve greater social equality, and its failure to modernize. In Burma, there were socialist experiments in workers' control of industry, and in co-operative organization of farming (mutual aid teams, producer co-ops etc.); Israeli and Yugoslav experiments were watched with interest. (Djilas, significantly, was one of the few important non-Asians to attend the First Asian Socialist Conference at Rangoon in 1953.) But only 10 per cent of the land nationalization target had been achieved in Burma eight years after legislation was passed. Moreover, actual political concentration of power and 'mono-lithicization' proceeded apace despite ideological lip-service to popular involvement and decentralization. Socialist parties and Governments were, in fact, very 'monolithic'. Here is Burma in the mid-1950s:

'It was sometimes difficult to distinguish the machinery of the League [the Anti-Fascist People's Freedom League (AFPFL) – the broad nationalist 'Front'] from the machinery of the government. The top positions in the League were held by the senior members of the Government: Nu – President and Prime Minister; Ba Swe – Vice-President, President of the TUC (Burma), and Deputy Prime Minister; Kyaw Nuein – General Secretary and Deputy Prime Minister; Thakin Tin – President of the ABPO [All Burma Peasants' Organization] and Deputy Prime Minister; and so on. . . . This combination of functions extended down to the local levels. . . . It was not merely that the two bodies had overlapping membership, in the way that the British Labour Government comprised the leadership of the Labour Party; it was rather as if Ernie Bevin, after joining the Cabinet, had remained General Secretary of his trade union. . . . [There was no notion of the] . . . incompatibility of [the respective] posts. . . .'[31]

There had been no conference of the League for nearly ten years. Vacancies on the Central Executive Committee were filled by co-option. Control over the local officials, themselves appointed from the centre, was exercised, again, from above. The Socialist Party, too, equally confusingly intertwined with the League itself, had called no congresses since 1947, and filled vacancies by co-option.[32] Members of the Socialist Party held nine out of twelve senior Cabinet posts, a majority of seats on the Executive of the AFPFL, and merged their organizational structure so closely with that of the AFPFL that a 'reference to "the Party" might mean the Socialist Party or the AFPFL. There was even a quite widely held view that the Socialist Party scarcely existed.'[33]

The parties of the Left which had most vigorously asserted the liberal tradition in the face of deep-seated pressures towards 'monolithic' organization thus ended up by assuming many of these features themselves. Social democracy thereby laid itself open to the charge of hypocrisy as well. Finally, its failure to deliver the goods made it appear increasingly irrelevant to peasants who had never known liberal democracy anyhow, and to whom the successes of the Communists, and the self-sacrificing readiness of the latter to fight, appeared more important than the appeals of pseudo-democratic political systems.

But no colonial nationalist movement could afford to be anti-democratic, either. In the face of colonial regimes possessing a monopoly of armed force independence could only be attained by counterposing to it the power of the organized masses. The way to independence, therefore, lay through the *extension* of democratic self-expression; colonial powers could be pressed to carry out their professed mission of civilizing, modernizing, and even democratizing. It was therefore possible, particularly in British and French territories, to press for instalments of political self-expression. The political strategy of the nationalist movements involved a twofold operation: the organization of a dynamic and integrated mass-movement at home with which to press for instalments of self-government in London and Paris.

After 1945, when attainment of independence without recourse to violence was often possible, Western social-democracy became important once more, notably for the African countries. The support of the Labour Party became crucial for any independence movement in the British Colonies. Reciprocally, as the importance of the independence movements grew, even more moderate elements in the Labour Party began to devote a little more time to colonial affairs (though the average colonial debate was still guaranteed to empty the House of Commons). The connection between men like Tom Mboya, Julius Nyerere, Kenneth Kaunda, and moderate-to-Right, 'official 'Labour grew. On the British side, Labour Party officials like John Hatch, journals like the *New Statesman*, kept up a constant pressure on colonial issues. An MP like John Stonehouse might actually find himself deported from the Central African Federation with great publicity. 'Colonial freedom' was no longer a private preserve of the militant Left. The nationalists themselves were happy to use both wings: 'official' Labour in their advance to constitutional reform, and the Left to mobilize extra-Parliamentary support. Tom Mboya succeeded in securing aid from *inter*national Labour, via the International Confederation of Free Trade Unions, and thereby helped swing that organization, hitherto almost exclusively obsessed with the anti-communist crusade, towards a new interest in the emerging territories.

Liberal democracy was a key weapon in the independence battles: Western Social Democracy an ally to be courted. But as ideologies, neither was satisfactory. Social Democracy has been no more successful in the new Africa than it has been in Asia. Even those African leaders most familiar with Western Socialism, such as Julius Nyerere, or Tom Mboya, have already modified their social-democratic beliefs considerably in the direction of one-party populism, because they have become convinced that the problems of the new countries require novel and stringent methods of social organization, not British parliamentary democracy. The key problem is that of giving an illiterate, ill-equipped peasantry a standard of living that befits human beings still existing at minimal, animal levels.

The answers have to be found quickly, not with inevitable gradualness, for expectations have been revolutionized, largely because of improved communications. Radios and films have begun to penetrate into the villages; literacy has increased – in greatly varying degrees – but at least to the point where the peasant can be well exposed to the outside world. Indigenous governments and foreign 'information' services compete to modernize the villager's view of the world, and to propagandize him in the process.[34]

In the remote countryside of Asia or Africa, people became aware of American jazz, British teenage dress, motorcars, countries where workers lived in houses which cost more than the yearly cash income of 250 Asian workers, where food was thrown into dustbins, where people seemed to live lives of unending hedonistic delight. Wants increased enormously; but now, they were no longer wants for basic metabolic needs; they were increasingly wants for what they knew the twentieth century could provide.

For them, then, the key question, after independence, was that of the 'take-off'. This, it seemed, was a problem the Communists had tackled and solved, not in developed industrial societies, but in countries as backward as one's own. For they had recognized what the Asian socialists had sometimes talked about, but not acted upon: that the under-developed countries were faced with 'a lack of means of production', as Sjahrir had put it, that 'expansion was more important than appropriation'. The traditional Western socialist preoccupation with distribution was irrelevant in countries where production was so low. As Norman Manley of Jamaica once put it: 'You cannot nationalize nothing.' Western socialism seemed an ideology of plenty.

Finally, Social Democracy appeared to be irrelevant since it was hardly a distinctive creed at all. In Indonesia, even a religious party like Masjumi contained vocal elements who stood for much of the socialist programme. Some of them outflanked the socialists 'from the Left'. Had not Hadji Salim reminded the Left as long ago as 1921 that 'Mohammad preached socialist economics twelve centuries before Marx'?[35]

Work for all, collective economic action for the general prosperity of all, the moderation of private profit by religious taxes and charitable donations, the elimination of 'socially harmful' capitalism and 'excessive' profit, a 'fair reward' to labour; profit-sharing – all these were quite consistent with modernized Islam. These policies might not satisfy those wanting something more radical: this they would get from the Communist Party. But they were enough to seriously weaken moderate socialism. Nor did the Muslims merely talk. The Muslim peasant organization, Sarekat Tani Islam Indonesia, financed out of *zakat* religious tithes, shifted its expenditure from traditional fields – schools and mosques – to the purchase of land for the needy, the financing of consumer co-ops, and the provision of rural credit.[36]

Mass support was vital for the success of a party – modernization a *sine qua non* of policy. Every party with any pretensions to power therefore preached some form of socialism. Indigenous capitalism was too weak to undertake the modernization of a whole society. Foreign capital would not do it either. It was exploitative, and a menace to national sovereignty. It had a wicked past to live down, and even more wicked neo-colonialist designs for the future.

For all these reasons, the sentiment that 'we are all socialists now' took very firm hold in the new countries. The only question was 'What kind of socialism?' In this competition, traditional Social Democracy, ill-adapted to the revolutionary demands of the environment into which it had been transplanted, was scarcely a distinctive and challenging faith. Its challenge was easily absorbed by parties which incorporated socialist planks into traditionalist ideologies. Where something more radical was called for, Communism lay to hand. Social Democracy, in Asia and Africa, never got off the ground.

CHAPTER FOUR

POPULISM

The Populist Ideology Detaches Itself

To COMPARE a political address by a West African leader from one of the ex-French territories with a speech by a leader in the ex-British countries is an illuminating and startling experience. The gap between the cultures seems so immense. Can one seriously, for example, imagine the President of an ex-British territory writing a poem to a trade union leader, as Senghor has done?[1] Belgian Platonism, British empiricism, and French Cartesianism seem indeed to have produced three different types of African.

Yet despite these inherited divergences, social and political thinking in the new African states – and in the new states outside Africa, too – exhibits newer convergences amongst peoples who have been subject to these very different colonial experiences, and who inherit also radically different pre-colonial traditions. They converge because the specific differences are over-ridden by the general common experience of the colonial past, and by their common present concern with the same central problem: how to achieve the take-off in a Cold War world.

Since the Gallic tradition is one which places a high premium upon lucidity and systematization of thought, it is to be expected that an African intellectual 'd'expression française' would attempt a serious confrontation with the major world-views of his time, and endeavour to develop a coherent theoretical system of his own. Conversely, one would expect to find Africans accustomed to British empiricism, both in formal education and in political life, to operate with a much more eclectic and rough-hewn set of notions.

Of the contemporary political leaders in former French West

Africa, Léopold Senghor and Sékou Touré are outstanding for the thoroughly Gallic style of their political theorizing, ardently Africanist as it is in content.

French African politics have always been intimately focused on the metropolis. No representatives from Kenya or Malaya have ever sat at Westminster, as deputies from colonies across the French possessions did in Paris after 1946 (and had done for much longer in the case of Senegal and the Antilles). But their participation was deeper than a participation in parliament: it was a participation in the totality of French culture.

Senghor, himself an outstanding poet in the French language, embodies this cultural association more than anyone else, though he was to use his French education to develop *négritude*. For men like him, the trap of assimilation had always been there. Had not Governor Faidherbe declared to the Senegalese, back in the nineteenth century, that 'the road is open to all of you alike'? And had not African leaders responded to the invitation – men like Blaise Diagne, President of the first Pan-African Congress, and deputy for Senegal in the French National Assembly, who had written to Marcus Garvey, rejecting his extreme black nationalism:

'We French natives wish to remain French, since France has given us every liberty and since she unreservedly accepts us upon the same basis as her own European children none of us aspires to see French Africa delivered exclusively to the Africans. . . . The French native *élite*, who are responsible for the natives of the colonies, could not allow, without failing in their new duties, the revolutionary theories of separation and emancipation . . . to introduce trouble and disorder where calm and order are the indispensable factors of the security of all.'[2]

Had not a black Governor-General led French Equatorial Africa behind de Gaulle in 1940? The civilized (European-controlled) world was open to the talents, in theory, for those who succeeded in 'evolving'. Bitterly, an Algerian was later to remark to Krishna Menon that the British might have called the Indians many things, but at least they had not called them English![3] The African in French Africa, if he was not to evolve into a Frenchman with a black skin, and thereby cut himself off from his own people, had to confront French and European culture much more frontally than those for whom a crude colour-bar solved the problem, since assimilation, for them, was impossible. This is why *négritude* developed as a consciously militant creed defining the African much more strongly in French Africa and the Antilles than in the British territories.

Yet *négritude* only developed as a reaction against European cultural imperialism. Africa had to debate on Europe's terms before she could debate on her own. And the key European *system* she had to consider is Marxism. Senghor, for example, in his address to the Founding Convention of the Parti de la Fédération Africaine in Dakar in 1959, when making his report on the doctrine and programme of the Party, delivered a lengthy exegesis on classical Marxist theory. No less than three-quarters of his oration dealt with Marx's theories of alienation, value, and social class. Much of what he had to say is in the classic tradition of generations of European Marxist 'revisionism' from Bernstein onwards. As one reads Senghor's criticisms of Marx: that the numbers of the traditional working-class do not increase, since the proportion of productive workers declines, and the proportion of white-collar and service workers rises daily; that working-class solidarity, equally, does not become stronger, for there are rival trade union centres; that the postulated increasing concentration of capital does not occur, since small enterprises become more numerous; that economic crisis-cycles diminish; that socialism is established first in backward countries, where the peasantry are the revolutionary class, not 'rural idiots', etc., etc.: one is reminded of Bernstein's classic notes in the margin of his copy of *Capital*: 'Peasants do not sink; middle class does not disappear; crises do not grow ever larger; misery and serfdom do not increase.'[4]

These criticisms of Marx from an African, then, are no different from criticisms familiar from the intellectual history of twentieth century Europe. Similarly, attitudes towards 'institutionalized Marxism', in the form of the Soviet Union, inevitably reiterate the criticisms of European critics. African leaders want radical decolonization, but they do not want a repetition of fratricidal collectivization and forced-march industrialization in their countries. Nor do they want a second edition of Britain's Industrial Revolution either. Apart from the intense misery for millions entailed in both these transformations, capitalist and communist, the new countries fear that their new-found independence might disappear in the process.

It is for this reason that African politicians and economists, though strongly attracted towards the idea of planning, are also very careful not to commit themselves to draconic and centralized direction of the economy. (True, with the 'commanding heights' in foreign hands, they have little opportunity to introduce Soviet-type planning. In political organization, though, they show little reluctance to centralize.)

Economists like Mamadou Dia have tried to work out an alternative economic system which will be at the same time Africanist and democratic-socialist, preserving the best in the values of traditional society, and fitting them to modern conditions. His critique of Soviet Communism is often an 'immanent' critique, to use Marcuse's term,[5] since it operates from within some of the postulates of Marxism itself. We are vitally interested, says Dia, in industrialization. Without it, our society cannot effectively decolonize itself. But not 'industrialisation à l'outrance' (flat-out industrialization), not autarchic, closed economies, or the sacrifice of human happiness to the requirements of heavy industry or of one generation for the benefit of the next. Dia therefore advocates 'middle-way' solutions: 'industries of transformation', using local agricultural products and raw materials first, rather than steel plants; co-operative and communitarian 'grass-roots' transformations of technique and work-methods at village level. They are naturally interested in Yugoslav 'workers' control', and in the experience of Israel's *kibbutzim* and *moshavim*. Already, indeed, many Israeli experts are at work in West Africa.

In theoretical terms, Dia elaborates further: Marx, he believes, was wrong to attack, and thereby help to condemn to oblivion, Proudhon's emphasis upon syndicalist and co-operative alternatives to capitalist enterprise. *D*ecentralization; *gradual* industrialization; workers' and peasants' *participation* in the shaping of economic policy, are all emphasized. For the new socialist Africa, human values must not be sacrificed to dogmatic hypotheses about 'economic efficiency'. But he uses the Marxist metaphor of base and superstructure to criticize Marx:

'Any authentic ethic for the economy of Africa must be based on a new humanism. . . . The economy . . . is only a means, an instrument for constructing society; the economy is a base only; it does not fulfil its role except in so far as it safeguards African culture. This is a new and essentially fertile idea in an epoch when the notion of material reward dominates everything and when geography is dehumanized to the point where everything is expressed in purely economic terms alone, assimilating social progress to statistical indices.'[6]

Here, clearly, Dia asserts the priority of human values over the claims of a spurious 'economic logic'. On returning from a visit to the USSR, his principal reaction was to condemn the 'materialism' of both the USSR *and* the USA. Our choice, he declared, differs from either: we choose a democratic-socialist way of life.[7]

Dia, however, has not displayed the same moderation in his political behaviour as he does in his economic theory. He is at present serving a life sentence for staging an unsuccessful *coup d'état* against President Senghor.

Important as the solution of the problem of poverty is in the new countries, then, they are not willing to achieve it at *any* cost. They remember Stalin, though again, the critique is an 'immanent' one: it uses Marxist terminology and concepts. Thus Senghor remarks:

'The concern for human dignity, the assertion of the right to freedom – freedom for individuals, freedom for groups – which permeates Marxist thinking and gives it its revolutionary ferment . . . are ignored by Communism in which Stalinism constituted the major deviation . . . [Stalin had created a society in which the State became] . . . an all-powerful, soulless monster, extinguished natural liberties of the human being and dried up the sources of art, without which there is no reason to live.'[8]

The sources of the new African ideology, then, are threefold: firstly, from the thinking of Europe, whether taken up or rejected; from the Pan-Africanism of the New World, the Diaspora; from African experience itself. The last is now pre-eminent: a new kind of Pan-African thinking has displaced the earlier lyrical and often mystical thinking of the pioneers of *négritude*. But *négritude* has been of immense importance, historically. It was largely a 'French African' product. Africans in the British territories, did, it is true, celebrate the African cultural heritage,[9] but, typically, they did not construct a coherent philosophy out of it. *Négritude* emerged effectively when a new generation of students displaced the older generation of leaders of Pan-Africanism after World War II. They were forced to define a philosophy which would be characteristically *African* as opposed to Old World or North American: whether conservative, liberal, social-democratic, or communist. Since these notions have not been widely studied in the West, they call for some closer examination.

One of the more intellectual, if extreme, expressions of Pan-Africanist thinking, occurs in the writings of Cheikh Anta Diop, a major writer of the *Présence Africaine* circle.

The basic tension of the Westernized African is visible in the challenge Diop throws out. Though a Mamadou Dia may praise Senghor, his poet-President, as 'l'helléniste africaine';[10] though the second Congress of Negro Writers and Artists, meeting in Rome, might pay respect to the contributions of the Eternal City to the spiritual life of the whole world, including Africa, among their ranks were men who had had quite other things to say about Graeco-Roman culture. According to Diop,[11] the Greeks were little more than competent 'implementers' of Egyptian (African) discoveries and inventions. In the process, they removed the spiritual content; they reduced the unity and richness of African thought and action to a 'dry materialism', consonant with the harshness of their Eurasiatic nomadic steppe life. The values and moral codes of Egyptian life, deriving from an easy, rich, peaceful, and settled social order, and permeated by a 'vitalist' philosophy, were brought down to the level of earth-bound Man. Greek art, typically, unlike fiercely imaginative African art which creates fantastic images of the gods, is naturalistically reproductive: it aims no higher than producing a 'copy' of Man himself. Hemmed in and oppressed by hostile Nature, the Greeks, who shaped the thinking of Western Man, *opposed* themselves to Nature. Africans, on the other hand, immerse themselves in the vital stream of the cosmos; they see themselves as part of a beneficent natural order, created by an All-Powerful Being.

Other major African theorists, including in their ranks many heavily influenced by Marxism, even a Sékou Touré, either ostentatiously avoid outright attacks on religion,[12] and affirm a policy of religious toleration (in order, explicitly, not to divide the nation on matters of 'private conscience'), or go out of their way to criticize Marxism in so far as it attacks religion.[13] Indeed, leaders like Nkrumah and even Touré have publicly participated in traditional libation-rites and cult-rituals, rationalizing this in terms of traditional national custom – and it is difficult, of course, to know to what extent such actions are merely concessions to popular sentiment. Such reaffirmations of African traditional belief, and corresponding expressions of hostility towards European culture, are not peculiar to Negro Africa. In Morocco, al-Fāsi has written of the African (Berber)-plus-Semitic culture of the Maghreb as a continuous tradition from the Semitic Phoenicians to the Arabs, in contradistinction to the intruding Latin and Anglo-Saxon culture which has oppressed North Africa from Carthage to the present day. From the beginning, he asserts, Berber and Arab mixed happily and were 'integrated into the life of the country'. The Carthaginians, the Romans, and the French imposed their government by force on a resistant North African population.[14] For these thinkers, the White crime is not dehumanization, but despiritualization.

Some apostles of *négritude*, under the direct influence of Jean-Paul Sartre,[15] blended it with modern existentialism.

The African is not the questing, driven, thought-dominated man of the West, they claim. He is a *total* being, whose mere persistence in being himself, living his way of life, constitute his uniqueness, his 'personality', his separateness from Western man. Aimé Césaire wrote the great hymn of this school of *négritude* in his poem, *Cahier d'un Retour au Pays Natal*:[16]

'Exult for those who have never invented anything
for those who have never invented anything
for those who have never explored anything
for those who have never conquered anything
but who yield themselves, captivated by the essence of things
ignorant of appearances but captivated by the movement of things
caring nothing for conquest, but . . .
truly the elder sons of the world . . .

. . . . .
Spark of the World's sacred fire. . . .'

Those who never invented anything, who were ignorant, but who were also in reality the true 'elder sons of the world', who preserved the sacred spark for mankind as a whole. Senghor, in similar vein, explored the horrors the White man had created in New York. At first he was overwhelmed by it:

'. . . confused by your beauty, by those great golden long-legged girls.
So shy at first before your blue metallic eyes, your frosted smile. . . .'

A sense of the underlying inhumanity of the city soon displaced
the initial impressiveness:

'. . . two weeks on the bare sidewalks of Manhattan
– At the end of the third week the fever seizes you with the pounce of
    a leopard
Two weeks without rivers or fields, all the birds of the air
Falling sudden and dead on the high ashes of flat rooftops.
No smile of a child blooms, his hand refreshed in my hand
No mother's breast, but only nylon legs. Legs and breasts that have
    no sweat nor smell.
No tender word for there are no lips, only artificial hearts paid for in
    hard cash
And no book where wisdom may be read . . .

         . . . . .

Nights of insomnia oh nights of Manhattan! So agitated by flickering
    lights, while motor-horns howl of empty hour⌐
And while dark waters carry away hygienic loves, like rivers flooded
    with the corpses of children.'

But life did throb beneath the skyscrapers:

'I saw in Harlem humming with noise with noise with stately colours
    and flamboyant smells
– It was teatime at the house of the seller of pharmaceutical products –
I saw them preparing the festival of night for escape from the day.
I proclaim night more truthful than the day.
It was the pure hour when in the street God makes the life that goes
    back beyond memory spring up
All the amphibious element shining like suns.
Harlem Harlem! A green breeze of corn springs up from the pavements
    ploughed by the naked feet of the dancers
Bottoms waves of silk and sword-blade breasts, water-lily ballets and
    fabulous masks
At the feet of police horses roll the mangoes of love from low
    houses. . . .'

And the life of the White man, too, could be transformed – if he
opened his soul to the spontaneity of the Negro:

'Listen New York! . . .

Listen to the distant beating of your nocturnal heart, rhythm and the
    blood of the tom-tom, tom-tom blood and tom-tom
New York! I say to you: New York let black blood flow into your
    blood
That it may rub the rust from your steel joints, like an oil of life,
That it may give to your bridges the bend of buttocks and the suppleness
    of creepers.
Now return the most ancient times, the unity recovered. . . .
Thought linked to the act, ear to heart, sign to sense

      . . . . .

. . . it is enough to open the eyes to the rainbow of April
And the ears, above all the ears, to God who out of the laugh of a
    saxophone created the heaven and the earth in six days.
And the seventh day he slept the great sleep of the Negro.'[17]

For some activist, revolutionary African political leaders and
thinkers, this celebration of mysticism and passivity was too much.
Gabriel d'Arboussier, the firebrand of the Rassemblement Démocratique Africaine, the militant mass party which swept French
West Africa after World War II, and the man who had forged its
link with the French Communist Party, attacked Sartre, Césaire,
and others furiously.[18]

The Negro peoples, he declared, had become conscious of themselves, had reasserted their personality, in *struggle*, not just by
'being'. Others, like Diop, on historical rather than political
grounds, roundly denounced the conception of an African heritage
'without culture', and pointed to the rich history of African civilizations and cultures. Diop even translated an essay on relativity
theory by the noted French Communist physicist, Paul Langevin,
into Wolof, to prove the richness and adaptability of African languages.[19] Yet Diop himself, in his assertion of the spirituality of
African culture, had laid the basis for the 'mystification' of the
Orphée Noir school.

But whatever the differences between them, racial-mystics,
political militants, poets, and African historians, could agree that
traditional African society enshrined important human values
which, they believed, the West had lost because of their proud but
also sad history as the pioneers of modernized industrial society.
The humanist critique of Western and Eastern economic assumptions developed by Dia (easily married, too, to Catholic social

philosophy); the delineation of a distinct 'African personality'; and the reassertion of the vitality and importance of a continuing African culture, could all be summarized as an assertion of the 'communitarian' nature of African society. Paradoxically enough, this stress on communitarian values, of the living *Gemeinschaft* of African village society, was quite consistent with a Man-centred humanism principally derived from the much-criticized Marx – and ultimately from the very Greeks Diop despises!

But the thinking of the new populists posits more than a peculiar *humaneness* in African social relations. It asserts that traditional society was peculiarly homogeneous in a way that is now un-familiar to Euro-America. The decolonized society, especially, is held to be *classless*, indeed conflict-less. Where conflict does exist, or where division into classes is incontrovertible, this is explained away in various (often mutually-inconsistent) ways. Some hold that these divisions of interest still persist from the old 'feudal' order of things – but that they will be eliminated during the process of modernization. Others find the major source of such discord in colonialism.

As a Marxist-influenced thinker, Sékou Touré, for example, cannot deny that 'contradictions' do exist in contemporary society. Society, he declares, is still 'cellularized' into fractional groupings with different interests: the intellectuals and the illiterate, the young and the old; producers and consumers; men and women; peasants and urban-dwellers; bureaucrats and their clients; and so on and so forth. But these are not *classes*, and the differences of interest between them will disappear as people lose bad old habits of protecting their vested interests, and as a new social ethic becomes more general. Their common interests, in any case, out-weigh their particular interests. Politically, his conclusion is that there is no longer, in a decolonizing society, any need for multiple political parties, which are nothing but the specialized organs representing the sectional interests of these rival groupings. The single 'National Front' will effectively subsume all interests within it.

Other African 'Marxists', however, take a somewhat different tack. Madeira Keita, for example, has this to say:

'. . . If a political party is the political expression of a class, that class representing *interests* – then clearly we can only agree that Negro

Africa is a class society. But we say that class differentiation in Africa does not imply a *diversification* of interests, least of all any *opposition* of interests.'[20]

Asian theorists similarly have developed 'populist' theories which emphasize the homogeneity of their societies. Asian society was, they hold, basically an agrarian order, and remains so today. Mohammad Hatta, for example, recognizes that

'... the old Indonesian states were feudal states, ruled by autocratic kings.... Nevertheless, in the villages, a democratic system remained in force ... [it was] ... able to maintain itself under feudalism, because the soil, the most important factor of production, was the communal property of the village people. It did not belong to the king ... on the basis of the common ownership of the soil, each individual, in carrying out his economic activities, felt that he had to act in accordance with common consent. Consequently, one finds that all heavy work that could not be done by one individual person, was performed by the system of *gotong-rojong*, mutual assistance. ... All decisions concerning matters of common interest were taken by mutual consent, or in the words of a Minangkabau saying: "Water becomes one by passing through a bamboo pipe, words become one by mutual agreement". ... All adult and indigenous members of the village community had the right to attend [village] meetings. ... In the original Indonesian village ... there are two further [democratic] elements, the right to make joint protest against regulations issued by the king or prince, regulations that are felt to be unjust, and the right of the people to leave the territory over which the king has authority, when they feel that they do not like to live there any longer.'[21]

President Soekarno, on the other hand, emphasizes much more strongly the extent to which the brotherhood of the Indonesian people is something new that has been developed in the course of colonial pauperization of the people of that country. Their life-condition has united them, across class-lines dividing peasant and worker, in opposition to the Dutch. In characteristic style, he coins a new Indonesian term, Marhaenism, to describe this condition of common immiseration:

'... The people of Indonesia are primarily Workers and Peasants, that is true ... [though] ... there are yet many other groups who are neither workers nor peasants [he cites tricycle-carriage drivers and street-vendors]. ... The term proletariat was used in 1926 to describe the whole of the poor, the common people; but they are by far not all proletarians. . . . To whom does the term proletariat apply? . . . The proletariat are the workers who do not participate in ownership of the means of production. But our nation . . . is composed of tens of millions of people not all of whom are covered by the term proletariat. There are great numbers indeed who are not labourers, very many who do not sell their labour-power to others. Formerly I explained to my comrades . . . why I used the term "Marhaen". It was for no other reason but that on a certain day I was walking in the rice fields to the south of Tjigereleng, and I came across a man hoeing the field, and I asked him. "Brother, who owns this field?" "*Gaduh abdi* [I own it]," he said. And so he participated in ownership of the means of production, owning that rice field. "And the hoe, who owns that?" "*Gaduh abdi*." "These tools, who owns these?" "*Gaduh abdi*." "But, Brother, you live in poverty?" "That's right, I live poorly." And I thought to myself then, this man clearly and certainly is not a member of the proletariat, he is a pauper, he is poor, but he is not a member of the proletariat, for he does not sell his labour-power to another without participating in ownership of the means of production. His rice field is his own property, his hoe is his own, his sickle is his own, his rake is his own. Everything is his own property; the crop of his rice field is for his own use. But he is still a pauper, he is poor. Nevertheless he is not one of the proletariat, he is a small farmer, a very poor farmer, barely making a living. "*Tani sieur*" I said at that time, "*Tani gurem*".* He is not one of the proletariat. Then, Brothers, and Sisters, I asked him, "What is your name?" "I am Marhaen," he said. He said that his name was Marhaen. I had an inspiration: Now, this name I will hold to; I will use this name to describe the destitute People of Indonesia.

'And of poor Indonesians there are not one million, not two million or three, but almost the whole of the Indonesian People are paupers. Almost the whole of the People of Indonesia are Marhaen! They are the poor common people, yes, the poor peasant, yes, the poor fisherman, yes, the poor clerk, yes, the poor stall vendor, yes, the poor cart driver, yes, the poor chauffeur – all of these are embraced by the one term, Marhaen.'[22]

The reason for this common poverty is Dutch 'investment imperialism', he goes on, an imperialism which, unlike British imperialism in India, pauperized an entire nation up to the time when after 17 August, 1945, that 'explosive force . . . all of

---

* *Tani sieur* (Sundanese); *Tani gurem* (Javanese): literally a chicken-flea peasant, i.e. a peasant with a plot of land no longer than a flea [note by G. McT. Kahin in original].

Indonesia's Marhaens, yes, those who were young men and women, who were workers, who were peasants, rose and acted'.

The societies of Asia and Africa, then, are commonly seen by theorists in those countries not so much in terms of the class-divisions that the Westerner almost instinctively begins to look for, but in terms of the common life-situation of whole populations which derives from their past and present tradition of village-level democracy, and from the unifying experience of common political oppression and economic impoverishment at the hands of foreign imperialisms.

To what extent does this ideological emphasis upon the 'unity' of the nation and the homogeneity of society reflect a real absence of social differentiation in the new societies, and to what extent is it merely another instance of the familiar rhetoric of all nationalists who, from Fichte onwards, have always appealed to an often-spurious solidarity, embracing all classes and conditions of the nation, even to the extent of denying that any significant divisions existed at all? To answer this question, we must look more closely at social class divisions – and at other divisions – in the new societies.

Social Class in the Emergent Countries

(i) *Bourgeoisie and Petty Bourgeoisie*. The countries which had fallen under European occupation by the nineteenth century were, as we saw earlier, frequently quite advanced economically and in general cultural level. Under European domination, however, what indigenous industry there was rapidly went to the wall. But where the wealthier classes in the traditional order of things were able – and permitted – to adapt themselves to participation in the new world-market economy, traditional wealth could be invested in the new sectors of the economy, and gave rise to a new class of indigenous capitalists.

Japan was perhaps the most striking case: here the ruling classes in an agrarian feudal society – though one which possessed a significant urban and commercial sector even before the arrival of Commodore Perry – were able to come to terms with modern capitalism by investing heavily in the new industrial economy which was rapidly constructed after the Meiji Restoration. The result was a peculiarly centralized and concentrated pattern of political control and economic ownership, in which indigenous finance-capital was closely interlinked with industrial enterprise, but where older feudal-paternalist traditions persisted, and affected relations between management and workers. From this launching-platform, Japan successfully built up a modern capitalist economy.

Indian economic development also displayed many of the features found in Japanese development, whether the capital involved was British or Indian. One of its outstanding character-istics was the early development of the joint-stock company under 'managing agents', who began as traders, and later became organizers and managers of industry:

'It was mainly through their agency that European capital and skill found their way to India. They used these in the organization of industrial undertakings and the development of India's resources which paid for the increasing import of foreign manufactures. . . . The whole system was in fact integrated with the imperialist economy. . . . The managing agency system introduced a degree of administrative control and financial integration in business which had never existed before. It preserved the legal and functional independence of each of the concerns opened up by a pioneering managing agency firm, and yet the firm exercised an overall control by putting up most of the capital in the concerns so floated.'[23]

Factory industry grew phenomenally from the 1880s onwards; so did joint-stock companies. Initially, the capital was predomi-nantly British. Even in 1949, nearly a half of India's total capital investment (Rs. 596 crores) was foreign; until this century, the proportion of Indian capital was relatively insignificant. In 1911,

'a group of 15 Managing Agents controlled and managed 189 industrial units . . ., 93 of which were controlled and managed by the "Big Five" Managing Agency Houses of Calcutta, viz. Messrs. Andrew Yule, Bird, Shaw Wallace, Duncan and Begg, Dunlop and Company, all of which were foreign owned and operated. With the exceptions of Tatas, there was no Indian Managing house which controlled or managed more than five industrial units'.[24]

But from that time onwards, especially after the large-scale repatriation of British capital in the 1930s due to the depression and to political instability, the number of Indian directors grew rapidly, particularly in cotton textiles (Gujaratis and Marwaris) in steel (Parsis – the Tata family), and in sugar (Marwaris and Punjabis).

The pattern of Indian capitalism, then, was peculiarly centralized and rationalized from the beginning: the emergence of a small number of big enterprises operating in various industrial fields and closely linked with finance-capital was not the end-product of a long period of *laissez-faire* competition between small firms. Indian capitalism began quite differently:

'Historically, the expansion of business in India had proceeded from the top downwards, not from the bottom upwards. An Indian plutocracy had even earlier formed a separate caste by itself, and those who carried on business under them did so as their servile agents, not as free merchants. A managing agency firm, Indian or European, similarly held the bulk interest in the several industrial units whose administration it controlled by a system of multiple directorships. Capital remained concentrated under both. Indeed the directors of Indian industries were . . . members of the upper rather than the middle classes; for the industrial power of the country was in the hands of a few persons only . . . about 100 persons held as many as 1,700 directorships of important concerns; 860 of these were held by 30 persons, and of these 30 10 only held between them as many as 400 directorships.'[25]

We will consider the wider significance of modernization, economic and political, 'from the top downwards', later. It has left those societies which have achieved independence without military and political revolution, and without radical change in the ownership of land and industry, with a very distinctive legacy in terms of popular predisposition to leave social initiatives to government and to external forces which they commonly see as something alien and external to their village world. To energize such populations, and to transform society without initiating disruptive social revolution, is the problem that non-revolutionary governments are continuously faced with.

Indian capitalism was able to develop quite rapidly as a 'compradore' junior partner of British business. It ran into major opposition, however, when it began to challenge British industry directly. Under free trade, the battle went to the strongest – British industry. For many decades, too, the new Indian capitalist class had to fight restrictive policies imposed by the British government which hindered the free development of Indian-owned industry. Indian capitalists fought unavailingly for years for government assistance in fostering indigenous industry. Only during the two World Wars did they get it. For these reasons, Indian capitalism came into conflict with the alien Government. India's most famous capitalist enterprise, the Tata steel firm, has long been a major source of strength to Congress (and today a Tata combines his direction of the great private empire with responsibility for the State-owned India Airways). Indigenous capital thus divested itself of its original compradore associations. After Independence, it was able to build a new image of itself as a major *Indian* contributor to national development and prosperity in an economy still half-controlled by foreigners.

In consequence, class-opposition to Indian capitalism could be fairly easily muted or deflected by skilful appeals to national solidarity. Indonesian capitalists, likewise, could always draw a distinction between 'sinful',[26] foreign capitalism and their own contributions to national growth and stability. Class divisions could therefore be relatively easily overcome by the nationalist movement. For this reason, much Marxist analysis of political alignments in backward countries has been wide of the mark. Unity in the face of imperialism has, for the most part, over-ridden class hostilities; national independence taken priority over class struggle; for the nation as a whole, not merely its workers and peasants, has suffered – admittedly in different degrees and in different ways – from alien rule.

Similar antagonistic relationships between indigenous capital and foreign capital are visible in countries with much less-developed colonial economies. In Nigeria, for example, the United Africa Company dominated the economy.

'By the late 1930s it controlled more than 40 per cent of Nigeria's import-export trade, and as late as 1949 it handled 34 per cent of commercial merchandise imports into Nigeria and purchased, on behalf of Nigerian marketing boards, 43 per cent of all Nigerian non-mineral exports.'[27]

In association with five other firms, the UAC formed the Association of West African Merchants which by 1949 handled about 66 per cent of Nigeria's imports and nearly 70 per cent of her exports.

Foreign domination on this scale was bound to produce conflicts in a society where indigenous trading was highly developed
and had been for many centuries. During the inter-war period, it
is estimated, no less than 100,000 people were engaged as middle-
men in the marketing of major Nigerian exports.[28] The average
net income of these traders was very high indeed for an 'under-
developed' economy: £650 p.a.[29]

The economies of countries like these, then, were far from
being pure subsistence economies. And increasingly, the national
and international money economy made increasing inroads: by
1950, 79 per cent of the adult male population of Ghana was
involved in the money economy; in Nigeria, 43 per cent; even in
Kenya, 30 per cent were involved.[30]

The great bulk of these 'traders', however, were 'micro-traders':
the 100,000 little men who clipped a few shillings off the handling
of minute amounts of palm-oil; the tens of thousands of market-
women who made pennies or fractions of pennies out of selling
relish, matches, fish, mirrors, or kerosene in the markets. It is
ridiculous to label them and wealthy giants like the United Africa
Company as 'capitalist entrepreneurs'. Among the hundreds of
thousands of African traders, there are indeed a few rich men;
there are even more men of moderate wealth. Of the 8,000 traders
operating in Kumasi, Ghana, for example, 150 had a turnover of
£500–£2,000 a year, and a few of these as much as £100,000.[31]
But the term 'bourgeois' – or even 'petty bourgeois' – can scarcely
be used to describe the mass of petty traders and hucksters, such
as those who form the bulk of the West African market trade.
In Koforidua, 3,000 sellers – some *70 per cent.* of the female
African population – participated in the market trade.

'Numerically, the great majority of these market traders will be small
and poor, making a few shillings, sometimes a few pence in the day,
pin money for women, a little cash from surplus vegetables or a handi-
craft. Their skill is in selling, in carrying in their head figures of pennies
and halfpennies, in finding a bargain from each other and selling to a
stranger. Few of them depend on trade alone. . . .'[33]

This last characteristic is of great importance in understanding
the readiness of these 'micro'-traders to support mass nationalist
movements, for they are very commonly occupationally indeterminate, 'floating' between self-employment, employment of others,

and sale of their own labour-power. They do not constitute a distinctive and consolidated social class. The petty market-traders, and notably the women who, in accordance with traditional West African culture, predominate in this sector of the economy, were one of the principal groupings which assisted Nkrumah in his rise to power. The market-women of Lagos, too, were

'. . . the main mass base of Nigeria's oldest political organization, the Nigerian. National Democratic Party. . . . The market women were constituents whom any urban politician or nationalist leader would ignore at his peril.'[34]

Nationalism in countries like Nigeria and the Gold Coast, therefore, though developed largely, originally, under the leadership of the small indigenous bourgeoisie proper, was also able to mobilize the numerically important micro-traders in common opposition to the big foreign interests. Its ideology, therefore, was much more populist than it was bourgeois. In a few territories, such as the Ivory Coast, relatively prosperous and differentiated, the prosperous farmer was dominant in the leadership. Its characteristic spokesman was Houphouët-Boigny. But though the son of a wealthy planter, and a chief and large planter himself, he led the great mass party of French West Africa, the Rassemblement Démocratique Africaine, into alliance with the French Communist Party – and into the 1949 violence at Dimboko, where thirteen people were killed and thirty-eight wounded.[35] But the attraction of the Communist Party was its militancy, not its communism. The more bourgeoisified *élites*, once they have gained political control, quickly lose their radicalism, especially in the more prosperous territories. There is a great gulf between the socialist theory even of a Senghor and Dia and their social practice. After his flirtation with the PCF, Houphouët-Boigny settled down to a more congenial role as a pillar of the French Establishment. Before long, he was Minister in the Cabinet that planned Suez.

A fully-developed *laissez-faire* ideology could scarcely flourish in the regulated world of the colonies. Something very close to it is reproduced in this passage from Awolowo, where Anglo-Saxon 'common sense', Puritan homilectic, Smiles-ian self-help and plain petty-bourgeoisdom find a congenial lodgment in the breast of a self-made Nigerian politician:

'I read as widely as possible . . . Shakespeare, Dickens, R. L. Stevenson, Emerson, Lord Avebury, Sir Walter Scott, Hazlitt, Elbert Hubbard. . . . But there were two books which helped me to evoke a philosophy of life to which, with some modifications which my experiences dictate, I still cling. The first book was *The Human Machine*, which was a free gift to anyone who took a correspondence course with Bennett College, Sheffield. The book was a collection of terse, powerful articles, loaded with the practical and well-tested doctrines of applied psychology . . . previously published . . . in . . . *John Bull*. The second book was written . . . by an American author, and its title was *It's Up To You*. The philosophy of the latter book is very simple, but also very true and fundamental. I will state it in a nutshell. . . . Take a jar, put in it small beans as well as big beans, making sure that each of the big beans is heavier in weight than each of the small beans; put the big beans at the bottom of the jar and the small beans at the top; shake the jar and, Behold! the small beans rattle to the bottom and the big beans shake to the top. . . . Now the world is like a mighty jar, and all of us are in it . . . like beans with varying sizes and weights. In normal circumstances, each of us is where he is because of his size and weight. By means of favouritism, or of some other deliberate and iniquitous tinkering with the contents of the jar, some beans which are small . . . may get to the top . . . but they are sure to rattle to the bottom sooner or later. Said the author in words which I vividly remember: "Nobody can fool the jar of life." The sine qua non for anyone who wants to get to the top, therefore, is to increase his size and weight in his particular calling – that is mentally, professionally, morally, and spiritually. Getting to the top is one thing and remaining there is another. To maintain your place at the top you must make sure that you do not at any time shrink or lose in weight. . . . I am a firm believer in this philosophy.'[36]

Here, Victorian drive is admixed with the American 'frontier' ethic of expansion and opportunity, plus lingering traces of the great Protestant Ethic, spiritually thinned down, as Weber has shown,[37] via the American sects, and finally secularized in the Rotary clubs and masonic lodges of the Mid-West,[38] and the whole infused with Nigerian business acumen.

But a bourgeoisie in close contact with thousands of micro-traders, face-to-face with the British Empire and the United Africa Company, could not be satisfied with a nineteenth-century ethic. Even in Europe, the 'small man' driven to the wall has turned to collective radicalism – even to the Nazis or Poujade. A purely bourgeois party could not hope to succeed, for whatever the numbers involved in the cash-economy, the mass of the people were only marginal producers of cash crops. The rest were sub-sistence producers. The really capitalized sector of the economy was controlled by foreigners. Even not-so-big business was com-monly controlled by 'ethnic' trading 'castes': the Indians in East Africa, the 'Syrians' in West Africa, the Chinese in South-East Asia, Greeks and Armenians in the Middle East. These alien ethnic groupings were oriented, not to the internal and local markets, but to import–export trading. They established them-selves in the seaports predominantly, and were usually in close 'compradore' dependence upon the overall colonial economic strategy.

They could be quite numerous and influential, but they could not easily form close ties with other, indigenous middle-class elements. In a society such as Egypt, for example, long involved in international trade, the 'middle classes' – described by Berger as composed of merchants, clerks, professionals, businessmen and agents, plus the 134,500 members of the 'agricultural' middle class (about 5 per cent of all landowners) – amounted to some 6–10 per cent of the gainfully-occupied population in 1947 – around half a million people.[39] He goes on to point out, however, that these people did not constitute a very distinct *employing* class. Most of the smaller landowners, indeed, were self-employed or even employed. They might well be ranked on a wealth or status scale as 'middle class', but they are hardly a distinct class of small capitalists. Indeed, this 'middle class' rag-bag includes a number of occupational groupings, like clerks and professionals, whose economic interests, whether in terms of ownership, job-situation, market-situation, or work-situation,[40] or in terms of status, educational level, style of life, etc. were not at all similar. Sharply-marked-off bourgeois or petty-bourgeois classes, with their appropriate political organs, were unlikely to emerge amongst ambiguous, fragmented and ethically-divided middle strata of this kind. Not only do they lack definition and corporate identity as a class, but, for many of them, their alien ethnic status makes it dangerous to draw attention to themselves corporately and politi-cally: they would invite attack as foreigners. Foreign-ness thus disqualifies these active and powerful elements from giving the leadership that an effective 'national bourgeoisie' might have provided.

The pattern of 'ethnic' monopolization of business opportunities, where 'economic class becomes coterminous with ethnic group',[41] means that the educated indigenous population has to find alternative outlets for the exercise of its talents and for the satisfaction of its desires for wealth, power, and status.

In the more backward countries, where business was poorly developed, the only other openings normally available to the ambitious and the capable were in the public service. In many colonies, too, teaching, medicine, social work, were largely Government jobs, not 'free professions'. But even in more advanced colonies, Government service was the main avenue of upwards mobility. In Indonesia, for example, the Chinese trading-class, early entrenched in the traditional trade between China and Indonesia, became under the Dutch regime of the 'Company System' and its successors, the hated operators of a Government-controlled system of forced deliveries, forced labour, and monopolies. The earliest Indonesian nationalist movement therefore developed out of the struggle of Javanese entrepreneurs to break the Dutch–Chinese stranglehold on business, with the formation in 1911 of the trading-association, *Sarekat Dagang Islam* (The Islamic Trading Society), an organization which then give rise to a political movement, *Sarekat Islam*, in the following year.

By 1919, it had completely changed its character. It had turned into a mass movement with two and a half million members. In the following year, the Indonesian Communist Party was formed. Middle-class traders were clearly unsuitable leaders for dynamic mass movements of this kind. Instead, the leadership came increasingly from a new and more militant social stratum – the western-educated Government officials. *Sarekat Islam*, typically, had been founded by a merchant, Tjokroaminoto; the young man who stepped into his shoes, and who built the new movement into a mass organization, was a young engineer called Soekarno.[42] He was able to draw on vast reserves of talent, resentment, and enthusiasm amongst young, Western-educated Indonesians barred from business by Dutch and Chinese monopolization.

They flooded into Government Service. By 1918, they occupied 98.9 per cent of the lowest positions – but only 6.4 per cent of the highest. Europeans, on the other hand, occupied 92·2 per cent of the highest, and only o·6 per cent. of the lowest.[43] Bitterness at this blatant discrimination, reinforced by a deliberate system of dual rates of pay for the same job (as in Kenya and many other colonies), was exacerbated by long periods of high 'graduate unemployment', when as many as 25 per cent of them might be unable to fill their stomachs with rice despite their Western education. Inevitably, then, they rapidly became consciously and militantly nationalistic.

It was a similar story elsewhere; and improvements were slow:

'In 1946 in India the proportion of Indians to British in the senior ranks was 504 to 623, and in Ghana the same year, 36 to 171. In Nigeria in 1949 there were 245 Nigerians to 2,541 British. In French West Africa, Frenchmen held the 5,000 senior posts. The remaining 37,000 posts were filled by Africans, a comparatively high figure. In Indonesia, also in 1940, Indonesians held 7 per cent of the higher positions.'

In the least-developed colonies, the 'new men' in the public service became particularly important as leaders of nationalism.

Their relationship to other segments of the middle classes emerges from this description of Leopoldville on the eve of the explosion in the Congo:

'Normally the contradictory interests of a bourgeoisie and the wage-earning mass of [sic] which it depends finds one of its manifestations in the articulation of a self-consciousness, a *morale*; what we find in the Congo, and more especially in Leopoldville, is that a bourgeois psychology and consciousness is viable not so much among the shop-keepers and taxi-drivers as among the relatively educated neo-bourgeoisie which acted as subaltern intellectuals and administrators of colonialism. Traders and artisans of course do not constitute a bourgeoisie in the strict sense but are dependent on the creation by a European middle-class of a large, consumer proletariat; naturally, there was opposition created by their speculation at the expense of the wage-earner's consuming power, just as they resented the development of a relatively skilled worker *élite* whose incomes were in many cases equal to their own and more stable. It was in the educationally-privileged, white-collar staffs . . . that a self-consciousness . . . first . . . appeared. . . . Lumumba was first politically active in the African Staff Association at Stanleyville. Black Trade Union organization commenced not with proletarians and depressed craftsmen, but with these professional associations of fonctionnaires. . . . The conclusion remains that it is highly misleading to talk of social classes; at best, we can discern tendencies towards the creation of such groups, whose consolidation would depend on the relative stage of capital development. There can be no proletarian as long as family and ethnic ties hold him psychologically and to some extent economically . . . from total dependence on the sale of his own labour-force; there can be no African middle-class as long as Europeans monopolize properly bourgeois economic functions, and as long as the two discrete elements of the 'economic' and 'intellectual' Congolese neo-bourgeoisie do not harmonize into a self-conscious class with special interests, and as long as they remain responsive to traditional allegiances.'[45]

The uneasy shift from 'bourgeoisie' to 'neo-bourgeoisie' indicates the ambiguity of this category, here used with an imprecision usually reserved for the term 'petty bourgeoisie', one of the spongiest catchalls in the Marxist vocabulary. Clerks, shopkeepers, taxi-drivers, sanitary inspectors, all sorts of strange bed-fellows are caught within the net. And yet these 'intermediate strata' ('middle' classes) *are* indeterminate congeries of occupations which defy precise schematization. What the passage does indicate well is the importance of the Western-educated civil servants in the emerging nationalist *élite* leadership, and the comparative weakness both of the specifically *entreprenurial* 'petty bourgeoisie' and of the 'working-class'.

The role of the Western-educated Civil Servant was even more crucial in the nationalist movements of French West Africa. Half the Grand Councillors in 1952, and 160 of the 227 deputies elected to Territorial Assemblies in that year, were civil servants (generally minor ones). On the occasion of the historic Conference of the RDA held at Bamako from the 25th to the 30th September, 1957, 60 per cent of the delegates were in public service: out of 254 delegates, eighty-three were administrators, forty-four teachers, and thirty-five health workers.[46]

As a result of the Lamine Guèye law, these were relatively privileged people. They were to continue to maintain this privileged status when independence had been attained. The new *élite* was often drawn from the traditional upper strata or the new wealthy. Traditional prestige was important: even on the Left, a Sékou Touré, despite his mass base in the trade unions and his Marxist proclivities, claimed descent from Almamy Samory, hero of resistance to French conquest in the nineteenth century.

Traditional wealth and high status themselves opened new opportunities for Western education: the new *élite* was thus doubly
imbued with a consciousness of the gulf between it and the ordinary people. The biographies of African leaders in former French
West Africa reveals the importance, indeed, of a single school, the
William Ponty school at Dakar, as a breeding-ground of the new
élite.[47] French official policy, indeed, had encouraged sons of
rulers and other upper-class individuals to acquire Western
education from as early as 1856, when the quaintly-named Ecoles
des Otages were set up.[48]

As a result, political leadership normally came from people
accustomed to high status in their communities. But even if they
could claim no traditional prestige, their new status as educated
men gave them prestige enough. Even on the Left, the leadership
was drawn from the ranks of this new intelligentsia. In Asia,
Burma's entire postwar history has been shaped by Western-
educated men like Aung San and Ko Nu, respectively Secretary
and President of the Rangoon University Students' Union in 1935,
the former a 'moderately prosperous' landowner's son, the latter
son of a merchant.[49] And the theoretical notions developed during
the struggle for independence were to bear the marks of their
formulation by this kind of *élite*. In the case of India, Clemens
Dutt had had to write to P. C. Joshi in 1928: 'I hope that you are
finding it possible to draw in actual proletarian workers in to the
WPP' [Workers' and Peasants' Party: an open, legal mass organization in place of the then-banned Communist Party.] The
situation had hardly improved by 1934: Soviet politico-Indolo-
gists were only able to produce, as evidence of the increasingly
'successful' Communist challenge to Congress, a rise in Party
membership from around twenty to 150 during a whole year.[50]
Even by 1945, when the membership had reached some 25,000,
eighty-six of the 139 delegates to the First Party Congress were
intellectuals, as against twenty-two workers and twenty-five
peasants; the high proportion of intellectuals was even more
accentuated amongst the full-time leadership. The Indian
Socialist Party, too, was overwhelmingly middle class.[51] Even in
would-be mass Left parties, then, the leadership was overwhelmingly a leadership of intellectuals.

But in the less developed societies, the intellectuals, despite

their (normally brief) Western education, remained in close
contact with the ordinary people. Increasingly, too, the sons of
ordinary peasants found their way into the schools. A French
sociologist who knew Patrice Lumumba well has described his
return to his home village in Kasai after an absence of ten years
(before Lumumba had become a major political figure):

'As we got nearer our destination, we had to stop more and more often.
Relatives and friends from every direction and of all ages . . . came to
greet him delightedly. They snapped their fingers, smacked their
thighs, ran their hands along the hero's forearm. Exclamations, con-
gratulations, and laughter. Babies were brought for admiration, children
had grown into adolescents, adolescents had become adults. . . .
  Finally we arrived. The local boy returned was greeted in triumph.
The whole village was there, his family, the chief, village notables, and
the small fry. The old historian-genealogist is present, too. . . . The
new spreads like wildfire. It is carried hurriedly to neighbouring
villages. Emotion is at its height, joy everywhere. . . .
  For more than a month, I saw my friend living in his childhood
surroundings. He had a word for everybody, he asked about everybody
and everything; he was invited everywhere. He was a "monsieur"
now . . . '[52]

Political leaders of this kind enjoy a special intimacy which is not
lost despite their new status as 'messieurs', in which, rather, the
villagers find vicarious satisfaction. For despite the efforts of
colonialists to build an African élite which would be European in
outlook, kinship still tied the élite to the ordinary people, and the
colour-bar constantly threw him back into the arms of his less-
educated and privileged fellows.

The new politicians therefore share many of the attitudes of
the ordinary villager – or at least, understand their needs and
likely reactions intimately. Patrice Lumumba, at the time of the
visit described above, had only just begun to engage in public
life. Even in a book written several years later, in 1956–7, he was
still the young intellectual in transition, struggling to develop a
political theory which would connect with the needs of the people
of his country, but as yet quite unable to step beyond the intellectual limits of Belgian paternalism.[53] His demands are the classic
limited demands of the évolué. The first demands of this kind
of élite invariably reflect their particular concerns with their own

problems: demands for 'indigenization' of the higher ranks of the Civil Service; for equal pay where 'natives' and 'expatriates' do the same work; claims for citizens' rights for 'civilized' men; or for better and wider educational facilities. As Lord Hailey accurately remarked of Nigeria in 1937:

'Local politics ... has not proceeded beyond the ideals of early Victorian radicalism; its ambition is a larger representation in the legislature, and a greater share in Government employ; it seems to make little appeal to the uneducated or rural elements.'[54]

Examination of the social background of the new *élite* abundantly confirms the predominance of the new intelligentsia, even in those countries where 'bourgeois' and 'petty bourgeois' strata are well developed. In the Indian Parliament of 1952–7, for example, lawyers were the most numerous occupational group (21·6 per cent), then landowners (9·2 per cent), then businessmen (7·4 per cent).

In less-developed Nigeria, paradoxically, the picture at first appears to be different, for business is strongly represented. In the Western Region Legislature in 1956, 32 per cent of the Members belonging to the dominant party, the Action Group, were 'traders or businessmen', and in the Legislature of the Eastern Region, 31 per cent of the Members of the dominant party there, the National Council of Nigeria and the Cameroons, were so classified.[55]

Yet the most recent authoritative study of the Nigerian *élite* is quite emphatic on the lack of cohesiveness and self-consciousness of the business *élite*. Indeed, they comment, 'As yet, there is only a nucleus of a business *élite* ... the business *élite* of Nigeria in no sense ... forms an economic "power *élite*".' Nor do farming or organized labour constitute important organized interest-groups: they are 'under-represented' and 'weak'.[56]

'Business', then, despite its being strongly represented in the higher councils of the new nation, is not a self-conscious organized grouping displaying classic capitalist attitudes, as is more often the case in more developed economies. Mechanistic political science which relates ideology directly to one or two simple attributes of social groups, usually to self-interest as implied in class-position, cannot adequately cope with the problem of analysing the complexity of historically-conditioned attitudes such as those of the Nigerian business *élite* in politics.

In the colonial situation, foreign rule has cut across the sectional class-interests of 'business'. Indigenous business, confronted with the entrenched power of large-scale foreign-owned commerce, becomes much more radical and nationalistic than the business class in developed economies. Because the business leadership is attached to a 'trading proletariat' of hundreds of thousands of 'micro-traders', it constitutes a mass force with radical tendencies. In those regions where entrenched 'feudal' rulers resist modernization, the radicalism of 'business' is even more marked. A classic instance is Northern Nigeria, where the programme of the Northern Elements Progressive Union is couched in a distinctly socialist idiom. This party finds its main support among the alien urban enclaves of traders and wage workers in the large Northern cities, and appeals also for the support of the *talakawa* peasantry. Other modernizing urban minority groups, such as the Action Group and the Bornu Youth Movement, have supported minor opposition parties on an ethnic basis.

In the Northern Region Legislature of 1956, however, 56 per cent of the Members on the NEPU and Bornu Youth Movement party-tickets, and 50 per cent of the Action Group Members, were 'traders or businessmen'. 49 per cent of the reactionary Northern People's Congress, in contrast, were 'central officials', another 24 per cent 'district heads'. These were not the new bureaucrats we have been discussing, but pillars of the old-entrenched 'feudal' order, as the educational data indicate more accurately: only 3 per cent of the NPC Members were 'headmasters or principal teachers', as against 25 per cent of the United Middle Belt Congress Members, for instance. Here, the 'new men', the business interests, and the urban masses, come together: the result is a radical programme with a socialist tinge.

NEPU claims to speak in the name of 'the simple people of Nigeria: the teachers, the clerks, the petty traders, the farm peasants, the lorry drivers, the truck pushers, the women and the ex-servicemen, etc.' (The order of groups is instructive). NEPU attacks NPC feudalism as a corrupt and inefficient ruling class regime, founded on 'first and last defence of property and privilege and rear-guard action against equality', and entrenched over the years by the 'Family Compact', the 'undemocratic electoral college system, and the evil of 10 per cent nomination'. It deplores the low educational and health standards in the Region, and advocates agricultural development, reform of the judicial system, and the allocation of more civil service posts and contracts to Northerners. The problem of the chiefs is to be handled by adopting the Indian method of dealing with Princes, Maharajahs and other potentates (a model also followed in Ghana) – what one might call the 'honorific tactic': plenty of honour, but little power. They are to be accorded, NEPU says, 'special and glorified status in the Local Government System', and guaranteed 'dignity and respect outside party politics'.[57]

NEPU thus advocates instalments of modernization which might seem elementary enough outside the North, but which is revolutionary in the Northern context, since it means the dismantling of feudal political control, the introduction of political democracy, modern social services, and the modernization of the agricultural economy. The socialist flavour of their language reflects this militancy. For NEPU, the political struggle is essentially a 'class struggle':

'. . . All political parties are but the expression of class interest, and as the interest of the "Talakawa" [peasantry] is diametrically opposed to the interest of all sections of the master class, both white and black, the party seeking the emancipation of the "Talakawa" must naturally be hostile to the party of the oppressors . . . this emancipation must be the work of the "Talakawa" themselves.

. . . The Machinery of Government, including the armed forces of the nation, exist only to conserve the privilege of this selfish minority group, the "Talakawa" must organize consciously and politically for the conquest of the powers of Government – both national and local, in order that this machinery of Government, including these forces, may be converted from an instrument of oppression into the agent of emancipation and the overthrow of Bureaucracy and autocratic privilege.'[58]

To label NEPU, then, as a 'petty-bourgeois' party, simply because of the predominance of traders and businessmen in its ranks is singularly unilluminating. The majority of political leaders in most societies, historically, have always been drawn from the upper strata of society: wealth and education equip those who possess them with the capacity to lead others, to inspire respect in their followers, to become familiar with affairs of state. The wealthy and the educated are therefore highly represented both on the Left and on the Right, whether in Europe or in Africa. But an analysis of the social background of MPs which had only this observation to make, would not take us very far in understanding the complexity of historical forces producing the very *different* ideologies of British Labour and British Conservatism, French Gaullism and French Socialism, African Caesarism and African Populism.

Business in Nigeria, is clearly markedly different from European 'Big Business', or even Indian 'Big Business'. Its programme is not markedly distinct from the programmes of other groupings, and the 'business *élite*' is able to subscribe to 'populist' values. It displays the classic 'progressive' attributes that Marx described for the bourgeoisies of Western Europe, which also had to fight their way into the sun against the entrenched power of the landed nobility. But where all-important external business and trade is run by aliens, the progressive capability of the indigenous bourgeoisie is frustrated: it is isolated from the mass nationalist movement, and usually concentrates on preserving its own skin.

Even in a relatively 'bourgeoisified' country like Nigeria, however, the business *élite* is overshadowed by the 'new men' in the political leaderships. In every Regional Legislature they are well outnumbered by civil servants, teachers, and lawyers. This predominance of the Western-educated professionals and government officials is again borne out by Table 1.

Hunter's recent study of selected African territories shows that this predominance of teachers, professionals and civil servants, with a smaller admixture of traders and businessmen, is not peculiar to Nigeria, but fairly typical of the new African *élites* (see Table 2).

This predominance of professionals, teachers, and lawyers, in the Legislatures of the new countries is, as we remarked earlier, not peculiar to these countries. It is markedly the case in Britain, for example, where 48·4 per cent of the Labour MPs in the 1945 House of Commons, and 61 per cent of the Conservatives, were in the liberal professions, managers, or officers. The reasons for this high level of participation of such occupational groupings are obvious enough: such people are guaranteed 'a great deal of in-

TABLE I. OCCUPATIONS OF TWO GROUPS OF ELITE NIGERIANS[59]

Occupation	Study of 156 (1958)		Who's Who in Nigeria (1956 edition)	
	Number	%	Number	%
Professions	90	57·7	340	35·6
Government and Politics	28	18·0	374*	39·1
Business	19	12·2	113	11·8
Clerical and Technical	13	8·3	59	6·1
Farming	3	1·9	28	2·9
Skilled Labour	—	—	11	1·2
Miscellaneous	3	1·9	31	3·2
TOTAL	156	100·0	956	100·0

* Includes 126 who listed occupation solely as 'legislator' and 18 as 'government minister', both of which categories were omitted from the other sample in favour of listings of permanent occupations. If these are omitted from the category of government and politics, the total for this group is 218 and the percentage 26·9.

group interaction in many activities and roles . . . which involve leadership skills and knowledge about large problems, are more politically aware, vote more, and have a greater commitment to such occupationally linked organizations as trade-unions.'[61] The lawyer, for example, possesses a network of social contacts, oratorical skills, technical knowledge, high social status and authority, plus ample leisure, opportunity, and financial independence, which place him in a supremely favoured position as candidate for public office, a fact well known to university students from the emergent countries, who, for many years, have contributed far more than their due proportion to the Law Departments of British Universities and to the Inns of Court. In addition,

'. . . occupations like . . . law and journalism . . . are dispensable in the sense that the practitioner is able to leave them for extended periods and enter politics without any loss of skill during his period of absence (perhaps the opposite is true in the case of the lawyer) and return to the

TABLE 2. PREVIOUS OCCUPATION OF MEMBERS OF PARLIAMENT IN SELECTED AFRICAN COUNTRIES[60]

	Teachers	Trader Business-man	Lawyer	Civil (a) Servant	Professions (b)	Farming Fishing	Village or local Chief	Clerical and co-operative	Miscellaneous (c)
Nigeria – Federal	98	44	23	87	20	8	1	15	5
East	34	17	5	9	13	4	1	1	2
West	43	34	14	7	6	4	—	6	7
North	26	16	—	76	3	2	7	—	2
Ghana	38	24	9	22	7	6	—	—	3
Kenya	19	4	2	5	3	4	—	—	4
Tanganyika	11	7	—	7	1	1	3	6	12
Uganda	21	6	5	8	2	—	—	6	4
Senegal	21	9	12	23	5	—	—	5	4
Mali	22	8	1	9	13	—	—	20	4
Republic of Congo	18	9	—	—	6	3	—	13	9
TOTAL	351	178	71	253	79	32	12	72	56

Notes: (a) 'Civil Servant' includes staff of Native Authorities, but 'Scribe' is included under 'Clerical'.
(b) 'Professions' include medical, journalist, engineer, Church, veterinary.
(c) Miscellaneous includes craftsmen, foremen, a few Trade Unionists, a political organizer, and some 'unknown'.

practice of his profession without too great a financial loss or dislocation'.[62]

The law, too, opens the gateway to business and administration.

In the more backward colonies and ex-colonies, such occupations have often been unavailable to the indigenous people; they have been monopolized by foreigners, especially where a direct colour-bar has operated. Thus the world well knows that on the eve of independence, the Congo had only a dozen graduates out of a population of $13\frac{1}{2}$ millions. Until his meteoric rise to fame, Lumumba had never been outside the Congo. In one typical backward country, Nyasaland, the expected yield of graduates from internal sources – from the VIth Forms of that country's secondary schools – has been calculated thus:[63]

1966	4	1969	8
1967	5	1970	11
1968	6	1971	12

'The number of African VIth Forms in the whole of Nyasaland, Northern and Southern Rhodesia, and the three East African territories put together did not reach ten in 1960'.[64]

As a result, Tanganyika, Uganda and Kenya will have to fill more than half the 4,000 or more senior posts in those countries with expatriates for several years to come.[65]

The point at issue here, however, is not the number of trained leaders, but their social composition. The former occupations of some current leaders of nationalist movements are instructive: Tom Mboya was an assistant sanitary inspector; Patrice Lumumba a postal clerk; Kenneth Kaunda a teacher; Joshua Nkomo a social welfare worker.

Because of the under-developed nature of the economy, the African *élite*, therefore, was commonly in peculiarly close rapport with the ordinary people. This does not, of course, prevent their adopting styles of life which, in extreme cases, like that of Houp-houët-Boigny, amount to the demagogic flaunting of Hollywood-style luxury in the faces of poor people who get vicarious satisfaction – for a time – from their leaders' opulence. The temptation is equally great for leaders from relatively humble backgrounds; for them, education and political power opened the world's oyster.

But the new *élite* can use this special closeness to the ordinary people, the kind of affection we saw revealed on the occasion of Lumumba's home-coming, to build a peculiarly strong backing for themselves by deliberately maintaining a simple, rather than a glamorous style of life. Their relationship to the masses is thus a two-edged one, at once intimate and distant.

Conventional discussions of the quality of 'inspired' leadership known as 'charismatic' concentrate on the personal and 'superhuman' aspects of such leadership. To be sure, without magnetic appeal, the politician is unlikely to make a mass leader. But there are many competent spell-binders who never become mass leaders; they remain oddities at Hyde Park Corners, prophets without honour, or leaders of microscopic sects. To become a mass 'charismatic' leader, the personal qualities of the leader must be yoked to a social policy which engages the hearts and minds of men because it all answers their needs. To *persist* as a mass leader more than ecstatic religious or emotional appeal is needed. The analysis of these aspirations, and of the way in which they are harnessed to a political or religious programme, is crucial: the social and 'this-worldly' aspects of leadership, as well as the personal and 'superhuman', are thus central to sociological analysis. Without such analysis, all we are doing, in speaking of 'charismatic' qualities, is drawing attention to personal magnetism.

'Charismatic' appeal then, does not derive solely from some mysterious, inexplicable quality: it also depends upon the political rapport the leader has with his followers, and on his ability to enunciate policies which connect with popular needs. Bonds of attachment between leader and followers are not based upon 'superhuman' qualities alone; rather, they depend for their efficacy on close identification. In so far as he is a Westernized 'monsieur' and later the powerful figurehead of a mass movement, the leader is remote. To succeed, he must remain 'one of the people'. It is this peculiar combination of mass rapport and social distance that characterizes populist leadership: it cannot rely on tradition and the 'deference vote'.

Once in power, too, this kind of *élite* leader faces problems of a different kind from those which beset traditional rulers. He becomes further distanced from his people. His education, his history as a Government official and then as a party organizer, predispose him to bureaucratic modes of thinking and acting. The perils of rule by such privileged bureaucratic castes, now in charge of whole societies, have already manifested themselves.[66]

The less differentiated the society, the stronger the likelihood of this kind of bureaucratic rule. To establish the pattern of differentiation further, we need now to move from an examination of the upper and middle ranks of society to an examination of the social characteristics of the urban working force.

(ii) *Workers and Peasants.* In the backward colonies, not only was the private sector of the economy minute, but also the State sector. In the Sudan, in 1953, for example, there were only 24,831 industrial workers.[67] In Tanganyika, a mere 2 per cent of the population lived in towns.[68]

Even if we take wage-earning as a whole, embracing agricultural labour as well as urban, commercial and service employment as well as industry proper, the labour-force was still tiny (see Table 3).

In countries like these, an urban industrial working-class scarcely existed. True, their influence might be out of all proportion to their members, as the role of the Sudanese Labour movement, particularly the railway workers' trade union, had shown in the development of Sudanese nationalism. And classically, in Europe, a tiny but concentrated Russian industrial working-class, led by a microscopically small Bolshevik Party, had been able to gain control of a nation of over 100 million peasants. If capitalist development was weak, the importance of the State as *the* modernizing force was correspondingly significant. In the Sudanese economy, for example, Government was the largest single employer of industrial labour, with 450,000 workers in its employ. Under such conditions, a dispute with one's employers becomes a dispute with Government. Trade unionism becomes politicized, and *nationalistically* politicized. The employer is Government, and foreign Government at that. The professions, the educated *élite*, and the working-class commonly shared this common employer – the State. This was particularly the case, in the capital cities. In Accra, for example, in the mid-1950s, Government and the Municipal Council together provided the greatest number of jobs: 13,578 jobs in government service alone (29 per cent of the total employed population), plus another 3,239 employed by the

TABLE 3. LABOUR-FORCE IN SELECTED AFRICAN COUNTRIES[69]

Territory	Number of Wage-earners	% of total Population	No. of Trade Unionists
French West Africa	350,000	2·0	70,000
French Equatorial Africa	190,000	4·2	10,000
French Cameroons	125,000	4·0	35,000
Nigeria (and British Cameroons)	500,000	1·5	150,000
Gold Coast	200,000	4·5	25,000
Sierra Leone	80,000	4·0	20,000
Gambia	5,000	2·5	1,500
Belgian Congo (and Ruanda-Urundi)	1,000,000	8·5	6,000
Uganda	280,000	4·0	1,500
Kenya	450,000	8·0	32,000
Tanganyika	400,000	6·0	400
British Somaliland	2,000	0·3	nil
Somalia	25,000	2·0	3,700
Zanzibar	5,000	4·0	900
Northern Rhodesia	250,000	13·0	50,000
Nyasaland	120,000	5·0	1,000
Southern Rhodesia	530,000	24·0	nil
Sudan	200,000	2·0	100,000

Municipal Council, as compared with only 3,000 employees of the largest private employer, the United Africa Company.[70] Even in agriculture, at times, Government might be involved, as in the case of the Groundnut Scheme, or the more successful Gezira scheme in the Sudan, where Government combined with tenantry in large-scale irrigation schemes, the 28,000 tenants hiring a further 150,000 migrant seasonal labourers.

The growth of class solidarity is maximized in situations where large-scale enterprises bring workers together under common conditions of work and life. Where the employer is Government, or where Government is importantly involved in the economy, the likelihood of economic interests growing into political ones is considerable.

But Government is normally not so predominantly the major employer. Plantations and extractive industries are normally the largest private employers of labour, apart from the commercial and merchandizing sector. The plantations of Eastern Sumatra, or the mines of Central-South Africa, are well-known instances. They do not usually operate with a stable labour-force. Migrant labour is the more usual labour-pattern here, particularly in the formative phases. Tens of thousands of men, year after year, have travelled southwards down the Great North Road from East and Central Africa to the mines of the Copper Belt and the Rand. In some areas as many as 75 per cent of the able-bodied males might be absent from the villages, throwing a heavy strain on old men, women, and young children who had to take over their work. Village society, nevertheless, does adapt, perforce: the tribe becomes dependent on the cash earnings of the young men in the towns. 'Wage-earning' Mayer remarks, '. . . is a normal part of . . . peasant life'.[71] In East-Central Africa, migrant labour has become built into a new stabilized pattern of rural life.[72] More usually, it leads to imbalances and tensions which the experience of Russia, Mexico, and other countries has made familiar.[73]

Though a new, 'industrial' consciousness may develop on the job, the pattern of labour-migration – the one-, two-, or three-year contract, with the eventual return to the village, temporarily or for good – impedes the consolidation of this consciousness. It also makes the sheer organization of the workers difficult, since the population is constantly turning over.

Significantly enough, trade unionism has been most effective on the Northern Rhodesian Copper Belt, where men live in mining-compounds with their families, and are not leading split lives. Most of their needs are satisfied by mine and township authorities, so that there is a notable absence of that proliferation of innumerable urban associations which one finds in Freetown or Nairobi. The existence of one dominant African organization – the African Mine Workers' Union – later followed by one parallel predominant political party, reflects this unity of Africans in the face of the mining companies which employ them and shape their entire lives.[74]

Solidarities thus develop in work itself; they develop in relationship to a common employer and they develop through common residence. The Congolese situation, on the other side of the border, might seem to refute this thesis: here an even more stabilized labour-force, with even heavier paternalization, has not produced trade unionism: the explanation is a political one: in Northern Rhodesia, trade unionism, after initial resistance, was tolerated. In the Congo, unionization and political organization were forbidden to Africans by the Belgians. In the Union of South Africa, high labour turnover and rigid repression of African trade unionism occur together: they have effectively prevented the emergence of African trade unionism on the mines.

Large-scale enterprise in the shape of mines or plantations, then, is not enough by itself to generate trade union consciousness and organization. Stability of the labour-force, and a political climate which is at least not totally repressive, are both necessary also.

The emergence of trade unionism is even less likely in those employments which are small in scale as well, as is the case, for example, in 'settler' farming, in indigenous farming where labour is employed, or in petty urban enterprise. It is least likely to develop where the labour is only seasonal. Here, workers are isolated from each other, and directly influenced and controlled by their employers. Personal service, where the African servant is isolated in the very house of his employer, is particularly infertile ground for trade unionism, and in settler societies, it is very important. Even in Durban, in Africa's most industrialized country, the (then) Union of South Africa, there were 28,708 domestic servants as against a total of 53,906 craftsmen, factory-operatives, manual workers, and labourers, in 1951.[75]

Even in non-settler countries, the domestic-servant component of the urban working force is usually high. In the Sudan, messengers, watchmen, and unskilled domestic servants constituted some 10 per cent of the industrial labour-force, which was predominantly unskilled, general labourers being the largest category.[76] The working force is not only predominantly unskilled: it is also rural in its orientation. For these are 'new' workers. Countries like South Africa, it is true, have had their urban working-force for decades. The case of the Sudan, then, where 82 per cent of the railway workers had fathers who were nomadic pastoralists, might

seem an extreme one. But a recent study of a South African city
has shown that the urban African population – ever-growing, ever-
changing – is not as fully 'urbanized' as surface impressions might
suggest. Many of the immigrants are recent arrivals; they obviously retain close links with their rural home areas. They are not
'committed' city-dwellers at all: they start off, indeed, *intending* to
return home ultimately. For them, city-life is to be merely an
interlude. The 'interlude', however, often stretches out to years,
even decades. But men who do thus remain, trapped by the town, –
the 'Red' people (so-called from the rural custom of smearing
their bodies and their clothes with red ochre), still think, basically,
in the value-terms of traditional rural society, and even after
decades of town-life never become fully urbanized.[77] They look
forward to ending their days 'back home'. The distinction between
'Red' and 'School', however, is not merely the simple one between
country and town dweller: many Bantu are converted to 'School'
ways in the countryside, and as 'School' people, still continue to
live in the country by preference. Not all of the 'School' people, by
any means, opt for town life; their 'Schoolness', rather, consists
in their attachment to Western ways and ideals, as acquired via
school or mission:

'The Red migrant, then, after fifteen, twenty, or twenty-five years in
town, may be just as Red as he was after five. . . . "Z", for example,
aged 46, had worked for nearly thirty years as a boss boy in Springs, a
labourer in Cape Town, and a building contractor's labourer in East
London, and intended to stay working in town until old age prevented
him.
    But these many long years in town, and the less usual intention to
stay even longer, in no sense mean that he has become town-rooted.
He is still a migrant, not an immigrant. "My real home", said "Z", "is
in Tshabo, in the country, where one is free to keep any number of
cattle and sheep, and money does not matter so much. My wife and
children are staying there permanently. There is nothing I like about
town life. I am only here because this is the place where people come for
money. Since I have been in East London I have visited my home every
Friday night and returned on Sunday night. I have spent all my
holidays at home. When in the country I do what I can on the land, or
repair the fences or the house. When I have free time in town, I always
spend it visiting the other Tshabo men who are here, and we drink
together and discuss home matters.'[78]

Such people never become fully urbanized psychologically. They remain attached to a code which is denied by the code of the city that younger people, born and raised in the urban environment, absorb. The intensity of conflict between the new, urban-born generation and their rural-migrant seniors was dramatically and tragically revealed in the East London riots of 1952 and 1958, when 'pent-up feeling about the rottenness of location life in general' exploded into anti-White violence on the one hand, but also into a witch-hunt carried out by older men against the youth.[79]

This persistence of ties with the countryside is not unique to East London. A Royal Commission on East Africa has pointed out, for the Africans of Nairobi, that the majority retain their land-holdings in their areas of origin: 'they have not established in the town homes in which they live with their families, nor do they share in the life of the urban community'.[80]

One of the principal reasons for the maintenance of the rural connection, of course, is that the land, and one's relatives in the village, constitute an ultimate safety-net in a world of insecurity where the Welfare State has never been heard of. Life in the towns and cities is hard, as hard as it was for the hundreds of thousands of peasants from Russia, Italy, Scandinavia, or Ireland, who flocked to the new expanding civilizations of North America. For those people, however, there was no going back. They were immigrants, not migrants. Their Rubicon was thousands of miles wide. Like those Africans who today are fully committed to the urban life, the European immigrant in the nineteenth century had to develop their own institutions of self-defence and self-protection. Like the populations of the expanding towns in Britain's Industrial Revolution, the new urban African associations were concerned with mutual aid, religious consolation, recreation, security in sickness, unemployment, bereavement, and security in the after life, too.[81] Negroes in African cities, Negroes in the cities of America, British working-men in 'Friendly Societies', prepared for death as an immediate reality and a triumphant release. In Sekondi-Takoradi today, one writer remarks,

'the community's concern with funerals . . . should be viewed against the gloomy background of poor housing conditions and harshness of town life, the high incidence of disease, the frequency of death, and the short expectation of life. These are the grim facts which lie behind the façade of gaiety and colourful dress.'[82]

But there was one alternative to the city world of burial societies. There was always the countryside. In times of depression, particularly, the urban population fled back to the protection of the village. Kahin records of Indonesia during the depression of the 1930s:

'A large part of Indonesian labour working outside of the village, much of non-village-based plantation labour as well as probably the majority of urban labour, maintained close contact with the village through former domicile and/or blood relationship with its members and in times of economic crisis was able to rely to an important extent on the social security that the village provided. The fact that these groups could look to the agriculturally-based village for minimum food and shelter in times of prolonged industrial and plantation unemployment is essential in understanding the political orientation of Indonesian labour.'[83]

Since 1945, however, there has been no major depression. The cities of the backward world keep expanding. But they are backward cities, the progeny of backward societies, 'urban agglomerations' which exist primarily to funnel out raw-materials, and to funnel in the manufactures of Europe. They are cities without industry: funnels, not workshops; cities of imperialism, quite unlike the industrial cities of Europe. Nevertheless, they are growing at rates similar to the expansion that took place in the era of the Industrial Revolution in Western Europe, America in the late nineteenth century, or the Soviet Union in the 1920s and 1930s. Here is the jump over one generation:

TABLE 4. GROWTH OF URBAN POPULATIONS IN SELECTED AFRICAN CITIES[84]

Dakar (Senegal)	30,000 in 1926	205,000 in 1953
Lagos (Nigeria)	99,700 in 1921	230,000 in 1950
Accra (Ghana)	38,400 in 1921	135,000 in 1948
Abidjan (Ivory Coast)	17,500 in 1936	86,000 in 1951
Freetown (Sierra Leone)	44,100 in 1921	85,000 in 1953
Saint-Louis (Senegal)	32,000 in 1936	63,000 in 1949
Conakry (Guinea)	13,600 in 1936	52,700 in 1951
Porto-Novo (Dahomey)	21,643 in 1928	33,525 in 1951
Bathurst (Gambia)	9,400 in 1921	19,600 in 1951

Even in South Africa, despite apartheid, which – in theory – consigns Africans to separate rural 'Bantustans', in reality the same process is going on, since the demand for labour in an expanding economy continues: from 1951 to 1958 the African population of Johannesburg increased from 465,000 to 576,000, nearly 24 per cent.[85]

And though the rural ties persist, the city population consolidates itself. In Kenya, '40 per cent of the African population of Nairobi before the declaration of the emergency [1952] had been resident there for five years or more'.[86] In the Sudan, 'even when unemployed, 65 per cent of the single men and 56·3 per cent of the married ones stay in Port Sudan, and 53·1 per cent of those who do go home do so because of family obligations, and not for the sake of agriculture or their flocks and herds'.[87]

For the hundreds of thousands of newcomers, however, city life is strange, in a strange place, amongst strange people. The life is hard, but even harder in the villages. The city attracts, not only in terms of money, but because life there has vigour and gaiety, bustle and movement, as well as danger, hunger, insecurity, and misery. Moll Flanders or Macheath would have been quite at home in the atmosphere pierced by the vibrant Highlife music of Ghana, or Johannesburg's Kwela, or in the Leopoldville of the mid-twentieth century:

'Pride and centre of Congo city life is the bar. . . . On the main road through the old township *Congo Bar* is as brilliant as the proprietor's lighting system can make it. . . . There is gaiety and light and noise, dancing and jiving, the making and taking of sentimental vows. . . . The girls of the town are much in evidence . . . *femmes libres*, more or less brilliantly dressed and made-up, with bold eyes and lacquered finger-nails, audacious, determined, frivolous, fickle, seizing life with both hands. . . . They flock to the bars, laugh the innocents out of their fears, initiate the village boys into the city, corrupt the solidly married husband, organize in their own defence, fleece the lascivious European, and generally carry on in gross defiance of Morality and Family Order.'[88]

Men adapt. They live in two distinct social worlds – which sometimes they get mixed up. A man's wife from the country may come to town unexpectedly, and encounter his town 'woman'. One wife described how

. . . she had originally come to town for a short visit only when her suspicions were aroused. "One night my husband had gone to church. I heard a loud knock. I opened the door and saw a woman standing there, with hands on hips. 'Is this the said Dickson's wife, this?' she said, looking at me very contemptuously. 'Yes', I replied, 'I am the rightful owner of this room, I and nobody else'. I closed the door, I heard her grumbling outside. 'East London is ours, with the men in it', I heard her say, 'and we will not tolerate being kept from our men for days on end by such sickly little country creatures". . . .'[89]

City life is not only more varied and lively, it is better materially – for those who are fortunate enough to get jobs. The urban wage-earner is not necessarily, by any means, the worst-off section of the population. When compared with the 'lower depths' of the city population, and especially when compared with their country cousins, far from being the most miserably-situated class of the population, the urban worker is a privileged person. Hence Senghor's sarcasm directed at unionized Government officials, self-proclaimed 'proletarians', who however 'propertyless' in means of production, earned around 360,000 frs. CFA, compared to the 180,000 frs. of the employee in the private sector or the mere 10,000 of the peasant.[90]

There is a direct correlation between the degree of urbanization and industrialization and the level of cash income per head. Liberals are often surprised to be told that the incomes of Africans in the Union of South Africa are the highest in that continent.[91]

The urban worker, then, is privileged compared to his country relative. But he does not always have work. Baghdad, Dakar, Bangkok and Lagos are full of people to whom Norman Cohn's description of the urban plebeians of the cities of Europe in the Middle Ages could equally well apply:

'In all the over-populated, highly urbanized and industrialized areas there were multitudes of people living on the margin of society, in a state of chronic insecurity. There industry at the best of times could never absorb anything like the whole of the surplus population. Beggars crowded in every market-place and roamed in gangs through the streets of the towns . . . peasants without land or with too little land to support them, beggars and vagabonds, the unemployed and those threatened with unemployment. . . .'[92]

Cities of this kind have been the breeding-grounds of the 'city

THE THIRD WORLD

mob', from ancient Rome and Constantinople to eighteenth-
century England and twentieth-century Baghdad and Cairo.
Vastly different from the 'class conscious' worker, they are likely
to produce more than their share both of Villons and villains; their
participation in political life is likely to be sporadic, violent and
extremist.

But even of those who do have work in the cities, by no means
all are wage-workers. In Lagos in 1961, for example, 'only 40 per
cent of those at work earned a wage, and many of these traded on
the side'.[93] Those who do work include many to whom another
classic description of a quite different time and place applies:
Parisian wage-earners in 1789, George Rudé has shown, were far
from being ideal-typical 'workers'. Their position was much more
ambiguous:

'Even when they formed a majority of the local population, the wage-
earners lacked the attributes of a distinctive social class. In eighteenth
century France, the term *ouvrier* might be applied as readily to individual craftsmen, small workshop masters – or even, on occasion, to
substantial manufacturers – as to ordinary wage-earners; in its most
frequent use it was synonymous with artisan. . . . Such usage cor-
responded to the social realities of the time, when the wage-earner had
as yet no defined and distinctive status as a producer and there were
often numerous intermediate stages between workman and employer.
The typical unit of production was still the small workshop which
generally employed but a small number of journeymen and apprentices.
Even in Paris, where the proportion of workers to employers was large
and the restrictions imposed by the guild-system had become more
relaxed than elsewhere, the journeymen still often ate at his master's
table and slept under his roof. The distinction between a wage-earning
journeyman and an individual craftsman, or even a workshop master,
was ill-defined: the 2,000 Parisian stocking-weavers who struck against
wage-cuts in 1774, while depending for their living on a wage, still rented
their frames from their employer, and worked in their homes. . . .'[94]

The likelihood of class consciousness and organization emerging
among unstable urban populations of this kind is therefore slight,
because they have not yet *become* a class. They are not even necessarily committed to life-careers as workers. Their skills – where
they possess any – are the traditional skills of village craftsmen,
not the skills of a Birmingham fitter, a specialized cog in an indus-

trial organization itself as complex and integrated a system of interrelated parts as the motor-cars he works on. The African worker does not work to a rhythm dictated by a moving belt. These are not, then, modern industrial workers at all. They are people only beginning to transform themselves into permanent city-dwellers, learning the habits of industrial and urban society, struggling to piece together a new identity and community out of the kaleidoscopic fragments of their lives. Contrary to what is generally assumed, the adjustment to the demands of factory work is relatively easily made. Accommodation to the multifarious demands of a totally new city culture is much more difficult. The adjustments outside the work situation are the more complex, and the more difficult.

Urban people not only maintain their ties with the countryside; they also import rural social relationships into the towns and cities. The raw newcomer has to orient himself somewhere in the chaos and flux of the dynamic, thrusting cities. Inevitably, he commonly settles down at first among people from his home region – the only familiar reference-point he can find in the ceaseless flux. They do, at least, literally speak his language. Often, whole city districts become preserves of people of one particular ethnic origin, much like Chicago in the 1920s.[95] These divisions inhibit the emergence of consciousness of common citizenship or common social class, and prevents the development of institutional arrangements cutting across ethnic barriers. Where occupational specialization and ethnic divisions coincide, the divisions are even sharper.

In Southern Nigeria, for example, the better-educated Yoruba originally monopolized skilled jobs: in 1921, they occupied 5,769 'artisan' jobs as against only 2,318 held by all other ethnic groups.[96] Later, however, Ibo also flooded into the urban centres. Finally, both these large ethnic groups, and other southerners, took up the bulk of the posts available for the educated in Northern Nigeria. As a result, northerners began to fear that southerners would soon be in charge of their country. The 'feudal' leaders of the North were able to insulate the local population from these dangerous southerners by confining the latter within *sabon gari* ghettoes.[97] But the modernizing influence of the southerners eventually began to affect the *talakawa* peasantry. When the radical Northern Elements Progressive Union, based on the southern elements in the cities, broke away from the cautious dominant party, the National Council for Nigeria and the Cameroons, the feudal leaders of the North countered by throwing their weight behind a rejuvenated Northern People's Congress as a conservative and 'northern-nationalist' party, which now, for the first time, appealed to mass support.

Ethnicity, then, in the present phase of development in the new African countries at least, is a much more important bond between men than class; it is the ready-made basis for the mass party. In the towns, since the town-dwellers still retain links with the country, and since membership of ethnic associations give him a social identity and provide him with real services, ethnicity is still crucial. The newcomer commonly settles with established fellow-tribesmen through whom he finds a job, or on whom he lives in what the French call *'parasitage familiale'* – a substitute for unemployment services, health services, and the whole apparatus of social assistance to the unfortunate. In the countryside, obviously, men are much more closely affected by 'tribal' membership. Conversely, the new bonds of class often have no place in the villages.

Over vast areas of Africa, men pass their lives farming their small plots of land – so small that anthropologists usually speak of African *horticulture*, not *agriculture* – within the context of a 'communitarian', traditionalistic social order. They rarely travel more than fifty miles from their homes, except when they go out to work for cash. They do not hire labour; they are not racked by money-lenders; they are not working on land owned by another – they are independent peasants. They are becoming sucked into the world market-system rapidly. In relatively advanced countries like Ghana, three-quarters of the adult male population are involved in the money economy. The rest are predominantly subsistence farmers. In other less-developed African territories, however, they constitute the overwhelming bulk of the population. That is why Sékou Touré's view of the class structure of Africa, though it over-simplifies, nevertheless enshrines the truth: 'L'Afrique', he remarks, 'c'est sa brousse . . . ses paysans qui forment 85 à 90 pour cent de ses populations'.[98]

Africa is its peasantry, subsistence-producers or cash-crop producers, but independent peasants. This is the basic fact about the social structure of the new African states – and of many new states elsewhere. Other social classes, to put it simply, are either not there or are only in process of formation, or, if they do exist, are impeded by a variety of factors from developing their own institutional and ideological identity.

We have already seen that an indigenous capitalist class is usually absent or weakly developed: foreigners control the 'commanding heights'. A lesser bourgeoisie is often more numerous, but where it exists, is normally engaged in trade rather than industry, is often 'compr'adore' in character, and, again, is commonly monopolized by ethnic minorities. The vast majority of indigenous entre-preneurs are only 'micro-traders', and have closer links with the ordinary worker or peasant than they do with the wealthy business *élite* amongst their own people. The 'middle class' elements who provide the political leadership are the Western-educated minor civil servants, not the small or large businessmen. This, then, is a quite non-entrepreneurial and markedly bureaucratic 'middle class', not a classic 'petty bourgeoisie'. To speak of a fully formed working class, or proletariat, is premature and inaccurate. It is the *peasantry* who form the mass of the population. The penetration of the money economy into the countryside, and the development of modern communications, make *them* – not the more fortunate urban workers – potentially a revolutionary force.

It is not surprising to find *sets* of classes 'missing' in this way. For class, basically, is a *relationship*, not a thing. No class can exist in isolation. Its existence implies the existence of other classes over and against which the class defines itself as a separate entity. There can be no proletariat without a capitalist class; no petty bourgeoisie except in contrast to an *haute bourgeoisie*; no 'middle strata' without higher and lower strata between which they locate themselves. All classes among the indigenous population, with the single exception of the peasantry, are normally extremely small and often only in a state of formation. There does exist in the more advanced of the new countries a more numerous and long-established proletariat, often a numerous petty trading bour-geoisie, a land-owning class, and sometimes some large capitalists. Even so, all these classes are unified by common opposition to foreign imperialism and race-oppression in a way that creates bonds between them that are absent in Western capitalisms. Colour is the index of this common inferiority which unites

Africans and Asians not only across class-lines, within their own states, but also across international, cultural, and geographical boundaries. These classes exist, then, not in a closed society where each faces primarily each other, but in a social system whose past was determined by alien rulers and whose present is still crucially affected by private foreign ownership of the commanding heights of the economy. The class-relations which are significant are global, not national.

Internally, and externally, the colonial world is conditioned by its situation in a world-system. Its internal structure and values, then, can never be identical with Europe's; for the colonial society is

'. . . divided into two, inhabited by different species. The peculiarity of the colonial situation consists in the fact that the economic realities, the inequalities, the enormous differences in living-standards, never succeed in concealing the human realities . . . what divides the world is first of all the fact of belonging or not belonging to a certain species, a certain race. In the colonies, the economic infrastructure is just as much a superstructure. Cause is effect: one is rich because one is white, white because one is rich. That is why Marxist categories have always to be slightly stretched when they are applied to the colonial problem.'[99]

Populism: Rural Idiom in a Modern World

We embarked upon an examination of class structure in the new Africa largely because of assertions by the ideologists of the new states that their societies were 'homogeneous', that they lacked the antagonistic class divisions of the Euro-American world, and that they were, in consequence, peculiarly *solidary*. We now have to agree that the evidence shows them to be largely correct. All nationalisms, of course, stress brotherly community in their rhetoric, even though, in reality, profound class and other divisions cross-cut the 'nation'. In Marxist terms, nationalism of this kind contains a large dose of 'false consciousness'. It constitutes an 'ideology' in that it is not an objective representation of the reality of the pattern of social relationships, but an illusory one which presents the desired state of solidarity as if it were actual reality.

To the extent that class and other divisions *do* really divide the new nations, the populist stress on 'social homogeneity' or 'classlessness' is so much ideology. But, in very many of these countries, classlessness *is* a reality. Classes are only slightly developed; the major antagonisms arise between the indigenous population and foreign capitalist or trading classes, and the *indigenous* population is not sharply divided by class. And even where there are class divisions amongst the indigenes, these are, in reality and not just as a matter of illusion, overridden by common solidarity vis-à-vis the alien exploiter and/or ruler. The ideology of nationalist populism, then, is to a very real extent, *not an ideology at all*, in Marx's sense of the word. Neither is it an 'ideology' in Mannheim's sense of the word; it is, rather, 'utopian', to use his terminology, in so far as it reflects the interests of 'certain oppressed groups . . . [which are] . . . so strongly interested in the destruction and transformation of a given condition of society that they unwittingly see only those elements in the situation which tend to negate it'.[100]

Populism has been quite inadequately recognized as the very important genus of political philosophies it is. Its general characteristics, therefore, need spelling out.

The first point we have already elaborated: the populist asserts that there are no divisions in the community, or that if they are discernible, they are 'non-antagonistic'. Thus class-divisions can then be dismissed as *external* ('imperialist') intrusions, alien to the society. Ethnic differences can equally be dismissed as consequences of 'divide and rule' or as vestigial, disappearing legacies of the past ('tribalism' or 'feudalism'), though, of course, in this case, it is necessary to accept that ethnicity *did* divide society in the past: only *now* is a truly homogeneous society emerging. All these divisions, it is held, will soon disappear, leaving a united society.

The populist commonly holds that the indigenous society is a 'natural' *Gemeinschaft*. Usually this implies an agrarian economy, based on the peasant or small farmer, as distinct from an industry-dominated economy. City-based capitalism, its banks, its factories, the whole array of urban existence, is believed to be unnatural and based on false values. It is individualistic, and devoid of any sense of community responsibility; worse, it is grasping, and does not recognize that we are members each one of the other. Big Business thus comes in for strong criticism; a complementary stress upon small rural handicrafts and manufactures is not unusual (as in Gandhi's Swadeshi movement for the revival of cottage-industry).

Co-operative forms of organizing the economy are strongly favoured (consumer co-ops, producer co-ops, credit co-ops, etc.) rather than collectivist ones. The co-operative is an ideal form of organization, of course, for the small farmer. Economically weak by himself, he is as terrified of losing his independence to the State as he is of losing it to the banks. He is at once extremely private-property-oriented in his psychology, but equally ready, of necessity, to pool his resources with others for their mutual advantage. The populist is thus strongly *communitarian*: he is an enthusiast for *local* government, suspicious of the State and of all large-scale, centralized and bureaucratized, organizations, towards which he commonly evinces that combination of envy, hatred, impotence and fear, which Max Scheler has termed *ressentiment*. But the organizations that *he* belongs to, he participates in very actively, and controls. Populism thus easily shades into anarcho-syndicalism. Both seek to devolve power down to the local level, to reduce the State to a minimum, and to build a new social order around the factory or the rural community. The anarchist, however, departs from *individual* liberty as the starting-point of his critique of the social order and his vision of the future. The populist departs from *community* values; for him, 'no man is an island'.

The populist, then, is usually some kind of radical, hostile to Big-ness in general. It is not difficult, however, to lead him either Left or Right and to extremes. He is predisposed towards action because he is too severely buffeted by events and forces beyond his control to be disposed to listen to mild doctrines. And when he does act, he does not leave it to others: he acts *himself*, and seeks to galvanize his neighbours.

Since the society is undifferentiated, organic, undivided, it needs only one single political organization to express its common interests, only one party. 'Class' parties are divisive: they weaken the society, and allow the enemy to split the ranks. The party does not represent a particular, narrow, sectional interest: it represents everyone, or at least, the threatened and disinherited mass – 'Marhaen'. The party then becomes co-extensive with 'the nation' or 'the society'; it is a *mass* organization both in terms of numbers, and in so far as it maximizes direct contact between the rank-and-file and the leadership, and minimizes bureaucracy. The rank-and-file constantly participate in policy-making. Finally, a mystical top dressing of quasi-religious appeal to the unity of people, land, and society is not unusual.

Some American Cases

Clearly, this is basically the ideology of small rural people threatened by encroaching industrial and financial capital. For this reason, populism is inherently radical: it is not, however, 'inherently' either 'Right' or 'Left', as the contrasting cases of Saskatchewan and Alberta demonstrate. For though we have so far looked at modern manifestations of populism in the backward regions of Africa and Asia, it has also been the characteristic response of the small farmer and peasant not merely in contemporary Afro-Asia, but in the Russia of the 1880s and 1890s, in recent Latin America, and is even found in the most affluent countries in the world – in North America.

In his authoritative study of the Co-operative Commonwealth Federation of Saskatchewan,[101] Lipset has shown how this movement grew up amongst a small-farming, 'homesteading', population dependent upon a single crop, wheat, which was subject to both natural and man-made fluctuations. Drought and grasshoppers might be serious enough, but the grain-exchanges of Winnipeg which sold the prairie farmer's wheat were worse in his eyes. So were the banks and the big agricultural-machinery firms. All of them did very well out of the farmer, who could afford it while times were good, but who was desperately pressed when, as in the depression of the 1930s, the world no longer bought his wheat, and Nature, too, was as hostile as she could be.

These farmers had mainly arrived in Saskatchewan since the turn of the century. Many of them came with strong communitarian or socialist convictions. Religious groups looking for toleration in a land where they could build utopian communities in accordance with their beliefs; men of enterprise, energy, and ambition, moving to the frontier to create a new life in which no man would be their master; socialists and radicals quitting an Old World which repressed them – all these were strongly represented amongst the immigrant population.

This new, unfixed population did adapt to the new conditions, but adaptation did not lead to conservatism because of the farmers' dependence upon unstable world wheat prices. They threw up their own protective organizations very early indeed; before long, they moved into co-operative marketing of grain, against the opposition of the railroads, the big grain companies, and the grain elevator companies. By the time the depression hit the prairies, the socialist content of Saskatchewan prairie-radicalism had been sharpened. The result was a turn towards politics, in the shape of a new political party, the Co-operative Commonwealth Federation.

The CCF ultimately came to power in 1944, on the leftwards wave which affected the whole world.[102] The innovations it introduced were similar in many ways to those introduced by the British Labour Government of 1945–51 (apart from the special stress in Saskatchewan, of course, on support for the farmer): the introduction of a series of measures of social security, 'infrastructural' improvements, and state intervention in the economy to the minimal extent necessary to ensure its continuing efficiency overall. The old communitarian emphasis is still strong even today. Recently, for example, proposals to reform local government by amalgamating units rendered unviable (because of the decline in rural population and because of improved communications which permit concentrated settlement in rural townships) met with opposition amongst farmers for whom the belief in 'grass-roots' democracy is a cardinal article of faith. Equally characteristically, the Provincial Government went out of its way to hold public meetings all over the province at which the proposals were explained and debated back-and-forth by the citizenry.

Saskatchewan populism is thus socialistic in content. But it is only one of a large number of such movements which have sprung up over the decades in the Plains/Prairie region of North America: Jacksonianism, Greenbackers, Populists, Farmer-Labor Alliances, Independents, and the Non-Partisan League, to name only a few. Lipset has written of this tradition:

'Agrarian radicalism, although it is rarely explicitly socialist, has directed its attack against big business domination. In certain economic areas farmers have openly challenged private ownership and control of industry. American agrarians have attempted, either through government or co-operative ownership, to eliminate private control of banking, insurances, transportation, natural resources, public utilities, manufacture of farm implements, wholesale and retail distribution of consumer goods, and food commodity exchanges. The large measure of "socialism without doctrine" that can be found in the programs of agrarian political and economic organizations is in many respects more socialistic than the nationalization policies of some explicitly socialist parties.'[103]

Alberta, on the other hand, produced a different variety of populist movement, one which concentrated on the small farmer's chronic condition of debt. Because of their helplessness in the face of price-changes, and their need for credit, currency quackery is always attractive to farmers. Social Credit was able to take up where earlier 'funny money' movements, such as the Greenbackers of the 1870s, had left off. *Monetary* reform, on the lines of Major Douglas' prescriptions, was to be the principal answer to the society's economic problems.[104]

Populist farmer-radicals had long explained that the cause of society's ills lay in the competitive social order dominated by the 'plutocratic classes'. Farmers and other 'democratic classes' should combine to build a producers' co-operative economy. The farmer, 'both capitalist and labourer', would transcend the class war between capital and labour, and achieve a revolution. The party system was merely a technique for dividing the masses: every party became bureaucratized and undemocratic. Parties, therefore, should be replaced by 'corporatist' organizations in which the legislature would be filled with the representatives of occupational groups.

Such notions were easily wedded to Major Douglas' economic theories, and to his anti-democratic political theories. In 1935, Social Credit came to power. But they failed to fulfil their promises to revive the economy on Social Credit lines. The war, however, saved them from incipient revolt. After the war, the Albertan economy flourished mightily, since the expansion of the oil and natural gas industries, plus farming prosperity, brought a high standard of living all round. 'Social Credit' in Alberta then settled down as conventional conservative government. But it remains, as Macpherson points out, only a 'quasi-party' system. To-day, it holds sixty out of the sixty-four seats in the Provincial Legislature; the other four are split between four other parties. The result is, *de facto*, a one-party system within a Parliamentary Government-and-Opposition framework: a striking parallel to populism in the backward emerging countries. Social Credit is still in power in Alberta, with minimal opposition, and has since spread not only to British Columbia, but has emerged as a national force at the Federal level, owing to its newfound support among the backward peasants of Quebec.

The importance of populism, then, has been infinitely greater than has been recognized, and its potential underestimated. It has shown a marked capacity for change and adaptation, and has successfully expanded its appeal to new sections of the population. Just as Social Credit has spread to British Columbia and Quebec from Alberta, so the CCF has teamed up with urban labour to form a Federal party, the New Democratic Party, which won seventeen of the seats in the Federal Parliament in 1963. The North American experience may be highly relevant for the emergent countries, where the divergence of originally parallel populist movements in leftwards and rightwards directions may be expected.

Finally, another populist movement from North America calls for some attention. McCarthyism, Trow has shown, drew its support from moderate and right-wing conservatives. It drew support also from 'labour-liberals', favourable to trade-unions and hostile to large corporations. But support for McCarthy was almost twice as great among 'nineteenth-century liberals' – those who were opposed to trade-unions *and* to large corporations – as among those holding other political positions.[105] McCarthy, he remarks, expressed for the small businessman his 'fear and mistrust of bigness, and the slick and subversive ideas that come out of the cities and the big institutions to erode old ways and faiths'. So did Poujadism in France. This attitude, then, parallels the anti-bigness and anti-city outlook of the small farmer to an important degree.

It is for these reasons that Macpherson characterizes Alberta populism as essentially *'petit-bourgeois'*. The farmer in the market economy, he suggests, is neither a seller nor a buyer of labour, yet is dependent on a price system 'which is ruled as a whole by the rate of profit on the productive employment of wage labour.[106]

His position is ambiguous, in appearance one of independence, but in reality highly determined by forces beyond his control. He lacks class consciousness, therefore, and oscillates perennially between conservatism and radicalism. He develops an *agrarian*, not a *class* consciousness.

Illuminating as it is, this analysis fails to develop the insight contained in his later remark that 'the conflict of class interests is not so much within the society as between that society and the forces of outside capital (and of organized labour)'.[107] Here, evidently, the failure of prairie farmers to develop a class ideology is seen not as a matter of 'a false consciousness of society and of themselves'[108] but as a sober recognition of the major division between the farmers as a whole and the outside industrial order. This is precisely the sentiment that we have found so strongly present in the emergent countries: not the internal class-struggle, for society is homogeneous, but the external, 'national' struggle against imperialism and neo-imperialism.

The categorization of the prairie-farmer radical populist as an individualist, moreover, only describes one dimension of his psychology. The populist does not, as in the classic liberal model, combine with others solely in the furtherance of his *individual* interests. He holds to a *communitarian* tradition which can by no means be adequately described as an ideology of 'independence'.

As we have seen, the early pioneers were commonly religious or political (often socialist) communitarians. They were enabled to begin farming by virtue of Government action. Government cleared away the Indians; Government built or financed the railways; Government surveyed and gave the land away for nothing or virtually nothing. The virtues of public action at the *highest* (Federal and Provincial Government) levels were thus abundantly evident to the pioneers. Deep faith in 'grass-roots' participation, therefore, does not preclude belief in government action; it does not mean anarchism. The farmers, characteristically, built a University in Saskatchewan as early as 1908, to provide scientific agricultural research and general education for the farming community. These, then, are scarcely individualistic 'petty bourgeois'.

Moreover, their sheer physical situation, isolated as they were by hundreds of miles from urban amenities; cut off from the next community by distance, culture and language (since ethnic groups settled together); periodically thrown back on their own and their neighbours' resources in times of depression; all these, of necessity, helped develop very strong community traditions at the local level, whatever their ideological predispositions, and effectively counteracted 'petty bourgeois' habits of mind that small-farming otherwise encouraged.

The involvement of independent farmers in the world market economy has thus produced a very distinctive set of related ideologies. In older European societies, too, this kind of ideology has appeared wherever capitalism has penetrated into traditionalistic peasant society. One of the great debates of our time centred round precisely this question: Lenin's famous dispute with the Russian Populists (Narodniks) over *The Development of Capitalism in Russia*. Today, because the debate was settled in favour of the Bolsheviks, we pay little attention to Populism. The greatest weakness of Soviet Communism, however, still remains their inability to modernize agriculture, a task only successfully completed in a few advanced capitalist countries, notably the USA.

But outside the USSR, populist ideas analogous to those of the Narodniks are by no means extinct. As Professor Isaiah Berlin has remarked:

'. . . It is Populist ideas which lie at the base of much of the socialist economic policy pursued by [the emergent] countries today.'[109]

Like Africans who sing the praises of the village society, or the prairie farmers who believe that farming is 'a good way of life' which the cities should subsidize even if it is economically inefficient, Russian Populists built their creed round the rural community. They celebrated the village commune, which, like the African village, was the ultimate 'owner' of the land in a society where *private* ownership of land as we know it did not exist, only the right to be given land by virtue of membership of the social group and to maintain rights in land by virtue of work done on it. The Populists saw the village as the 'natural' society upon which capitalism was encroaching, dividing brother from brother, creating classes where before were men. Equality was the great watchword, capitalism the enemy, the Revolution the panacea. Men were not determined atoms, governed by the 'laws' of history of the positivists, they declared. They were free spirits. The

Russian Narodniks would have responded to Léopold Senghor's words:

'The unique property of man is that of detaching himself from this earth, of raising himself above his roots to stretch himself towards the sun, to escape, in one single act of liberty, from his "natural determinations".'[110]

The Russian village community, the *mir*, was a reservoir of pre-industrial human values which could be drawn upon by those who challenged the inhumanity of industrial capitalism. Society and industry had been rationalized and modernized; now they needed to be *humanized*. Men like Chernyshevsky realized that the State had come to stay, but for many it was an enemy to be destroyed. The destroying force would be the peasantry, transformed into an historical agent by violence. Decentralization and participation would be the hallmarks of the new society.

Modern populists in Africa or North America no longer dream the anarchist dream of society without the State. Both prairie-farmer and African nationalist, indeed, have a particularly important place for the State in their scheme of things. The African nationalist still insists upon local democracy and mass participation, because without this social transformation cannot be effected, the prairie farmer wants to preserve 'grass-roots' democracy, to resist domination from outside and from on top.

But this anarchist strain has somehow to be reconciled with support for a strong State. The new nations have been particularly influenced by Soviet experience in creating a modern industrial society out of backwardness. The 'demonstration effect' of this achievement by a strongly-centralized Party and State has not been lost on the new countries. But neither has the other lesson of the Stalin era: the dangers of a bureaucratized and centralized regime, for if the new countries are developing nearly a century later than the Narodniks, and can observe their failure, they are also developing nearly a generation later than Stalinism, and can observe its horrors. They have no wish to repeat Bolshevik mistakes – or Bolshevik successes, if the cost of success is so high in human terms. For theirs is a people-centred society, not a society obsessed with things, with industrialization at all costs, and with indices of production as the measure of human happiness. They have been ruled for long enough by people who reduced Africans to the status of 'a cocoa-producing machine',[111] and who installed an order in which 'robots stood at the peak of the hierarchy of values'.[112] In oratorical ardour, Senghor passionately invokes 'Man, inscribed in black on our Malian flag. . . .' The anthropologist, more dispassionately, points to the root of this man-centredness, singling this out as the major generalization that can be made about African culture:

'. . . Life is conditioned by certain attitudes towards property and persons . . . in which opportunities and power depend upon status within social groups rather than upon control of investments; where, indeed, the safest form of investment, and often the only one, is still to be found in the building up of claims against persons.'[113]

This is narrowly put, focusing as it does on 'power' and 'opportunity', but it highlights the radically different emphases of pre-capitalist life. Today, ex-colonial man, who is also often pre-capitalist man, hesitates; he rejects capitalism, but he is uncertain and ambivalent about the ambiguous lessons of Soviet experience. Can he preserve the positive values he cherishes in his own culture, or must they be sacrificed to modernization?

CHAPTER FIVE

THE STRUCTURE OF THE NEW STATES

WE have noted before the eclecticism of the populist theories from the new countries; those from the former British territories, in particular, draw upon a variety of sources in developing their theories.

Many of them live in countries with rich and various indigenous cultural traditions. In addition, they draw upon the modern culture of Europe and America. In Indonesia, for example, nationalism appeals to a complex traditional heritage which contains Hindu, Muslim, and other elements: but a Soekarno also draws upon French Revolutionary ideals, Social Democracy, the Four Freedoms, the lessons of Soviet, Indian, and Chinese revolutionary and nationalist experience, Sun Yat Sen *and* Ibn Saud, Lenin *and* Gandhi.

But it would be a mistake to conclude that, because, say, Gandhism and Leninism are incompatible within the Indian context, any populist synthesis of such elements within the cultural context of the newer nations is necessarily contradictory, incoherent, or unsystematic. This would indeed be the case if we took as our departure-point the 'cultural logic' of the various world-views which new populists draw upon, for these appear to be mutually incompatible. But if we bear in mind the fundamental principles of populism outlined in the last chapter, the apparently contradictory pieces borrowed from various philosophies can be seen to fit together. We need, however, to start from the standpoint of Asia and Africa and not from that of Euro-America, for the borrowed 'pieces' are, in fact, only being used as confirmations or exemplifications of various aspects of a basic populist position. European and American borrowings, paradoxically, are particularly attractive because of their 'authority' as parts of dominant world cultural systems.

To say that populism is 'coherent' does not mean that it is a closed system, a tight-knit and rigid dogma. Indeed, its internal stresses and strains are such as to leave a wide area of indeterminacy and latitude when it comes to making political decisions and creating political systems. Modern populism, though systematic, though radical and innovatory, is also pragmatic and empiricist, cautious and open-minded. Every theory, every remedy, every plan, every philosophy, is inspected. Does it fit African or Asian traditions and conditions? Does it fit our present and future needs? Can it be *used*? Sékou Touré, in particular, elevates pragmatism to the status of a cardinal principle:

'. . . Philosophy does not interest us. We have concrete needs. . . . One should compare results rather than principles. Society is not made for principles, for a philosophy, for a doctrine, for a given science; on the contrary, science, philosophy and principles of action ought to be determined for the people, with reference to the realities of the people.'[1]

The borderline between such empiricist-pragmatist thinking and pure opportunism is often thin: the justification is always the success of the national-liberation movement. Politically, it means that all positive relationships – alignments, alliances, friendships, co-operation – are entered into, and maintained, only in so far as they help further the decolonization process. Everything else is subsidiary. Enmities and oppositions, equally, are determined by reference to the same criteria. Hence, different circumstances involve adopting different tactics – but the goal remains the same. So Indian National Army leaders fought alongside the Japanese in Burma; Soekarno and the Indonesian nationalists could use openings presented by the Japanese, who encouraged a certain degree of Indonesian self-organization, at the very time that other nationalist leaders like Sjahrir were fighting with the Indonesian underground against the Japanese. In the name of nationalism, a Sékou Touré could reject the French embrace, and a Bourguiba welcome it:

'If we opt for co-operation with the West, it is because it is profitable. It allows us to avoid dangers and gain real advantages in the present situation'.[2]

This philosophical flexibility of populism is reflected in its institutional manifestations and it can take a variety of forms. It is neither 'inherently' authoritarian or democratic: in North America, it has been appealed to by Right-wing movements and by Left-wing ones. It has been a decentralizing and 'grass roots' movement in Saskatchewan, and an anti-parliamentary, corporatist, and authoritarian ideology in Alberta. It has generated a conservative regime in the latter Province, and a socialist 'Welfare State' regime in Saskatchewan. It is an 'intellectualist' and non-sociological illusion to assume that the form and content of the political system which emerges in any given situation is determined predominantly by the internal logic of the reigning ideology alone.[3] An ideology is only one of the variables in any given situation: it exists within a particular culture and social structure. Ideas *are* important 'in themselves'; they *do* possess an 'internal logic', but they may 'fit' certain situations better than others. They have to be modified and adapted to the specific institutional contexts within which they lodge. For if men are influenced by ideas, they also tailor them to suit their needs and interests; the ready-made general principle, too, has to be applied to specific situations.

So the new societies in which populist thinking is important display, like North American movements, a variety of types of actual political organization. A preliminary simple typology would recognize two broad divisions: the 'solidarist' type and the 'pluralist', sub-dividing the latter into those societies where ethnic divisions predominate, and those where class divisions are more significant.

The One-Party States

The first type of society, the solidarist, emerges under specific conditions: where the society is markedly homogeneous in class terms; where political centralization has over-ridden ethnic divisions; or where both sets of conditions occur together. The latter is likely to be a particularly highly integrated society. The archetype is Guinea, where society is undifferentiated, and bitter struggle against an intransigent France* has further consolidated

---

* 'Intransigent' in that de Gaulle, although he offered independence to Black Africa, did so on the virtual condition that France would abandon countries

the population under a militant and solidary political party. A strong single-party regime is even more likely to occur where actual *military* struggle has to be waged for independence, as in Algeria, in Cuba (despite marked class-differentiation), and in the one-party Communist ex-colonial states from China to North Viet Nam. In these societies, the one-party state is the norm. Communist or non-Communist, State and Party are closely integrated. Minor parties usually disappear rapidly, whether in free and equal competition with the mass party, or because they are suppressed or forcibly merged into a single 'National Front'.

Under these conditions, it becomes impossible to operate a conventional parliamentary 'Government-and-Opposition' system, even if the political leadership wanted to. Here are a few cases:

Cambodia, 1955	82 per cent of the vote for King Sihanouk's Popular Socialist Community
Tunisia, 1956	597,813 votes out of 610,989 for Bourguiba's *Front Nationale*
Soudan, 1957	64 seats out of 70 for the *Union Soudanaise*
Ivory Coast, 1959	all seats won by Houphouët-Boigny's *Parti Démocratique de la Côte d'Ivoire*
Tanganyika, 1960	70 out of 71 seats for candidates backed by Nyerere's Tanganyika African National Union
Senegal, 1960	Senghor's *Union Progressiste Sénégalaise* win all seats

The list could go on. It would show, too, an *increasing* trend in most countries towards the consolidation of the power of the majority party, as when the Union Soudanaise's sixty-four out of seventy

---

which chose independence to their own devices, and to their own poverty and weakness – a threat which came to pass: '. . . de Gaulle [was] so poorly advised that he ordered the withdrawal of all French functionaries [from Guinea]. Only about fifteen of the 4,000 were left a few weeks later. Cash registers were emptied, and the weapons of the police, the library of the Ministry of Justice, the furniture of the governor's palace were stripped and shipped back to France. Some Frenchmen went so far as to tear out telephone wires and electrical fixtures; fruit trees were cut, gardens decimated, walls torn down, obscene curses scrawled on buildings, and a ship bringing five thousand tons of rice re-routed. Guinea found itself on the brink of catastrophe. . . .' (Italiaander, *The New Leaders of Africa*, p. 274.)

victory of 1957 was turned into a total sweep of the board in the elections of March 1959.

The single party is thus the norm in societies of this kind, where the sense of unity deriving from a fairly homogeneous social structure is further intensified in the course of the nationalist struggle. Guinea is an outstanding case: here, 'integral' organization has been carried to the maximum. Guinea's exercise in *Gleichschaltung* is a result both of her backwardness in social terms and Marxist influence upon the thinking of her leadership. More precisely, it is Leninism rather than Marxism that Sékou Touré draws upon as a model of State and Party organization and of the relationship between State and Party. Leninism obviously commends itself to a militant labour leader. Some of Stalin's authoritarian developments of Leninism appear too.

Recently, for example, the doctrine of *intensified* class struggle familiar from the Moscow Trials epoch has been revived by Sékou Touré:

'After eighteen months of independence, we are moving into a phase of struggle which is peculiarly difficult since the motives for engaging in revolutionary struggle are less obvious, and actions of sabotage less perceptible. Reaction, dispossessed of the authority which the illegal colonial regime conferred upon it, has put on an impressively "sympathetic" countenance and adopted "friendly" manners, but its destructive intentions are still there. . . . Independence . . . is only a stage on the road to emancipation, only a battle won in the struggle for the well-being of the people. . . . In the face of imperialist conspiracy, which, far from having laid down its arms, on the contrary seeks to redouble its efforts . . . we must carry on with the mobilization of the patriotic consciousness of the people [and] *we launch these calls to vigilance today with the same force and for the same reasons.* . . .'[4]

An earlier pronouncement shows that this was no new theme:

'. . . If the interests of the people demand that a thousand or two thousand people be killed, we will do it without hesitation, so that the masses may be permitted to live happy lives, in honour and dignity . . . countries which have been the first to apply the death penalty to murderers and thieves are the countries where theft and homicide are unknown today'.[5]

He goes on to give Saudi Arabia [*sic*] as a model in this respect, and to advocate the death penalty for motorcar drivers who kill people through speeding or because of drunken driving, and for other criminals:

'In future no pity will be shown to thieves. We shall impose extreme penalties on them. We have said that if you catch a thief in the act of breaking open your door, you can shoot at him'.[6]

In actual fact, one or two public executions did take place – leading to great popular revulsion.

There is a marked contrast between this readiness to use revolutionary violence and the more pacific injunctions of the political leader of another backward country which has achieved independence via a peaceful and parliamentary transition to independence. In Tanganyika, there was no bitter struggle, no legacy of animosity on both sides, as in Guinea. The background of Tanganyika's leader, moreover, is that of British liberalism and Social Democracy. Far from being a Marxist, Julius Nyerere is a Roman Catholic, educated at Edinburgh University.

The results of this difference in experience are obvious: we find no scathing denunciation of adversaries as 'deviationists', 'fractional elements', and the like. Nyerere, indeed, goes out of his way to point out the negative aspects of one-party society:

'Of course such overwhelming social unity has its dangers But the danger lies not in the absence of an artificially created opposition organization, but in the possible exclusion of the eccentric, the one who does not conform to the social mores. It is by the existence of a place for the 'odd man out' that a newly independent country can be judged to be fully democratic.

He must not only be allowed to live without any restriction on his personal freedom; he must be able to contribute to his society through his work and ideas. The all-pervading, nation-building nationalist organization must be able to incorporate and use the man who deliberately stands apart from its institutions. . . .'[7]

Nyerere, then, is sensitively aware of the dangers of the mono-centric society, of the rights of minorities, and of their value to society. He understands the significance of a legitimate Opposition, too. But he also emphasizes what liberal Western critics often forget, that two- or multi-party parliamentary democracy cannot possibly flourish in present-day Tanganyika:

'The notion that democracy requires the existence of an organized Opposition to the Government of the day is false. Democracy requires only freedom for such an Opposition, not the existence of it'.[8]

In this kind of situation facing these backward new States, the conventional wisdom offered by the West seems not only irrelevant but also insolent. How can you mechanically transfer institutions developed in differentiated industrial societies to societies whose condition is radically different? How can you operate a two-party system when you have only one party that embodies the common aspirations of a whole country, and which the overwhelming majority insists on voting for? The spokesmen of the new countries get angry at this point. What do you expect us to do, they ask – *invent* an opposition? The situation is not unlike that of J. P. Morgan, who, when under fire from anti-trust legislators, remarked that he could be hardly expected to do business against himself.

The single party does *not* become dominant solely because of its supremacy in disposing of the means of violence and opinion-formation. It does represent the popular choice. Criticism may legitimately be directed at the 'single list' system in Algeria, and at the absence of elections at all in Cuba. Yet who can doubt that if open elections were held in these countries, the mass party (FLN in Algeria: ORI in Cuba) would win hands down?*

There are real dangers that the leaders of the new societies may be tempted to throw out the positive *principles* of Western liberal democracy along with the unworkable parliamentary *institutions* that have traditionally embodied these principles. The tight-rope is difficult to walk, but at least many of the new leaders are aware of the problem, and recognize the strengths in the liberal position. Nevertheless, even those educated in British parliamentarism inspect the whole range of both Western assumptions and institutions critically. Why accept the theory, Nyerere asks, that '. . . the public services are and ought to be politically impartial', when we know that 'Civil Servants are human beings . . .

---

* American opinion surveys in Cuba in 1960 revealed, in fact, overwhelming support for the regime. The extent of support might well, today, be somewhat diminished, especially among the middle classes, but any party leader in the West would be delighted to receive the enormous percentage of the vote that Castro would undoubtedly receive in an election.

[and] have political views [which] . . . must affect their work'.[9]

There are, he agrees, real dangers in a partisan Civil Service. But there are also dangers in an uncommitted, a nominally neutral, or an actively hostile Civil Service. 'Neutrality' is an attitude which affects social action every bit as much as partisanship. And the crucial need at the moment is for engagement, not detachment:

'. . . The system of "checks and balances" is an admirable way of applying the brakes to social change. Our need is not for brakes – our lack of trained man-power and capital resources, and even our climate, act too effectively already. We need accelerators powerful enough to overcome the inertia bred of poverty. . . .'[10]

As a practical deduction, the President is to be elected directly by adult suffrage; he will be Head of State, Commander-in-Chief of the Armed Forces, and will have full executive authority; he is also to be leader of the majority in the Assembly, not an extra-Parliamentary figure, and in addition will not be bound to accept the advice of his Cabinet. The President will also be able to 'appoint, promote, dismiss and exercise disciplinary control over the Civil Servants and the police. In fact, except in the case of the more senior posts, he will delegate his power to the Commissions, but he will be able to override their decisions. . . .'

'In practice', the President, 'like any politician in a democratic country', cannot operate with as much freedom as these formal powers might appear to suggest:

'He governs by consent; if he cannot get the consent of his own chosen colleagues he is likely to have some difficulty in getting it from the country as a whole.

The Government are aware that some of our friends may be over-conscious of the dangers of dictatorship. But they recognize an over-riding need to provide leadership. . . . In practice the main difference between our new proposals and those which really operate in Britain may well be our recognition in law of something that happens anyway. Where they have no power, Ministers must – and do – use uncon-stitutional pressures to get in their offices men with whom they can work. We are simply making the law accord with the facts.'

The *Observer* editorially commented that Mr Nyerere's case was 'in many ways convincing':

'Who can deny, in the light of recent experience, that the new countries are going to need firm and powerful control from the top? Provided the sovereignty of parliament and of the courts remains real, the essential safeguards should remain intact. But we have serious doubts – despite the logic of Mr Nyerere's arguments about a political Civil Service – whether it is wise to provide a constitutional impediment to the growth of a truly independent and impartial body of public servants. This may take time, but it should not be ruled out as an objective.'

In the West, we have never had to revolutionize and democratize a society from the top in this way. Little wonder that the *Observer's* editorial pronouncements were cautious; there was a hesitancy in recommending the usual Western panaceas. Gunnar Myrdal, one of the few social scientists who had seriously grappled with problems of freedom and control in the new societies has pointed out that while institutions for local self-government and co-operation should ideally be run by the people and only minimally by officials,

'. . . in a stagnant society these institutions do not come into existence except as a result of state policy. The officials have the function of propagating them, starting them, and guiding them. . . . This process is a totally different one from the historical process . . . in the Western countries, and the problem is a totally new one which the Western countries have never faced'.[11]

Once independence has been attained, the role of the State increases rather than diminishes. Projects as large as Egypt's High Dam or Ghana's Volta River Scheme, or the modernization of a whole country's agricultural practice or its system of land-tenure, require massive finance, certain authority, and mobilization of resources on a scale that calls for major governmental intervention: the resources of even the largest corporations become inadequate. The State, too, as a political power, has to guide the general direction of the economy, for the acceptance of foreign aid, unless carefully controlled, can lead to a new subservience. Indigenous private enterprise also needs to be bent to national purposes. And if private enterprise is allowed to flourish unchecked, the socialist objectives of many governments would be impossible of attainment: apart from the technical and economic need to plan and invest on a large scale, there is also an ideological predisposition in favour of public enterprise. For all these reasons, a vigorous and strong government is needed.

The extent to which the common problems facing these countries produces parallel developments, despite other marked divergencies in history and culture is strikingly revealed in the political convergence of two such diverse figures as Sékou Touré and Julius Nyerere, both in their general populist ideology and in their advocacy of a strong state and a single party.

For though each of these countries has its own idiosyncratic features, they share a basic life-situation in common. The central fact, internally, is backwardness. In both countries, therefore, we find that class-divisions are not well developed: naturally, therefore, neither country has thrown up class-based parties or a pluralist political system. There are, of course, other divisions in society on the basis of which a pluralist system might be erected, the most important being ethnicity. But no ethnic group is large enough or well enough organized to impose its hegemony over the whole country, or even to dominate a region: Tanganyika has many scores of 'tribes', but of these, even the Sukuma, the largest people (around a million strong), possessed no centralized political institutions.[12] The second basic sociological fact is the legacy of colonialism, which engenders a nationalist movement opposed to 'tribalism' and devoted to national consolidation.

The case of Alberta shows that the emergence of one-party systems under such conditions is not confined to the contemporary ex-colonial world. Macpherson has shown how, even *before* Social Credit's rise to power in that Province, a conventional party system was absent. Instead, prairie movements historically tended to produce what he calls a 'quasi-party' system, in which, although the institutions of parliamentary Government-and-Opposition, checks and balances, and divisions of powers between executive and legislature, were still formally maintained, in fact, a single party reigned supreme. The party in power under such conditions reigns virtually unchallenged; if inherently anti-democratic, it can easily establish outright dictatorship.

In Alberta, of course, the Province is merely a unit, with limited constitutional powers, within a wider, Federal system of government. This sets important limits on any tendency to abuse the powers the Provincial Government does have, and precludes it from acting unconstitutionally. In Saskatchewan, a more significant opposition has persisted within the Provincial Legislature.

Early experiments in replacing hostile senior Public Servants by more sympathetic individuals were abandoned, since the public servants, by and large, gave their loyalty to the incoming Government, and did not seriously sabotage its programmes.

Internal restraints on single-party rule of this kind are virtually absent in the new one-party states, though world opinion does exercise a most important external influence over their actions. The running barrage of Press criticism, though often unfair, has been an important brake on illiberal tendencies in Ghana.

Restraints upon monocentric governments and authoritarianism are least likely to be effective in those countries where independence has had to be achieved through armed revolutionary struggle, in so far as discipline, authority, and obedience become institutionalized and are carried over from the war into the peace. On the other hand, mass guerilla warfare does make for a high degree of political consciousness and involvement in political life on the part of the ordinary people; to gain their support, serious instalments of social reform have to be accepted as part of the independence programme.[13]

In a recent study,[14] Finer has suggested that social backwardness inevitably means also a low 'political culture'. Societies which are very simple in social structure are not only eminently likely to succumb to 'strong' government, but in particular to *military* government, for unlike advanced and complex societies, such societies are simple enough to be run by the relatively crude methods of military administration. A rapid glance at the history of South America and of the Middle East show the force of much of his argument.

Most of his most striking cases are drawn from Latin America in particular. One of the key factors he neglects, however, is the role of the USA in Latin America (and of Britain, France, and the United States, the oil-Powers, in the Middle East) in frustrating advance to modernization via peaceful and parliamentary means, in alliance with reactionary indigenous ruling classes. The military in Latin America have been the ultimate force maintaining the *status quo*, firstly, because they have had the tacit or explicit support of the greatest Power in the world, and secondly, because whatever other conflicts of interest which might exist between them and the landowning and Big Business classes have been subordinated in recent decades to the task of containing the ever-growing revolutionary upsurge of the lower orders.

The US proclivity for 'strong rule' is not, of course, confined to Latin America. US-supported military regimes have played a similar role in repressing democracy as well as revolution in countries like South Korea. In South Viet Nam, the fascistic regime of Ngo Dinh Diem was only kept going by the expenditure of more than $2,000,000,000 since 1955, by the participation of nearly 15,000 American 'advisers' in the war against the Viet Cong, and by the repression of dissent. The elections called for in the Geneva Agreement of 1954 (not signed by the USA) have not been held because the Communists would probably win them. The reactionary Ayub regime in Pakistan similarly depends upon US support.

In the Middle East, however, in Egypt, Iraq, Turkey, and elsewhere, the military has played a different role of late. Kept in subjection to other foreign imperialisms for decades, its position was symbolized in Glubb Pasha's control of the armed forces of Jordan. To the local military, as to all Arabs except the puppet 'Kings' ruling over them, the national struggle against the Ottoman Empire had only been rewarded with the betrayal and balkanization of the Arab world. The military continued to suffer intense humiliation, as, notably, in the Egyptian–Israeli conflict, when its attempt to play the role of a loyal national force met with disaster. Social backwardness, foreign interference, and domestic corruption, has prevented the creation of efficient military machines. The nationalist revolts of the Army in the Middle East, therefore, have classically come from the colonels, men like Nasser who experienced the incompetence and corruption of their own senior military leaders, who had become the tools of foreign interests, and of vicious and inept kings and parliamentarians. For these military men, the national struggle, successfully accomplished in South America, still remained to be carried to its logical conclusion.

Many of them were of humble origin, not scions of the prosperous ruling class: Nasser's father was a rural postmaster. They had also experienced repression: his uncle, with whom he lived in younger days, had been imprisoned for several years.

After the defeat in Palestine the young officers drew their conclusions:

'The Mother-country is besieged by enemies. It has also been duped in its turn – pushed into battle unprepared, and vile ambitions, invidious intrigues and inordinate passions are toying with its destiny. It is also left there under fire unarmed. . . .

In the Army . . . [defeat in Palestine] . . . wrought a radical change, in both the spirit and disposition of the officers. They formerly talked of nothing but enjoyment and pleasure. They now spoke of sacrifice and devotion to duty – of readiness to give up their lives for the dignity and integrity of the Mother-country. . . . We used to say to ourselves if the Army would not undertake this task, who would?'[14a]

The role of the military has thus been quite different in Latin America and the contemporary Near East: the one preserves the *status quo*, the other has become a revolutionizing and modernizing force.

In the other new countries, only those which experienced armed revolution have seen serious Army intervention in post-Independence government. Normally, however, the Army came into being only as part of a general independence struggle in which the mass nationalist party was the senior partner, indeed the progenitor of the Army. The Army, therefore, continued to play a subordinate role after independence. In Indonesia, Col. Nasution's interventions as representative of the Army have been limited. The danger, however, is always present, as in the case of Burma – another country whose Army was forged in the actual independence struggle – where General Ne Win, after initial intervention and subsequent withdrawal, has finally taken over the reins of government. Col. Boumedienne's role, and those of other military leaders of *wilayas* in Algeria, again points to the likelihood that armed revolution will leave a tradition both of authoritarianism and of direct military intervention in politics. The analogous growth of the influence of the military in the United States of America in recent years, under the stimulus of practically incessant 'hot' international war and continuing, ever-present 'cold' war, from World War II through the Berlin air-lift crisis to Korea and the Lebanon, Viet Nam and Cuba, shows that in conditions of chronic war-emergency, the hand of the military in shaping government policy is inevitably strengthened.[15] A similar picture could no doubt be drawn for the Soviet Union, had we more adequate documentation for that country. It is abundantly true of post-1945 France, where officers schooled in repression in Viet Nam and Algeria actually revolted against the civil government and at one time threatened the metropolis itself. The social objectives of the Army, however, have varied enormously in all these cases. True, they all share a common vested interest in a strong modern Army. Finer rightly remarks that in view of the fact that they are an independent social grouping within the wider society, disposing of immense power, and inherently self-contained and well organized,[16] the extraordinary thing is not that they have intervened in politics in countries of 'low' political culture, such as those of Latin America and the Middle East, but that they have not done so more often in *every* emergent country, and in countries of 'high' political culture, too.

In those new states where armed revolution has not taken place, particularly in Africa, where independence was handed over freely by Britain and France to a score of countries, the Army has played no such central role. Not only has it remained quite subordinate to the Party, the real architect of independence, but it has been unimportant for a much simpler reason: it virtually does not exist. The military, therefore, has *not* been a significant factor in these countries. Where it has taken over the reins of power, it has by no means always been conservative. Military rule has been merely an extreme case of authoritarian rule. And tendencies towards military authoritarianism, as with tendencies towards one-party authoritarianism, though strong, are held in check by countervailing forces.

Countries with 'low' political culture are undoubtedly wide open to military take-over bids not merely because simple soldiers can run simple countries, but also because the peoples of these countries have been habituated to authoritarian traditions, often over millennia.

In traditional Hindu thought, an authority points out,

'individual rights are related to the performance of individual caste functions. Therefore, rights tended to be social or caste rights, and it is individual duty to caste which is emphasized – not individual rights against the state administration'.[17]

Civil status and civic duty were thus determined by group membership – by caste in a system of castes. And although priestly Brahmanic theorists might try to interpret *dharma*, not as 'social conformity' within a specific polity, but as an 'eternal system of morals and law' which transcended human society and bound even the earthly sovereign, in practice the king suffered few restraints on his freedom of action. There was no place, traditionally, for 'organized competing interests':

'Basic law or tradition was considered inviolable and the royal commands constituted specific applications of the sacred law. The ideal was that of a stable society governed by an established king-leader, ruling under fixed law'.[18]

Brahmins and kings might have their differences, but the reconciliation of a traditionalistic social order with a transcendental world-view was not difficult, since both were ultimately concerned with the maintenance of their traditional joint authority. Moreover, earthly struggle, especially by the lower orders, was inconsistent with a religion that enjoined upon men the scrupulous pursuit of the moral life whose aim was spiritual progress towards *nirvana*, not the achievement of material advantage in the here and now. Moreover, man's duty lay towards the whole society, not merely that section of which he was a member:

'Under the classical Hindu scheme of values, the struggle of group against group and individual against individual for the sake of material political advantage was not morally valid. . . . Contentious leadership for the seisure and exercise of power within the state was not considered a desirable form of political activity'.[19]

Popular revolt was virtually precluded: the various castes were held to be complementary, not antagonistic. Occasionally, the Brahmins themselves might withdraw support for a monarch whose behaviour they judged to be inconsistent with Hindu religious values; then the way was open even for lowly believers, too, to dissociate themselves from their ruler. But generally, otherworldly religion acted as a guarantee of earthly stability.

These societies, attached to a stationary agrarian order, conceived of the earthly order as only a very insubstantial moment in the infinite flux of the cosmos. They also validated the power of the state, integrated the individual into the group, and the groups into a wider polity.

For the Muslim, again, Islam:

'. . . while essentially a religion, and as such profoundly personal and also finally transcending all particuliarities . . . of this mundane world . . . none the less . . . has been distinctively characterized by a deep concern for these affairs. . . . The true Muslim life includes the carrying out in this world of the divine injunction as to how mankind, individually and corporately, should live. It has been characterized, equally . . . by an intense loyalty towards its own community. . . . In essence, Islamic history, therefore, is the fulfilment, under divine guidance, of the purposes of human history'.[20]

In 'integral' polities of this kind, there was no room for the concept of an institutionalized, official, and legitimate, Opposition.[21] But despotic as they were, such authoritarian regimes were rarely *totalitarian*.[22] They allowed for the independence of different levels and areas of institutional life. Although subsumed within an overarching world-view, and subject to the ultimate absolute authority of the ruler, the ruled did have rights as well as ruler, no matter how unequal their relationship. At village level, too, the lively self-government of the Indian *panchayat* might flourish; at the centre, an authoritarian system.

But it was the *duty* of the individual that was emphasized most strongly; he existed, not as an isolated individual, but always as a member of a group articulated into a social order, much as European feudalism saw the earthly order as part of an hierarchical earthly order which embraced peasant, lord, and King, and was itself subsumed within a wider divine order with God at its apex.

Later, political thinking in post-feudal Europe, expressed in theories as different as those of Hume and Marx, viewed social institutions as the outcome of conflict between particular interest-groups within society, a struggle in which both force and persuasion played their part.

Pre-capitalist political theory, then, both in the West and the Orient, eschewed class conflict, and preached instead complementarity and the subordination of sectional interests to the higher interests of the whole, and the rights of those who ruled to determine what these higher interests were. Rational and devout conduct, both, demanded the resolution of conflict, not revolution.

So far, we have only isolated the authoritarian and solidarist elements in the pre-European heritage of the regions later to be colonized. We have not yet considered the democratic strengths enshrined in these traditions. But the recognition and performance of one's traditional duties towards the local community and the remote State, whether accepted voluntarily and internalized as legitimate or imposed by force, breeds habits of mind quite different from those of intransigent liberal-Protestant individualism or the class solidarity of the Western European socialist tradition.

And superimposed on these traditional bases is the legacy of colonialism – as we have seen, essentially a bureaucratic system.[23] Colonialism might innovate radically in some spheres – industry, education, etc. But in the political sphere it maintained dependency and resisted the stirrings of self-movement among the ruled. When nationalist leaders demanded the extension of democratic rights: the vote; elected instead of chiefly or appointed representatives; rights of assembly and expression: they were normally met with the reply 'But you are not ready yet. . . .' Their reply, in turn was always: 'But how can you expect us to be democratic if we have never been allowed to practise democracy?' Millions of television viewers in Britain and the USA had this argument sharply brought home to them, for example, by Tom Mboya, when he returned the classic assertions of liberalism, humanism, and socialism against defenders of colonialism.

In the colonized society, where administration takes the place of politics; where solidarity becomes the key weapon of the oppressed; and in the post-colonial society, too, where individualism and partisan sectional interests are seen as divisive, a high premium comes to be placed on discipline and unity, virtues which are also vices. The critic becomes suspect – and critics are often right. In the history of nineteenth-century European nationalism, too, one finds a similar ambivalence: a tremendous desire for liberty, 'anarchist' decentralization of power, appeals to individualism, libertarian humanism, and anti-Statism; and contrary tendencies for movements with huge and difficult tasks to accomplish, and with the constant problem of welding together into one solid force groups with discrepant sectional interests, to emphasize *duty* rather than *right*. The prominence of the former rather than the latter in the writings of Mazzini is a reminder that, whatever the retrospective myth created by democratic nationalists, nineteenth century European nationalism was by no means always libertarian and democratic, and that 'solidarist' nationalism is by no means a purely African phenomenon.

In Latin America, again, Bolívar, 'the Liberator', had nevertheless absorbed enough of Spanish political culture to build authoritarian principles into the draft of his first constitution. The president was not only to have life tenure, but also the authority to nominate his own successor:

'The President of the Republic becomes in our Constitution the sun, which, from the centre, gives life to the universe. . . . I have never been an enemy of monarchy, as far as general principles are concerned; on the contrary, I consider monarchies essential for the respectability and well-being of new nations. . . . The new states of America . . . need kings with the names of presidents'.[24]

The leadership of a nationalist movement that has had to struggle for independence finds itself in control of an all-powerful machine. Once in power, it is strategically placed to consolidate its control still further. As it penetrates into every area of social life, the Party becomes the principal avenue of advancement for the ambitious, who climb on to the bandwagon. Everything depends on securing its favour. Party membership, party office, party influence and patronage, are the high-road to power, wealth and prestige.

In Europe, we have become accustomed to thinking of the party as the instrument of a *class* or other sectional interest-group, and of the *class* as an entity which exists *prior to* the party. We have seen, in many countries, the rising bourgeoisie chafing under the restrictions imposed on it by a landed aristocracy which controlled the political machinery of the country. We have seen the bourgeoisie – as a socio-economic *class* in the first place – begin to claim political rights for itself.[25]

The new working-classes of Europe, in their turn, struggling to improve their grim conditions of life and finding themselves oppressed and trammelled by Combination Acts, and unrepresented in Parliament and party, had to develop their own organizations. The movement was again one from 'economic' self-defence to political offensive – from the trade union to the political party.

But in the emergent countries, the Party, rather than being the expression of the economic interests of a class, is itself the opening to economic opportunity. Wealth derives *from* political power; it does not create it. Other means of acquiring wealth, prestige, and power, both for individuals and as groups, are strictly limited. For those connected with the successful dominant Party, however, rapid mobility is possible. The political *élite* therefore develops common economic interests, precisely the point made by Djilas in relation to Eastern Europe.[26] Of course, as in Eastern Europe, or anywhere else for that matter, the very possession of power is a good independently of economic or other rewards. Only the most naïve of psychologies holds that Mr Krushchev fights to keep his position merely because he likes big cars or eating well. Men seek power: to attain and retain it, they will sacrifice many things, including wealth. But in so far as 'material' motivation *is* concerned the Party does symbolize opportunity.

The distinction between economic power and political power, is, of course, a familiar theme from the literature on late capitalist as well as socialist societies. In particular, much ink has been spilled on the question of 'managerial capitalism', in which, it is posited, 'nobody' really owns the giant corporations at all. These analyses differ on the question of the ultimate focus of decision-making. Some hold that authority is diffused between legal 'owners' (the shareholders), directors, and managers; others, that the managers manage in their own interest; yet others, that the managers operate in the interest of the holders of big blocks of shares, and that the 'commanding heights' of the economy are in fact controlled by an ever-diminishing class which controls key directorates, and recruits into its ranks a proportion of Organization Men, the 'managers' whose skills they use to maintain the efficiency of their enterprises. And some believe that the shareholder is effectively dead: the managers operate industry in the general interests of 'the enterprise', and/or for the benefit of society at large.[27]

The most striking cases of control without ownership, however, are to be found in non-capitalist societies, where even the key large share-holders are missing and all that exists is the control – exercised ultimately by politicians.*

The new countries are capitalist economies, but of a peculiar

* Granick, in *The Red Executive*, decisively rejects the notion that the 'technocrats' really run the Soviet Union.

kind. Despite their political independence, their economies are still 'colonial'; major enterprise is owned by foreigners, and staffed by foreigners. Private enterprise is still scarcely a golden highway for the indigene. But *political* office now opens up incomparable opportunities. Most sectional interest-groups, however, are quite pleased to join behind the new *élite*, since for them, too, the removal of alien control is the precondition for the advancement of their own interests.

Indigenous businessmen; young intellectuals looking for jobs; civil servants anxious for promotion; trade unionists who hope to improve their wages and conditions of work under a more amenable Government; peasants for whom the removal of the White man is the quintessential condition if they are to aspire towards a human existence at all – all share a burning interest in independence and in the success of the Party and of the new State.

The Party consolidates its power by building up satellite organizations from which it draws fresh strength, and by means of which it penetrates into all spheres of social life. In England, by contrast, the trade union movement emerged long before the political party of the working-class, the Labour Party. In consequence, trade unionism has remained independent of the political 'wing' of the Labour movement. (Many, indeed, argue that the trade unions control the Labour Party.) The Co-operative movement, too, had its separate origin, and has maintained its autonomy to a significant degree. But trade unions and co-operatives in the new states are of very recent growth, and have often only really developed since independence.

No one would argue that *they* control the Party. Indeed, they often only come into existence at all as a result of the initiative of the Party, which organizes them as satellites round the sun, itself. Even where they are not actually called into being by the Party, the unions come to maturity in a state dominated by a single party. It is not surprising, therefore, to find the Party insisting that the prime function of the trade union movement is to co-operate actively with Government in the political and economic development of the country – a rhetoric familiar enough to Europeans in both 'West' and 'East', it is true, but much more telling in Senegal or Ghana. The dangers of a trade unionism which gives up its autonomy and the militant defence of its members' interests are only too well known from Soviet and capitalist experience,[28] but the first steps in the argument justifying the subordination of the trade unions are compelling enough:

'In the independent countries of Europe, Asia or America, the working class is the class which produces, but whose share in the distribution of goods is minimal: there follows a struggle between this class and the exploiting class whose interests are totally antagonistic to it. In the heavily industrialized countries, the proletariat cannot develop towards progress and social justice except after having fought and overcome the forces which exploit it.

Thus class struggle . . . [is] . . . the only way to achieve power and final liberation from all forms of injustice.

In the colonized countries, the situation is quite different, for the contradiction between the different strata of the population are minor in comparison with the principal contradiction, that between the interests of the people of the colonized country as a whole and the colonial system itself. . . .

. . . the particular activity of the UGTAN [L'Union Générale des Travailleurs d'Afrique Noire: General Union of the Workers of Black Africa, Guinea's trade-union movement and 'centre'] is inseparable from the general activity of the peoples of Africa for their emancipation. . . . The fundamental objective of the UGTAN . . . in the present situation . . . [is] . . . the liquidation of the colonial regime . . . *internal contradictions are less significant than the principal contradiction* between the interests of Africans and those of the colonial regime. . . .'.[29]

From here, the argument is easily extended to deny independent action to sectional interests at all, and to maintain the principle of the subordination of class to national interests in the era of de-colonization. Class action, therefore, *de facto*, is put off until the Greek kalends. Here is John K. Tettegah, then Secretary General of the Ghanaian TUC:

'In the minds of the Ghana Labour movement there are not two parties in Ghana today. There is only the CPP . . . the CPP is Ghana and Ghana is the CPP. . . . We in the Trade Union Movement therefore have no other objective than to organize working-class opinion and ensure that . . . the workers record their highest vote for Comrade Nkrumah [in the Presidential elections]. . . . We shall analyse the votes ward by ward, and we shall know the places where people have refused to go and vote and they can be sure we will take the necessary action against those traitors of our cause. . . .'.[30]

The trade union movement now becomes an 'inseparable arm' of Government and Party. It fights vigorously against 'any attempt to divide the country into two social classes'. Now this *can* mean – as it has meant in Ghana – Government action to force wage-increases on employers; it can also mean the arrest of trade unionists who lead strikes 'to the detriment of the national economy' as at Sekondi-Takoradi in 1961, where spontaneous protests against budget measures which hit workers' incomes, culminating in an 18-day strike, met with the severe disapproval not only of Government, but also of the official trade union movement. As an autonomous force, the trade union movement can scarcely be said to exist in this kind of situation; the interests of the organized workers are subordinated to the political objectives of Government; indeed, any distinction between the two is held not to exist. Naturally enough, this development receives the blessing of orthodox communists. The French-speaking Africans even have a phrase for this state of affairs: *'syndicalisme participant'*.

The same picture could be drawn for the other major groupings: the co-op movement, the farmers' organizations, the women's movement, the youth movement, etc. These, too, are developed as party organizations. In Accra, the welding-together of these bodies is even physically and dramatically visible, since the tall modern 'sky-scrapers' of the Convention People's Party, the Ghana TUC Workers' College, and the building of the United Ghana Farmers' Council, stand together on one huge site.

The long-term consolidation of party power is further insured by the building of a youth movement, so that a new generation of party supporters is reared upon the ideas of the dominant party; it constitutes a reservoir of activists from whom reliable 'cadres' can be drawn in the future.

The ideological content of this education is, of course, determined by the party. It varies considerably from country to country. But the structural phenomenon of the one-party state recurs in states with quite different social objectives. President Houphouët-Boigny, on the Right, as much as President Sékou Touré on the Left, have used long-established leadership of a powerful political machine to progressively drive rival groups and individuals out of politics altogether, or – more usually – to incorporate them into their parties.[31]

It would be tedious to go on and show similar developments in other new one-party states. Enough to note that where the trade union movement has attempted to maintain its independent role, the result has been ignominious defeat. For Ahmed ben Salah, Secretary-General of the Union Général des Travailleurs Tunisiens, his stand against President Bourguiba, in defence of 'socialist planning' for Tunisia, meant the loss of his job. Only later, was he re-accepted back into the fold, though now as Secretary of State.[32]

There is little chance, therefore, that independent class or other sectional organizations will flourish in the one-party regimes at present. Overshadowing all is the party, so all-inclusive an organization that the term 'party' with its sectional implications to British ears, is quite inappropriate. This kind of movement has little in common with the party as we know it. It is a form of organization inherited from the West, but it is by no means a sectional or purely parliamentary associational grouping. The Party is largely what it claims to be – the country.

Party and society merge. The Rassemblement Démocratique Africaine, a spokesman once remarked, was 'the expression of the masses *and* the masses themselves'. In a country like Guinea, where the PDG had 800,000 members (not votes) out of an electorate of 1,405,986 people in 1958, this is scarcely rhetoric; the Party *does* become coextensive with 'the masses themselves'. This is generally recognized by the leaders themselves, who distinguish their 'movements' or 'fronts' from Western-style 'parties':

'[The Rassemblement Démocratique Africaine] is the union, in one large political organization, of all ideologies, all ethnic groups, all social situations, all the territories round a platform for concrete achievements. . . . It goes without saying that [such a union] cannot be realized on the basis of one ideology, since our movement must include all tendencies, nor can it be achieved on the basis of the demands of any one particular class or social stratum, since the grouping must include the whole social structure'.[33]

'Our disaffiliation from the French Communist Party was forced upon us; the R.D.A. is a movement and not a political party. . . .'[34]

'We are not divided into followers of different parties; we belong to a single Front, the National Front, face to face with colonialism. . . . Tomorrow, perhaps, parties with different views of what internal political order is best for the country will develop within the National Assembly. But today all of us stand for the independence of the country and for establishing that independence on a democratic basis'.[35]

'The PDG . . . is not a political party in the European sense of the word . . . it is not the political instrument of a given social class. . . . European parties [express] contradictions of interest between existing classes. . . . The European party . . . [is] . . . by nature conservative or revolutionary. . . .
    The PDG cannot preach policies based on class, for the differentiation of social strata in Black Africa is not characterized by a fundamental difference or even opposition of interests. . . . A mass political movement must carry out the defence of the interests of all social strata in the country, and cannot remain indifferent to the activities of other cooperative or cultural movements. The specific activities of each organization should be closely integrated into the framework of major objectives set for general achievement by the political movement'.[36]

'As there [is] no division among the people about the need for independence, so there will be no division about the need for an organized attack on the economic and social forces which restrict the practical expression of the human dignity proclaimed by that independence'.[37]

In the national 'Front', the Party is the senior partner, pre-eminent, the force which achieved independence, which maintains it, and which guides the battle for decolonization. Western-style Government-and-Opposition and plurality of parties are seen as irrelevant:

'Does democracy imply a plurality of parties? We say no. We believe that there have been forms of democracy without political parties. . . . We cannot afford . . . the . . . luxury of a ministerial crisis every six months . . . [or of] . . . sterile [and] fratricidal opposition'.[38]

All this means a different conception of 'party'. It means, in particular, the rejection of the conception of society as a constellation of competing interest-groups, each, on the political plane, represented by one or more political parties. Robespierre and Rousseau, rather than Hume or Montesquieu, are the appropriate Western thinkers here: the rational, revolutionized society is characterized by the existence of a 'general reason' over and above the 'particular reason' of its constituent individuals and groups. The people are the fount of instinctive 'natural reason': the leadership, therefore, must never become alienated from them, but must immerse itself in, become co-extensive with, the people. The party confounds itself with Society; within this mass party, the people constantly involve themselves in the governmental process; they operate what Renan called 'une plébiscite de tous les jours'.[39]

To people brought up with respect for the rights of the minority as well as the rights of the majority; for whom the legitimacy of dissent is as important as the right of the majority to rule, the new one-party states exhibit features which arouse antipathy in their breasts. And not without reason. In the last few pages, we have pointed to the dangers inherent in this kind of political system. This concentration of power into the hands of a centralized party headed by an *élite* with a charismatic leader at its apex, unless actively combated, engenders the 'cult of personality' and luxury and self-seeking amongst the *élite*.

As we have seen, the main opportunities for the indigenous 'new men' occur in the public sector of the economy, particularly in Government and Party service. The bright young man can get ahead quickly. Guinea has the youngest Council of Ministers in the world: in 1959, the average age of Ministers was thirty-nine years; of Secretaries thirty-six. The Minister of Finance was 29.[40]

The Party controls the Government, and both together control the public sector. Inevitably, therefore, before long, the Party is flooded with 'carpet baggers'. Peculation and misuse of public resources become common – hence the periodic 'purge' of those who publicly overstep the mark by their ostentation. Whether they are any more guilty than their accusers is often dubious, for very many enjoy the delights of the Paris cuisine in the Ambassador Hotel in Accra, or the new Casino (built with Government assistance) whose membership was confined to those with an income of over £1,500 a year. These are scarcely the institutions appropriate to a society which claims to be a 'social' as well as a 'political democracy'.

A Houphouët-Boigny can go so far as to flaunt luxury as part of a Hollywood-style appeal to the masses:

'Far and away the most splendid residence in Africa is that of the Ivory Coast's President, M. Houphouët-Boigny. . . . Over £3 million has already been spent – out of French aid funds – and further work on the landscaping of the grounds is likely to cost a further million at least.

THE THIRD WORLD

In keeping with Houphouët's unflamboyant nature, the palace doesn't look so extraordinary from the street. It is in three separate buildings: the Presidency, the Residence, and the reception halls. Not until the dinner-jacketed guest penetrates to the latter, past fountains, cascades, statues, and descends a regal staircase into a vast marble reception hall, there to shake hands with his host and his beautiful wife, does the extent and beauty of the place register. Nothing is missing: from chandeliers and antique-style furniture in subtly contrasted colours to embossed chinaware and cutlery for over 1,000 guests, and a single table that seats hundreds. . . . Many visitors – both tax-paying Frenchmen and delegations from less favoured African states – were, I am told, shocked at such extravagance. But an Ivorian journalist who inspected the palace on the day after the big reception, exclaimed: "My God, anyone could live here – the Queen of England, President Kennedy. It makes me thrilled to be an Ivory Coast citizen".'⁴¹

'No caged bird, but a delicious, capricious worldling, the Ivory Coast's sensuous, luxury-loving Maria-Thérèse Houphouët-Boigny, 31, delights Parisians even more than Jacqueline Kennedy or the Empress Farah. . . . The Ivory Coast's First Lady is coiffed by one of the most exclusive Parisian hairdressers (Carita), and dressed by Dior, whose salon is strategically located across the street from the Houphouët-Boigny's apartment. . . . The affluent Houphouët-Boignys also have a villa in the stylish Swiss resort of Gstaad (her six-year-old adopted daughter, Hélène, is attending school in Switzerland), an Ivory Coast beach house, an ultra-modern five-story tower in the fashionable Cocody sector of Abidjan, the Ivory Coast's capital. Thérèse loves orchids and sables, pilots a fast Lancia. . . . Frenchmen, who call her the Ivory One and see her as the forerunner of a new Europe-influenced African woman, delight in her exuberant, ultra-feminine wit. It did not go unappreciated at a recent luncheon party at Bobby Kennedy's house, at which, latching on fast to New Frontiermanship, she switched tables after every course. Murmured Thérèse, raising male expectations: "I suppose I'll be in the swimming pool for dessert".'⁴²

Across the road from the luxury residences where poor people's money is thus squandered are the petrol-tin *bidonvilles*, shanty-towns for the semi-unemployed of the industry-less cities. The African countries under more militant Left-wing leadership, notably Guinea and Mali, show more sense of reality; though still not enough. Algeria, however, a country with one million dead and four-fifths unemployed, is understandably relatively free from the

THE STRUCTURE OF THE NEW STATES

curse of *la dolce vita*; and Dr Banda's government in Nyasaland has also instituted a salary cut of 10 per cent for ministers.

Luxurious living is not merely morally objectionable: in under-developed economies, it can be a very serious barrier to de-colonization. In Dahomey, for example, 60 per cent of internal budgetary income goes on the salaries of Government personnel (not unusual under colonial regimes, either.) Tiny Gabon has one MP to under 7,000 people; France only 1 to 100,000. But these MPs get far *more* than their French counterparts, and over twice as much as the British MP – all this in poverty-stricken banana or groundnut republics.

In ex-French Africa as a whole, there are several thousand such MPs, fifteen governments, and hundreds of cabinet ministers. An MP who works three months out of the year receives as much in *one and a half months* as a peasant who works for *thirty-six-and-a-half years* – a lifetime. Moreover, the 'work' for parliamentarians (particularly in one-party states!) is often derisory. Civil servants, too, scarcely work themselves to death. In Brazzaville in May 1961, the majority were at their place of work – not necessarily, however, working – for three to four hours a day. They spent more time in bars and dance spots than at their desks. Yet most of the new countries waste money on sumptuous Parliament buildings: 10 millions of francs in the Senegalese Four-Year Plan for a 'palace' for regional – not even national – assembly buildings at Tambacounda alone – to accommodate twenty members; whilst on the other hand – a mere eight millions for the development of production. At the very worst, lunatic 'Versailles' are built, such as Houphouët-Boigny's palace, for which hundreds of tons of malachite were specially *flown* in – from Russia![43]

The Prime Minister of Uganda, Mr Obote, and even a former labour leader like Tom Mboya, have been criticized both by their political opponents and their friends for staging weddings which were noted in the world Press for their lavishness in the high style of upper-class European elegance. Devoted supporters of organi-zations like 'War on Want' have become disillusioned in the face of the squandering of scarce capital on a luxury car for Mr Ken-yatta. Much of this behaviour, perhaps, is merely an understand-able assertion of the right to do things Europeans do. The poor masses in the Ivory Coast, evidently, do feel admiration for the worldly glamour of their successful leader and his wife, as the poor have always felt for the glittering heroes and heroines who have climbed up out of the ranks of the poor and have become socially accepted by the traditional *élites* – here the Whites.[44] Unlike the American Negro boxer or jazz artist, Houphouët-Boigny has all this and real *power* too.

But in countries where the wage-earner only receives between £1 and £3 a week, and the mass of the peasantry considerably less in cash income, it is highly dangerous for the *élite* to be as blatant as this about its privileges. Moreover, most *élites*, in varying degrees, are sincerely restrained by an egalitarian ideology of dedication to the well-being of the nation.

Where luxurious living does rage in poor countries, it must usually be hidden, and victims periodically sacrificed on the altar of austerity, in the name of 'oneness' with the people. Ghanaian Ministers have been removed from office for becoming too financially successful. In the United Arab Republic, all titles save that of 'Minister' have been abolished.

In the typical ideology of the new states, therefore, equality of wealth is heavily emphasized, both for tactical reasons *and* out of sincerity.

This privileged style of living on the part of the new *élites* is partly a continuation of traditional patterns: people expect rulers to live like rulers and they defer to the great. Colonialism has also accustomed them to expect the ruling stratum to develop a very removed and lofty style of life. But they do not always resent this; often, they feel pride in the new magnificence of their leaders, for it mirrors their own changed status. They feel that they have achieved not merely political independence, but much more: a new dignity, and a new prosperity, too, for in the more energetic and radical countries, from Indonesia to Ghana, independence has often meant immediate improvements in the lives of the peoples measured in terms of more schools as well as more cash and food. In Indonesia, for example, peasant indebtedness was largely wiped out at Independence (owing to inflation).[45] Between 1955 and 1960, Ghanaian industrial workers doubled their average monthly earnings. In both Ghana and Nigeria, education has expanded very rapidly indeed since the establishment of self-government.

All this has been achieved under the leadership of the political party. It is natural, then, that the leadership of the Party, and especially its Leader, should be fervently acclaimed.

This devotion to the Leader is strikingly visible for example, in West Africa, where party-leaders who have switched their policies most radically have yet succeeded in carrying their followers with them. The most striking case is that of Houphouët-Boigny, who took his political party from alliance with the Communist Party to membership of de Gaulle's 'Community' with no significant loss of support from the mass membership and the electorate.

The extraordinary personal power of the new leaders has attracted much publicity in the overseas Press. Kwame Nkrumah, disliked by Lord Beaverbrook and by liberals alike, has come in for special criticism, and the newspapers have been flooded with stories of the most blatant and repulsive leader-worship. The truth is – quite simply – that the stories are mostly true. There *is* a tremendous 'cult of personality' in Ghana. President Nkrumah is *normally*, nowadays, referred to by such terms as 'Osagyefo', 'The Torch', 'The Messiah'. 'He who all Ghana, all Africa, Hail'; 'Comrade Nkrumah Knows what is Best for Ghana', the Ghanaian public is told. Press pictures show him, for example, meditating in the wilderness for seven days before making a crucial political decision. A great deal of this is public-relations propaganda which the un-frantic people of Ghana take with a smile. But foreigners read it cold; it sticks in the English gullet and stinks in English nostrils.

There is nothing peculiarly African about such adulation, however. Russian as well as African peasants have inclined before 'Little Fathers', from the Tsars to Stalin. And peasants who go to the cities, as in the mass immigrations of the 1920s and 1930s in the USSR, carry with them habits of dependence upon their superiors, reverence for the 'tall poppies', deference to authority, and attitudes of identification with the solidary community which they transfer from family and village to the State. French peasants, too, worshipped a Napoleon, even a Louis Napoleon, who '[sent] them rain and sunshine from above', in Marx's classic phrase. Nor are the people of civilized Germany in any position to reproach the people of Ghana for their peccadilloes when one looks back only a generation ago.

The 'cult of personality' is, however, unpleasant and alarming.

It is also often ludicrous – and it is probably inevitable. But however 'inevitable', those who wish to see the new states consolidate their independence and advance to decolonization do not accept these things without criticism. For them, humanity consists in imposing human values on the world, not submitting to the 'inevitable'.

For some, all this appears to confirm those pessimistic theories which emphasize the increasingly 'mass' character of modern society, where autonomous 'secondary associations' – trade unions, women's organizations, youth organizations, etc. – are either eliminated, or, more usually, are not effectively supported by their members, who thereby lose control of them to the *élites*.[46] This situation opens up 'totalitarian' possibilities, since it becomes easier for a political leadership to capture existing organizations from apathetic memberships, or to create new state- or party-controlled organizations.

Either way, they gain control over peoples' lives by depriving them of their own independent organizational means of expression. In this situation, it is said, far fewer people express opinions than receive them; communications are so organized that it is difficult or impossible for the individual to answer back immediately or with any effect; the realization of opinion in action is controlled by the authorities; and the mass has no autonomy from the official institutions of society.[47]

Clearly, the more 'integrated' of the new states have gone a long way in this direction. They lack a richly-developed network of independent secondary associations. For this reason a potentially 'totalitarian', and not merely 'mass', situation already exists, for the newly-created organizations of workers, youth, women, farmers, co-operators, etc. are all controlled by the dominant Party.

The new populism, then, might appear to be inherently headed towards totalitarianism. But the picture we have drawn so far has deliberately dwelt upon the negative elements in the situation, and upon institutional forms as distinct from cultural content.

On the other side of the ledger we should enter the fact of the very backwardness of the traditional society, for though it may be a poor basis for the development of a classical, Western-type parliamentary democracy, it is also a tremendous 'natural' barrier, too, to totalitarianism. African society may lack modern secondary associations, but it possesses deeply-entrenched traditional ones. As in any society, the heritage of the past is far from being uniformly positive: the African past contains illiberal traditions inherited from a 'feudal' past. Nigeria's North, for example, is described correctly by Coleman, not as the routine paragraphs of the British Press commonly describe it – as the very model of cautious and admirable constitutionalism – but as 'monolithic' and 'totalitarian'. Pre-European society was by no means as beautifully 'constitutional' as many modern nationalists and even anthropologists – reacting against the nineteenth-century view of Africa as a blood-soaked 'Dark Continent' – would have us believe.

But it has been the colonial system which subsequently tended to freeze traditional institutions, and actually shield them from indigenous pressure for change and modernization. In India, for example, it has been argued that:

'... in their determination to administer Hindu law without introducing any changes ... [British judges] ... imparted to it a rigid character which it had not previously had, by their exclusive reliance upon ancient authorities. ... "The consequence was a state of arrested progress, in which no voices were heard unless they came from the tomb".'[48]

Even centralized monarchies, in fact, possessed mechanisms for the handling of institutionalized change. In the Barotse legal system, for example, the citizen did have rights, there was a mature body of law, based on consensus about underlying moral postulates, and a judicial system in which people could participate and criticize, and in which modification could take place.[49]

In 'stateless' societies, where no permanent, specialized structure of overall, centralized political authority existed, men ran their own affairs themselves: they co-operated in joint economic activities, settled disputes, worshipped, married, and fought, without any specialist judges, chiefs, police, or military leaders to tell them what to do. Moreover, the notion that 'stateless' societies are entirely governed by fixed, unchanging customs and law has long been challenged, even by orthodox functionalists. In 1926, Malinowski rejected the view that submission to custom was automatic in primitive societies,[50] and a more recent study has demonstrated how men may well subscribe to a commonly-accepted body of legal and moral principles, and yet nevertheless 'bend' them to fit their own private interests, e.g. by appealing to different sections of the same code, or simply because principles have to be stated in very general terms, and 'interpreted' when applied to actual situations.[51] And even where the rules *are* unambiguous, actual social behaviour does not necessarily follow them.

Traditional society, even the African despotic monarchy or the Asian bureaucratic empire, was not as 'totalitarianized' as is sometimes believed. Particularly at village level, people participated directly in the affairs of their society: in *panchayats* and caste assemblies in India, for example, or in African village institutions of mutual aid and regulation. Nor has this tradition disappeared with the advent of the modern state. Indeed, those trying to impose modernization complain precisely that the villages are so independent of the state that they are extraordinarily difficult to influence.[52] The *élite*, then, does not have it all its own way, even though it does control the state machinery, for the state machinery is weak, and the traditional independence of the village strong. Traditional village independence therefore constitutes an important 'countervailing' check on the unrestrained use of centralized state power.

But the range of choices, fortunately, is not as restricted as this. It includes the possibility of democracy. For many theorists, 'democracy' is essentially entailed in constitutional arrangements, and particularly in the structural organization of central parliamentary institutions. But democracy is, in fact, much more than this, and much more, too, than the striking of a balance between the various power-centres in the total society. Lipset has suggested, indeed, that quite undemocratic institutions – authoritarian trade unions, for example – can contribute to the *overall* functioning of political democracy since their autonomy inhibits the total concentration of power in the hands of one single entity. A gangster 'trade union' may thus contribute towards democracy. But democracy is, in fact, much more than a matter of structural arrangements, important as these are. It is built into a whole texture of life; it is 'indivisible'. If lost or threatened in one area, the whole suffers. It is, certainly, importantly maintained by the existence of laws on statute books, but these, too, are only part of a whole culture, a whole balance of alignments, institutional arrangements, and of ways of thinking and behaving, even at the level of the individual personality. In the absence of this 'pervasive' democracy, democracy cannot effectively flourish in enclaves or parliaments. In Britain, for example, democracy does not consist in Parliament alone. Indeed, in the era of increasing insulation of *élites* from people, in the era of manipulation of the 'Lonely Crowd' by 'Hidden Persuaders', the parliamentary forum becomes a decreasingly effective democratic institution, however vital and desirable its functions. Ultimately, however, democracy depends upon the permeation of society by democratic values, upon a proliferation and diversity of open, democratic institutions, upon a *praxis* of democracy in a thousand different contexts: public meetings, demonstrations, lobbies, soap-boxes on corners, little meetings in little halls, letters to MPs and local papers, the give-and-take of the branch meeting, and the no less important consequent readiness of the individual to speak his mind without first looking over his shoulder.

So too, in Africa, a whole fabric of life contains *its* praxis of toleration, of participation in public affairs, of moral codes which enshrine mutual and reciprocal rights and obligations. It is a quite different tradition from ours in Europe, because it arises out of a sharply dissimilar cultural background. It is quite unconnected organically with the institutions which have been imported from Europe and deposited on top of African society in the name of 'democracy'.

If 'democracy' is taken to mean 'parliamentary democracy', there is no need to go on arguing about its chances of survival in the one-party states at least, for in these countries, quite simply, it has never even been born.

In an African society where 97 per cent of the voters cast their lots for him as President of Tanganyika, Julius Nyerere has this to say of democracy, African and European-style:

'. . . This idea of "for" and "against", this obsession with "Government" balanced by "Official Opposition" . . . though it *may* exist in a democracy, is not essential to it, although it happens to have become so familiar to the Western world that its absence immediately raises the cry "Dictatorship".

. . . I consider to be essential to democratic government: discussion, equality, and freedom. . . . Those who doubt the African's ability to establish a democratic society cannot seriously be doubting the African's ability to "discuss". That is the one thing that is as African as the tropical sun. Neither can they be doubting the African's sense of equality. . . . Traditionally, the African knows no class. . . .

. . . If democracy, then, is a form of government freely established by the people themselves; and if its essentials are free discussion and equality, there is nothing in traditional African society which unfits the African for it. On the contrary, there is everything in his tradition which fits the African to be just what he claims he is, a natural democrat. . . .

. . . To the Anglo-Saxon tradition, the two-party system has become the very essence of democracy. It is no use telling an Anglo-Saxon that when a village of a hundred people have sat and talked together until they agreed where a well should be dug they have practised democracy. The Anglo-Saxon will want to know whether the talking was properly organized. He will want to know whether there was an organized group "for" the motion, and an equally well organized group "against" the motion. . . .'[53]

It is true, as Soviet experience indicates, that low-level discussion and participation is quite compatible with a centralized and totalitarian system. But Tanganyika is not the USSR, and the tradition of free discussion is a living force restraining tendencies to illiberalism.

A second important characteristic of traditional society is the high value placed on mutual aid and on the redistribution of wealth. Many studies have shown how difficult it is for would-be African entrepreneurs to accumulate capital because of the demands made upon them by their kin, demands which can only be flouted at the risk of social condemnation, even ostracism.[54] Individualism is growing, but it has to contend with a 'communitarian' sense of obligation to one's fellows that is deeply rooted in the culture of centuries. It is, of course, a loyalty to narrow groups: kinsmen; fellow-villagers; members of the same ritual congregation. The extension of sentiment of mutuality to other 'tribes' or to the nation involves a quite new kind of 'universalizing' of morality.

Such universalization has been strengthened rather than weakened by the experience of the colonial struggle. 'Divide and rule' policies have been more notable for their ultimate failure than their short-term success. For people who have experienced decades of monocentric colonial rule are reluctant to see it replaced merely by the monocentrism of a new élite. 'Democracy', 'equality' and 'fraternity', are words which often produce a wry smile in the

West, where the responses of a whole generation have been deadened by the experience of Hungary and Suez, the concentration camp, the hydrogen bomb and brainwashing. But in the decolonizing world, slogans like 'Liberty or Death' still move men – and move them to action.

So if the new countries have no experience of Western-style democracy, and lack the structural institutions which underlie that particular kind of democracy, they are nevertheless not without reservoirs of indigenous democratic experience upon which to draw. As Lipset has shown, formerly apolitical masses entering into politics often display a proclivity for violence and authoritarianism,[55] but these have been situations where 'democratic' solutions to their problems had totally failed. Where democracy does deliver the goods, in Africa, or elsewhere, the masses are not seduced by authoritarian creeds. The objectives of both masses and leaders in the Third World call for an extension of human rights, not repression, violence, and hatred of others. These peoples are asking for far more than bread: they are asking for access to the world's culture, and for dignity, both for themselves and for others. They expect their leaders to embody their aspirations, and though they do occasionally throw up a Houphouët-Boigny, they produce more often a leader who offers self-sacrifice and equality: *Uhuru na Kazi* (Freedom and Work) is the watchword of the new Tanganyika. The drab-uniformed revolutionary leader, in fact, is one of the major figures of the twentieth century.

The Pluralist Polities

We turn now to those new states which fall into the 'pluralist' category. So far, in fact, we have only discussed one crucial kind of division – class division – and have found it relatively unimportant in the more backward states. But if classes are little developed, other kinds of division do exist, and cut across this homogeneity. The major social divisions are, in fact, those between ethnic groups. In some societies, ethnic divisions are so deeply-entrenched that the political system of the new states is built around 'ethnic' parties. The result is some kind of federalism. Nevertheless, *within each ethnic region*, a single party is normally dominant.

The crucial fact, however, is not that of traditional ethnic diversity, but the restructuring of pre-existing ethnic divisions under colonialism. *'Tribalism' of this kind – 'party tribalism' – is a quite new and modern phenomenon.*

A classic case is Nigeria, where British rule, broadly speaking, consolidated the emirates of the North into a Muslim Northern Region, the multiplicity of stateless societies of the East into an Eastern Region, with an Ibo/Ibibio majority-core, and the various Yoruba kingdoms into a Western Region. The modern political system developed from the beginning, then, as a federal structure, and all subsequent developments have been shaped by this inescapable heritage. At the same time, although British rule did mean common government, common laws and common experiences, ethnic divisions did not disappear, partly because of 'indirect rule', but largely because of the recency of the centralizing colonial apparatus and the scale and diversity of the traditional social structures cobbled together to form colonies.

Ethnic divisions thus became politically institutionalized. They were reinforced by highly uneven modern economic and social development. The modern economic backwardness of Northern Nigeria, formerly the centre of great civilized states, and the early predominance of the Ibo in education, are typical instances. Today, the political divisions between North, West, and East are so well established that they seem unlikely to be altered without a massive social transformation. The Action Group, by penetrating the forbidden North, and because of its electoral inroads in the East, threatened the ethnic parties in those Regions. Awolowo's appeal to a new kind of nation-wide mass radicalism brought retribution in the form of combined counter-attack by the two larger parties. He is now in gaol, beaten by entrenched ethnicity. And where the ethnic parties *have* had success in 'outside' Regions, they have won only the votes of ethnic minority enclaves (e.g. Yoruba in the East; Ibo and congeners in the Western towns). At other times, they have won the votes of minority 'tribes' claiming autonomy (e.g. Action Group success amongst the 'Middle Belt' minority in the Eastern Region); they have been glad to take up these claims as a means of weakening rival Regional Parties. *Both* these apparent exceptions to the rule that ethnic allegiance is the primary allegiance, do not, therefore, undermine our thesis. They confirm it. Ethnicity still predominates.

In other countries, the 'new' ethnic divisions have not been so strongly-entrenched. In Ghana, for example, the only major ethnic grouping opposed to the CPP was Ashanti. Outside Ashanti, the opposition consisted largely of chiefs and an older generation of intellectuals, both conservative elements who were easily isolated in the general enthusiasm for modernization and who lacked mass contacts and support. The destruction of the opposition by the mass party was therefore relatively easy.

But where regionalism is more marked, and the emergence of centralizing institutions inhibited, the country, on reaching independence, flies apart into its constituent elements – not horizontal divisions of class, but vertical regional divisions of 'tribe'. The Congo, as the world knows from Katanga, was extremely unevenly developed economically. The only unifying and centralizing force was the grid-iron of the Belgian administration stamped on to the living raw material of dozens of 'tribes'.

Because of Belgian suppression of all independent forms of African self-expression, no African unifying institutions really existed. Only the White colonial apparatus held the society together, and once this was removed, the Congo disintegrated into its component tribal segments, each producing its own party. Lumumba's Mouvement Nationale Congolaise alone attempted to create a new sense of Congolese identity, but was frustrated: the direct military and political intervention of the Belgians, the 'divide and rule' policy which culminated in the separation of Katanga, and the murder of Lumumba, prevented the incipient federalism of the MNC from maturing and spreading. The Congo still remains divided between shifting coalitions of the various political parties, which mainly represent traditional ethnic divisions as modified by the colonial experience: thus Abako has been a party of the BaKongo people; MNC-Kalondji, the party of the BaLuba of Kasai, etc.[56]

Finally, Kenya provides another, more recent, example of the separation out of rival political parties on an ethnic basis. The Kenya African National Union, on the one hand, draws its support largely from the numerically-superior Kikuyu and Luo who achieved comparatively rapid social development under colonialism. The less numerous and more backward (largely Nilo-Hamitic) peoples backed the rival Kenya African Democratic Union. The former, naturally, believe in a strong centralized state; the latter wish to protect themselves under a federal constitution. And KANU is obviously winning, as Nkrumah won in Ghana.

For societies divided vertically by ethnicity, the problems are not those of class war, but of schism and separatism. Where the conflicting groups are inextricably mixed up residentially, the process of disengagement may give rise to most bloody scenes, as during the Congolese debacle, or – more horrifyingly – in the mass 'communal' killing during the division of geographical India into political India and Pakistan.

Federal constitutions, or regional and 'tribal' parties in a centralized state, thus make for a pluralist, not a unitary political system. They are much admired by people from the West, because they are believed to be a good insurance against totalitarianism and disorder. Yet within each 'tribal' area, the party's social base is normally just as homogeneous, and its grip quite as powerful, as that of the single-party in Guinea or Tanganyika. Nor are they, in fact, ensured against bitter fratricidal conflict or against inroads on democracy, as the Nigerian case has shown.

Finally, we may note that 'ethnic' pluralism is also present in much more advanced ex-colonized societies, where traditional differences in culture, poor communications, an understaffed structure of government, and marked imbalances of social and economic development inherited from the pre-independence era, all combine to perpetuate 'vertical' schism.

India since 1946 has reorganized her political divisions on the basis of 'linguistic provinces'. Since independence, Indonesia, too, strung out over thousands of islands inhabited by many different cultural groups, and where Javanese dominance is resented by the less populated and more backward 'outer' islands, has succeeded only with the greatest difficulty in consolidating the nation, and has vacillated for years between 'federal' and 'unitary' constitutions. As in the Congo, federal integration was further artificially impeded by the activities of the Dutch.

Little wonder that federalism does not seem as attractive to nationalists who wish to see the nation united for rapid all-round development as it appears to some apostles of pluralist political theory:

'The consciousness of common nationhood, of unity exists. But so also do many of the old customs which emphasize the differences between groups within the society. This is an understandable situation. . . . But such slow evolution is not a practicable proposition in Africa today. The nationalist movements which are largely responsible for the existence of the national feeling must consolidate their position in this respect if they are to be successful in their next tasks. . . .'[57]

But in the more developed of the new countries, a new kind of multi-party system is emerging. Here, nation-wide, *class*-based parties, not ethnic regional parties, have emerged to form an effective opposition.

In India, for example, the elections of April 1962 to the Lok Sabha (Lower House) showed a marked increase in the votes for the conservative Swatantra Party on the Right and the Communist Party on the Left, principally at the expense of Congress. Congress lost 6¼ million votes; the Communist Party gained nearly one million; and Swatantra over seven million. These changes were not reflected closely in terms of seats: the number of Congress Members declined from 371 to 361; the CPI stayed steady at twenty-nine; and Swatantra emerged as a Parliamentary force for the first time with eighteen. Yet in the first two Parliaments of independent India, so weak was the opposition to Congress that no party could muster the fifty seats (10 per cent of the total membership of the House of the People) needed under the Constitution to be recognized as an official party in opposition.[58]

Nevertheless that huge 'umbrella', Congress, still holds 371 out of 489 seats, and 45.06 per cent of the votes; the CPI, by contrast, obtained only 10 per cent, and Swatantra 6.48 per cent.

India, which was too culturally unified for ethnic parties to be of any real importance, is clearly witnessing at last a challenge to the dominant nationalist-populist party from class parties of both Right and Left. Despite this, Congress still commands overwhelming support.

The chief reason for the failure of class parties in the past – despite several decades of indigenous capitalism – probably lies in the persistence of the retarded agrarian economy:

'. . . five-fifths of the population live in villages, while 70 per cent are engaged in agricultural occupations . . . The proportion of people living in the towns hardly increased between 1881 and 1931, while the proportion of industrial workers in the total working population actually declined between 1911 and 1941'.[59]

Class divisions were not strong enough to divide a nation united in the independence struggle behind a single party, Congress. Even today,

'five-sixths of the population live in the 550,000 villages of India, and a large proportion of the other sixth lives in small towns. In 1951, there were only 76 towns with more than 100,000 inhabitants and only five (Bombay, Calcutta, Madras, Hyderabad, and Old and New Delhi together) with populations exceeding one million. . . . Only in the last twenty years, and especially since 1947 [has] urbanization proceeded rapidly'.[60]

But the last sentence is the significant one. Increasingly, therefore, the Communist Party finds a favourable situation for class appeals in the cities, and is beginning to establish roots in the countryside. It is still hindered by the fact that in a nation of villages, its main cadres live in the cities, among intellectuals and workers, though not so seriously hindered as the enfeebled socialist movement:

'A study of the Praja Socialist Party in Bombay (1953) showed that of 469 active members, 136 were industrial workers and virtually all the others middle class'.[61]

The Communist Party is undoubtedly making ground even in the backward provinces, as class increasingly dissolves populist solidarity,[62] though it still, however, tends to find its support structured along the lines where caste and class coincide, rather than on a purely class basis.[63]

The Communist appeal is strongest among workers and peasants. It is a class appeal essentially. It has been suggested that Communist success in Kerala, where the Communist Party formed a Provincial Government, depended not on class, but on the fact that this was the most highly-*educated* population in the whole of India, and that the large unemployed intelligentsia transmitted their discontents to the masses. Detailed figures, however, show that it was the *less*-educated who voted heavily for the CPI in Kerala, not the better-educated.[64]

In Indonesia, another more developed ex-colonial country, the major nationalist 'umbrella' party, the PNI, has been able to maintain its lead with much less certainty. In the 1955 elections to the House of Representatives, it emerged with 57 seats, as against 57 for Masjumi and 45 for Nahdlatul-'Ulama, the two Muslim parties, and 39 for the Communist Party. In the December 1955 elections to the Constituent Assembly, the PNI returned 119 representatives, Masjumi 112, Nahdlatul-'Ulama 91, the Communist Party 80, and the Catholic Party 10. The socialists returned only ten members to the Constituent Assembly, and five to the House of Representatives.

Since elections might ultimately produce a Communist victory, new general elections now appear to have been delayed indefinitely. Democracy has been sadly reduced; instead, we have a variety of ineffective experiments with 'Presidential rule', 'guided democracy', and 'transcendental cabinets' (in which the Communists as well as the Army now have representation).

The crisis in the more advanced of the new countries like India and Indonesia has its parallels in Latin America, where national independence has been established for well over a century, but where the social revolution needed to dissolve the legacy of colonialism has not been achieved anywhere except in Cuba.

Recent developments in Latin America suggest that the analysis we have presented for Africa and Asia could be applied with considerable benefit to that part of the world. Hobsbawm, in particular,[65] has noted, firstly, the apparent senselessness of Latin American politics when interpreted in conventional Western terms: that states like Colombia, with familiar liberal-and-conservative parliamentary systems and 'comparatively few military coups and dictatorships . . . [have] . . . produced massacre as a permanent political institution'; that the mass trade unionism of the Argentine has been Peronist, not socialist, or that Castro's Communism has been extremely unorthodox.

Further, both socialism and communism have been remarkably weak; like 'Western democracy', they have been easy to overthrow and contain, not just because the military have been ruthless, but because these political creeds have not had the support of the masses.

What they have supported, Hobsbawm suggests, has been *populism*: Peronism in the Argentine; Getulio Vargas' movement in Brazil; the National Revolutionary Movement in Bolivia (which has nationalized the mines, elevated the Indians, and armed the people); the Aprista movement in Peru; the Democratic Action Party in Venezuela. Sartre, too, has pointed out the essentially populist nature of the *original* ideology of the Cuban Revolution, which was highly pragmatic and as remote from Communist thinking on the subject of class and revolution as it was from institutional Communism.[66] Not for nothing had a representative of the Communist Party once sat in a Cabinet of the very Batista whom young men like Castro were going to destroy.

With new guerilla peasant revolutionism astir in Guatemala, Colombia, Venezuela, Peru, Ecuador, Paraguay, and Brazil, the prospects for Castroism are by no means dim. Castroism, however, does have one peculiarity: it is a product of a small country, very closely and directly exploited economically and controlled politically by the US, even to the extent of quite recent actual military occupation. *National* resistance was thus joined to populist dissatisfactions. But the two are separable (as we have seen them separated in the Canadian prairie movements).

For most of Latin America, this nationalist element is lacking. As Hobsbawm points out, these countries had achieved national independence of Spain and Portugal by 1830. But the new states became the property of the rich Creole *élites* which then took over economically, since they owned the land, and politically, since they owned the state. For the Indian peasantry, excluded from politics, the liberalism of their rulers was a rhetoric masking vicious exploitation and violent and corrupt manipulation of arms, money and votes against them.

As we have noted for Africa and Asia earlier, in Latin America socialism and communism have for many decades been regarded by the indigenous peasantry (where they have heard of them at all) as foreign ideologies, rather than as creeds rooted in American soil. The bearers of these systems, again, have been labour aristocrats and small circles of rich intellectuals in the cities, and especially foreign immigrants (e.g. Spanish and Italian anarchist and other rationalist and secularist groupings). The masses were thus effectively insulated from these orthodox unorthodoxies. Indeed, they never entered political life at all. Now they are doing, and they are entering with their own, peasant-conditioned unorthodoxy: populism. The big differences between this populist upsurge, however, and that of the regions we have been examining so far, lies in the absence of nationalism as a superadded element, since formal national political independence was achieved over a century ago. But the independence *is* only formal and 'unfinished'. After Cuba, nobody can be under any illusion that the 'national' element will not soon be provided in the form of a vast upsurge of (always latent) anti-US sentiment. At this point, the Latin American, the Asian, and the African movements converge ideologically. But in Latin America, in countries vastly more developed than India or Ghana, populism, instead of coming into conflict with Communism, merges into it. The streams of revolution come together, and presage unexpected syntheses and unorthodox transitions to new kinds of socialism and communism.

Differentiation and Conflict

In the more economically developed of the recently colonized countries, then, the familiar outlines of the class struggle are thus becoming discernible. Latin American States, long politically independent, share two crucial features in common with the new countries of Afro-Asia: backwardness and lack of full autonomy. In this huge reservoir of agrarian backwardness, foreign capital, notably from the USA, has exercised the final vote, a 'vote' occasionally expressed via the bayonet rather than the ballot-box. In the past, much of the frustration of the ignorant and disoriented masses was worked off in hopeless illusory struggle, such as Euclides da Cunha has classically depicted in his epic picture of the rising under Antonio Conselheiro.[67] More recently, Hobsbawm has shown how desperation has turned the Colombian countryside into a theatre of the most terrible violence in which individuals and groups torture and kill each other on a scale which he calls 'genocide'.[68] Here is one portent of the desperate future awaiting countries which fail to use political independence as a springboard for social transformation. Eventually, of course, the kinds of leadership provided by millenarian prophets and local bandits give way to organized revolution. The beginnings of peasant revolutionism are already present; in the cities, too, there are signs that a watershed has been reached, with the entry of the masses into politics. The mass demagogy of Getulio Vargas in Brazil and of Juan

Perón in Argentina marked the beginning of this new period. These city-based movements appealed to new masses of city workers who lacked a strong tradition of urban industrial living and whose trade unions had had to fight for their existence. Perón may not have solved either the major internal or external problems of a still-capitalist Argentine: he did, however, enormously improve the standard of living of the Argentine industrial worker.[69] Little wonder that the faithful still vote for him overwhelmingly, long after he has been forced to flee the country.

At this point, 'Western democracy' breaks down. It does not allow popular choice of quite other systems. When in the Argentine and in Guatemala and Kerala, the people vote for a left-based Caesar or for Communism, *they are not allowed to*. Force is used to stop them, or 'politics' is replaced by administration, as when Nehru brought Communist Kerala under 'Presidential rule'. Thenceforth, the likelihood of stability in government is slight: the parliamentary system is discredited; the bayonets behind the ballot-box stick too far out, and any resulting government can only be unrepresentative and minority. Government becomes, in fact, government *against* the people: if it continues to leave the social problems underlying the political crises unsolved, dissatisfaction is merely driven underground, and smoulders until the next explosion.

Growing class struggle can thus lead to the undermining of the entire apparatus of the parliamentary state, and produce among the masses a revulsion against both the ruling classes *and* parliamentary institutions. In those new countries where class alignments have already jelled into party form, the class parties are not yet strong enough to constitute such a threat to parliamentary democracy – nor, indeed, are they necessarily anti-parliamentarian at all. What is likely to divert class-struggle into authoritarian channels, Left or Right, is the failure of 'bourgeois' democracy to achieve the social revolution. In the backward countries, *this has never yet been accomplished by any 'bourgeois' democracy*. The countries which have seriously tackled land redistribution, housing, illiteracy, and malnutrition, have been countries where political revolution has taken place: in Egypt, where the military *élite* has distributed land and nationalized industry; in Cuba, where a gigantic and imaginative experiment in modernization is taking place; in China, North Viet Nam and North Korea, under Communist leadership; even – from an earlier epoch – the unfinished Mexican achievement in distributing land to the *ejidos*, and in nationalizing foreign-owned oil. And in these countries too, where Western eyes see only the negative aspects of revolutionary control, the people have gained far more than houses, latrines, medicine, or even land. They have gained something which depends on all the foregoing, but is more than their sum: human dignity.

Gellner has shown for Morocco how the apparently 'meaningless' pattern of revolts – where rebels are (quite untraditionally) gently treated; where people rebel against their own, nominal leaders; where they are repressed by people in whose name, allegedly, they are rebelling – does make sense when seen as struggle and manoeuvre for *future* advantage by people who want to test the limits, but who do not wish yet to commit themselves totally or unequivocally in an open run for power, a struggle which will, in fact, be a Left–Right struggle.[70]

Sharpening class-struggle is thus the order of the day in the more advanced countries, and is not too far distant in even the less-advanced. The critical reader will have observed that two classes we avoided discussing in Chapter Four above are, in fact, of great importance in agrarian economies: landowners and landless agricultural labourers. The omission was deliberate, partly because these two classes scarcely exist in the more undeveloped societies, and partly because the conflicts of interest between them have so far been successfully contained, or cross-cut by other loyalties. But India has by now an agricultural proletariat numbering 33 millions, and a powerful and entrenched landowning class. And despite what we noted above about the 'non-proletarian' nature of the urban working-class in the newer countries, it must also be observed that there was an urban labour-force of over 300,000 in Nigeria in 1953, 153,000 of whom were organized into trade unions.[71] Plantation-labour and mine-labour, where they exist, constitute a potentially independent political class-force of enormous power, as the cases of Northern Rhodesia and Indonesia show.

We have already seen populist nationalism in head-on conflict with the newer class-organizations in one of the leading new African states, Ghana, where workers at Sekondi-Takoradi staged a strike against Government 'austerity' policies, and were met by force. They found themselves, too, up against the Party-controlled, 'official' trade-union leadership. This was no aberrant happening. In the Presidential election of 1960, Dr Nkrumah received seven votes for every one cast against him in the country as a whole, but in the most socially developed part of the country, in the capital of Accra itself, he succeeded in obtaining fewer than two votes to one.[72]

In the West, the common liberal answer to the problems of the new countries, apart from the conventional recommendation of parliamentary institutions, is the assumption that future socio-economic differentiation will provide the basis for the emergence of social classes, parties, and other groupings which will form the basis of a 'pluralist' instead of a monocentric, society. Social differentiation, the argument runs, will produce democracy.

The protagonists of this viewpoint have perhaps not looked at the picture of class-differentiation in Russia and China on the eve of their Revolutions. The statistical analyses made by both Lenin and Mao of rural class structure in their countries are healthy correctives to liberal confidence. For parallels to Russia and China are already strikingly visible in some of the new countries. In part of Buganda, for example, the following situation has been reported:[73]

Large farmers	2	per cent
Well-to-do peasants	19	,,
Middling peasants	27	,,
Poor peasants	32	,,
Landless labourers	20	,,

Such a table hardly requires comment; these are the statistics of latent revolution.

But one comment *is* necessary. It is frequently assumed that 'development' is the great need of the emergent countries, not least in those countries themselves. Many of them express a merely verbal 'socialism' which fits the facts of increasing class differenti-ation, *élite* control, and foreign economic dominance only very awkwardly. There is, in fact, no such thing as development 'in itself', or 'modernization' *per se*. Development of the Buganda kind is capitalist development, and leads to the emergence of property-based classes which, sooner or later, will express their economic interests in political terms. As social classes become more pronounced, ideologies of populist solidarity will become increasingly irrelevant in their turn. Julius Nyerere has foreseen that new interest-groups within the dominant *parti unique* will eventually split away from the party, and that a multi-party system will emerge:

'In the newly-independent countries it is most unlikely that there will be a two-party system for many years. The nationalist movements are going to be very powerful indeed: they will control the Government, and organize local development in the economic and social sphere without there being any effective challenge to them from within – and any challenge from outside will only strengthen them.

This development of a one-party Government will in fact be the inevitable result of both the recent history and the environmental conditions. It will be a long time before any issues arise in the new countries on which it will be possible to build a real opposition organization. This will eventually happen, and it will be brought about by a split in the nationalist organizations.

There is no alternative way in which it can happen because the nationalist organizations are not real political parties in the Western sense; they are coalitions for national purposes. The first of these purposes is political independence. The second is nation building.'[74]

Nyerere's assumption that the growth of political opposition will inevitably take place assumes that society remains reasonably open and democratic. It is by no means impossible, however, that a 'new class', in those underdeveloped societies where political power is the highroad to self-advancement, might use its power to maintain its position indefinitely by use or threat of force.

Recruitment of young people allows for a degree of mobility, but the mass of the people, in the nature of things, cannot *all* be officials (though, in some countries, they are trying hard to bring this about). And parties which restrict recruitment to their families and followers are likely to sow the seeds of future opposition, future demands for the cleansing and democratization of the public machinery. But mass parties also normally launch youth movements which educate a new generation in the official ideology, and prepare the enterprising among them to take office in future. The possibilities of a more or less 'closed' political *élite* manipulating power for itself are thus considerable, even if, in the process, it will also produce reaction and a new kind of vigorous opposition. Leaving aside the crucial limitation on Governmental freedom of action represented by foreign ownership of the key resources, nearly all other power is concentrated within the State in the hands of the *élite* which staffs the machinery of the party, and pre-eminent power lies with him who controls the Party itself. Although the leading politicians normally do not privately own really major economic assets, their *de facto* control over the whole society, including powerful controls over the foreign-controlled sector of the economy, does place them in a special 'relationship to the means of production', when alternative avenues in private enterprise are meagre as compared with those available through occupancy of party, administrative, and governmental office. This is one situation in which a gulf could open between rulers and people – the class struggle here will not be the classic Marxist one between socio-economic classes whose antagonisms stem from the contradiction between private ownership and social production, but from the antagonisms between a political *élite* controlling the society as a whole, and the rest of the population. This is the 'new class' situation.

The other possibility is the classic Marxist class struggle in the more developed capitalisms of the new countries. This we have seen already taking shape in India and Indonesia.

The third possibility, of course, is a Communist society of the North Viet Nam–Chinese type. But short of a general disintegration of Cold War positions in South-East Asia, future Viet Nams are only likely on the actual Chinese borders. Southern Viet Nam is the obvious candidate, for only massive American expenditure and military intervention has kept Ngo Dinh Diem and his successors in power.[75]

We can understand why, therefore, the splitting of the newly-forged nation into warring classes does not necessarily strike people in the Third World as the epitome of social advancement. Steps *can* be taken, too, to prevent the accumulation of private wealth, property, and privilege, and socialist-inclined governments, controlling new and growing nationalized sectors of the economy,[76] may succeed in preventing a repetition of Europe in Africa. The single-party system might, that is, be perpetuated, and turned in a socialist direction.

This is indeed what official Communist policy seems to envisage. They anticipate such a situation as one in which they could flourish, and turn the usually already-socialist single-party system in the direction of Communist single-party society. Cuba here seems to them an attractive model. There are three relevant comments. Firstly, the Communist Parties or elements (for there are few organized Communist Parties in Africa as yet) are post-Stalin Communist organizations. They are not, then, likely to work for the establishment of the ruthless centralized despotism that was the pre-1956 model. Secondly, nothing is changing more rapidly than the Communist world, and further changes in the heartlands of Communism will have their impact on the communists in the 'proletarian nations'. The current indications are still in the general direction of liberalization, or at least flexibility, rather than regression to authoritarianism. Thirdly, the weak Communist Parties in the Third World, if they grow towards and synthesize with the mass nationalist-populist parties, will be mice marrying elephants. Only those mesmerized by paranoid terror of communism will assume that the influence will be all one-way, i.e. in the direction of 'communization' of the mass-nationalist parties. They forget, too, the impact of experience of the negative facets of communism which caused, for example, the recent exodus of African students from Bulgaria, or the later clash between Ghanian students and the Soviet authorities. The most dynamic possibility in the entire scene – one which could transform the present division into a 'communist world', a 'capitalist world', and a 'Third World' – is the nationalization of communism. The emergence of Peking as a Medina to Moscow's Mecca; the growing 'polycentrism' of the Eastern bloc; the increasing self-assertion of countries like Poland, Albania, and now Roumania, within the bloc; the defection of Yugoslavia; the current rebellion of the Italian Communist Party and its CGIL trade union centre, the largest communist forces in the capitalist world – all these suggest that a more flexible communism, adapted to local needs, may not be long in coming, both in the under-developed countries and elsewhere. And the Chinese influence is stimulating a revival of colonial revolution long muted under Soviet influence. Two American students of communism in India, indeed, end their study by commenting:

'It is probably not an exaggeration to say that the greatest obstacle to the success of the Communist movement in India was Josef Stalin'.[77]

That obstacle, expression of only a phase in the development of Communism, has now been removed, both for the ex-colonial peoples and for the peoples of Eastern and Western Europe. Young Russians maturing to adulthood today only know of the Stalin era at secondhand. Windmiller and Overstreet go on to remark that the Indian Communist Party, which has never fully followed the blueprints exported from Russia, has been 'neither monolithic nor unchanging . . . *should it become even a little Indian, it will be truly a force to be reckoned with'*.[78]

The kinds of communism we are most familiar with from the past, therefore, notably communism in its Russian or even its Chinese forms, are unlikely to set the pattern of future communism too closely. Instead, if either 'national communism' were to develop, or truly internationalist forms, instead of heliocentric Russian or Chinese types, it would inevitably be suffused with the national and internationalist traditions developed during the era of populism.

Cuba may well be a harbinger. In that country, the small Communist Party, despite the moral and material support a Russian ally brings it, dares not press too hard on a movement with which it now forms a 'unified' party, but which in actuality contains only a small minority of orthodox Communists. The orthodox Communists, notably Anibal Escalante, when they did press too hard, were quickly exported – to Moscow.[79]

This is one potential direction: a convergence between a liberalized communism and a socialized nationalism: something quite different from the paranoid picture of a Communist 'take-over'. But the dominant communisms are still extremely powerful. China's bid for militant leadership of world communism, indeed, has only begun. And in new countries where class-divisions are allowed to develop, a classical communism-of-opposition (as in India today) could still come into conflict with the dominant nationalist party and emerge as the major alternative, fighting, not fusing with, the nationalist party. In those countries which fail to achieve the take-off, and relapse into the hungry frustrations of stagnation or regression, all kinds of conflict from anarchic protest to regional schism or even communist revolution could flourish. A revolutionary leadership could easily replace those nationalist parties which have lost their social-reforming zeal, or who were restrained by 'Western' pressure from proceeding with social transformation. The appeal of the 'Caesars of Asia', to use Chéverny's scornful phrase,[80] to their glorious nationalist record, cannot make up indefinitely for their failure to provide land, homes, food and intellectual light. If the still-capitalist new countries do continue to stagnate, and fail to achieve the social revolution required, future historians might well conclude that while Stalin successfully kept the Communists out of power in Afro-Asia, the State Department put them in. The dilemma is serious for conservatives in the Western camp. Whatever they do at home, East of Suez and South of St Louis, they must support revolutionary social change, or face a world in arms against them.

Only those curiously mesmerized by a peculiarly obsessional and anachronistic view of communism – including, unfortunately, many of the political leaders of the Western world – and lacking in confidence in their own political values, can be unresponsive to these new possibilities. Despite the rigidities of the Cold War, there are enormous areas of choice open to all countries. This is especially the case for the new countries, whose choices are limited by poverty, it is true, but whose uncommitted position in the Cold War makes them the object of elaborate courtship by both sides, so that Germany, the USSR, and Britain have *all* built steel plants in India, and – for a while – America and Russia were both possible financiers of the Aswan High Dam.

Unfortunately, social theory does not develop as rapidly as its subject-matter. Possibly it is too difficult for a generation reared in an epoch of Right and Left totalitarianisms to think in sufficiently flexible terms about new countries that fit neither category easily. It also appears to be necessary to remind some people that in the crucial battle against the most vicious totalitarian system in history, the Soviet Union was aligned with the Western Powers against Nazi Germany.[81]

Simplistic dichotomies between 'totalitarian' and 'democratic' societies ignore the innumerable shades of grey between the two; they are usually more illuminating for the light they cast on the

Cold War assumptions of writers than for any light they may shed on the political systems they purport to describe.

The fundamental choice the new countries have to make, in fact, is not one between the polar extremes of 'totalitarianism' or 'democracy', nor between 'parliamentarianism' and 'dictatorship'. It is increasingly defining itself as a choice between a socialist pattern of society or a capitalist one.

The peoples of the new states are by no means insensitive to the dangers of one-party rule. After Madeira Keita had delivered the defence of the single-party system from which we quoted earlier, a young African got up and asked whether the single-party system was, in fact, always a good thing. What of such 'single-party' states as Spain or Portugal, he asked, which we abhor? The answer he received was that there are 'good' and 'bad' one-party systems, and that the Spanish and Portuguese systems were not based upon parties of the people.

Probably a more relevant answer is that they are quite different phenomena altogether from the systems in the new states. Some parallels are obvious enough between one-party systems in Louisiana, in Alberta, in the pre- and post-war fascist countries, and in the USSR. But the situation in Georgia, USA, is radically different from that in Georgia, USSR, let alone that in Tanganyika. And it is not merely that every country has its unique, historically-conditioned legacy of culture. Such a view would lead us to a total empiricism, for every society, like every person, is a unique 'personality' in this sense. Rather, the fascist systems, the Soviet system, the white-supremacy states of the USA, and the new countries, represent different types of social formation and belong to distinct sequences of human social development. The content of political relations, the meaning of the whole society, is different for each type. The desperate struggle to maintain White supremacy in the southern USA; the last-ditch resort to illegal violence by a coalition of military, capitalist, political, bureaucratic, and landowning elements in the effort to preserve capitalist society against the threat of disintegration and its replacement by socialism or communism – these are distinctly different in content from the emergence of a single-party National Front system (for which the term 'national democracy' is increasingly being used) out of the struggle for liberation and modernization by hungry and 'inferior' peoples.

One-party states in the Old World are responses to long-developed and deep-rooted division in society. The one-party state in the new countries, however, expresses the opposite; the genuine unity of the country. As Brenan's classic analysis of Spanish history shows, the triumph of Franco was only the last act in a long-drawn-out struggle, ultimately stemming from the division of Spain into radically different socio-economic regions with characteristic class-patterns, whose political expression took the form of successive parties which changed from era to era but were always renewed.[82]

When a society is chronically divided in this way, tensions which generate periodic protest and violence inevitably ensue, and evoke counter-reactions. France today presents a similar picture of chronic crisis, and has done for a long time. It is the product of a balance of forces in which there is no overwhelmingly predominant working-class as in England, but a working-class which has had to contend with a numerous peasantry and an unusually numerous and militant shop-keeping petty bourgeoisie, as well as a Church and a powerful capitalist class.[83] Even at its post-war height, the French Communist Party could never command enough support outside the working-class to consolidate its power and withstand the inevitable counter-offensive (leaving aside the fatal effects of subservience to Moscow.) In a situation of tensionful stalemate, 'strong government' is usually one of the 'answers' thrown up. In 1936, Spanish reaction tried precisely this 'solution'. De Gaulle produced a less violent, characteristically Gallic, 'Bonapartist' variant.

The kind of polity that is emerging in the new states may thus formally resemble other one-party systems, but is, in fact, a distinctive phenomenon: the response of seriously-under-developed countries, with democratic aims, to the demands of decolonization. As to the less attractive aspects of this kind of political system, it is necessary to remember, too, that both West and East have provided some of the models used. The Soviet one-party system and the Gaullist One-Emperor system have been particularly influential. The Old World has not taught the Third World democracy alone, as Western ideologists would have it.

It has also taught much that is quite inimical to democracy: the theory and practice of un-democracy. But these models would probably not have been used had they not proved congenial. Had they not been there, they would have had to be invented, like the Devil. The single-party in the new states has one major feature distinguishing it from Old World types. While it disposes of almost total political power and controls the state machine, it does not have unqualified control over the economy. The major industries, if any, the plantations, the mines, the communications systems, the banks, generally remain in the hands of foreign Big Business. This Big Business does now have to reckon with the uneasy presence of a Government which can seriously harm it, and which – in the more radical countries – is actively determined to bend the economy of the country in new socialist directions. Big Business can be seriously harmed. If it plays safe, a *modus vivendi* can be reached. Ashanti Goldfields, though obliged, along with other firms, to raise wages, and to devote, in future, a large proportion of its profits to reinvestment in Ghana, could still make net profits of £1,135,624 in 1961. The relationship between private business and government remains unsolved and problematical.

In most new countries where the single party does flourish, overt political differences still persist, though in some, the holder of anti-government opinions is not likely to sleep easily of nights. After the Preventive Detention Act and the dismissal of Ghana's Chief Justice, it becomes less comforting to tell ourselves that there are still Royal Commissions, and still a Parliament, in Ghana, or that the initial period of stabilization of a new state is bound to be attended with extreme challenges to the legitimacy and authority of the state. (The historically-minded point to the number of incarcerations during the similar period of formation of the Gold Coast as a colony.)[84]

But the one-party state of Africa, for example, is quite simply *not* a party organized on thoroughgoing Leninist principles. An observer at the Second National Conference of the Parti Démocratique Guinéene at Kissidougou remarked that 'Guinea may be a stridently one-party state, but it seemed a lively party'.[85] Nothing is more striking on the ground than the divisions within these formally 'monolithic' organizations which have not had time, in fact, to bed down into rigid orthodoxy. The divisions are usually only of a personal or factional kind, more rarely those of principle or ideology. As the Sekondi-Takoradi strike indicated, unless a party sets out on a wholesale, deliberate policy of repression, differences of interest will out. Trade unions, youth organizations, women's organizations, etc. are susceptible to the pressures of the people they represent as well as susceptible to Government and Party pressure. And even if such organizations are dissolved or lose their autonomy, this does not, of course, mean that the sectional interests which they cater for thereby disappear. If open expression of differences of interest is suppressed, it only goes either underground or into the dominant party itself. We have seen, in Europe, much more rigorous and 'rationalistic' attempts at creating monolithic societies, where differences have yet persisted and have been carried right into the councils of the single party. 'Sovietology', especially 'Kremlinology', after all, largely consists in the evaluation of the relative size and influence of the contending interest-groups within Soviet society and within the Party: technocrats, workers, peasants, youth, intellectuals, consumerists, partisans of heavy industry, liberalizers, the military, Stalinists, pure factionalists and so on. The 'suppressed' differences are merely carried into the committees of the party, and fought out within their confines. A pure 'monocentric' society is, in fact, a logical impossibility, and an illusion. To take the supreme case of a Right-wing, late-capitalist attempt at 'monocentric' Party rule – the Nazi state – we know that its internal unity was in large measure fictional, and that even given Party domination and co-ordination, the Nazi Party still had to dominate and co-ordinate men according to criteria which had to be decided upon. Those decisions were fought out between contending groups. The Nazi Party was, as Neumann put it, a 'ruling class with four wings'.[86] This society, formally and to a large extent in reality, too, organized on 'the principle of absolute and magical leadership . . . in a strict hierarchy', was in fact 'to a considerable extent held together by a network of rackets' and a further fantastic complexity of 'private rackets'.[87]

References to Nazism and to Stalinism serve to remind us that Europe has no monopoly of political rectitude. The tone of much of the criticism levelled at the new states, therefore, seems particularly offensive to leaders of emergent countries who may have imprisoned some of their opponents,* but who themselves have 'graduated' in the colonial prisons their critics endorsed. They feel that their modest peccadilloes offer no serious competition to a Europe which has killed, tortured, and imprisoned tens of millions within living memory. To the new countries, hydrogen bombs and concentration camps are as much a part of the European heritage as penicillin and parliamentary institutions.

Moreover, when they examine Western parliamentary democracy, or some of its extra-parliamentary manifestations at least, they are genuinely puzzled. Which of the many variants, exactly, is the 'best' democracy – the British, French (*sic*), or American systems? And if each of these 'democratic' countries has evolved its appropriate variant of democracy, so that none can be said to be 'better' than another, why not similarly develop a democracy relevant to African culture and history and African contemporary needs? Is it 'freedom' for one man to influence the opinions of eleven million readers of his newspaper, or – as in Ceylon – ought the Press to be in some way responsible to the *public*?

Once we begin asking these questions, we begin to see that they constitute a challenge to the weary thinking of the Old World, with its assumptions of ineffable superiority. For though the single-party system of some of the new states contains dangers for democracy and for world security, so does the France of de Gaulle, the America of Johnson, the Britain of Home, and the USSR of Krushchev.

Nevertheless, in renewing the institutional impediments to potential totalitarianism, in the one-party states at least, one cannot, with great confidence, point to any definite feature that seems to ensure the preservation of democracy. The strongest insurance appears singularly intangible and weak – yet it may, in fact, prove so ultimately significant that it will preserve freedom more effectively than any formal constitutional devices. This is the cultural inheritance of independence, self-reliance, co-operation, and equality; the belief in freedom, in participation, in decentralization, all of which, as we have seen, are as much part of traditional culture, particularly at low level, as are more

* In Ghana, Nigeria, and Senegal at least there have been plots to overthrow the new governments by force; in Togo and Gabon they succeeded.

negative traditions at higher levels, and have been augmented and adapted to modern conditions during the struggle for independence. Though the past leaves legacies which hold the Third World back, it also offers living and positive traditions which are a powerful source of democratic, egalitarian and socialist sentiment and action.

CHAPTER SIX

THE HUNGRY PEOPLES AND THE AFFLUENT BLOCS: POSITIVE NEUTRALISM

So FAR we have largely been looking at the new societies from the inside. Yet we did stress that they have become what they are under the quite specific conditions of an emergent world-system, and that it is this essentially *external* impact that has shaped their internal development.

Now, these countries, for the first time, are turning their eyes outwards, beyond their boundaries. They, too, have begun to act on the world stage, with such remarkable co-ordination that within a very few years they have emerged as the third major political grouping in the world.

Conservative and militant alike, reactionary and progressive, socialist and royalist, have shown an extraordinary tendency to adopt similar positions in international affairs. 'Conservatives' can be extremely militant: a Tungku Abdul Rahman could take the lead in driving South Africa out of the Commonwealth; a Northern Nigerian Prime Minister break off diplomatic relations with France over the Sahara atom-tests; a Bourguiba promote the bloody battle of Bizerta, and a 'non-violent' India take Goa. In Cambodia, a former King has become leader of a militant mass party.

For no matter what their other interests, they are still faced with the consequences of colonization. They are eager to help others who have not yet achieved political independence to strike off the yoke. So Tanganyika provides a haven for nationalists from Mozambique and Southern Rhodesia; Algeria trains guerillas from Angola. 'Conservatives' and 'militants' both share a common antipathy to colonialism, whether it takes the form of alien political rule, as in the Portuguese African territories, or continued foreign economic domination, as, say, in Nigeria. Decolonization keeps the ex-colonies united to this degree. Whatever their internal divisions, the Other still stands there, a constant spur to the harmonization of diverse interests.

Afro-Asian nationalists, of course, sometimes pretend that these common interests override all other divisions between them. They do not. There have been most bitter and acrimonious disputes between the Islamic countries of the Middle East; between Pakistan and India; between countries 'd'expression française' – or, more to the point, 'd'expression gaulliste' – and those of English 'descent', or 'obedience', to use the French terminology. There are differences of ideology between militant Leftist countries like Guinea or Mali, and states like Mba's Gabon, or Houphouët-Boigny's Ivory Coast, whose 'independence' of France is not very obvious. There are obvious competitors, too, for Pan-African leadership – Nkrumah, Nasser, Touré, Senghor. Rival trade union organizations also continuously jockey for position.

But much more striking than the disputes between the new states has been the extent of their co-operation. Before the 1950s, the division between 'pagan' Africa, South of the Sahara, and Islamic, Arab-Berber North Africa, was the accepted division of Africa. Today, it is not. Traditions shaped over centuries have been overthrown in a few years. Now, Morocco and Liberia, Ghana and Egypt, Angola and Algeria, co-operate. They co-operate because, despite other differences, they share a common past of domination by the White Other, a linked history of struggle for independence, and a common present of struggle against poverty in a Cold War World.

It is because of this that a distinct pattern is discernible in the external as well as the internal political orientation of the new countries. By now, we are all well aware of the rapid growth in influence of the 'Afro-Asian' grouping at the United Nations, whose actions are based upon a philosophy of 'positive neutralism.'

They are bound together, then, by a continuing shared interest in the anti-imperialist struggle. But in addition, large contiguous areas of the globe, formerly divided among the European Powers, are re-discovering older cultural links, obscured or suppressed under colonialism. Their history as colonies has provided them

with new allegiances that formerly did not exist. Following independence, new kinds of solidarities begin to assert themselves.
The legacy of local particularism remains, but there are very
strong and growing pressures towards unity on a higher plane than
that formed by the boundaries of the state. African nationalism,
for these reasons, operates – unlike the classic Western European
nation-state – not just within the boundaries of, say, the 'Nigerian'
nation, but at both narrower and wider ranges, and these affiliations command just as much, often more, emotional allegiance
as the 'Nigerian nation'.

Countries still fighting for independence have little leisure to
devote to considering the future shape of the nation. Asked
recently about his views on a Federation of East Africa, Dr Banda
replied sardonically: 'At this time I am concerned with another
federation down here, and we are fighting to get out of that!'[1]

To the already-independent countries, the liberation of the
remaining colonies is a primary preoccupation. The very last
page of Kwame Nkrumah's book, celebrating the independence
of Ghana asserts firmly:

'Our task is not done and our own safety is not assured until the last
vestiges of colonialism have been swept from Africa'.[2]

They are not merely paranoid, or deluded, in being so concerned.
They have seen political and military threats to Morocco and
Tunisia from *ultras* in Algeria, and challenges to Indonesian
sovereignty from the Dutch. For the new African States, South
Africa, leagued with Southern Rhodesia, Portugal-in-Southern
Africa, and industrial interests in Katanga, constitutes a dangerous
and ever-present threat.

The colonial boundaries are, inevitably, the point of departure
for the new nationalisms, for the independence of the particular
colonies is the only practical kind of independence for which these
territories can realistically agitate, and normally the outgoing
colonial Power has, in fact, transferred sovereignty over the whole
of the former territory. Only the viciously intransigent, like
the Dutch in Irian, have attempted to hang on to portions of the
new national territory. To Indonesians, the demand for Irian was
not, as foreigners frequently assumed, merely a device to promote
internal solidarity in a sadly-divided country – though it was that

as well – but itself a stimulus to this very disunity, with foreign adventurers, US fliers and Dutch mercenaries, bombing Indonesian towns, operating underground, setting up 'independent republics' in the Moluccas, using Irian as a *place d'armes*, and repressing movements favouring union with Indonesia in Irian itself.[3]

The really serious unfinished problems of the boundaries of the new states, however, are not these local disputes over marginal zones: Irian, Kashmir, or the 'lost provinces' of Bunyoro. They concern the viability of the new states as totalities. The most serious legacy of colonialism is in the economic sphere, in the form of backwardness, monocultural economies, foreign ownership of major resources, uneconomic 'dwarf states', poverty, and an extremely poor economic base for the kind of political 'rationalization' that Pan-Africanism envisages.

Countries like Gabon, with a population of only 420,000, Chad with 2,730,000, or Congo-Brazzaville with 795,000, do not make serious sense. Whole countries are vast farms producing palm-oil, peanuts, bananas, or cocoa. This economic specialization makes them desperately dependent upon world buyers. In the extreme they may be dependent upon only a single crop. In Mali, for example, the basis of the modern economy is, literally, peanuts; in Zanzibar, *cloves* alone have been the basis of the market economy for decades. The import trade, too, is commonly in the hands of foreign firms: in Ghana, 85 per cent of imports are controlled by European firms (the United African Company, the Unilever subsidiary, pre-eminent among them). For the more backward, monoculturally specialized, dwarf states, their room for manoeuvre is minimal, despite formal political independence.

Nevertheless, nationalists continue to demand independence, even for dwarf territories. The most recent tragi-comic case has been the setting-up of the West Indian islands as independent states, with consequences in British Guiana already which may well be reproduced even in the other, better developed islands in the future. Nor have nationalists hesitated to break up wider federations into 'unviable' components, where – as in Central Africa – federation was a device for holding back African-majority control. But political break-up has not only frustrated White-constructed federations; it has also, for the time being, deferred the realization of the hopes of Pan-Africanists, and of Pan-Negro, Pan-Arab, and Pan-Islamic, enthusiasts. Nationalists have insisted on independence, despite immediate negative consequences, because for them, to invert Lenin, it is a case of 'One Step Backward, Two Steps Forward'.

The African nationalist argues that colonialism is neither an economic nor a political system, but a *total* social system. Political independence is the prime prerequisite for freeing the society from foreign economic domination; following political independence, federation is the next step for economies which are too unbalanced or weak to constitute 'viable' economic units on their own.

Many Western economists, however, insist upon the irrelevance of political considerations to anyone engaged in making 'purely' economic calculations. Nationalism, and 'Pan' movements, are, to them, 'non-rational' factors which, at worst, get in the way of dispassionate, objective economic analysis, and therefore impede the taking of sound decisions about development, or at best, have to be taken into account as irritating, non-rational 'facts of the situation'. They are, in short, 'values' which run counter to 'economic logic'.

The African nationalist thus finds himself under fire on the grounds that no economy can be autarchically 'independent', least of all the raw-materials-producing ex-colonial economies which depend essentially for their foreign earnings on trade with the developed world. 'Rational' economic organization, it is argued, calls for the maintenance of established relationships with the advanced countries (though – to use Weber's terminology – 'substantive' rationality does require recognition of the existence of 'non-rational' (e.g. nationalist) sentiments). Political independence is therefore held to be an *economically* retrograde step. The belief that industrialization and the mechanization of agriculture can rectify this built-in weakness of colonized economies is also questioned: the 'mystique of the tractor' is challenged by reference to disasters such as the Groundnut Scheme or China's 'Great Leap Forward'. The 'Third World' seems eternally doomed to be the barnyard of the whole world. Finally, the glaring lack of complementarity between the economies of the various African states is stressed. As a final, crushing argument, the examples of New Zealand and Denmark – specialized agrarian economies closely dependent upon Britain – are held to demonstrate (*a*) that political independence is quite compatible with tied markets and with close political association with an industrialized power, and (*b*) that agrarian, and not solely industrialized, economies can produce very high living-standards. 'Imbalance' and 'viability' are therefore held to be subjective, value-loaded, and unscientific terms; Pan-Africanism a dream and a delusion.

Finally, political scientists influenced by linguistic analysis point out that 'total' or 'pure' independence are metaphysical terms; logically, no country can be wholly independent.

Theorists in the new African countries sometimes reply to these arguments with more heat than logic. Senghor, for example, quite misses the point of Marx's insistence that 'humanity', 'liberty', 'equality', 'fraternity', and 'independence' are not absolutes, but concepts which take on different meanings in differing social contexts and which are often cynically manipulated by ruling classes to suit their ideological book:

'You hear: *independence*. If the founder of scientific socialism returned to the world, he would perceive, with amazement, that these 'chimeras', as he calls them, and especially the Nation, are the living realities of the twentieth century'.

A more relevant riposte to this kind of critique of nationalism is developed by those African thinkers who stress the inter-relationship of the economic and political orders. The economists amongst them, for instance, accept that the New Zealand or Danish cases are interesting. But they also point to the worries, even for countries like New Zealand, currently presented by the European Common Market, precisely because of the extreme specialization, and hence vulnerability, of the economy of that country. 'Viability', they suggest, is not a 'purely' economic concept; 'purely' economic choices, uninfluenced by values, do not exist. Concepts such as 'viability', they hold are, in fact, neither purely 'economic', nor 'political'; the political and economic orders are not dissociated spheres, but dimensions of the single realm of *political economy*. Their own guiding values are quite explicit: they want to maximize their freedom to manoeuvre to create a humane and modernized total society, and to associate with countries of like mind. These goals, they believe, cannot be realized within the framework of a country of two million people who survive by supplying France with bananas. And they point out that New Zealand's position, in fact, involves a deep political dependence on Britain, something which African countries are endeavouring to escape from, not to recreate.

They also reject the notion of 'the economy' as an enclosed sphere of production and market activities within which the production and exchange of 'things' takes place in a manner somehow unaffected by social values. 'Economic' choice is, they hold, directly affected by values. There often follows a kind of Afro-Asian variation upon the Galbraithian critique of the a-morality of Western economies, as contrasted with the human-centred values built into African traditional economies. Economic philosophies which accept individual competition and the consumption of material goods as the highest ends of human life are treated scornfully.

But they do recognize the limitations of the dwarf society. The establishment of national independence, therefore, they say, is only a first step. The nation is not an absolute, but a 'vocation', to use Mamadou Dia's term. Internationalism is the other face of the new nationalism. But the problem of choice remains: with whom does one associate, for what ends, and on what terms? Association with other decolonizing states or continued association with the Great Powers of Euro-America?

In the former French territories of Africa, with the notable exception of Guinea, fear of the negative consequences of 'balkanization' frightened most territories into retaining membership of the French 'Community', even leftish Mali or Senegal, as well as – obviously – conservative, francophile regimes like the Ivory Coast or Gabon. These countries feared what, in fact, did come to pass in the Congo and Guinea: that the imperial Power would pull out, totally and immediately, leaving chaos behind it. Some states genuinely desire the French connection; others are terrified of the alternative, poor and ill-equipped as they are; yet others see it as a bridge to a more real ultimate independence.

Despite nominal commitment to Pan-Africanism, most of the new countries remain economically dependent upon the 'reformed' imperial Powers.

The only major alternative available at present is the equally undesirable one of economic dependence on the Soviet bloc, the very condition that has been forced on Cuba by the intransigence of the American ultras, and very nearly upon Guinea by French intransigence. Cuba's experience in becoming sucked into the Soviet–American nuclear struggle is hardly likely to reassure the new countries of the virtues of the Soviet connection.

The two positive alternatives which offer hope of avoiding Cold War entanglement and 'neo-colonialist' dependence are economic co-operation between the emergent countries themselves, and international development under world-organization auspices.

The first of these is naturally the most attractive. The colonial boundaries are clearly unsuitable: they are clearly not going to determine future political or economic arrangements. To that extent, Pan-Africanism is a built-in technical necessity. From Nigeria's Jaja Wachuku to Nyasaland's Banda, African politicians have lamented the dismantling of inter-African organizations, from West African airways and currency systems to educational systems and shipping companies. For a while, however, demolition has been the order of the day, part of the conditions of independence.

Yet Pan-Africanism is rapidly becoming a technical, as well as a political fact. Initially, Pan-Africanism meant political co-ordination alone. The effects of the numerous political Conferences and Congresses have been very real, not merely an accumulation of paper resolutions, as the recent founding of a unified military organization for Africa demonstrates. This co-ordinated pressure helped bring independence to most of Africa, and to make African and Afro-Asian groupings international forces. But in infrastructural fields, too, a series of less spectacular but equally effective agreements: on the harmonization of communications systems, on surveys, customs arrangements, on health and educational programmes: have been concluded. Most notably, a Plan for the development of higher education for the *whole* of Africa has been agreed upon by a Conference of African States at Addis Ababa in May 1961. Rather than each state trying to establish its own small university, the number of future universities is to be limited to thirty-two, which will provide facilities for the continent as a whole.[5] The outlines of a co-ordinated Plan to eliminate illiteracy by 1980 have also been worked out.

Intra-African or intra-Third World economic co-operation is much more difficult, however. Some hard tokens of intent have indeed been given: Ghana's loan of £10 million, for example, helped Guinea survive the blow of French withdrawal. But the task of co-ordinating the economies of the new African states is fantastically difficult in a situation which looks like this:[6]

TABLE 5. DISTRIBUTION OF TRADE OF SELECTED AFRICAN TERRITORIES, 1950–7; PERCENTAGES OF TOTAL TRADE

		Imports %	Exports %
French African Community (a)	Trade with French franc area	74·7	75·3
Congo	Trade with Belgium	37·1	52·7
Sterling Area Africa (b)	Trade with Sterling area	66·7	63·6
Sterling Area Africa (b)	Trade with UK	46·0	51·0
Union of South Africa	Trade with Sterling Area	45·9	51·0

(a) French Cameroons, French West Africa, French Equatorial Africa, Guinea, Malagasy.

(b) Federation of Rhodesia and Nyasaland, Kenya, Tanganyika, Uganda, Nigeria, Sierra Leone, Mauritius.

Source: UN Economic Survey of Africa since 1950, pp. 154–7.

TABLE 6. INTER-AFRICAN TRADE: SELECTED AFRICAN TERRITORIES, 1950–7; PERCENTAGES

	Imports %	Exports %	Total %
French West Africa	8·7	12·6	10·4
Congo (incl. Ruanda Urundi)	7·7	4·6	6·1
Ghana	6·1	2·5	4·2
Kenya, Uganda, Tanganyika (a)	4·2	8·0	6·0
Nigeria	0·8	1·3	1·0
Federation of Rhodesia and Nyasaland (b)	36·4	18·1	26·9
Union of South Africa (c)	8·5	10·8	9·5

(a) including trade between these countries
(b) including trade between members of the Federation prior to 1954.
(c) including South West Africa from 1955.

These tables indicate two things: the extraordinary dependence of all the agrarian states on their former colonial masters or on 'the West' combined, and the exceptionally small amount of trade between African states. All they have to pool and exchange is their poverty: only the mineral-producing and industrialized states of southern Africa trade to any important extent with other African territories. The rest have little to send each other except the same raw materials and foodstuffs – and what is the point of exchanging peanuts? Little wonder that Nigeria – which only sends 10 per cent of her exports to other African countries – is not very interested in Pan-Africanism, or that the ex-French territories with a much larger trade between them retain closer political links.

The political independence of the new states of Africa is real enough for all but the dwarf states of former French Africa. But no country can be freed overnight from the ties which bind every peasant to the markets of Europe. Guinea, for example, the country which has most ruthlessly accomplished total political decolonization, had to be kept afloat by aid from the Soviet bloc, and from the dollar earnings of the foreign-owned bauxite mines at Fria and the Loos Islands.[7]

Even the militantly socialist leaderships, therefore, are very careful not to jeopardize their economic survival by nationalizing foreign-owned enterprise, lest they kill the goose that lays the golden eggs. Even Guinea has now made a *rapprochement* with France. The usual course for the socialist governments has been the kind of tactic adopted in Ghana, where the rate of company tax was stiffened, wage-increases of 20 per cent were insisted on, plus an increased investment locally of 60 per cent of net profits after tax. Since this left the mining companies still with dividend rates of 45 per cent, the prospect did not terrify them. The companies now scrupulously steer clear of any suggestion of direct interference in the national economy, and are rapidly 'indigenizing' their staffs.

But the 'colonial' character of the economy remains. The African countries can help each other little. Capital is accumulated internally all too slowly. Recourse to external aid seems inevitable. Yet here, once more, the 'proletarian nations' find themselves in the same life-situation. They come with palms outstretched to ask for bread, and they are offered – capitalism or communism. They get aid largely as part of the world strategies of the two rival blocs. 'Aid' is neither disinterested Christian charity, nor proletarian internationalism; it is a political and military weapon in the world power-struggle.

At this point, the new states boil over. Between their society of hoes and goats, and the Euro-American world of space-rockets and blast-furnaces, there is a Grand Canyon full of bitterness and mutual mistrust. This is the great 'alienation' of the twentieth century, to them far more vicious and dehumanizing than any gulf between worker and bourgeois in capitalist society. On the one hand, the capitalist *and socialist* 'millionaires', to use Nyerere's words; on the other, 'the damned of the earth', as Fanon calls them.

Sékou Touré has expressed this view most explicitly of all: 'The major division in the world today', he remarks, 'is not between East and West, but between the under-developed and the developed countries of the world.' Senghor goes further, and asserts that although the European or American worker is oppressed and alienated under capitalism, he, like the capitalist and everyone else in the 'over-developed' world, benefits from the exploitation of Afro-Asia, and Latin America. His formulation is important:

'In brief, the proletarians of Europe have benefited from the colonial regime; *therefore they have never really – I mean, effectively – opposed it.*'[8]

This view has also been expressed by some Left-wing European writers on the Third World, notably by Sartre and by the geographer Buchanan, who cites with approval Moussa's statement that the 'efforts of Western workers to raise their standards of living have contributed more to the deterioration of the position of the under-developed countries than has the profit motive of industrial or commercial leaders'.[9]

Such views have, of course, long been current on the Right, when they have been used as an argument from self-interest to 'justify' the retention of imperial holdings. They now occur on the Left. More extreme forms of these theories circulate in the Third World itself; in essence, traditional socialist internationalism has been replaced by a new kind of revolutionary theory in which the major conflict is seen as one between the hungry 'proletarian nations' and affluent Euro-America, capitalist or communist. A mystique of 'the colonial disinherited' replaces the solidarity of *all* the exploited in class-society. There is too, a kind of Sorelian celebration of 'cleansing' violence which will rejuvenate the earth and transform former slaves and former masters alike into human beings. Though the socialist terminology remains, in the course of this argument, international class solidarity has been subtly transformed into inter-*national* antagonism.

The temptations of such a view are obvious enough, especially in countries like Fanon'a adopted Algeria, where the betrayal of the French Left has been so patent.

When the new states speak of themselves as 'proletarian nations', they see themselves in the image of Marx's working-class, as an emergent social grouping which, under the politico-economic domination of the wealthy propertied states, have been exploited and robbed of human status. Under this oppression, they have developed a consciousness of their common fate; they have thrown up, initially, 'defensive' organizations (the equivalent of Lenin's 'trade union consciousness'). Ultimately, they have made the transition to revolutionary and collective *political* consciousness and action, through which they will bring about not only their own liberation, but also the world-historic destruction of the power-apparatus oppressing all humanity. The imperialists themselves will be freed from the curse of dehumanizing superiority which distorts their lives as much as inferiority distorts the lives of the oppressed. The particular struggle of the proletarian nations thus has a universal significance. Their revolution will be a *socialist* one which will permanently alter the 'human condition'.[10]

Since the 'proletarian nations' have appropriated for themselves the role of Marx's proletariat, as grave-digger of capitalism, there is little historical role left for the proletariat of the advanced countries. In the new theoretical model, they are either passive or active accomplices of imperialism, so long corrupted that they have become historically insignificant as a revolutionary force.

If the proletariat of the advanced countries has been displaced by the revolutionary peasantry of the backward countries, so has the country which produced the first major revolution of our times. To thinkers like Ly, capitalist imperialism is the primordial enemy, but Soviet imperialism is no less imperialism.

Some of the political leaders of the new countries, too, have been quick to take up this theme. Julius Nyerere, for example, speaks as a socialist and a Catholic:

'I believe that *the purpose of Socialism was to remove the sin of Capitalism, and to return wealth to its original use – the satisfaction of simple human needs, the banishment of poverty* . . . this is happening in the socialist countries. . . .

But . . . the socialist countries themselves, considered as individuals in the larger society of nations, are now committing the same crime which was committed by the capitalists before. . . . On the international level, they are beginning to use the wealth for the purpose of acquiring power and prestige! . . . Socialist countries, no less than capitalist countries, are prepared to behave like the millionaire – to use millions to destroy another "millionaire", and it need not necessarily be a capitalist "millionaire" – it is just as likely to be a socialist "millionaire". In other words, socialist wealth now tolerates poverty – which is an even more unforgivable crime!

I believe that no under-developed country can afford to be anything but "socialist". . . .

. . . Karl Marx felt that there was an inevitable clash between the rich of one society and the poor of that society. In that I believe Karl Marx was right. But today it is the international scene that is going to have a greater impact. . . . the world is still divided between the "haves" and the "have-nots". This division is not a division between the poor countries of the world and the rich countries of the world . . . the poor countries . . . should be very careful not to allow themselves to be used as the tools of any of the rich countries. . . . And don't forget that the rich countries . . . may be found on either side of the division between capitalist and socialist countries.'[11]

This theme has already made its way into organized politics. At the Afro-Asian Solidarity Conference at Moshi, Tanganyika, in February 1963, Nyerere returned again to the 'Scramble for Africa' theme, called for federation and socialism, and appealed for unity and non-interference. After deploring the assassination of the President of Togo, he remarked:

'The imperialists, old and new, will exploit the differences *within* African nations *and between* African nations . . . the weaker amongst us are regarded as no more than pawns in the Cold War conflicts. . . .'[12]

Two months later, in Kenya, the Kenya African National Union issued an election manifesto proposing a socialist republic, non-aligned with either East or West. Referring specifically to Tanganyikan ideas, it declared that the Marxist theory of class warfare had no relevance to the Kenyan situation, and warned against 'more subtle' forms of imperialism, Western or Communist.[13]

One can easily see why the Soviet Union no longer seems as revolutionary a force in the Third World as it still appears to be to Western leaders. In a world in which the major division is that between poor and rich countries, Western and Eastern blocs are *both* advanced, industrial – and White – countries. They struggle between themselves, neglecting the problems of two-thirds of humanity, and using their poverty as a means of extending their rival political systems. The African visiting the Soviet Union feels as alien in the face of Soviet industrial strength and ever-increasing affluence, as he does when he visits the cities, factories, and pleasure-domes of the Western capitals.

The Third World, basically, is not very interested in the wrang-lings of Europe. For them, the future of the hungry two-thirds is the dominating issue. Their attitudes towards the world outside their boundaries are thus largely dictated by the state of society within their boundaries. It is the obverse of their common poverty, their first concern. But they know, too, that this poverty is itself an historical product, that their societies are products of colonization, that they have been *made* like this by human action, and that they can now be *un*-made, or *re*-made, into something new and higher, by human action.

Independence is merely the beginning of this process. True, there are those, like President Léon Mba of the client Gabon Republic, who declared on an official State visit to Paris that 'Gabon is independent, but between Gabon and France nothing has changed, everything continues as before'.[14] But the peoples of Africa certainly *expect* significant changes to take place, and quickly. Most political leaders have to pay at least lip-service to the aim of social transformation: no government dare profess anything else – even more serious, no government dare fall behind in the race to turn those words into action. Otherwise they fall, unless they are a Gabon, whose uranium merits intervention by French paras.

Even the most conservative are interested in a certain minimum of decolonization. For some, it has scarcely gone beyond running up a new flag to the sound of a new national anthem. It was not unexpected that a Houphouët-Boigny would defy majority opinion in the Third World by participating in the Mollet Suez cabinet; more surprising, perhaps, that a Senghor could casually comment on the French Sahara tests: 'If two hundred and seven bombs have already been exploded, why protest about the two hundred and eighth?'

In flouting Third World feeling so openly, these leaders are playing with fire. More normally, even figures so far removed from radicalism as Their Majesties Hassan II of Morocco and Haile Selassie of Ethiopia may be found supporting China's admission to the United Nations or denouncing American pressure on Cuba. The conservative Muslim leaders of Nigeria were quite as decisive in their reaction to the French tests as the militant leaders of Ghana or Guinea.

Even for the conservatives, things can never be quite the same again. Neither Britain nor France can command the automatic support of their former ex-colonies for old-imperialist policies or for neo-colonialist policies. Totally undemocratic regimes like Pakistan's or South Korea's military governments, or Diem's South Viet Nam, can, of course, be relied upon to slot without question into the NATO–SEATO–CENTO set of alliances. But no new state struggles to be free merely in order to surrender to new forms of alien control, whether the aliens are old acquaintances, or new ones. They are no more attracted by Soviet society, either, except as a model of rapid socialist modernization. Africans are not interested in the internal consistency of Marxism or in its theoretical dogmas; they *are* concerned with the relevance of Soviet institutions and Marxist ideas to the African situation. As the pragmatic Touré puts it: 'Philosophy does not interest us. We have concrete needs:

You must understand that all our thoughts, all our actions are mobilized by Africa, and essentially for Africa. Ours is not a formal neutralism, and neither events in Iraq, nor in Tibet, will make us modify this appreciation. The world needs peace, but we, too, need peace in the world. We wish to stand aside from the quarrels and antagonisms whose development does not impinge upon the historical development of Africa.'[15]

The tone of detachment is severe, intended, and highly significant. People in 'East 'and 'West', convinced that the whole meaning of the world is the meaning given it in Bonn, London, New York, or Moscow, genuinely cannot understand such 'neutralism'. In crude but honest extreme, Mr Dulles thought it 'immoral'. Mr George Meany, President of the AFL–CIO, remarked as recently as 1955, the year of Bandung, that:

'. . . Nehru and Tito are not neutral, they are aides and allies of Communist imperialism – in fact and in effect, if not in diplomatic verbiage.'

It is difficult for a man who assumes that the 'American century' is a reality and not just an aspiration, or who sees the world as a Western soap-opera of 'baddies' versus 'goodies' ('Communists' versus 'democrats') to understand that there can be such a thing as a genuinely neutral position. In the Communist world, too, the non-aligned Powers were long denounced as 'running dogs of imperialism'. For anyone departing from the assumption that the struggle between labour and capital is fundamental, this statement by a Moroccan nationalist could be nothing more than a bourgeois obfuscation of the centrality of the class struggle:

'Our creeds must be of our own creation, or, if derived from [elsewhere], adjusted to suit our own needs and temperaments. So *a labour union should not be regarded as anything more than one aspect of organizing the Moroccan nation.*'[16]

It would not, of course, be difficult for Soviet (or even American) trade unionists to comprehend nationalist desires to integrate trade unionism within the total social system of which it is a part. What is quite inadmissible for the 'East' is al-Fāsi's tacit rejection of proletarian internationalism; what the West finds unacceptable is the omission of any reference to the overriding struggle of 'democracy' against 'Communism'. Equally offensive to both camps is the realization that this nationalism is not old-style nationalism at all: it is part of a new kind of *international* allegiance which pulls against the bloc-system, its primary loyalties not to nation or bloc, but to the poor nations first, and the world next.

The new nations therefore prove difficult to discipline, at state or lower level. African trade unions, for example, have increasingly asserted positions independent of either WFTU or ICFTU. Even those who stayed within those world 'centres' helped turn them away from Cold War towards concern with world development.

But the most emphatic breakaway from Cold War trade unionism came with the establishment of UGTAN as a purely *African* trade union centre, in which Guinea played the leading role. She was not, however, successful in maintaining UGTAN affiliates in the other ex-French West African territories. Only the more militant independent African states – Ghana, Algeria, Mali, the UAR, and Kenya – followed her lead. Ghana, in particular, produced both her own strongly independent national trade movement, and co-operated with Guinea in the setting-up of another African international trade union centre – the All-Africa Trade Union Federation.[17]

Most national trade union federations, nevertheless, still maintain the international trade union links they had developed before independence, notably to the ICFTU, which has been denounced by Pan-African trade union leaders as a 'ravenous monster of subversion, sabotage, and vicious propaganda'.[18]

The world trade union movement is thus affected by the overall competition between doctrines of general international class solidarity on the one hand, and the doctrine of prime allegiance to the Third World on the other. Even those who profess socialism most vigorously nevertheless do so in terms which emphasize unity rather than division, empiricism rather than dogma. With Nkrumah, they see themselves as 'marching neither Right nor Left, but forward'. The forms of socialism historically evolved in Europe and America seem to them irrelevant to their situation; the East-West conflict as a fundamentally inhuman, perversely blind, and parochial obsession. For them, the wealthy third of the world, which prepares to destroy everything for the sake of illusory ideologies, while two-thirds of the world starves, has forfeited all claim on human respect; their high-sounding professions seem so much hypocrisy.

The touchstone of genuineness, for the Third World, is how one *acts* on the issue of colonial freedom. In Africa, it is the test of South Africa which divides the sheep from the goats. On this issue, Tanganyika and Algeria, Ghana and Senegal, Morocco and Ethiopia, stand together in the one camp; Britain, France, and Portugal, in the other. Here, Africans believe, the limits of European liberalism are reached, and the self-interest of the advanced world overrides all else.

Southern Africa permits no compromise. The soft 'winds of change' might blow in Tanganyika, even in Kenya, where the much-discussed White settlers numbered only a few thousand families anyhow, but in South Africa and Southern Rhodesia, in the Copper Belt of Northern Rhodesia, and in Katanga, the most valuable part of the whole continent is at stake.

South Africa's economic importance is extremely great: British investment alone amounts to £250,000,000.[19] But South Africa is important, too, as another 'extreme': it approximates closely to a 'pure' model of a totalitarian society.

It is split right across the middle by the division into White and Other. All the major clashes of interest are *between these same groupings of people*. Whites employ Blacks; they work at different kinds of work. The orders flow one way. For Blacks, menial jobs only. In Church, White and Black worship separately. Blacks cannot form trade unions, nor can they vote. For them, the city slums of Johannesburg and the rural slums of the reserves. For the others, the 'European' areas.

In Britain, according to the 1951 Census, 89·67 per cent of the occupied population were 'operatives'; only 2·04 per cent 'employers and managers'. But Britain, though sharply divided in this one very crucial field of relationship, is not South Africa. Twelve million people might have felt enough solidarity and common interest to vote Labour in 1959. Yet a third of British trade unionists did not. Nor do 'Conservatives' constitute a very homogeneous category in a mass democracy. Some are Roman Catholics, some Protestants. White collar workers commonly feel distinct from industrial manual workers, though under certain circumstances they, too, unionize very quickly.[20] Class solidarities thus certainly exist, but they are cross-cut in very complex ways by other important lines of cleavage. As G. D. H. Cole has remarked, in British society:

'... groups are ... fluid and diverse ..., their membership overlaps considerably, *élites* tend to emerge more on a functional than a general basis. ... A society organized in this manner will not have either a single *élite* presiding over all its affairs, or a number of rival *élites*, each at the head of a distinct faction of its people ... it will have instead *numerous élites*. ...'[21]

In Britain, therefore, it is possible for managers and directors to share some elements of common identity with clerks, anti-unionists, and Liberals. Roman Catholic businessmen and unskilled labourers may unite on issues like State aid for independent Roman Catholic schools, across class lines. But in South Africa, the cross-cutting allegiances are minimal. There are, it is true, divisions in the ranks both of White South Africans and Black South Africans. But they are increasingly overridden by the unifying, levelling pressure of racism which forces them all into a single mould. Non-White and White face each other in total opposition – in church, state, school, house, mine, cinema, bus. Repression has to be *total*. *All* aspects of life: the schooling children get or do not get; the jobs one is allowed or forced to do; the churches one can worship in; the places where one can live: everything is regulated. To enforce the regulations, police, soldiers, armoured cars, torture, jets, informers, become part of the normal conditions of life. For totalitarianism allows *no* 'free' areas of social or personal life: in Mills' terminology, it involves the co-ordination of *all* 'institutional orders'.[22] Without any effective cement of common ideology, force alone keeps the social structure in being.

Such a political system is very fragile: it depends on only one of the elements of government identified by Confucius, and the weakest one at that:

'Tzu Kung asked about governing, and the Master said, "Adequate supplies of food, adequate stores of munitions, and the confidence of the people." Tzu Kung said, "Suppose you unavoidably had to dispense with one of these, which would you forgo?" The Master said, "Munitions." Thereat Tzu King asked if of the remaining two he had to dispense with one, which he would forgo. The Master said "Food; for all down history death has come to all men (and yet society survives); but the people who have no confidence (in their rulers) are undone." '[23]

Confucius knew, as did Max Weber, that mere political power, reliance on force, is not enough. 'You can do anything with bayonets,' it was once remarked, 'except sit on them.' The strong government has in addition to the means of force, a stronger weapon – *legitimacy*. The people accept its *right* to rule. Such a government has *authority* as well as *power*.

In South Africa, there are no common values pervading the whole of society, accepted by all, which might provide such a basis of legitimacy. Step by step, what little community there was between White and Black has been eliminated. It has led to total division and total domination. It will end, as in Algeria and Angola, in total conflict.

Internally, the struggle is likely to be very different from the pattern in agrarian societies, for industrialization has brought into being a force which the rest of Africa lacks: an urban labour-force which, paradoxically, has grown mightily during the period of theoretical *apartheid* (for industrialists cannot afford to be shackled by the ideologies of politicians; they need labour). The involvement of this mass in the struggle for elementary democracy, under increasingly more uncompromising leadership, is only a matter of time. It will be encouraged by world opinion, by nationalism now rising in armed rebellion as nearby as Angola, and by more constitutional movements in Northern Rhodesia, Nyasaland, and Southern Rhodesia. But South Africa can hardly emulate any of these countries. The country lacks suitable mountains which a kindly Nature provided in Algeria. Ballot-boxes are out of the question. There remains straight mass conflict, especially industrial struggle and sabotage in the towns.

Just as the Tsars, in nineteenth-century Russia, or the British in India, succeeded in turning humane, cultured upper-class liberals into bomb-throwing terrorists, and ultimately in unleashing mass rebellion, so *apartheid* is doing today. The outcome, however, is likely to be profoundly affected by events outside the Republic. South Africa is scarcely purchasing jet planes merely to suppress riots in the native reserves.*

Neither White nor Black can realistically expect that South Africa will settle its internal problems without drawing in the outside world. For South Africa is the centre of an industrial network which dominates the rest of southern Africa. It draws labour from all over Central and East Africa. These places now have independent governments. They are involved in the whole Bandung world outside Africa. American and British capital, too, is involved. South Africa's diamonds, gold, and uranium weigh much heavier in the balance than Guinea's bananas, or the frankincense and myrrh, camel-hides and bananas, which figure so

---

* More than £200,000,000 worth of warships, jet aircraft, and artillery has been purchased from British arms manufacturers alone during the past five years (*Sunday Telegraph*, London, 31 March, 1963.)

largely in the exports of the Somali Republic. If imperialism does hold on in southern Africa, it can only expect to risk its remaining holdings and influence, not just in the rest of Africa, but in the rest of the world. Nor can one envisage the USSR, in a more polarized situation, continuing to sell her diamonds politely through De Beers. If she does ever take the decision to become involved in the southern African battle, as nearly happened in the Congo, the Last War might well be upon us.

Today, there can no longer be any remote 'frontier incidents', any 'little far-off countries of which we know nothing'. Before 1939, 'disturbances' on India's North-West Frontier could be handled by bombing the tribesmen; bayonets were usually enough. Today, India's frontier problems imperil the security, even the continued existence, of the whole world.

Because of conflicts in remote 'backwaters', the world has come near to total destruction on at least three major occasions since 1945: once, when General MacArthur sought permission to use nuclear weapons to bomb Manchuria; again, when the French generals at Dien Bien Phu called for US carriers off the coast to launch a nuclear strike; and again at Cuba in 1962. South Africa, similarly, could be the cause of a major war in Africa. Such a war could not be confined to African states alone. For no country can opt out of the world social system. As Haile Selassie put it at Belgrade: 'We can no more refrain from political activity in the year 1961 than man can voluntarily refrain from partaking of . . . radioactive fallout.' Even in Europe, home of the classical nation-state, new 'supra-national' economical and political groupings of states are emerging.

Although the new states commonly feel estranged from either camp in the Cold War, therefore, they do not isolate themselves; no country can afford to do so. But when they do take positions in the world arena, they are different positions. They steer clear of direct alignment with either side. Slowly, they have built up co-operation, in the first place, with their fellows in the under-developed world. The pioneering key role, in the Afro-Asian world, was played by India, whose 'non-involvement' was never of the negative, Swiss-Swedish type, and had deep roots in Hindu and Gandhian traditions of non-violence. This neutralism was always an activist neutralism.

Twice – in Korea and in Viet Nam – India played a decisive part in bringing hostilities to an end, and – by the device of partition – helped achieve a temporary stabilization, even, in the case of Viet Nam, without American approval. The habit of neutrality proved inter-continentally contagious in the era of the Thaw. It helped international relaxation in Europe as well, for Geneva led to the independence of occupied Austria, and ushered in a whole period of disengagement, including a halt in atomic testing.

But the new Asian states in the immediate post-war period had been far too weak and preoccupied to do very much. They emerged into nationhood, in the words of Hashim Jawad:

'. . . [in] a climate of defensive isolation when their principal purpose was to safeguard their freedom and independence and avoid getting involved in the power politics of the Big Powers.'

At the international level, therefore, notions of disengagement and neutralism were most notably canvassed on the European Left, where the Cold War conflicts were sharpest, rather than in Africa or Asia. The 'Third Force' conception was largely a European product at that time, and in the infertile climate of the Dulles–Stalin era, the seed perished. Despite this, the rejection of the Cold War, in very sharp and bitter form, was forced upon one country, Yugoslavia, which defied the Soviet, starved proudly for a while, and then accepted American aid, without, however, accepting political direction. Finally, the USSR, too, made her peace.

Yugoslavia's role in the development of what was to become a coherent neutralist doctrine did not stop there, for she also worked actively to lower the temperature of very 'warm-war' relations with Greece, and with Bulgaria. Finally, Europe reached out to non-Europe: Tito's contacts across the Mediterranean with Nasser were crucial in turning UAR policy, hitherto largely preoccupied with Arab questions, towards neutralism. Egypt's interests began to transcend even the three worlds described by Nasser[24] – the African, the Arab, and the Muslim. Under the influence of Nehru and Tito, Nasser himself became increasingly aware of the common interests not only of the Afro-Asian countries but of others who were struggling to 'disengage' from the blocs.[25]

These important and bold initiatives by weak countries like

India and Yugoslavia gave inspiration to peoples struggling for self-expression everywhere. In particular, it gave moral leadership to the growing number of ex-colonies which were coming to independence, as did the more violent independence struggles in Indonesia, Viet Nam, and Algeria. In Europe, too, Stalin's apocryphal remark 'And how many battalions has the Pope?' was shown to be a typical *realpolitik* underestimation of the power of ideas which were to move men into the historic battles of East Berlin, Poznan, and Budapest.

By 1955, the Afro-Asian states had become numerous and self-confident enough to take their first major step towards defining themselves as an independent force in the world. The Bandung Conference was essentially a compromise, however: it was not yet fully a *positive* neutralism, for it sought to accommodate its neutralism to the Eastern-bloc formula of 'peaceful co-existence', at that time skilfully enunciated at Bandung by Chou En-Lai. At Belgrade, six years later, Tito, looking back at Bandung, remarked sardonically that co-existence of that kind was 'better than war', but was, in fact, 'more like an armistice – and we actually had such co-existence between the world wars!'

The Bandung Declaration certainly paid important tribute to 'positive' principles. But in practice, the major emphasis at Bandung was largely *negative*: *abstinence* from intervention in other countries' internal affairs; *refraining* from threats or acts of aggression; *contracting out* of Big Power 'defence' arrangements, and so on.

The result was not so much a positive solution of international problems outside the framework of the blocs altogether (as with the neutralization of Austria, or, later, Laos), but usually the slicing-up of countries like Korea and Viet Nam, in the words of Prince Sihanouk of Cambodia, 'as if they were so many common or garden birthday cakes'. Panmunjom was the symbol of this wearing, hostile 'living-together'.

This kind of neutralism, then, was hardly positive, but as a first step towards sanity it was epoch-making. Countries which strove for real non-involvement, like little Cambodia, found themselves victims of infiltrating rival forces. The series of proddings by China all along her southern borders, within her traditional South Asian sphere of influence, was part of the 'hard' line which followed the brief interlude of the 'hundred flowers'. Its effect was to emphasize the gulf between positive neutralism and Communist 'co-existence-from-positions-of-strength'.

In 1957, the Third World, by now visible as a distinct force, received a new accession of strength. Arab Africa had already begun to detach itself from external control with Nasser's assumption of power in Egypt. Africa south of the Sahara did not begin to move until Ghana became independent on 6 March, 1957. Before long, militant African nationalism had three foci: Accra, Cairo, and Algeria. Within a few years the 'Afro-Asian' grouping at UNO became a significant force. With the beginning of the era of Macmillan's 'winds of change' and de Gaulle's Referendum, the numbers of the UN member-states swelled to such an extent that, in the 'Year of Africa', 1960, a specifically *African* grouping emerged within the now large Afro-Asian grouping. The original signatories to the UN Charter were soon far outnumbered – largely by states that had never existed in 1946.

The era of Big Power domination of the UN was effectively over. Automatic American majorities were no longer certain. Nor could the new countries be predictably aligned the same way at every vote. Most important of all, the poor nations began making their own initiatives.

They brought a new strength to the United Nations, not just as so many votes, but because their conception of the purposes of the organization was strictly internationalist, as distinct from bloc-oriented, and because, too, they sought to use the facilities of Lake Success to promote positive action to eliminate poverty and war, and not merely to make propaganda for Cold War advantage.

As a spokesman of a country that had been cruelly betrayed by the League of Nations – and one not renowned for its democratic enlightenment in other respects – Haile Selassie expressed his continuing faith in internationalism, despite everything, in moving words:

'For us, the small, the weak, the under-developed, there is nowhere else to go. If we turn to one or the other of the major power groups, we risk engorgement, that gradual process of assimilation which destroys identity and personality. We must, from force of circumstances, look to the United Nations, however imperfect, however deficient. . . . This is not a counsel of despair. Our own life has demonstrated that we are incapable of despair. Men will die in defence of principle.

Let us not delude ourselves; it is not the great powers that need the United Nations. It is the small powers which . . . have the most to gain through the successful achievement of its goals. . . . Unilateral action outside the United Nations is . . . a luxury denied to the poorer weaker nations.

But . . . in the face of world opinion, massed in support of right and justice, we venture to suggest that even the great nations, powerful as they are, will hesitate to breach the peace and violate fundamental rights of mankind and of nations in defiance of the United Nations, and thus face universal condemnation. This is our hope, our only hope. . . .'

Today, the new countries respect UNO as few do in the West, on the Right or the Left. To them, it has meant actual aid as well as moral encouragement, a place where they have taken their national causes, country by country, to lay them before their fellow-men. They know UNO is important and effective; their own independence proves it. On the occasion of Guinea's entry into UNO, Sékou Touré declared:

'I should be remiss if I did not express to you . . . the sincere gratitude of the people and Government of Guinea. . . . For the destiny of Africa, the importance of the moral and political support which this Assembly brought us . . . can never be fully realized.'

For their needs, however, the UN is not effective enough. Too much power is still concentrated in the hands of the 'over-developed' nations:

'Of the current UN staff with the rank of Under-Secretary or its equivalent, 22 are from North America, 18 from Western Europe, 11 from Asia and the Far East, and only 4 from Eastern Europe, 4 from Latin America, 2 from Africa, and none from the Middle East. The position is nearly the same with regard to the lower ranks of the Secretariat.'[26]

The UN thus recruits fewest of its staff from countries most committed to its objectives.

Too much power in 'over-developed' lands, and too much wealth. Even the conservatives in the Third World become incensed at a situation in which world armaments in one year consume resources which would meet the present-day import requirements of the Sudan for a thousand years.[27] They know that it is technically possible to banish brute poverty and hunger from the earth within a generation.[28] 'The total external cost of industrializing the under-developed regions of the world would . . . be of the order of $100 billion – about a two-year's world arms' bill. . . .' The reduction of military expenditure to one-third of its present value could provide the funds needed to industrialize all the under-developed countries within ten to twenty years. Bernal, indeed, has done some of the sums: such an allocation of funds, he considers, would make possible the creation of fourteen new industrial centres, each one with the capacity of the whole of British industry, and another thirty centres each as large as Paris, in addition to enlarging eleven existing major centres.[29] The mind may boggle at the immensity of such development programmes, but the majority of mankind no doubt thought, too, that space-travel on its present scale would be unattainable before many decades.

Yet present trends, unchecked, mean an *increasing* gap between the rich and poor nations, not a narrowing one. Falls in raw materials prices outweigh aid given by foreign powers and international agencies; expanded production is soaked up by worsening terms of trade;* capital is flowing increasingly to the rich, not the poor, countries. And much of the aid given is predominantly military-political in purpose; it frequently goes to the most loathsome of regimes rather than to 'democratic' countries; it rarely reaches the peasant; and it distorts the economy of the recipient in the interests of the economy of the donor. Nor does it help modernize agrarian economies. 'In Pakistan,' a recent study notes, 'a steady move away from industrialization policy has taken place.' [26a]

Inevitably, then, the new states want international economic planning and credit-arrangements which would break through these barriers to modernization, and which would integrate and bring into mutual benefit the economies of both the advanced and the backward countries.

Their central objectives, then, are peculiarly similar to those

* The expansion of production by 70 per cent over several years in Nigeria only brought in 5 per cent more from the sale of these products. The decline in the prices of raw materials is, of course, a long-established trend. It enabled the favoured classes in the favoured countries even to benefit during the Depression of the thirties, for example (see Dobb, *Studies in the Development of Capitalism*, p. 333).

enshrined in the UN Charter, aspirations which have been frustrated for nearly a generation by the antagonisms of the Big Powers which have dominated that body. Today, there is a new possibility that the reservoir of hope and goodwill towards UNO accumulated in the new countries will provide that organization with the moral resources to actually implement long-overdue schemes like SUNFED. If these aspirations are not satisfied, the hope and goodwill could easily evaporate; hatreds and dissensions will be generated which would destroy UNO and seal the fate of the world. Or they may decide to sacrifice this generation in the interests of the next: the way that has cost so many millions their lives in this century.

The peoples of the new countries are no more and no less better human beings than most of their fellows. A despotic monarch like Selassie; a *marxisant* mass labour leader like Touré; a Buddhist socialist ex-King like Norodom Sihanouk; an old-style General-dictator like Abboud are not always model vehicles of the rationalist, humanist, liberal, and socialist values rightly held so dear in the Old World, nor are they very compatible bed-fellows, on the surface. But they stand in a special position in the flow of world-history. And behind them stand hundreds of millions of people.

It is therefore no starry-eyed mystique of the 'proletarian nations' as the Deliverer of the twentieth century to suggest these values and policies do have a universal quality, and that their actualization would be to the advantage of the whole world, not merely of the Third World. At this phase of human development, then, we are witnessing a very significant phenomenon: the taking-up of aspirations as old as human history: peace, co-operation, production for creative ends, human emancipation and enlargement, for the first time, not merely by individual idealists or utopian sects, nor even by particular movements or nations, but by the majority of the world's population.

In the eighteenth century, rising bourgeoisies, striving to make their voices felt in societies dominated by land-holding aristocracies and established Churches, took up older notions of freedom of the individual, the development of the personality, of liberty, equality, and fraternity, and mobilized the human aspirations of the 'dis-inherited' behind them. Once established, these values, and the institutions in which they were enshrined, became part of the culture of whole societies and of humane men generally. In the nineteenth century, similarly, the working-class expanded the notion of 'fraternity' into a philosophy which enriched human relations with a new sense and practice of solidarity and community, and a new confidence that in a 'society of equals' Man could be emancipated from the bondage of Nature. It is the new societies, today, which are reviving these themes and relating them to the condition of man in the twentieth century.

Like the liberal bourgeoisies of the eighteenth century and the Romantic era, they are self-interested. Their self-interest, however, happens to be the self-interest of the world. Like the working-class of the nineteenth century, they are unwashed, illiterate, and often intolerant and insensitive.

Not until they are relieved from the pressures of desperation will more refined values emerge. But those who can only see the illiberal aspects of the new regimes forget that the words they use are echoes of concepts formed in the eighteenth and nineteenth centuries in Europe and America: they are *our* concepts, too, and they are *still* liberalizing forces today. But now they come increasingly from Africa and Asia, rather than from a Europe prepared to hand over its political choices to a consortium of officials.

The new populism *could* become the source of a revived humanist internationalism. It *could* as easily disappear, just as Russian Populism gave way to Bolshevism. But the issues so ardently debated by the Russian Populists are still the crucial issues for the Third World. Is capitalism inevitable in these countries? Can non-Communist governments achieve the take-off? Does 'modernization', or 'socialism', inevitably entail rigid mobilization and 'forced marches' for the development of heavy industry? Must the emergent countries necessarily go through the miseries of the USSR in the 1920s and 1930s? These issues are important, too, not merely for the new states. They are crucial for the future of the older industrialized societies, too – and not merely as 'foreign policy', for they raise fundamental questions about the nature of our own societies; questions about affluence, depersonalization, community, and the very ends of life.

In Europe today, as the new countries uncomfortably remind us, we face the consequences of our kind of 'modernity': of hedonistic materialism, of the breeding of Organization Men, of the feeling that men have lost any real say in the running of their own lives. New urges, and even actual experiments, show the depths of these concerns, as the history of Yugoslav 'workers' control', and the widespread interest in it outside Yugoslavia, demonstrate.[30]

The biggest single moral question raised for us, however, is the extent of our humanity. Is the hunger and explosiveness of the world beyond Suez in fact only 0·7 per cent of our national concerns? It is a question which Britain in particular must face.

Identification with the struggles of the colonized peoples has been a basic theme in the popular culture of the Western countries. The Labour movements of Europe and America still adhere to the position stated by Marx: that 'labour in the white skin cannot emancipate itself until labour in the black skin is free'. The Left has continued to cleave to that line of tradition. But there has also been a powerful and popular counteractive ideology: that of pride in Empire and unquestioned White superiority often allied, paradoxically, to a parochial 'Little England-ism'. When Mr. Macmillan, in a recent speech, turned from home affairs and asked 'What about abroad?' 100,000 viewers switched off their television sets.[31]

Many of the resolutions passed at trade union branches, therefore, do not necessarily reflect the feelings of those not present, but rather of the more politically-conscious minority; the votes on colonial issues are often traditionalistic and hollow, devoid of that burning content which could translate them into action. Much of the uncertainty in the note of the Labour trumpet, too, reflects a wider uncertainty about socialism in general. And particularly after 1945, the anti-colonial struggle became confusingly intermixed with the Cold War. Malaya and Cyprus, in particular, were struggles in which colonialism was able to represent itself as anti-communism; the non-communist Left was therefore thoroughly confused and divided.

One of the reactions to this diminished internationalism on the Left in the advanced countries has been a diminished internationalism in the Third World. Fanonism is one symptom of this loss of trust.

Yet the full logical implications of the metaphor of the 'proletarian' nations are not, in fact, followed through. It is not used to imply a revolutionary overthrow of the advanced nations. Apart from its impracticability, or the world conflagration which a struggle of 'proletarian' *v.* 'millionaire' nations would involve, there is no such mood abroad in the Third World, nor does Fanon himself suggest the use of violence except to expel colonial rulers from colonized territories. Colonial liberation, he assumes, will set in train democratizing processes in the metropolitan countries themselves. But the 'revolutionary' task of the 'proletarian' nations is *not* to capture the machinery of economic and political power from the Euro-American 'millionaires', as the historic task of the proletariat, in Marx's schema, was precisely to smash the apparatus of dominance of the ruling-class. The problem, for these 'proletarians', increasingly, is that the 'millionaires' are less and less interested in exploiting them. Today's 'super-profits' are being made in Western Europe, not the Third World. But *politically*, the Great Powers cannot afford to lose their influence in the new countries, nor dare they allow them to starve. The 'proletarian' countries badly need association with the advanced world, too, for this is one 'proletariat' that *cannot* stage a revolution; the 'proletarian' nations cannot finish the revolutionizing process on their own – basically because they are not significantly 'proletarian' at all: they are nations of peasants.

The metaphor of 'proletarianism' thus breaks down at many points, primarily because it runs counter to the growing unification of the world. The Third World needs a wider internationalism than itself, a relationship which must be *between* advanced and under-developed countries, and with the international agencies which straddle and transcend these divisions.

The release of UNO from the stranglehold of the two giants; the thaws in the Cold War won by Europeans who 'destalinized' Eastern Europe, and by Asians who damped down hot wars in Indo-China and Korea, ushered in an era when colonial powers no longer feared that to quit the colonies was an invitation to a Soviet take-over. The actions of men across the 'development-barrier' have had reciprocal effects – and mutual benefits.

World problems, ultimately, can only be resolved by world action, not by the activity of the Third World alone, and even less by the Great Power blocs, for they are least easily moved. The transformation of the backward world would also transform the life-situation of the advanced countries. The backward world, where most men live, could offer a stable and expanding market – at present ridiculously small – for the enormously-developed productive powers of Euro-America, not to mention the markets in Eastern Europe which the West at present largely denies itself. (In 1960, British exports to Nigeria were worth more than the value of exports to Eastern Europe.) But the *purely* agrarian, *backward* economy cannot hope to emulate Canada or even Denmark. And as long as the aid they receive fails to modernize their agriculture and develop their industry, it will be useless.

Some half century ago, the agrarian colonies of Australia were relatively minor outlets for British exports. By mid-century a modernized and independent Australia, still largely dependent on the export of wheat and wool, but now from a modernized agricultural and pastoral sector of the economy complemented by a developed industry, had become Britain's leading trade partner,* and one of the richest countries in the world. Canada, too, has achieved great prosperity even though her top exports are still staples: newsprint, wheat, planks and boards, and wood pulp are her four most valuable commodities. So have agrarian Denmark and New Zealand.

To be successful, aid must stimulate social revolution. The second annual report of the Social Progress Trust Fund Alliance for Progress of the Inter-American Development Bank is instructive:

'During 1960–61, according to FAO, Latin American food agricultural production declined approximately 2 per cent and food production dropped below that of the previous year when there had been also declines relative to the prior year. There are no statistics showing any appreciable improvement in rural income levels; indications are to the contrary, showing that as a result of economic and demographic facts most *campesinos* are now in a worse plight than they were a few years ago.'

The moral is clear. We have to make choices, whether we like it or not: the internationally planned elimination of poverty is a choice that now presents itself as a practical possibility – but vested interests have to be challenged radically in the process.

* Australian exports to Britain in 1962–3 were valued at £160,880,000 (sterling); British exports to Australia at £262,360,000.

There is little doubt that the prospect of entering the Common Market aroused a great deal of excitement, particularly amongst young people, nᴜt so much because they were thrilled about the possibility of a reduction in the price of tomatoes or typewriters, but because they saw in this a movement towards a common society. This positive humanist sentiment is also increasingly visible in the new concern for the 'damned of the earth'. War on Want has doubled its income in six months; in the USA, the imagination of young people has been captured by the Peace Corps. Signs of a new conscience and consciousness are there. These 'soft-hearted' sentiments are 'hard facts' of politics which the professional politician ignores to his peril. But the lifting of the primordial curse of poverty from the globe can scarcely be achieved by individual charity. For all their excellence, War on Want or Oxfam are, in fact, latter-day equivalents of Victorian organized charity, which, in the end, became a barrier to serious 'welfare' reform, which only the State was fitted to undertake. The international attack on poverty, equally, will have to be carried out, ultimately, by the collective, corporate action of governments, states, and international organizations. The lasting contribution of the charity organizations will not be their material contribution, but the awakening of the 'conscience of the rich'.

Having said this, it still remains for us to see the other side of the coin of 'positive internationalism', for decolonization involves unremitting, dedicated effort on the part of the peoples – and leaderships – of the new countries themselves, too.

There is often an inverse relationship between the amount of socialism talked and the amount practised. Criticism of the new leaderships on these grounds has not been wanting from abroad. But when it comes from those whose enthusiasm for decolonization has never been particularly apparent in the past it has often been dismissed as mere hostility. Attacks on Nehru, Nkrumah, and Nasser in the Beaverbrook Press, for example, have done incalculable damage to the image of Britain in those countries, and have merely hardened the intransigence of the criticized. But – whatever their motivation – the critics have focused on real defects. And where the criticisms could be rightly dismissed as unjustifiable, much that was soundly-based tended to be dismissed along with it. In the end, criticism itself can be turned into a source of internal strength and rigidity if the credentials of the critics can be 'demonstrated' to be suspect; the repression of any kind of *internal* criticism can then be 'excused'. Thus Hitler used, occasionally, to print and circulate selected anti-Nazi cartoons in order to show the German people how the outside world hated and threatened Germany. The Moscow Trials, too, made great play with the theme of the external threat of Nazism, as a 'justification' of repression.

But criticism from people perceived as friends is different. Just as people in Eastern Europe, in the turmoil of 1956–7, did listen seriously to the voices of revolutionary socialists and Communist dissidents, whereas they did *not* respect 'professional anti-Communist' sources, so people in the new countries are more willing to take criticism from such proved friends of the Third World as René Dumont.*

Dumont's criticism of the Third World is doubly telling in that he combines an explicit, flexible and revolutionary socialist humanism with a specialist's understanding of the economic, social, and technological problems of the backward world, whose agronomy he has been studying – against a background of experience in France – for some three decades, firstly in Viet Nam, South America, and China, and now in Africa.

Called in to advise to the Governments of Mali, Guinea, the Ivory Coast, Chad, Congo-Brazzaville, Dahomey, Senegal, Malagasy, Caméroun, and Ruanda-Urundi, he found himself obliged to speak sympathetically but firmly to the leaders of the New Africa.

The contrast is very strong between this kind of principled and informed criticism and the traditional recipes of both Right and Left. On the Right, the critic often starts from the assumption that human evolution culminated in the British Empire (or the French Communauté, according to national taste). On the Left, traditional anti-colonialism has been slow to adapt to new developments in the new states. Reflexes have been long conditioned – the interests of the 'colonial' and ex-colonial peoples must be defended, often uncritically. On the one hand, there are those who never cease to stress that colonialism is not dead, and who point, with reason, to Southern Rhodesia and Angola. Since their

* Notably, in his critical examination of the new states of former French Africa, *L'Afrique Noire est Mal Partie*.

intellectual stock-in-trade is diminishing, however, they are increasingly obliged to play upon the theme of 'neo-colonialism' – again, with reason.

Unilever *is* still there; foreign capital still dominates the new countries. The freedom of political manoeuvre of the new states is thereby limited. But it is by no means entirely non-existent. Sir Roy Welensky is very sensitively aware, as some Left-wing critics are not, that political independence for Nyasaland and Northern Rhodesia is not meaningless; so are the Whites who have flocked out of those countries. (After fifteen years, the 'frozen Left' is at long last prepared to admit that India is actually, meaningfully 'independent'.) The acceptance of foreign aid does not, as extremists in both Washington and Moscow assume, inevitably involve political domination by the donor. The recent history of Egypt, India, Iraq, Yugoslavia, Afghanistan, or Guinea, to name but a few cases, is eloquent testimony. Though Communist Russia is building the Aswan High Dam, Egyptian Communists still languish in gaol.

Perhaps the most depressing feature of all this comment, Right, Left, and centre, is its essential political-ness. All will freely acknowledge that the political and social revolutions go hand in hand. Yet little of the interminable debate on the politics of the new states focuses on the *content* of this politics: the gritty reality of the 'take-off' for the poverty-stricken inhabitants of a bloc-divided world. This defect is as marked in the thought of Africans and Asians as in the thought of foreign commentators.

Analyses like Dumont's are all too rare. He establishes the connections between social, political, and economic problems, and technical questions of agrarian and industrial advance. He does not ignore the *natural* barriers to progress: disease, easily-eroded soils, and underpopulation (despite the 'demographic explosion'). But he emphasizes that the backwardness of Africa is a *human product*, not merely a natural condition. The 'human haemorrhage' of the slave trade, and the decades of subsequent colonialism, stamp contemporary Africa with their imprint, as they also stamp those who are leading the new Africa in her struggle to decolonize.

The effective decolonization of Africa also requires the decolonization of the new leaderships: teachers, now Ministers of Education, who want French standards of education for their pupils, French standards of comfort for themselves, and a French content to education itself; political leaders who flee the villages for the joys of town life, and who abhor manual work. Of the new generation of students – so revolutionary that they never penetrate beyond politics to the lives of their peoples – he asks whether they can be seriously considered as 'revolutionary' in any but a Pickwickian sense. Chinese and Algerian students have been forced to take life seriously. But elsewhere, the situation is too often that described by one worker in the Third World:

'. . . last year, in the course of a tour of West Africa and Morocco, I only met one student whose "revolution" took any real account of the problems of his people!'

Dumont's recipe is simple: work. He tells the African leaders to get their hands dirty, to replace Europeanized 'academic' education with teaching connected with the daily life-experience of hunger, sickness, and ignorance in the bush village. They could start by actually *going* to the villages, by emulating Cuba's 'Year of Education', in which illiteracy was eliminated. In Mali, 75 per cent of the children in the capital, Bamako, have been to school; in the remote bush villages, only 3 per cent. Schools under the village trees; school buildings built of local materials; the revival of the school farm: these are the only serious ways of building mass education in Africa. Official plans to recruit 7,000 *expatriate* teachers to staff African institutions of higher learning alone during 1962–80, plus another 14,000 African staff, seem, in the light of teacher shortages in Europe and America, and in the light of current allocations of resources to the needs of the new countries, most unlikely to be achieved.[32]

This does not so much mean that educational standards must be diluted, but that they should be decolonized. The maintenance of French or British styles of education means in fact that the ordinary villagers are getting *no education at all*. Only thirty years ago the Soviet Union showed how to tackle the problem of raising health standards in a poverty-stricken society by using *feldshers*, medical workers with only elementary training.[33] Today, that investment is paying off in superb standards.

A 'Welfare State', in fact, cannot be built, as India once rashly thought, on the basis of poverty. These countries face a basic and increasing food production problem that has been concealed – so far – by foreign aid. In 1890, India produced 270 kilograms of grain for every one of its citizens; in 1945, only 180; and by 1961, only 175. An agricultural revolution is an elementary necessity, and Dumont spells out, in detail, the kind of innovations, major and minor, that this would entail: replacing Africa's ubiquitous herd-boys by sheepdogs (the boys could go to school); the use of simple animal-powered and water-powered equipment; the avoidance of costly and relatively unrewarding giant projects; the introduction of unrefined sugar from locally-grown cane into the diet; the cessation of the export of Africa's minerals in the husks of the groundnut, etc., etc.

These technical improvements in agriculture need to be supported by industrial advance. This means building, not more ridiculous Nowa Hutas (where coal and iron had to be imported from the Donbas!), but factories to produce saws, bicycles, and agricultural tools – and not breweries either. (Alcohol forms some 10 per cent of imports, and of urban budgets, in the Ivory Coast, and the governmental *élites* in many parts of Africa are fast becoming alcoholic addicts. In Burundi in 1959, 120 million of the 200 million francs received by the African peasantry from their sales of coffee went on European beer alone, plus an unknown amount on banana beer.) It should not be necessary, for example, for West African countries which export palm oil to use their precious foreign exchange to import soap.

But to achieve all this a new kind of revolutionary dedication is needed. For a leader to work publicly with his hands, as Lenin worked in the Kremlin with his broom on 'Red Saturdays', may be in some cases, merely a demagogic gesture. In Dumont's view, however, the kind of 'animation' symbolized in this gesture is seriously needed; a socialist ethic is a *sine qua non*, not the values symbolized by the Mercedes in which so many new *élites* roll round from one luxury hotel to another.

In countries which bear the imprint of a fierce struggle for independence – such as most African states have never experienced – in Algeria, in Cuba, or in China, the poltroons, the self-seekers, the inefficient, and the reactionary have been weeded out of responsible positions in three decades of tough struggle. This kind of revolutionary efficiency, summed up in the Chinese phrase

'Red *and* expert', is badly needed in many new countries where the results of inefficiency and irresolution are magically 'explained away' by blaming all shortcomings on the 'colonial legacy' or on 'neo-colonialism'. In the West, where few people have had direct contact with countries battling to raise themselves by their own bootstraps, the positive and magnificent side of these revolutions is often forgotten: only the regimentation and central direction is observed, never the spontaneous upsurge and expansion of human horizons. But Asian and African peasants see things quite differently. In an age when the USSR appears to have lost a great deal of its earlier revolutionary dynamic, the appeal of China to people who *need* a revolution is very powerful, even though, at the same time, they fear the implications of massive social revolution in the nuclear age.

There are, however, other experiences, on which they can and do draw. Israel provides one set of lessons: a country which has had to fight for independence, and which has actually made the desert bloom, using 'communitarian' methods of organization and living-together which might well be adapted to African and Asian conditions. Yugoslavia provides yet another: there, independent peasant proprietorship, limited to a maximum of ten hectares, has been combined with socialized industry controlled by the workers, plus co-operative commercial and industrial organization in the villages. African independent peasants, working on their own patches, within the context of a traditional community culture, thus find the Israeli *moshav* a more relevant model than more strictly *collectivist* forms of organization such as the Soviet *kolkhoz* or the Cuban state farms (neither of which has been eminently successful). Scandinavian co-operatives, too, provide a valuable lesson in self-organization for farmers and consumers endeavouring to protect themselves against exploitation by great private and public corporations. But in impoverished Africa, instead of maximizing individual dividends, a greater share of the profits would need to be ploughed back into projects for the mutual advantage of the members. China, the Soviet Union, and Cuba all provide valuable lessons, positive and negative, in the strategy of industrialization and modernization. The new states, indeed, have plenty of lessons available, and can learn from the errors of the pioneers.

Plenty of lessons, indeed, but far too little being learned from them, and far too little being *done*. At this point, populist philo-sophy threatens to become truly an ideology, a screen between them and reality, used, too, to justify the masterly inactivity of many of the new leaderships. So in Britain, after the First World War, the wartime ideology of 'all pulling together' was so powerful that politicians and administrators actually assumed that harmony of interests was the reality, and so were blinded to real divisions of interest. Supremely euphoric, they did very little to promote social reform. By virtue of their ideology, 'they were effectively constrained from seeing the need to constrain groups to work together'.[34] Protracted 'verbal' populism can be just as illusory and ineffective. The decolonization of the new states, then, requires the demolition of myths.

For the peasant will not put up with this for ever. Myths do not feed him. When he does boil over in revolt against the privi-leged city *élites*, the result is hardly likely to be a copybook revolution, but a destructive and bloody jacquerie, a 'congolization' such as that described by Hobsbawm for Colombia, where des-perate and frustrated people butcher their enemies, their neigh-bours, and each other.

Somewhere along the line, this kind of blind, anarchic protest will give way to classic, organized revolution. In the Third World, this means *peasant* revolution, and, apart from Angola and Algeria, the first foreshadowings are already visible in Africa: in Caméroun, where young people between ten and twenty-five years of age formed the backbone of the *maquis* which fought both the French and their own independent government, and where terrorism has bred counter-terror until even government officials admit that the people would welcome the return of the Whites. The classic initial symptoms of peasant resistance are reported from other countries: in parts of Malagasy, only 15 per cent of the taxes are collected, and the villagers fail to repay loans.

From the new leaders, a reduction in salaries and privileges is called for. To pretend that Africa can afford such luxuries as the removal of taxes, as in the Ivory Coast, is dangerous delusion. Africa has little enough capital; she cannot afford to relinquish public access to what little does exist. What she *does* possess is people (though not over-many of these, either). Hence the stress upon 'human investment', which, in Dumont's view, ought to mean fifty days of work for social-development purposes per year from the peasantry. African males, in many regions, he believes, if better fed and trained, could work longer and harder; at present, the women are over-worked, and the men, at least seasonally, under-employed.

Many will shudder at these 'illiberal' notions, which awaken memories of colonial forced labour, British satanic mills, or Soviet collectivization. But dollars are *not* going to do the trick: the record of 'international aid' since 1945 is evidence enough of that. Nor are there likely to be enough of them in the visible future. Whether they are there or not, it is necessary to change *people*. Decolonization involves much more than a negative undoing of the work of the colonizers, or the mere replacement of expatriate personnel by Africans. It means training and creating *new men*, with new, non-colonial minds. Aid which does not do this cannot transform production, for without the enthusiasm, the participation, and the understanding of the villager, one can do little. Manual work thus needs to be respected, as it is respected neither in the West nor in Africa. This is no 'proletarian pastoralism' of well-fed White intellectuals, but a simple fact which must be absorbed by those who wish to see the energies of the world unlocked.

The transformation of the under-developed world does mean changes for the 'over-developed' world, too. It means that the advanced countries have got to contribute more than the 2 per cent of national income provided by France, the Soviet Union, or China, or the 0·71 per cent which Britain spends on the under-developed world. To raise living-standards in the Third World by a mere 2 per cent per year, thirty to forty-five billion dollars a year are needed: today, the total volume of international aid is about six billion.

If only a little of the new-found enthusiasm and spontaneous popular support for famine relief causes could be harnessed for the far less personal and visible, but infinitely more important, task of turning our whole economy towards the development of the backward world, we would begin to enter human history and leave pre-history.

We need, in brief, to harness this most admirable enthusiasm to a programme of planned international world-development if we are going to check the growing polarization of the world into affluent and poverty-stricken societies. The morbid concentration of purchasing-power in North America must be corrected, the whole mythology of aid, and the rationale of world prices, re-examined, for no serious development can take place so long as Africa continues to lose twice as much as she received in external aid through falls in world prices of raw materials, as she did between 1955 and 1959. In advanced countries farmers expect, and receive, government protection in the form of stabilization arrangements, floor prices, long-term forward purchasing agreements, etc.; in the Third World, they starve. It is as possible to store raw materials against speculation *internationally* (an FAO proposal torpedoed in 1946), as it is for the US Government to store vast quantities of farm produce in a single country.[35] Infrastructurally, the legacy of colonial division in Africa could be replaced by common services across territorial boundaries: today, it is still necessary to pass through the London and Paris telephone exchanges if you wish to phone Nigeria from adjoining Dahomey.

The 'take-off', then, demands very great readjustments on all sides. The African leaderships, by and large, have yet to hammer out sound development plans and to mobilize their peoples to carry them out.

They would be advised to take the criticisms of a Dumont to heart. Indeed, if some of them were a little more tolerant of both internal as well as external critics, they might oblige their opponents to make constructive criticism instead of driving them to underground subversion and bomb-plots by closing all other channels of dissent.

For people in the advanced countries, an equally sharp re-orientation is called for. Younger people are more responsive to the moral challenge of the hungry world than their elders. At present, unfortunately, much of this positive idealism is harnessed for power-bloc crusades or diverted into support for 'rich men's clubs'.

These new aspirations have not yet become the dominant mood of politics. But they are the 'utopian' aspirations that will increasingly shape the future. For the future *is* subject to human agency, and the pace of events is such that most 'historically'-minded social analysts have been caught napping.

Until the emergence of a consciously 'cosmopolitanized' culture appropriate to an internationalized world – a mental revolution which will accompany the real growing-together of states in economic and political terms – various kinds of traditional nationalism will persist, perhaps with higher and wider ranges of inclusiveness. Earlier conceptions of the dissolution of limited nationalisms in a wider, ultimately universal order, did, it is true, eventually run into the sand – inevitably, in eras which antedated the emergence of world society. But is anyone to deny, after the vivid demonstration of the appeals of *international* communism and socialism, that the transcendence of the nation-state is a spent appeal to human imagination?

It is possible to know too much history, to overemphasize the way in which the past, continuity, and tradition, condition men's present behaviour. 'Functionalist' social scientists have as often over-stressed the way in which a culture is an *existing* entity, to be understood predominantly in terms of the contemporary balance of forces in a society. This, they assert, can be analysed without having to explain how existing institutions and groupings came into being, or how they developed in the past.

The point is not merely that these two approaches are, in fact, *complementary*; it is rather that the dichotomy between 'historical' and 'functionalist' modes of analysis is analytically a bad one. The present can only be properly comprehended in terms of the past.[36] A good historian, in fact, makes a 'sociological' analysis of the period he is writing about; 'non-historical' sociology is bad – or limited – sociology; non-sociological history bad history. But the reintegration of these two strands of intellectual tradition is still not enough. For men are not determined entities, like rocks and trees. They have minds. Human beings can, and do, react *against* the past. They are affected *by* the past, in so far as they absorb behaviour-patterns of their culture. But they have also the faculties of imagination and creativity; they innovate as well as receive and absorb, they revolt as well as continue. They step outside the structural framework of the existing social order and the intellectual framework of received ideas to create *new* ideas and *new* ways of ordering their relationships with one another. In order to understand human behaviour, then, we have to be sensitive not only to the past and the present, but also to the future, to make a place in our thinking about society for what people want to be, to have, and to do – in a word, for Mannheim's 'utopian' element.[37] To put it paradoxically, perhaps, society is a product of the *future*, as much as the past and present.

As the great continental social thinkers of the late nineteenth century, reacting against deterministic positivism and evolutionism, insisted,[38] consciousness and value-orientation, 'Promethean' and 'Faustian' elements, are central to the human condition. From our analysis, therefore, we have not projected any 'inevitable trends' into the future. For there are no 'inevitable trends'. Quite simply, we can choose. Even in a Cold War world, the latitude is enormous, and the area of choice can be widened. If, Britain, for example, as an industrialized Western Power with great reserves of respect and prestige still to draw on, were to associate herself definitively with the emergent countries, the world would be transformed. One of the major props of the Cold War would have become a support for international development. Britain has a peculiar legacy from the past, in which, quite recently, she dominated the rest of the world. It has made us at once superior and self-centred, but also intensely aware that we are involved in the world.

Other countries, too, have internationalist traditions upon which the rest of the world might profitably draw. Some have been explicitly neutralist and anti-imperialist. Scandinavia has developed a political culture which has produced a succession of distinguished international civil servants dedicated to peace, and is still producing more positive variants of neutralism. In Norway, for example, Professor Ragnar Frisch has already outlined a plan to bring the complementary economies of the West and those of the poor countries into closer relationship.

One thing seems certain: if positive decolonization does not take place, we face another round of wars and revolutions. In such a situation, the Third World may well decide to begin the 'take-off' by hard, centralized discipline. That way, its characteristic 'man-centred' philosophy will certainly disappear, and go down into history, like Russian Narodism, merely as an 'ideology of transition'.

We conclude, therefore, by emphasizing the fact of choice, for two reasons. Firstly, because this poses the problem of world development as the *moral* issue it is. Though we have suggested that massive decolonization would be in the interests of the whole world, and even the narrow, short-run, *material* interests of the peoples of the advanced countries, we have deliberately avoided formulating the problem narrowly in terms of the effects such a world transformation might have on our pockets.* It would be worth doing even if it cost us a good deal. Even if joining ECM were to enable us to maintain or even raise our living-standards, it would be the wrong choice for the wrong reason. In this, we feel closer to an R. H. Tawney, who argued for social equality *from ethical assumptions*, rather than to those socialists like John Strachey who used to calculate how much better off each of us might be if capitalist wealth were to be divided up between us. Secondly, we emphasize choice instead of positivistically enunciating 'laws' and 'predictions', because social science cannot tell us what 'will happen'. It can enable us to understand what forces are at work, to assess the significance of the values according to which we act, and the likely practical implications of our choices. It enables us to choose rationally, and not blindly or dogmatically. What we lose, in dropping the spurious certainty of deterministic dogmas, we compensate for in other ways, for this width of uncertainty and relativity also carries with it a corresponding share of hope and freedom, an enhancement of human choice and human values, whatever the constraining conditions which sane men have to take account of. In the words of Gunnar Myrdal, 'the future is continually our own choice. There is no blind destiny ruling history.'

Men are not, in fact, atomic particles behaving according to inexorable eighteenth-century laws of mechanics; nor is it adequate to say that absolute, 'iron' laws have been replaced by laws of *probability*. For men have minds, and can always choose to die rather than submit, to keep hope alive rather than accommodate to the 'inevitable'; they can innovate and introduce *new* ranges of human vision. The emergent countries, by their very existence, are re-opening a discussion that has been closed for too long in the Old World. They are raising questions of value and human choice in a technologized and bureaucratized world. They are striving to

---

* Such arguments are liable to backfire: imperialism has been 'justified' on grounds of self-interest. After all, if it could be demonstrated that Empire *did* benefit the British working-class, ought that to make us advocates of imperialism? The judgments and human choices entailed in an interpretation of imperialism and its aftermath are *not* to be decided primarily on the basis of quantitive assessments of the effect of Empire upon our living-standards.

avoid the depersonalization and alienation so widely deplored in the literature of the West, to resist two sharply opposed camps, drifting – even speeding – towards final extinction. They ask themselves – and us – why it is 'necessary' for people to starve in an era of moon-colonization and planned consumer-goods obsolescence, why we are helpless observers of a 'population explosion' that may be as fatal as the explosion of the hydrogen bomb. These questions are a challenge: they place 'man-centred' issues on the agenda of human society for discussion and action. And they concern our societies as well as the new, growing ones, for we are far from convinced of the perfection of our own City.

If the Third World has raised the questions, the answers can only be found by the joint action of men everywhere. People in the Third World are unlikely to find the answers on their own. Nor is our 'conventional wisdom' likely to be adequate to the task. We have little excuse now for continuing to think of world problems in terms of the ineffable superiority either of late capitalism or late communism. The Third World challenges both – and offers even to transcend itself. 'This colossal task,' Fanon has written, '. . . consists in reintroducing Man into the world, man in his totality' – not Eastern man, Western man, or Third World man, but the creation of social institutions and the shaping of human values which, for the first time, would be appropriate to the world society that already exists in fact.

People who consider ideas and ideals unimportant might consider again the history of Christianity, Islam, or Communism, for they are ignorant of the real world. We *need* new ideas quickly. If men can learn to be torturers, they can also learn humanity. If they do not, the lesson is clear: 60,000 people found out the ultimate meaning of our present ideas in one blinding flash, at Hiroshima on 6 August, 1945.

CHAPTER SEVEN

TOWARDS WORLD WAR IV:
THE END OF THE WORLD?

'WESTERN' POLITICAL science – particularly American – has been dominated, over recent years, by an obsessional concern with the rivalry between the United States and the Soviet Union which has reflected itself in the proliferation of bipolar political models of the world social system: 'democratic' v. 'totalitarian'; 'pluralist' v. 'monocentric'; 'authoritarian' v. 'liberal', etc., etc. All this was natural enough in an era dominated by the Cold War as it was waged up to the 1950s, and in which the prospect of World War III haunted men's minds. Little wonder that this should be the dominant style of thought, since besides the confrontation between the two super-Powers all else seemed insignificant.

In the immediate aftermath of World War II, the Old World, Europe, had been the centre of the struggle; Czechoslovakia and Berlin the typical flash-points. But confrontation on such a scale could not be contained even within the bounds of the continent of Europe. It erupted in its most violent form, on a gigantic scale, outside Europe altogether: in Asia, with the outbreak of the Korean War (where MacArthur's landing at Seoul was larger than D-Day in World War II), and later, on America's doorstep in Cuba.

The 'World War III' which C. Wright Mills wrote and worried about was conceived of as a war between the two major industrial Powers, the USA and the USSR. But the rest of the world continued to display an obstinate interest in its own problems, and resisted being relegated to the backstage of a play with only two actors. The non-Communist 'Third World' tried, precariously, to manoeuvre between the blocs. Then, in Korea, the decisive shift took place, when China directly committed large military forces to a war in which the Communist forces had initially been supplied and supported primarily by Moscow. A new world-communism had emerged on the scene, one with interests independent of the USSR, and therefore potentially liable to conflict with the 'elder brother', and liable to act most vigorously and independently especially in those sensitive areas on the periphery of the Chinese heartland. And so it proved: at Quemoy and Matsu, in Korea, in Viet Nam.

World War III never became a full, global, permanent military commitment of forces in active combat. But hot war, and 'incidents', kept on breaking out and constant, vicious Cold War was waged regularly right across the globe: in this sense, World War III certainly took place. So over-riding seemed the contest between the two super-Powers that there was a period of distinct 'cultural lag' in political consciousness before men became aware that a new and more severe Cold War was growing up just as the Old Cold War showed signs of slackening. From the time of the death of Stalin, there began that process of gradually accelerated rapprochement which is still being worked through. By the time Mills attempted to formulate a general awareness of the dangers of World War III in 1958, the causes of that conflict were slowly being eroded away – and the outlines of World War IV were beginning to become visible. World War III did not wind down easily or inevitably. There was no theatre-script, no inevitability in the dénouement. Mills was right to worry. At Cuba, in 1962, the two super-Powers came within a hairsbreadth of destroying each other and the world. They may yet still do so. But that particular trial of nervous stength not only focused the conflicts of an epoch. It also began the process of resolving them. Loosened travel controls; reduction of tension; recognition of spheres of influence; minor military concessions; cultural exchanges; visits by Heads of States – all the symbolic apparatus of reconciliation was put into motion.

Today, the primacy of the New Cold War over the Old Cold War is obvious, and it is the prospect of World War IV that matters, not World War III. For we are no longer dealing with the bipolar conflict between the capitalist USA and the communist USSR. We live in a world where revolution has set in on a world scale, often without benefit of Marxism, and where counter-revolution has passed from containment to intervention.

All this took some time to imprint itself on men's consciousness. It was not easy to grasp that there could be any conflict deadlier and more menacing than that between the United States and the USSR, or to bring into focus the complex processes by which the struggle between the two industrial super-Powers gave way to uneasy reconciliation, as both began to find themselves confronted with a new Power that challenged both the capitalist USA and the very Mecca of the Communist world itself.

For now there are several communisms where once there was one. The old models of 'East' v. 'West', always inadequate, cannot, now, possibly represent the new alignments, ties and divisions. Today, such bipolar models are simply a barrier to clear thought. Any more viable model has to encompass the emergence to political independence of the former Afro-Asian colonies (and the subsequent decline of many of them back into dependence); the emergence of China as an independent Communist world-Power; the transformation of early nationalist-populist Cuba into a third major centre of revolution, particularly for Latin America; the growing restlessness of Eastern European communist states; and the parallel growing reluctance of some allies of the United States to follow her emerging policy of total resistance.

Communism in the 1950s produced new 'polycentric' tendencies within Europe in the period of Hungary and Poznan. But the serious divisions within communism today are not these. Far more fundamental is the division between the old communism of the developed, industrialized, and largely European countries, and the revolutionary new communisms of the underdeveloped world. Moscow and Peking are the two major opposed centres of these opposed communisms, but even they cannot contain a revolutionary process that is far wider than any particular form of communism, or even of communism itself, and which constantly generates new and original forms and ideologies. Cuba is symptomatic of this new revolutionary wave, for despite her economic and political dependence upon the USSR, and the retrospective addition of a little Marxism to the original revolutionary mix, Cuba is anything but an orthodox Soviet satellite. She is, in fact, an independent centre of revolution for a whole continent, and by that token, closer to the revolutionary communism of China than the staid 'socialism in Eastern Europe' of the Soviet Union. For Cuba, revolution in the backlands is more significant and more universal than the communism of the developed world.

The USSR, however, cannot divest herself of her history very easily. She is still a world-Power with a compulsive and entrenched official ideology of revolution, but more importantly, a world-Power whose political support still comes overwhelmingly from Communist countries and movements. She cannot easily abandon these allies, and so remains involved in revolutions, e.g. in the provision of matériel for Viet Nam. But her prior concern, increasingly, is her own internal condition, which cannot seriously improve unless she can release resources at present swallowed up in the insatiable maw of an enormous machine built to cope with nuclear warfare and a world in revolution. The Soviet population, too, whatever the degree of their sympathy for the people of Viet Nam, have also been waiting for the 'second stage' of socialism for fifty years, and are becoming a little impatient with arguments and commitments which stand in the way of a little more comfort right now.

The winding-down of World War III was largely brought about by a new realization that the nuclear arms race was likely not only to obliterate civilization, but also to impoverish humanity before finally destroying it. Cuba brought home the first lesson: that there could be no victor in a nuclear war: and the subsequent race to develop defences against inter-continental ballistic missiles further brought home the opportunity cost of an arms race which involved such a large-scale diversion of resources that no progress could be made towards resolving severe internal social and economic strains: neither in the USA nor the USSR could there be any effective 'war against poverty' as long as men poured the fruits of their labour into nuclear/space programmes.

The USA, of course, can bear this load better than the USSR, and some sizeable and influential segments of the community achieve short-run benefits from the war economy of a society described by Fred J. Cook as a 'Warfare State'. Nor is the USA inclined to extend the détente with Russia in the direction of a more positive joint approach to tackling the causes of revolution and war. The détente remains little more than an agreement not to join a suicide pact. Instead, the USA has become increasingly committed to handling revolution simply by applying force. In a world in which she is the richest member, she has an understandable, if shortsighted, commitment to keeping the world as it is.

But if the accommodation between the USSR and the USA, for all its tentativeness and limits, and despite all the remaining sources of antagonism between these two super-Powers, left American policy basically unchanged, it did mark an important turning-point for world communism, for it involved the de-fusing of what was once the major international explosive force – the Soviet Union. But although the Soviet Union has become less enthusiastic about world revolution, the world in turmoil has not, and there is a leadership vacuum which many are willing to fill. China has not hesitated to sharpen conflicts wherever they can be found or to generate them where they cannot, and manoeuvres to absorb local conflicts into her world-revolutionary strategy even if to do so she has to support 'feudalists' and other strange comrades-in-arms. Symbolically, the Soviet Union's major intervention on the world stage since the fall of Krushchev has been the quite opposite role of 'elder statesman': at Tashkent, where her efforts – unlike China's – were successfully devoted to stabilizing and mediating, not sharpening and exploiting, the Indo-Pakistani conflict.

Given this abrogation of the revolutionary leadership, the stage appeared well-set for bids by China and Cuba for world revolutionary leadership. But in reality, neither Cuba nor China have had much success. China's failure to maintain and extend the harmony generated at Bandung was a result of her shift from a policy of co-existence and non-intervention to a directly revolutionary policy, after her break with the Soviet Union.

Revolutions could only be practised against the existing Governments of the Third World. Relations with these governments became more and more strained, until the ultimate point was reached in December, 1962, when China became involved in large-scale war against the largest of the non-Communist Bandung Powers – India.

From that time onwards, all but a few Third World governments, such as Somalia, Tanzania, Indonesia, and Cambodia, flinched back from contact with China, who was only too visibly developing not just a political and diplomatic offensive in Africa, but was actively engaged in supplying arms. (That the Ugandan Army, for example, was equipped with British rifles shocked nobody, but the entry of Chinese weapons into Africa were somehow intolerable.)

By the time of Chou En-Lai's visit to eastern Africa in June 1965, the African continent he declared ripe for revolution was, with a few exceptions, set firm against China. 'Against whom, exactly, would these revolutions be directed?' a Kenya Government official statement inquired. By the time of the abortive Algiers Conference of 1965, mounting Chinese ideological and diplomatic pressure had conspired to bring about the opposite of what she had intended. A wedge had been driven between China and most of the rest of the Third World, whereas ten years earlier, they had been able to live together as parts of the Bandung grouping.

In addition to China's failure in the Third World, the struggle between China and the USSR, too, has, for the moment, been decided in favour of the latter. Even communist states and parties in the immediate Chinese orbit have aligned themselves on the Soviet side, notably the Japanese Communist Party and North Korea. Elsewhere, China has had to content herself with the support of Communist Parties in such insignificant countries as Paraguay, New Zealand and Albania, or with the formation of microscopic 'Chinese' splinter-groups which have broken away from the large pro-Soviet Communist Parties.

Perhaps the biggest single material blow to Chinese ambitions since the economically catastrophic break with the USSR, came with the elimination of the Indonesian Communist Party from the political scene in late 1965. Through the slaughter of several hundred thousand Indonesian Communists, the PKI, with its powerful influence upon Soekarno, its three million Party members and its control over twenty million members of trade unions and other organizations, was eliminated almost overnight, and this in the largest country in the world and the largest in South-East Asia. This major event, shifting the world balance of forces, evoked little commensurate response in the West, either in terms of any humane reaction to what has been described by the most vivid chronicler of the events as 'the most ruthless massacres since Hitlerism',* or in terms of any understanding of the magnitude of

* The phrase is actually from the cover of Tarkie Vittachi's *The Fall of Sukarno* and may not be actually the author's.

this event, in political terms, not just for Indonesia, but the whole balance of power in South-East Asia, and consequently, for the world.

To this disastrous blow, China could make no effective response whatsoever, just as she has been unable to achieve any of her other major aims. Nor are paper victories like the humiliation of the Portuguese at Macao any substitute. To a leadership conscious that power flows out of the barrel of a gun, it is becoming painfully obvious that the guns are not all in the hands of revolutionaries by any means. In effect, China lacks the industrial, agricultural and financial resources with which effectively to back up her ideological call to revolution. Hence the contrast between the fiery words and the cautious reality: the hundreds of 'serious warnings' over the offshore islands. The 'paper tiger', in fact, seems singularly substantial, the Chinese dragon no more menacing than those in traditional street-processions.

Frustration and impotence, however, rarely evoke moderation and patience in action, and the development of nuclear weapons by China is a recourse to the ultimate in violence in a situation where her enemies are able to contain and threaten precisely because they are stronger. But the Chinese bomb, instead of offering a short-cut military equality, is not as yet very 'credible', and, in its viciously circular turn, generates further nuclear and other military counter-activity by the USA, and, as in the USSR, drains off investment which would otherwise go to develop agriculture and industry.

The failure of China's bid for revolutionary leadership has thus been pretty general, and the shift from a tactic of wooing the Third World to a tactic of toughness and intensified pressure met with disaster at Algiers. Some of the divisions which divided the Afro-Asian countries were of the nature of private quarrels: India and Pakistan, Indonesia and Malaysia, intra-Arab and intra-African rivalries. Others arose from competition for leadership of the Third World, notably Indonesia's independent attempt to head up the 'Nefo' (New Emerging Forces). But what crucially split the Afro-Asian states was insistent Chinese pressure to follow Chinese policy over a wide range of issues: in the first place, to refuse admission of Malaysia and the USSR to the Conference table.

In the event, these quarrels did not come to the point of a head-on clash, because a way out of these multiple dilemmas was found. It was a mechanism familiar enough to anthropologists and psychiatrists: avoidance. The 'solidarity' of the Bandung world was maintained simply by not facing any of the contentious issues which would have forced countries to divide into pro- and anti-Chinese directions, and along other lines of cleavage. Such a negative avoidance was implicitly, of course, an effective expression of impotence, and at this point, 'non-alignment' began to turn from a political force into a Platonic ideal.

A recent indicator of the decline of the solidarity, effectiveness, and autonomy of the non-aligned grouping as a collectivity, was provided by the meeting in Delhi in October, 1966 between Mrs Gandhi, President Tito, and President Nasser. Whereas Bandung, in 1955, had announced to the world a new presence and a new set of initiatives on the part of an aggregation of states in which China was able to associate with the non-communist majority, the meeting of the three heads of state at Delhi not only had very little to say to the world, but was virtually ignored by it. It is a safe bet that even many readers of this book will be unaware that this particular meeting of non-aligned leaders from Africa, Asia and Europe ever took place at all.

The unity achieved at Bandung marked, of course, the major internal schism in that grouping: that between the revolutionary, mainly communist countries and movements, and the non-revolutionary ones. Since then we have witnessed the cumulative repression not only of revolution, but even of liberal democracy, in Brazil and Argentina, in the military African regimes and the client despotisms of Asia, and now, with Greece, in Europe. This tide of counter-revolution has reduced severely the possibilities of manoeuvre for those who try to remain non-aligned, and the Third World has been notably paralysed as a result.

It has always contained within its ranks states whose interests, whose regimes, philosophies, and policies were very different. The definition and composition of the Third World, indeed, was always situational and complex, an operational rather than analytical term, like those other key terms: 'self-determination', 'neutralism', and 'non-alignment': defined by Professor Mazrui in his study *Towards a Pax Africana*. Now any logician (or any intelligent man in the street who reads the newspapers), can show that, at times, the claims of African states to be 'neutralist', 'non-violent', or 'independent' appear to be little more than rhetoric, or, at best, to be taken in a Pickwickian sense: when, for example, a socialist-oriented state like Tanzania calls in British troops at the time of the Army mutiny, or when a Gaullist-oriented state like Gabon calls in French paratroopers.

Further, these states, which emphasize the sacredness of the principle of 'self-determination', are certainly not neutral vis-à-vis South Africa, or, in the past, Algeria, and would have happily 'intervened in the internal affairs' of these countries if they could have found a way of doing so.

But there is much more than rhetoric to their claims. To make sense of them, one has to understand that the terms have no absolute meaning 'in themselves', and can only be defined situationally. The kind of definition need, that is, has to be *socio*-logical as well as logical, and the relevant situational framework within which the operation of defining neutralism has to be performed is the double context of (*a*) the successive Old and New Cold Wars, and (*b*) the relationship between the developed and the under-developed states. 'Nonaligned', for example, means *non-aligned vis-à-vis Russia and America*, or, now, China. These 'master-principles' of non-alignment therefore by no means preclude other, subsidary alignments, e.g. the alignment of the francophone territories with France (herself experimenting with non-alignment in her relations with Moscow, and Washington, though calling it 'Gaullism'). Similarly, 'self-determination' means determination of Africa's future by *none other than continental African states*: that African affairs are not the prerogative of Powers outside this universe. This applies, certainly, to Russia and China, but especially to the ex-colonial Powers and to the leading Power in the capitalist world, the USA. 'Self-government', Mazrui suggests, primarily means 'government by rulers manifestly belonging to the same race as the ruled'.

This kind of situational analysis, applied to the definition of the 'Third World', makes more effective and explicit distinctions that were left undeveloped and implicit in the last chapter. (I shall confine myself here to the analyses of one sub-unit – the African continent – within the Third World as a whole.)

At the level of relationships between states, one important

feature, guiding one major definition of the 'Third World', is clearly implicit in the very label itself: they are held to constitute a *Third* World, as against the First and Second (capitalist and communist) Worlds respectively.* In other usages, however, the Third World is defined on the basis of the shared experience of a colonial past and a continuing 'neo-colonial' present, or upon the contrast between the world of Euro-America and the rest. The spokesmen and ideologists of these countries thus most commonly speak of them as the 'Afro-Asian' states. A yet wider distinction is the dichotomous one of the 'underdeveloped, versus the 'developed' states. In this model, the dividing-line cuts across the familiar dichotomy of 'communist'/'non-communist' or 'democratic'/'totalitarian'. These particular single-strand dichotomies are poor ideal types which cannot, and do not, adequately organize, let alone exhaust, the complexities of the reality upon which they are brought to bear. The multiple sets of allegiances involved do not fall neatly along the line of one single dominating articulating principle, but involve cross reference in thought and cross-cutting ties in action, since allegiances and the groupings shift according to the situation. There is not however, an infinity of such ties and divisions; in fact, they are few. But they are numerous enough to make the patterns of association often quite kaleidoscopic. 'Underdeveloped' versus 'developed', for example, brings China squarely within the camp of the poor countries, and puts the USSR on the other side of the fence. In this usage, common amongst French Marxists, the 'Third World' includes communist *and* non-communist countries. But this is only one line of division and association: at other times, a trichotomous Communist-Capitalist-non-communist 'Third World' model is used. A four-part model: Capitalist world/Russian-Communism/Chinese Communism/non-communist Third World: is perfectly possible, and commonly used; or a further trichotomy: 'developed' world (including the capitalist states *and* the USSR)/Chinese Communism/non-Communist Third World. Such oscillation of meaning are not by any means mere academic definition-spinning; they are the stuff of everyday international relations.

The voting record of Third World countries at the UN is one index not only of the flexibility of their attitudes, resulting from the

*As in Irving Louis Horowitz's *Three Worlds of Development.*

THE THIRD WORLD

multiple attachments already described, but also the reality of their claim to be 'non-aligned':

'The figures do not reveal either extensive bloc voting or overwhelming pro-Soviet voting on the part of the non-aligned states. In those instances where the United States and the Sovet Union voted differently, 26·1 per cent of the votes cast by the fifty non-aligned countries coincided with those of the United States, and 29·2 per cent with those of the Soviet Union . . . The twenty-three African countries voted with the United States 30·7 per cent of the time and supported the Soviet position 24·4 per cent of the time . . . Most significant, the votes of all the states differed from both the Soviet Union and the United States nearly one-third of the time, or 31·3 per cent.'*

This attempt to avoid identification with either bloc has, then, not been merely a verbal rhetoric. It has reflected the real kinship which exists between non-communist Third World countries which can never be fully distanced from those other countries which like them, are underdeveloped, but unlike them, are communist. Since they are non-communist countries, they do not make automatic partners for Moscow, Havana or Peking. Tied to the West by economic links, they can never be, unreservedly, pro-Western because these economic links are also chains. Many of the Third World countries, too, have maintained this difficult independence in the face of severe pressure to become aligned, notably when the UAR did not flee into the sheltering arms of the Soviet Union, even through and after Suez.

As a *positive*, coordinated international grouping, however, the non-communist Third World has clearly lost ground. Neutralism, therefore, still persists, but it is rarely, now, a 'positive' neutralism. This is not due to some sudden failure of will, but to a lack of real power due to their economic weakness. Even within these countries, though the ruling elites have decisive political power so far as the formal machinery of politics is concerned, control over their economies commonly lies abroad. This economic weakness at home makes them politically weak abroad, where at best, they can only pool their separate weaknesses: at worst, sell their foreign policies and their UN votes to the highest bidder.

The attempt to maintain a Third World position in international

* Francis O. Wilcox, 'The Nonaligned States and the United Nations', in *Neutralism and Nonalignment*, ed. Lawrence W. Martin, pp. 227–8.

affairs can only be effective when policies pursued at home lead to economic growth. Otherwise, country after country is forced back into dependence on one of the larger Powers, and thereby is sucked into its political orbit. Modern Afro-Asian populism, as we saw in Chapter 4, is essentially a response to the challenge of industrialism on the part of small producers, normally agricultural producers, who seek to preserve themselves against the inroads of capitalism, on the one hand, and the challenge from communism on the other. It is, then, an alternative philosophy of, and strategy for, development, not simply a backwards-looking nostalgia. As such, it is an activist creed, which places great emphasis upon popular participation and upon forms of organization that transcend pure individualism but stop well short of centralized collectivism.

Populism and the 'Third World' are not, of course, co-extensive, except at the level of aspiration towards non-communist, non-capitalist development. Those states which have actually institutionalized elements of populism in their internal policies, or which have talked about so doing, like Soekarno's Indonesia, Mali, Algeria, and Tanzania, have constituted an influential grouping within the non-aligned bloc, and have thereby injected their ideas and values into the thinking of the Bandung countries. But in reality, few of the Third World states have seriously put populist notions into operation internally. Rather more have talked populism, but only a few experimented with communitarian agriculture and participatory 'self-help' schemes.

The serious viability of any 'third way' could, of course, only be seriously tested once independence had been secured. From the beginning of the 1960s, many former colonies did secure their independence; most of them succeeded in consolidating the new states as sovereign entities. But now development, not independence, became the major issue, and the internal development programmes of the new states became their dominant concern, not their international political status.

Unattracted by the prospect of continuing 'neo-colonial' capitalism, on the one hand, or by the model of state socialism on the other, they evinced a lively interest in any viable alternatives. The existing 'great models', however, were peculiarly unattractive in one crucial respect. They appeared to offer no answer to the problem that most concerned the new states: the modernization of the countryside.

Chinese communism, for example, to maintain its appeal for the Third World, needed to demonstrate her relevance not so much as a model for the achievement of national independence (which they had already), but as a model for the economic transformation of an agrarian society. The most impressive Chinese achievements, however, were in the industrial sphere, where Soviet aid had been an important initial asset. But the countryside was another matter, for although Chinese performance outstripped that of India, well over a decade after the revolution she was having to import huge amounts of grain from capitalist Australia and Canada to feed her people.

There seemed no very strong reason, then, why, in societies which had only just emerged and consolidated themselves as viable polities, non-Communist leaderships should follow Chinese models whose results, in terms of agricultural productivity, were equivocal, but which certainly involved deliberate and massive radicalization.

Non-revolutionary India, too, which had invested heavily in industry during the first three Five-Year Plans, was obliged to turn back, in the fourth Plan, to the development of the agricultural sector, and, within the industrial sphere, to those industries, like the fertilizer and agricultural machinery industries, which could supply the farmers.

Exponents of, and apologists for, free enterprise, naturally strongly resisted any extension of socialism, whether in Chinese or any other form. Others hostile to action by the state were more concerned to protect pluralism rather than capitalism. Specially sensitive to any form of concentration of State power, they were not slow to point to the failure of the non-communist single-party regimes to register any serious successes in achieving the agrarian 'take-off'. Not only was communist agriculture unimpressive, but non-communist single-party regimes had also failed to substantiate their claim that, by concentrating State power and national resources, they could effectively overcome the fragmentation of petty capital in millions of separate hands, and thus facilitate centrally-controlled investment in large-scale programmes which the private entrepreneurial economy could not or would not undertake. The control of this investment by the State, it was held, would also prevent the growth sectors of the economy from falling into the hands of 'neo-colonialists'.

In reality, their critics pointed out, the one-party regimes achieved virtually nothing. Industrialization on any significant scale was noticeable by its absence, and, in the agricultural sector, 'villageization', 'self-help', and similar communitarian or planned agricultural developments not only failed more often than not, but had also proved highly capital-intensive, not labour-intensive, and had absorbed the services of skilled technical and managerial personnel who were in particularly short supply.

The failure of the single-party regimes is indeed evident. But more to the point is the more general failure of *all* the under-developed countries, whether single-party or multi-party; whether socialist or otherwise: whether militantly independent or client-states; whether controlled by military men or civilian parties; and, one should add, whether communist or non-communist. None have effectively succeeded in making the agricultural 'take-off', and there seems little reason for singling out the one-party regimes for special pillorying for their agricultural failures. Indeed, only advanced capitalist countries, the USA and Canada, and Western Europe since 1945, have cracked the problem of dramatically raising agricultural productivity (apart from satellite 'kitchen gardens' of industrial countries, such as New Zealand and Denmark, which, in economic terms, are more like overseas provinces of Britain, and have in any case, developed sizeable internal industrial sectors.) Even the USSR drags this particular foot limpingly behind its strong industrial limb.

The particular defects in the policies of agrarian modernization adopted by all these countries cannot be dwelt upon here, nor the reason for the success of modern agriculture in North America and Western Europe. They would include not only the availability of capital, but also a supply of suitable managerial, administrative and technical personnel; a developed scientific and educational infrastructure; a developed extension service; a programme of planned agricultural experimentation; and a highly motivated and skilled farming population. The conditions and resources that made success possible in Euro-America, one need only note here, are quite absent in Africa and Asia. Yet modern collectivist and cooperative schemes, which involve radical transformation of *all* social relations, and not merely relations of production – precisely the most complex and difficult of all operations on which one could conceivably embark – have all too often been the methods chosen. In the absence of these necessary factors, forced-march programmes only ensure that any mistakes made will be really big mistakes. The more successful agricultural ventures in the Third World do not involve transformation of all institutional orders, but simply support at the point of production or economies in marketing: improved small-holder peasant agriculture has been more rewarding than state, cooperative, or collectivist projects. (Improved productivity along these lines, does, however, carry with it social concomitants that will have to be reckoned with in the future, particularly the emergence of class-stratification in the countryside.)

These technical and social obstacles to improved productivity are daunting enough. It is necessary to add to them a further set of political constraints and inhibitions, for once the farmer has increased his production, he is all too often confronted with a rapacious or simply inefficient State which ensures that a great part of the product of his labour is taken from him.

In all too many countries, what Professor Andreski has called 'kleptocratic' regimes milk the farmer, and ensure that whoever gets priority – the military, the carpetbaggers of the Party, the townsmen, the capitalists, the governmental elite, or the traditional authorities – it will certainly not be the farmer. His role is simply to produce the spoliable wealth.

Even the most angelic of governments, however, operating the most rational of agricultural policies, have been fighting a losing battle on the world scene, whatever they have done within their boundaries. The constraints under which any underdeveloped primary-producer country has to operate have been of such a defeating and global order that even where the raising of productivity has occurred, it has solved nothing.

Firstly, and primarily, the 'scissors' phenomenon has operated throughout the whole of this period to the detriment of the producers of raw materials who have often increased production, sometimes quite sharply, only to find that the earnings from these increased exports have been negated by falls in world-prices.

In Nkrumah's much-denounced Ghana, for example, a great deal of attention has been paid to the shortcomings and extravagances of investment-policy, particularly the dissipation of sterling reserves, accumulated from cocoa sales, on irrational schemes, on 'prestige' projects' and simply into private pockets. But it is less frequently observed that the production of cocoa, the main source of foreign earnings, *doubled* under Nkrumah's regime, or that this increase was accompanied by a decline in the price paid for cocoa on the world market which entirely negated the achievements on the production side:

TABLE 7. GHANA COCOA BEAN PRODUCTION AND INCOME, 1956–65*

Year	Spot Price of Cocoa Beans in US cents/lb.	Ghana's Production in metric tons	Adjusted Revenue in US $
1956	27·3		
1957	30·6		
1958	44·3	209,800	$204,471,080
1959	36·6	259,500	
1960	28·4	321,900	
1961	22·6	439,000	
1962	21·0	416,000	
1963	25·3	428 400	
1964	23·4	427,700	$220,157,960
1965	Feb. 20·6		
	June 13·8		
	Aug. 14·0		

Source: *Cocoa Statistics*, January 1, 1966, A publication of the UN Food and Agriculture Organization.

*I am indebted to Dr Frank Chalk for this table. A similar table is presented in Fitch and Oppenheimer's 'Ghana: End of an Illusion', *Monthly Review*, Vol. 18, No. 3, p. 85.

The result was that the doubling of production produced very little increase in national income. Farm-income can often be cushioned against fluctuations for a short time, but not on this scale over such a long period. More commonly, swings in world prices are felt very directly and immediately by the peasant producer, who never knows what he is to expect. What happens on the New York and other commodity exchanges is directly experienced by plantation-workers and by every small farmer involved in the money economy in remote African and Asian villages. World economic fluctuations of this kind thus directly touch the lives of millions who have been hoping for, even expecting, improvement in their lives. The peasant who has doubled his acreage finds himself where he started. Running in order to keep in the same spot may be funny in *Alice in Wonderland*, but not when it means foregoing the food, shirts, education, paraffin lamps, and bicycles one has looked forward to. Then it is likely to produce blind protest, despair, bafflement, or even, eventually, revolution.

For governments seriously concerned with finding answers, the situation is as frustrating as it is to the farmer. They can get little assistance from experts, either, for the peasants of Asia share their helplessness with the economists and politicians of Europe and America. If the scourge were merely one of *fluctuation* – of business cycles, booms and slumps, or stop-go jerks – it would be bad enough. But today, overall, for most of the world, there is a general condition of progressive, secular *deterioration*. Fluctuation is bad enough, for it makes long-term planning almost impossible. Large projects cannot be stopped and started without serious waste of resources and dislocation of organization, since inter-related parts and phases of large-scale plans each depend upon the other.

'Inelastic' world demand is part of the explanation: the world supply of cocoa, for example, is increasing rapidly but the demand for it very little. In such a situation, producers do not command the market, and the price drops as production increases. The underdeveloped producer-countries find themselves at the mercy of the rich consumer-countries who are in a position to fix world-prices. For the more 'monocultural' countries, like Ghana or Cuba, the problem is particularly acute, and producers cannot even withhold supplies from the market, for the organization required would be considerable, and the temptation for one or more countries to sell as prices do begin to rise too great.

Even if such arrangements could be made, however, a new threat to the producing countries is becoming an immediate rather than a long-term threat. Substitutes are being developed for raw materials which have hitherto been necessities for the economies of the developed countries. Today, many of the key raw materials produced outside Euro-America become ever less important to modern industry, which now produces, from a few basic chemical elements, substitutes for traditional natural raw materials. A century ago, all this would have been an occasion for panegyrics on human inventiveness and on the inevitability and rightness of human progress. Today, we are more likely to be aware that one of the new artificial products not to be found in Nature is strontium 90, and that the development of substitutes for older raw materials sentences vast areas of the world to new, and perhaps irremediable poverty. The export of sisal alone accounts for a quarter of the value of Tanzania's agricultural exports: in the last three years the world price has tumbled catastrophically, and a new chemical substitute threatens to accelerate the speed of this economic decline. The 1963 fall in world coffee prices caused standards of living to drop very rapidly in Brazil, and was followed by political disorder and military take-over. In the Sudan, cotton provides some 65 per cent of the total value of domestic exports, some 17 per cent of the Gross Domestic Product, and approximately 20 per cent of the money incomes generated in the Sudan. Now, cotton has to compete with the man-made fibres.

Without international action to alter the relationship between prices for manufactured goods and prices for primary products, a very bleak future is assured for the world's peasantry. There are no signs that any effective action is being taken.

Instead, the underdeveloped countries are likely to continue to become ever more backward vis-à-vis the advanced industrial nations. Income per head in 1965 has been calculated at $2,220 for the rich countries, and only $190 for the poor countries. At present rates of growth, by 1970 the figures for the rich countries will be $2,610 and for the poor, $210. More and more, investment is being channelled towards the developed nations: towards Western Europe, North America, and the 'Old' (White) Commonwealth countries: South Africa, Australia and New Zealand: because these offer the highest returns on capital invested. The poor nations fear that the European Common Market will be yet another major step in this direction: that it will be a 'rich men's club' largely independent of the poorer parts of the globe, and therefore less and less interested in them as an area of investment, except where they still continue to serve as producers of irreplaceable – or cheaper – raw materials, notably oil. They fear an inversion of the Leninist model of imperialism: that from being areas producing 'super-profits', they may become such unattractive investment prospects that they can be abandoned, and condemned to permanent poverty.

Countries like Kenya, whose White Paper on 'African Socialism' is said by the cynical to read like an investment brochure,* appear already, despite verbal 'socialism', to be desperately willing to do anything to attract foreign investment in the name of 'development'. Their desperation is understandable. There are other countries which resist auctioning off their resources, just as they resist auctioning off their UN vote, precisely because they see the continuation of a predominantly agrarian and extractive economy is a prime guarantee of permanent backwardness and helplessness. They also appreciate that without industrialization, they are on the losing side in international trade, and that they cannot hope to solve their problems on their own, for Africa today contains more than fifty political units, with an average population of about four to five million people, 36 of them with a population of under fifteen million, 30 of these under five million, and twelve under one million.

To overcome these micro-national limitations; to create regional economic groupings; to replace the built-in orientations of trade towards single metropolitan centres; and to overcome the entrenched interests of new elites ruling the micro-states, and the different ideological orientations of the leaderships of adjoining countries, is a gigantic set of tasks. All these factors, taken together, conspire very effectively to frustrate coordination of radical and rational economic policies. Between the francophone territories of West Africa, for example, and their anglophone neighbours, no new links are forged or are likely to be while they all remain rival producers of the same crops primarily tied to France or Britain. On the other side of the continent, in East Africa, the divisive effects of differences in political orientation are similarly visible. Existing channels of economic and infrastructural coordination and communication have broken down in the face of new competitions and conflicts between a Kenyan policy oriented towards private investment from the 'West', and a Tanzanian policy aiming at her own variant of socialism open, both to the traditional

*African Socialism and its Application to Planning in Kenya.

'Western' connection and Eastern Europe and China. New banks and currency, new customs barriers, and competing investment in the same fields (such as the cotton industry) signify, not so much the failure to move towards federation, but the dismantling of what little serious institutionalized cooperation exists.

The effects of asymmetrical terms of trade, and the divisions within the Third World, produced or underlined by particular ties to particular developed economies and political groupings, have not been the only degenerative features of the situation of the poor countries in the last decade. They have all been confronted with the major problem of mobilizing capital. Most of them have relied heavily on the provision of aid from the developed world. Never very remarkable, the volume of aid has stayed at a rather uninspired level for several years. Nothing is more full of pitfalls for the unwary than the operation of trying to measure aid flows, for the statistics commonly fail to distinguish the aid component proper from general capital flow; do not always separate private investment from governmental grants and loans; and achieve the astounding vanishing trick by which military aid is made to disappear, or is re-titled 'support'. Nor, if we do distinguish, say, a food programme as 'non-military' aid does this epithet mean very much when that food is going to South Viet Nam.

Existing aid has been disproportionately allocated to those countries which have offered the best promise, not for 'development' or 'democracy', but for compliance with the politico-military strategies of the Great Powers. The most elementary general proposition that can be advanced about aid policy is that, from the point of view of economic growth, most of it goes where it is least needed. China, the largest and one of the poorest countries on earth, receives nothing. Up to 1960, she did receive Soviet aid, but in that year, underwent the traumatic experience of the whole-sale withdrawal of Soviet finance, Soviet technicians, Soviet industrial equipment, and, even, it is said, the blueprints of the factories under construction. The severity of this ruthless and sudden disruption of planned growth was almost as crippling as that which resulted from Guinea's break with France, but the scale was infinitely greater and the consequences world-historic, for this trauma underlies the whole of the subsequent movement of Chinese policy towards a militant, independent, activist and intransigent world-revolutionary policy, of which the 'cultural revolution' is merely the latest internal instalment.

Of the two super-Powers, the major capitalist contender for world hegemony, the United States, like the USSR, has been guided primarily by considerations of world-power in its aid policy. In 1956/7, it was calculated that of the $1,000M worth of US aid which had gone to 20 countries with an income per head of less than $100, $336M had gone to South Korea, $246M to South Vietnam, $41M to Cambodia, and $49M to Laos. Of the 18 countries with an income per head of between $100 and $200, $111M out of $464M went to Taiwan.

The direction of aid has thus a regular distribution – around the Chinese and Soviet peripheries. But its social direction as well as its geographical direction, has been equally pronounced, for the overwhelming top priority in aid programmes has been military aid. It has not been notably channelled to 'democratic' nations. Some, like Chile, have been parliamentary democracies; most of the major beneficiaries of US aid no kind of democracies.

Apart from this direct allocation of aid resources for military purposes, sharpening confrontation in Asia and Latin America and the increase of private internal Third World conflicts (exacerbated severely by the dabbling of the Great Powers) have caused Third World countries themselves to spend more and more on preparations for war. The massive defence budgets of India and Pakistan are perhaps the most striking cases, for these are countries faced with the intractable and enormous problems of civil development in a subcontinent of millions of human beings. Indo-Pakistani enmity is not, of course, a product of the Cold War; China's support for the much less democratic of the two countries and her military confrontations on India's frontiers, certainly are conditioned by her hostility to the Soviet Union, and her suspicion of the 'Western' orientations of the major non-Communist Power in Asia.

But having identified the major cause of the unproductive use of the exiguous resources that are available, it still remains the case that money and human energy is devoted to modernization of a more positive and creative kind. True, the scale of investment is far too low to bridge the ever-widening gap between what is achieved and the needs and wants generated by the world demographic explosion and the revolution of rising expectations. But even where money is expended on health, agriculture, education, and industrial and agricultural development, existing Development Plans and projects are marked by a degree of inadequacy and even plain failure that cannot be attributed solely to the world market, the world arms-race, or the Cold War.

Many of the difficulties encountered in modernization, however, do stem back to the distortions induced by the economic and political polarization of the world.

The flow of trained specialists from the Third World to the developed countries, especially to the USA, is one crucial and chronic haemorrhage that frustrates the implementation of plans that depend precisely upon the availability of experts. The brain drain to the USA from the poor countries of the world far outstrips the counter-flow of technical assistance under aid programmes. Nor is this solely a problem for backward countries. Lord Bowden and Professor Titmuss have drawn attention to the built-in frustrations, and the economic and social dislocations, caused by the 'brain-drain', even for a wealthy country like Britain, since the US space programme in particular, and American affluence in general, has attracted to the USA a body of foreign scientists in whose persons is locked up a financial investment greater than the whole of the aid these countries have received from the USA since 1949. The problem is even more tragic for the poor countries, whose doctors, engineers, agriculturalists, and students go abroad never to return. The insatiable sponge of the space/nuclear race in the advanced countries ensures, in Bowden's words, that 'fields in India and Africa will remain uncultivated so that America can put a man on the moon'. Put another way, in this respect the less developed countries are subsidising the most developed nation on earth.

Another major way in which national planning is frustrated by world anarchy lies in the field of finance, for countries which depend crucially upon a steady, calculable flow of capital from the outside world – as most poor countries do – find it impossible to carry out continuing and inter-related Development Plans when finance is liable to be suddenly, and unpredictably, cut off. Even without these 'micro'-traumas, the need to negotiate particular 'projects' separately and to have them evaluated before loan sanction is given, generates a piece-meal approach to planning that may hearten proponents of Popperian liberalism, but which constitutes an agonizing and sterilizing heartbreak for those struggling to achieve steady and balanced growth. The provision of aid on a 'project' basis, for example, makes it difficult to connect man-power budgeting with educational provision, and to relate these and project them over a time-span of years. Donor countries, too, are not always simply making donations, for a great deal of 'aid' includes a large component which has to be expended in the donor's own country. Nor is the financing of prestige projects confined to megalomanic despots in new states, for rich donor countries are usually far more interested in spectacular and visible dams and large buildings than in modest but vital campaigns to eradicate disease or provide water in remote areas.

Lying at the heart of another set of constraints is the peculiar intractability of the central problem: agriculture. At times, in particular countries, quite striking achievements have been registered with particular programmes – as when Kenya succeeded in elevating smallholder market production to the status of a 'major industry ... within an amazingly short period' (total agricultural production increased at an annual rate of 4·5 per cent, from £74M in 1954 to £117M in 1964, the most notable rise occurring in coffee production, which jumped from £170,000 in 1954 to over £5M in 1964.) But other sectors of the rural economy, other regions, and other sections of the farming population, have experienced no such improvement. It is no morbid preoccupation with gloom to observe that, in any case, 'Kenya is one of the few underdeveloped countries where agricultural production has been rising significantly within the last decade'.*

Successes like the Kenya case are worthy of special attention, because we may learn from them what to do. We can equally learn what not to do from the failures.

In neighbouring Tanzania, for example, the 'villageization' programme which was the lynch-pin of the programme to modern-ize rural production and rural life generally, has had to be virtually totally abandoned. The causes of this defeat lie not so much in the constraints presented by financial and technical difficulties, but in

* Hans Ruthenberg, *African Agricultural Development Policy in Kenya, 1952–1965*, pp. 1, 12.

298

weaknesses at the level of human and 'social' inputs: the shortage of suitable managers; the unfamiliarity of new settlers removed from their natal villages to share a new life with strangers from different cultural backgrounds; their unfamiliarity with new crops and new land; and the quite novel requirements of life in radically new cooperative, centralized communities initiated and controlled by administrative machines stemming down from Ministries in the remote capital. Sheer dedication and enthusiasm, where these were present – mainly in the form of the extraordinary explosion of 'self-help' movement in the euphoric post-Independence period – have been no adequate substitutes for agricultural, social, and organizational skills, and it is tragic to chart the history of the popular mobilization which produced a wave of construction-projects and studded the country with new 'home-made' schools, dispensaries, and roads, only for their makers to find that there were no teachers or medical assistants, no books or drugs, to turn these into living foci for the 'animation' of rural life. Under these circumstances, despair or resignation re-assert themselves. Where they do not, the contradiction between effort and expectation, on the one hand, and the actual achievement of little on the other, sharpens frustrations and sows the seeds of discontent. When Chou En-Lai spoke of Africa as ripe for revolution, he was premature. Before revolution, we may anticipate a period of growing dissatisfaction and disturbance, and of epiphenomenal political takeover bids by various kinds of authoritarian and 'tutelary' cliques. Indeed, the latter process is well-advanced: between 1958 and 1965, there were thirty-five *military* coups alone in underdeveloped countries, '18 of them in countries which had been independent for 20 years or less, and six for only five years or less.'*

These changes of regime are normally coups d'état by very small bodies of armed men – in Africa, normally, one or two hundred soldiers only are involved. Such major coups are possible because of the highly centralized structure, and the smallness of scale, of the formal machinery of politics and administration in backward countries, and because of the low degree of popular involvement in political life. The 'mass party, is commonly only 'mass' insofar as

* S. E. Finer, 'The Military in Politics', paper presented to Manchester University Conference on Political Development, September, 1965, p. 4.

it provides a mass audience for political rallies and demonstrations. Political 'participation' of this kind is much more analagous to that of the traditional city mob of ancient societies or the more recent variants familiar from Naples, Cairo, and Baghdad. This kind of 'mass', to use Kornhauser's terminology, is a 'disposable' instrument, rather than a self-activating and goal-defining manifestation of 'participatory' democracy. Such analytical distinctions, however, only provide ideal-type conceptual categories. A more valuable index of the reality of the degree of moral involvement of people in 'their' governmental and political institutions is provided by the record of the resistance offered by the masses when the governments which claimed their allegiance, and which appeared to successfully manipulate and mobilize support, are themselves overthrown. Universally (except for popular murmurs at the overthrow of Ben Bella), the mass party or its 'unquestioned, leaders are toppled with effortless ease, and popular protest, let alone intervention, is nil. In Finer's graphic phrase, 'not a dog barks': the nigh-total inaction of the populace is the most striking feature of these coups.

The low level of politicization reflected in this easy vulnerability of even the most apparently entrenched mass political machines, is not in any way modified by the accession to power of the new authoritarians; indeed, these effectively inhibit any kind of inquiry, debate, or commitment. Sectional interest-groups are denounced as part and parcel of the 'party politics' that has been exposed and deposed. Normally there is little need, however, for the military to disband parties and trade unions, or to bring them under control, because this has already been done, for the most part, by the previous regime. All that is necessary is to sweep up the elite minorities at the apex of the institutional complex: Government/ Party/Trade Union centre/Women's Organization/Youth Movement. If these are too deeply unreconstructable, because permeated from top to bottom by adherents of the old regime, they may be replaced, but the form remains the same. Indeed, a most striking feature of the military regimes is the continuity they display, both in their practice and their ideology, with the very regimes they have overthrown.

Even ideologically, they continue the internal and external policies that the old single-party, too, promulgated: at home,

modernization via a mixed economy, with a large part both for the
State and for foreign private investment; abroad, decolonization
and non-alignment vis-à-vis the Cold Wars. The sociological
reason for this continuity are not far to seek. They derive, firstly,
from the severe constraints within which *any* government of a
backward country has to operate, and, secondly, from the character
of the new military elite.

These men do not resemble either of the types of military
interventionist familiar to us from Old War or Latin American
history. They are not, on the one hand, – as 'class' theorists tell us –
simply instruments of some ruling class, dependent variables,
despite their activism in overthrowing constitutional forms and
political institutions. Nor are they – as 'elite' theorists would have
it – a developed *stand*, an 'officer caste', with independent proud
traditions, (like the Reichswehr in the Weimar Republic or the
French generals in Algeria), with a proclivity to define the interests
of the military as the interests of the nation; to present the armed
forces as the embodiment of the nation and the symbol of its
glory; and to make militarism at home and abroad central features
of national policy and national culture, if only to distract attention
from failures and from internal divisions of interest.

No, these are, rather, men without traditions, new men quite
as new as the Party elites they displace. Nor are they flamboyant
military adventurers but, rather, stolid bureaucrats in uniform who
forward no sectional corporate military interest, but who rule
through a consortium of civilian professional administrators and
grey professional conservatives. Since they lack the skills needed
to govern even these relatively uncomplicated societies, they have
to fall back upon technocrats, primarily non-political civil servants
and academics, to help them out. The new military, in any case,
can scarcely be a *stand*, for they have only been generals (sometimes have only been officers) for five or ten years. But as a rapidly-
advanced monocentric power elite, they have the same social
characteristics as the men they toppled from power, with one key
difference – they wear uniforms and control the machine-guns.
They do not, however, depend principally upon guns, certainly
not at this stage of political development, where the sense of
euphoria induced by a clean sweep of the old single party brings
them a fund of popularity. But unless they solve their countries'

problems – and they are unlikely to – they will be obliged, as discontent mounts, to rely more and more on bayonets. Few yet have tried the tactic experimented with by Nasser, of developing some form of mass base via an organization under the control of the ruling elite.

It is true that the economy, under these regimes, is much more receptive to, and attractive to, Western investors. It is also more cautious about Western aid, because many of the old regime's difficulties were the result of an over-easy acceptance of aid which has to be repaid. Loan servicing, the repayment of both principal and interest has become a serious burden for poor countries, for whom total indebtedness tripled between 1955 and 1964 to $406M. By 1965, 44 per cent of the value of official bilateral loans alone was offset by repayment and interest charges of previous loans. Total indebtedness was much higher. For thirty-seven countries, debt service payments rose from 3·8 per cent of their export earnings in 1956 to 10·8 per cent in 1964. 'Aid' is not, as some think, simply giving money away. Broadly half the aid has been in the form of grants, it is true, but the other half has been in the form of loans which have to be repaid with interest. In 1961, grants made up 63 per cent of the bilateral government aid. Grants had fallen to 56 per cent in 1964, though the terms of loans improved for the borrowing countries (interest rates fell from 4·6 per cent to 3·6 per cent and repayment periods rose from, on average, 19 years to 22 years, with improved 'grace' periods.)

In foreign policy, the neutralism displayed certainly leans more to the international Right. 'Directional neutralism', however, is nothing new, or peculiar to the Third World. In Europe, Claude Bourdet once classically expressed a Left-wing variant of it in the era of the Old Cold War, with typical Gallic wit:

'Let us suppose that the Communist peace offensive hides the darkest of strategems, let us suppose further that the Atlantic policy reflects the intentions of innocent lambs, it is still the consequences of the latter that we fear'.*

The caution of even the military regimes in the face of the snares of the Cold Wars, however, is marked. Western investment is one

* Claude Bourdet, 'Beaucoup de colombes', *Combat*, 20/4/49, cited in John T. Marcus, *Neutralism and Nationalism in France*, p. 33.

thing; Western conditional aid, Western political control, another. Verbally, certainly, non-alignment is still official policy. True, China is taboo, but she was to the civilian predecessor-regime. True, the continued assertion of implacable hostility towards South Africa by the new military regimes is a verbal matter rather than a statement of intention to confront – but so it has been for many years. Only countries like Tanzania and Zambia have been prepared to hurt themselves in this cause, and Zambia's capacity to do so is seriously qualified by an economic dependence upon Rhodesia and South Africa which cannot easily be dissolved.

These shifts towards the West are thus significant, but scarcely major, departures from the policies of the former, often more verbally militant, single-party regimes. It was Nkrumah's government, for example, which carried through a Volta Project in which the original aims – the creation of an integrated aluminium industry around a hydro-electric power-base that would also lay the foundation for other industrial development – have been virtually abandoned. Instead, Ghana now has a capital-intensive hydro-electric project, which, under a thirty-year agreement, will only involve a manpower requirement of 145 at its maximum. The aluminium factory has disappeared; the smelter remains, but the bauxite is not to be Ghanaian, but Jamaican, and is to be processed in the United States. Power is supplied to the Kaiser enterprise at nearly cost, and the ancillary irrigation and fishing projects, and the associated public utilities, have been separated from the aluminium project. Nor, so far, is there any likelihood that internal demand, or the needs of adjoining countries, will absorb the available power-supply. The Nkrumah regime had accepted, too, the prospect of facing interest and principal repayments of £34M per year, beginning to fall due in 1967, without any assured major revenues from the project, apart from the £2·5M worth of power which Kaiser contracted to purchase. Industrialization, irrigation, and fisheries potential, which could utilize both the power and water potential and produce further revenue, would require the investment of capital on a scale that simply has not been available.* These were scarcely, then, – despite the rhetoric of 'socialism' which they expressed – the economic policies of a government set upon breaking the classic pattern of the colonial-extractive

* Fitch and Oppenheimer, op. cit., p. 123–126.

industries. Nor are they so radically different from the policies of the new military, as far as these have become visible.

In practice, the gap between old and new regimes is not so wide as the gap between the professed aims of successive regimes and their substantive achievements. To a very large extent, then, the 'non-political' and 'national' military governments represent a closely-related 'functional alternative' to predecessor regimes that, too, were 'no-party' governments of 'national unity', which repressed, demobilized, or absorbed opposition, which centralized all power in their hands, and which operated a mixed economy.

Military intervention is nothing unfamiliar, particularly in the recent history of Latin America. Nor is the rhetoric of altruism and nationalism: it has always been used to deck out even the most flagrant maximization of sectional private interests, whether these be the special interests of the military or class-interests with which they identify. The maintenance of public order carries with it the maintenance of the domination of those who control that order. The military may often be 'radical' and 'innovatory' in their readiness to dispense with traditional or established institutions: parliaments, civil rights, etc. – even to the extent of appealing to the masses before more dangerous elements pre-empt them (as in early *peronismo* and *getulismo* in Argentine and Brazil) – but this radicalism is always ultimately oriented to the over-riding aim of defending civil society against the threat of social revolution. Such political and military 'revolutions', therefore, have been profoundly anti-revolutionary in social terms.

The conservatism of the military, today, however, is no longer the local conservatism of traditional nineteenth century armies, just as the capitalism of Argentina and Brazil is no longer simply the capitalism of the traditional meat and coffee interests. Today, particular local interests become quickly interwoven with world-wide groupings whose fields of force transcend national boundaries and sectional interests. For South-East Asia, the polarizing principle is provided by the challenge of China; for Latin America, by the new threat of Castroism. In the face of such challenges, old and new segments of ruling classes, civilian and military conservatives, close their ranks and fall in behind 'firm' (usually military) leaders.

Hence, in Latin America, 'since the rise of Castro the military have taken a pronounced rightist turn'.* In Ghana, the first reaction of the new military government to an attempted coup against the National Liberation Council was to:

'assure the public and the world that the investment climate in Ghana remains undisturbed by this morning's event. The N.L.C.'s policies which have fomented the favourable investment climate remain unchanged ... There are presently in Ghana a number of representatives of foreign firms negotiating with the Government for participation in various enterprises. These negotiations will continue.'†

Particular intra-national class-confrontations, like particular confrontations between states, today are more and more subsumed within a more inclusive and decisive international set of alignments. The orientations of those challenging, rather than maintaining, the established dominations have become similarly internationalized; in this process, the development of ever more efficient machinery for the worldwide dissemination of ideas has become of critical importance. Today, a high proportion of the population of Guatemala City listens to Radio Havana.

In this world society, the dividing-lines are drawn with reference to the over-riding confrontation between the varied forms which social revolution is taking, on the one hand, and the emergent centre of opposition to those varied revolutionisms represented by the USA, on the other. The relevant typology, therefore, is not one which establishes a basic dichotomy between 'democratic' and 'totalitarian' forms of polity, nor even between military and civilian regimes – however significant these distinctions may be – but between those movements and organizations oriented to radical social change and those resisting it, within the framework of the articulation of all these separate movements and organizations as part of an overall global struggle.

Professor Kathleen Gough has developed the broad outlines of such a typology. There are today, she notes, some 2,352 million people in 'underdeveloped' countries, that is to say outside Europe, North America, Australia, New Zealand, and Japan. About 773

* S. E. Finer, 'Military and Society in Latin America', *Sociological Review Monograph No. 11*, 'Latin American Sociological Studies', p. 150. One should note, however, that Finer's article emphasizes the *autonomy* of the military.

† Lieutenant-General J. A. Ankrah, *Ghana Today*, Vol. 11, No. 4, 19th April, 1967.

Table 8. Tentative Breakdown of 'Underdeveloped' Regions

	Millions 1961	%
Total Underdeveloped World (Exludes Europe, North America, Japan, Australia and New Zealand)	2,352	100
1. *Communist Nations* (China, North Korea, North Vietnam, Mongolia and Cuba)	773	33
2. *Colonial and White-Settler-dominated societies* (Largest – S. Africa, Angola, Mozambique, Rhodesia, Hong Kong, S. Arabia and Aden, Puerto Rico, and New Guinea)	49	2
3. *Satellite or Client States of Western nations' 'Neoempires'*	511	22
(a) Client States of USA (Largest – Argentina, Columbia, Peru, Brazil, Ecuador, Chile, Venezuela, Philippines, S. Vietnam, S. Korea, Thailand, Taiwan, Turkey, Iran, Saudi Arabia).	318	14
(b) Other regions possibly classifiable as client states of the USA. (Pakistan, Mexico)	146	6
4. *Total colonial, client or semi-independent underdeveloped states heavily influenced, if not controlled by the USA*	1,138	37
5. *Client States primarily dependent on European nations* (Largest – Malaysia, the Congo, Nigeria, Cameroun)	193	8
6. *Relatively independent and neutral nations* (Largest – India, Burma, Ceylon, Indonesia, Cambodia, Afghanistan, Nepal, Syria, Iraq, Yemen, UAR, Algeria, Morocco, Kenya, Tanzania, Sudan, Ethiopia, Uganda, Ghana)	873	37
7. *Countries which have moved or may be moving into client relationship with the USA*	901	38
(a) Guatemala, Honduras, the Dominican Republic, Guyana, Venezuela, Brazil, Argentina, Bolivia, Ecuador, Trinidad and Tobago, South Vietnam, Thailand, Laos, the Congo, Togo, Gabon	227	10
(b) 'Neutral' nations moving towards client status (India, Indonesia, Ghana, Afghanistan, Ceylon, Kenya, Ghana)	674	28

TOWARDS WORLD WAR IV

8. *States containing armed revolutionary movements*   *Millions* %
    (Guatemala, Peru, Venezuela, Ecuador, Paraguay,   1961
    Brazil, Honduras, Bolivia, Columbia, Angola, Mozam-
    bique, Congo, Cameroun, Portuguese Guinea,
    Yemen, S. Arabia, Philippines, Thailand, Laos,
    S. Vietnam)   266 11

9. *States containing unarmed revolutionary movements or parties with wide popularity*
    (India, Rhodesia, S. W. Africa, Nicaragua, Dominican Republic, Panama)   501 22

million of these 2,352 million, or one third, have become Communist states (China, North Korea, North Viet Nam, Mongolia, Cuba). Only 45 million people (about 2 per cent of the total) remain under colonial and white-settler dominated societies, 39 million of them in southern Africa (South Africa, Angola, Mozambique, Rhodesia, Hong Kong, South Arabia and Aden, Puerto Rico, and New Guinea being the largest).

Some 1,530 million people, or 65 per cent of the total, live in nations that are 'politically at least nominally independent yet are still within the orbit of western power and influence'. 511 million of these people (22 per cent of the total) live in what she calls 'client states' (the largest of these states – those with populations over five million – being Colombia, Argentina, Peru, Brazil, Ecuador, Chile, Venezuela, the Philippines, South Vietnam, South Korea, Thailand, Taiwan, Malaysia, the Republic of the Congo, Nigeria, Iran, Saudi Arabia, Cameroun, and Turkey). These are 'nations with indigenous governments which are, however, so constrained by western military aid, economic aid, trade, or private investments, that they have little autonomy. Many of their governments would collapse if western aid were withdrawn'. About 318 million of these people (14 per cent of the total) live in nations whose governments are 'beholden' to the United States; most of the rest, to Britain or France. If one were to add Mexico and Pakistan to the list of client states – though this is a matter of dispute – the population of the 'client states' would rise to 657 million, or 28 per cent of the underdeveloped world (instead of 22 per cent without these two countries) and the US share of client-states would rise to 464 million (20 per cent of the total).

There remain some 873 million people (37 per cent of the total)

307

in 'relatively independent and politically neutral' countries, the larger nations – those over five million strong – being Burma, Cambodia, India, Ceylon, Afghanistan, Nepal, Yemen, Iraq, Sudan, Ethiopia, Uganda, Ghana, Indonesia, UAR, Algeria, Morocco, Kenya, and Tanzania.

In recent years, however, 674 million in India, Indonesia, Afghanistan, Ceylon, Kenya, and Ghana, have moved into closer dependence on the United States, so that 'their future as independent nations is very uncertain.' To these must be added those states containing 227 million people, in 16 nations, who, during the last fifteen years, after a period of relative independence, have moved into, or back into, a client relationship, usually with the United States: Guatemala, Honduras, the Dominican Republic, Guyana, Venezuela, Brazil, Argentina, Bolivia, Ecuador, Trinidad and Tobago, South Vietnam, Thailand, Laos, the Congo, Togo, and Gabon – often following a military coup.

If we were to deduct those nations moving into client status, this would leave only 199 millions, or 8 per cent of the underdeveloped world, in the category of neutral nations, and brings to a total of 1,142, or 48 per cent of the underveloped world, the people who live in client or near-client states of the USA or in its colonial dependencies, with a further 901 million (38 per cent of the total) whose independence appears to be severely qualified or already lost.

Armed revolutionary movements, Gough observes, (though they are often very small) now exist in at least 20 countries with a total population of 266 million: Guatemala, Peru, Venezuela, Ecuador, Brazil, Honduras, Bolivia, Colombia, Angola, Mozambique, the Congo, Cameroun, Portuguese Guinea, Yemen, Southern Arabia, the Philippines, Thailand, Laos, and South Viet Nam. A further 501 million people live in seven other countries where unarmed revolutionary movements or parties have wide support: India (especially the states of Bengal and Kerala), Rhodesia, South-West Africa, South Africa, Nicaragua, the Dominican Republic, and Panama. 'In more than one third of the underdeveloped world, therefore, revolution is a considered possibility, while in another third it has already been accomplished.'*

* Data and Table adapted from Kathleen Gough, 'Dissent in Anthropology', chapter in *Dissent in Social Science*, ed. T. Roszak (forthcoming).

These major geological faults running across the world social system have, of course, been more or less perceived by analysts and observers, as well as by those closely involved in the process, but not always sharply enough brought into conceptual focus. In the 1950s, the geology of world society was presented in the language of 'the' Cold War, that global confrontation between the USA and its allies, and the USSR and its. Yet this model was crucially defective in one fundamental respect: it imposed the straightjacket of communism/anti-communism on a world balance of forces that was even then much more complex than this particular dichotomy, and which often could not be reduced to this simple distinction. Some of it could: Korea or Berlin. But much could not: in Europe, the Hungarian Revolution; in non-Euro-America, the events around Suez and the Algerian struggle for independence; Kenya, Cyprus and Cuba: these and more minor clashes were not primarily about communism at all, but about independence and imperialism. Some, confusingly, did overlap with the struggle over communism, as in the case of the Malayan Emergency, or the French struggle to hold Indo-China.

But in the 1960s, with the emergence of several communisms, with the proliferation of non-communist but radical or revolutionary movements in Cuba, the Dominican Republic, Angola, and elsewhere, it became increasingly difficult to cram all these manifestations of social revolt into the Procrustean bed of the Old Cold War. Instead of the absorption of world revolutionism by a monocentric communism, we witnessed the absorption of various communisms into the framework of spreading revolt in the Third World, as the Old Cold War visibly wound down in Europe.

Yet the language of a single 'Cold War' is still used in the ideology of the 'West', even at a time when the USSR and China are locked in mortal political combat. Such simplifying ideologies clearly possess a momentum of their own: it is hard for a whole generation reared on them to rework them, because to do so would be to raise dangerous questions about basic assumptions. The ideologists of Communism are similarly stuck with their own schemata. All such ideologies strain towards asserting their universal validity; all of them contain a unidirectional, ultimately optimistic, 'Whig' view of history. For the US, the strategy of defeating communism by using military might as a 'shield' behind which the work of 'winning hearts and minds' can be accomplished, depends upon the assumption that non-communist development programmes can be made to work quickly and can be successfully undertaken by governments whose principal raison d'être is their willingness to accommodate to United States leadership.

The Soviet version of modern evolutionism, again, assimilates the emergence of the new independent states to a general model of the 'crisis of imperialism', out of which – it appears to be implicitly assumed – new socialist and populist regimes emerge which can be induced, by Soviet aid and influence, to move towards the Soviet 'camp'. The model here would seem to be Cuba. The Chinese model, per contra, assumes that revolutionary praxis on the part of the people themselves in the backward countries will eventually accomplish the exposure and overthrow of 'bourgeois' reactionary and nationalist-populist regimes by a new revolutionary and peasant-based movements.

All of these ideologies are, of course, 'future-oriented', as *policy* about development inherently must be. The model of the ideal society which they ask mankind to strive towards, however, is not some unrealized future utopia, but the contemporary condition of the USA, the USSR, or China. The model is present in the here and now. In past centuries, the creators of 'utopian' myths used to locate their utopias in the remote past, not the future. They looked backwards to the Golden Age, to the paradisical state of Adamic innocence, to the era of the Goths, or the days before the Normans. With the advent of modern industrial society, the idea of progress and the notion of evolution of society through successive higher stages of development, all tending in one direction, gripped the imagination of generations impressed by the manifest success of the industrial societies in establishing their control over the whole world, and in displacing all other types of pre-industrial society and incorporating them into their new empires. Forwards-looking optimism was characteristic of Marxists, laissez faire liberals and reformist socialists alike.

All anticipated the conquest of traditionalism by rationality. Today, by contrast, the ideal models men look towards tend to be neither in the past nor the future, and are certainly not mythological. They are in the very contemporary real world. For some, they are the self-evident wealth and power of the USA or Western Europe; for others, the example of the Soviet Union; for yet others, the examples of China, Cuba, or perhaps even Israel, Mexico, or Japan. But the dominant contemporary models are really only the major contenders: the USA, the USSR, China and Cuba. Yet as we have already seen, none of them are very satisfactory as models for poor, small, agrarian countries. The USA appears to them quite inimitable. The sheer size alone of the USSR and China makes those models singularly inimitable also. And Russia and China fall short, in quite vital respects, of what is hoped for, especially in terms of human liberty and the more material field of agriculture.

Since no model represents even a largely satisfactory blueprint, bits and pieces are incorporated into a syncretic mélange in which State planning, private enterprise, and foreign investment all co-exist in a variety of combinations.

But in the event, whatever strategy is opted for, none of them produce the results. The situation of the 'underdeveloping' countries worsens: to call them 'developing' is presumptuous and inaccurate: vis-à-vis the advanced states, they are 'under-developing' fast, slipping backwards.

It would be naive, therefore, to assume that 'development' is an inevitability. There are already visible a number of 'non-development' alternatives: the slide into chronic disorder and bloodletting in Colombia; the endemic chaos of what Professor Tinker has described as 'broken-backed states',* or which Professor Galbraith describes as 'states in which the writ of government only runs up to the airport';† or the protracted miseries of the 'varieties of parasitism' listed by Professor Andreski for Latin America: 'kleptocracy', 'militocracy', the 'parasitic involution of capitalism', 'praetorianism', 'constitutional' and 'bureaucratic' oligarchy, 'decorative constitutions', etc., etc.‡

Such debilitated and unstable societies, however, are scarcely likely to be left to their own devices politically, however abandoned

* Hugh Tinker, 'Broken-backed States', *New Society*, No. 70, pp. 6–7.
† in *Second Thoughts on Aid*, (ed. Moncrieff), p. 21.
‡ Stanislav Andreski, *Parasitism and Subversion: the case of Latin America*, Chapters 3 and 5.

they may be economically, for sooner or later the interested rivals for international leadership will intervene. Any kind of serious challenge to the status quo has to be defined as 'Communism'.

Again, the rivalry between the USA and *institutionalized* communism in the shape of the USSR or China is injected into private quarrels which arise over quite other things. The problems of these countries which are not easily assimilable to any such simple schema as communism/anti-communism have to be manipulated until they do fit. Extraordinary intellectual operations are performed to provide a rationale for such simplifications of reality. So refined analyses are made, in the case of the Dominican Republic, in an attempt to discern those elements within a broad constellation of radical forces which can be labelled 'communist', even if these are a distinct minority. Sometimes the patent irrelevance of communism as an internal issue – as in the case of the support given by the USA and the USSR for opposite sides in the Arab-Israeli conflict – is not even ideologically justified at all, so discrepant are the very different concerns of the original parties to the dispute and those of the intervening Great Powers. Insofar as there is a struggle over communism, it is a struggle at a higher, completely external, Great-Power level. Whether the intellectual operation of justifying these power-struggles and interventions by reference to internal communist threats is carried out or not, therefore, other kinds of operations, political and military, rather than ideological and analytical, *are* carried out: troops are landed to forestall communist 'subversion' or intervention. All radical movements, whether visibly communist or otherwise, in whole or in part, have to be defined as 'communist' and visited with hard intervention. If the label cannot be made to stick, the intellectual operation is not seriously necessary anyway.

The ideology and practice of counter-revolution, when it takes the form of simple *Realpolitik* of this kind, or when the ideological rationalization is too patently unbelievable, often generates the very responses it seeks to forestall. After the US invasion of the Dominican Republic, Señor Juan Bosch is reported to have remarked that whereas there had only been 500 Communists before the invasion, there would soon be 50,000.

The unreality of these ideological definitions of the situation are equally visible in the case of the 'domino' theory in South-East Asia, for, empirically, the posited domino-policy on the part of China is equally shared by the USA, which has converted Thailand, independent even throughout the colonial period, into a military base from which Viet Nam is bombed. Evidently, the game of dominoes has more than one player, and it is empirically observable that one of the first domino-states to lose its autonomy has lost it, not to China, but to the USA. Such definitions of the situation, at this point, lose contact with reality. Increasingly, the effective definition operated upon is a military one, in which types of regime are not a prime consideration. States become merely disposable tracts of land, over which military operations are conducted, and sources of men and materials for war-machines which overstep in their scale of operations any restrictive barriers imposed by national boundaries and other constitutional niceties, let alone any consideration of the inhabitants' own definition of the situation.

Paradoxically, this is happening at a time when the impetus of the Communist bid for world-leadership has slowed down. The split between China and the USSR and the contrary marked rapprochement between the US and the USSR; the growing practice of unilateral action by Eastern European countries such as Bulgaria and Roumania; the effective non-existence of SEATO and the internal crisis of NATO;* the contrast between China's verbal bellicosity and the actual care with which she stays clear of direct, especially military, commitments outside her borders; the deep absorption of the USSR and China in their own severe problems of internal development; the latter's military, industrial, and agricultural weakness, plus the setbacks she has encountered across the globe; all conspire to produce a general de facto drawing-in of horns. Out of the confusions of China's 'cultural revolution' the two major alternatives of external policy which rose to the surface – whether to rely for defence on a mass Army and an armed population, or whether to have recourse to the latest military technology (i.e. Soviet nuclear weapons and rocketry) – were both predicated upon the assumption that China must prepare for an eventual attack, sooner rather than later, by the USA. For once, the word 'defence' was used to mean 'defence', for neither

* See Christopher Mayhew, *Britain's Role Tomorrow*, passim.

strategy was designed to prepare for large-scale Chinese offensive action outside her borders.

The pressures for other states to become aligned in this sharpening world-conflict have thus been severely intensified, and few of the weak and poor nations have been able to withstand them, as Gough's typology indicates.

Countries which offend the major Powers are quickly likely to find themselves deprived of aid, and the political space in which to play the political game of setting one side against the other as competing aid-providers has become very restricted. The non-availability of capital from outside inevitably thrusts the governments of poor countries back on their own exiguous internal resources and helps sharpen internal competition for these. Internal mobilization – 'going it alone' – becomes the only course left for those few governments determined to maintain non-alignment come what may, and yet continue with ambitious development plans. This would appear to be the significance of Tanzania's new policy, announced in the 'Arusha Declaration'.* Deprived of aid from Britain, owing to the conflict over Rhodesia, having no adequate alternative source of aid from the communist world, Tanzania has 'chosen' the only available alternative: mobilization of its own internal financial and human resources through nationalization of banks, food-processing firms, insurance, import-export agencies, and a controlling share by Government in other key industries (sisal, breweries, tobacco, shoes, light metal goods, wattle extract, and cement).

The rationale of this policy is made quite explicit by President Nyerere: foreign gifts and loans are not adequate to finance the Development Plan; the revenue from taxation is also inadequate; there is no effective world agency which can divert resources from the wealthy countries to the poor; and, finally – 'gifts and loans will endanger our independence'.†

The mobilization of internal capital is, of course, only the first stage of the process. The next problem is what to do with it. Here, too, the experience of the failure of the UN's 'Development Decade', and, in particular, the inability of poor countries to industrialize, has resulted in acceptance of the fact that these

* *The Arusha Declaration* and *TANU's Policy on Socialism and Self-Reliance.*
† op. cit., pp. 7–11.

countries are, for the visible future, destined to remain agrarian societies. President Nyerere thus declares that 'we have put too much emphasis on industries', which are capital-intensive, and which, being necessarily mainly located in urban centres, mean not only that the gulf between town and country widens, but that most of this development in the urban areas is paid for by the foreign exchange earned from the sale of the farmer's produce. This renewed emphasis upon the centrality of agriculture by the leader of an underdeveloped country has been paralleled by recent thinking from more academic quarters. Professor Gunnar Myrdal, for example, has argued that 'for several decades, little or even no new employment can be generated by industrialization', and that since the labour force will increase by between 2 per cent and 4 per cent annually, the greater part of this increase will have to be absorbed in agriculture, especially since modern industry is not very labour-intensive. The towns of the Third World at present are filling with an explosive population of unemployed and semi-unemployed people, with odd-job seekers and beggars, and will continue to do so unless agriculture absorbs them. He does not argue against industrialization, which he urges should be started as soon as possible and as fast as possible, but that in-dustrialization alone is insufficient. All this involves the rapid raising of the productivity of land and agricultural labour.*

A more revolutionary derivation from the evident predominance of the countryside in Third World economies departs from the traditional Marixst theme of the gap between town and country. Today, this theme is being elaborated much further, now in a international context. The 'gap' does not mean that town and country are *separated* from each other. Far from it; the cause of the backwardness of the country *is* the richness of the town; between them there are not simply differences, differences of separate structural and cultural forms: these are the products of a single relationship in which the town exploits the countryside. To Nyerere, on whom the influence of Dumont's writings is obvious, industrial development in the cities is 'paid for' by the farmers. For Fanon, the town/country theme becomes elaborated into a more active-revolutionary analysis and, at this stage, merges with

* Gunnar Myrdal, 'Paths of Development', *New Left Review*, 36, March-April, 1966 pp. 65 ff.

Chinese world-revolutionary theory about the countryside 'surrounding' and overcoming the city and its dominant bourgeoisie: the strategy of armed peasant-guerilla revolutionary warfare. In Third World countries where the problem of agrarian backwardness stays unsolved, this major option, peasant revolution, will sooner or later present itself. To this extent, Chou En-Lai was correct when he spoke of Africa's ripeness for revolution. Africa may well get there in the long run, and in our speeded-up universe, long runs have a habit of being surprisingly short. But even given the best will in the world on the part of would-be revolutionary leaderships, it is singularly difficult to speed up the secular processes of class-differentiation and the emergence of class-consciousness, just as it is difficult to speed up agriculture since new forms of organizing production and new crops have to be tested out over years, not weeks: plants still tend to grow by the season whatever the political regime. Developments in the countryside therefore may be slower than revolutionaries or agricultural modernizers would wish, and a period of chronic disorder, endemic unemployment, jacqueries, urban-plebian discontent, authoritarian 'solutions', Byzantine politics at the capital, the enrichment of the few and stasis or periodic crisis – and overall further impoverishment – for the many, are much more likely than a neat transition to either the 'take-off' or to revolutionism. In China, a century elapsed between the Opium War and the victory of the Communist revolution; it took from the 1860s to 1949 for the social revolution to work through its successive phases, and for national struggles to be displaced by class struggles.

In the meantime, elites in backward countries continue to try to handle the problem of development, some, relatively passively, by recognizing and accepting their own weakness, and settling for a client relationship which will endorse their contemporary dependent position in the world-economy; others, more actively, by inviting the more entrepreneurial peasants to 'enrich themselves' and become prosperous money-economy farmers.

The socialistically-minded leaderships have experimented with varied forms of alternative to the small-producer rural economy. These we may range along a continuum from collectivism to cooperation (though we need, for more refined analysis, to specify the areas in which 'collectivism' or 'cooperation' are being practised, e.g. in production operations, marketing, land-tenure, social services at community level etc.). Here, however, we have to content ourselves with these very crude general labels. At the 'collectivist' end of the continuum are the analogues of the Soviet State Farms: 'factories in the fields', not merely because they are mechanized, but because the social position of the agricultural worker in the production process resembles that of his industrial counterpart: both receive a wage from the employer-State (or some organizational derivative such as the Development Corporation). This form of organization of the rural economy is the least effective of all, not least in the USSR, for not only does it entail a very high level of work-commitment and work-methods and habits, but requires, too, the internalization of the work-style within the psyche of the worker. Social control by the knout, or the naked incentives of the cash-nexus, are not enough. Workers have to be induced to work well without obsessional direction and supervision: they need to be industrially educated enough to take positive work-initiatives themselves.* At the lowest level, they need to be trusted to work to the clock and to sustain a high volume of output, and not to wreck the machinery or produce a poor product. All these dispositions are quite absent in the labour forces available in backward countries, where the rhythms of work to which peasants are habituated; the levels of ideological commitment; educational and cultural norms and values; and experience of large-scale organization, are singularly lacking. Some of these elements of a modern 'culture of work' can be induced fairly readily; others come slowly. By and large, however, the State Farm is the most difficult, and least suitable, of all forms of non-individualist agricultural organization. The pre-Independence African experience – from the Niger Project† to the Groundnut Scheme‡ – is eloquent testimony enough, and even the major fact of Independence, though it eliminated the element of anti-colonial resistance to White direction,§ is not sufficient to reverse all the

* For an excellent examination of this problem in the history of European industrialism, see Reinhard Bendix's *Work and Authority in Industry*.
† Baldwin, K. D. S., *The Niger Agricultural Project*.
‡ See the very poor but lone general account by Alan Wood, *The Groundnut Affair*.
§ Such resistance was a major handicap in small farming as well as large-scale plantation agriculture. I am not referring to anything as formalized as collective

other negative factors we have mentioned. But in the absence of an internalized ethos, State farming generally entails a high degree of centralized and hierarchical control and compulsion – similar to the very 'colonial' patterns which proved so unpopular, and which most governments are seeking to avoid replicating in post-colonial society. (Significantly, the least disastrous State Farms seem to be those where existing estates and plantations, manned by a habituated labour-force, are taken under State control.)

At the other end of the continuum, we find very loose 'cooperation', in the form of the sharing of common resources (orchards, tractors, herds of cattle, etc.) or common services (marketing, retail-stores, schools, dispensaries, 'extension' and technical services ranging from advice to the provision of fertilizers, sprays, seed, etc.). Assistance from the State, centrally and locally, is normal in this pattern, though the basic farming unit is the independent family-farm household.

The normal social result here – whatever the result in productivity terms – is the continued differentiation of the rural community into incipient social classes: at the one end, the emergence of the largish capitalist farmer, at the other, the loss of land, reduction to 'proletarian' status, (and often exodus from the community, especially to the towns), or the slide back into subsistence agriculture. Underneath and within the cooperative forms, therefore, processes of the genesis of inegalitarianism work themselves out, to the chagrin, usually, of socialistically-minded political innovators who see the cooperative as a way of preventing the emergence of capitalism and class-differentiation.

Most elites in new states are not, however, socialistically-minded. Even where they are, they are also interested in holding on to power, so they are obliged to tolerate rural capitalism since it patently works better than collectivism or producer-cooperativism. Moreover, to do anything at all, governments need capital,

'peasant revolt' or protest, but simply the phenomenon which Ruthenberg sums up so well:

'Too many farmers for too long considered everything the European Agricultural or Veterinary Officer proposed as bad for no other reason than pure animosity towards colonial rule. Several politicians found it effective to exploit these sentiments and to encourage non-cooperation ... In view of the great numbers of such small holdings it was simply impossible to contact the mistrusting mass of subsistence farmers. ...' (op. cit., p. 24).

and to obtain this, they need to have a flourishing agricultural sector which can be milked. Whether the milk is converted into the cream of numbered Swiss bank-accounts, or used to 'build the country' or even 'build socialism', it is improved petty-farming which generally provides the revenue needed.

There appears to be one qualification to this generalization about petty-farming, for petty-farmer production is quite compatible with large-scale and centralized organization. There are two outstanding cases in Africa, both very little studied. The first set, Nasser's land-settlement programmes in Lower Egypt, are difficult to study for reasons of access. But they appear, according to observers, to be successful. The second is the enormous Gezira Scheme in the Republic of the Sudan, initiated as long ago as the 1920s under the Condominium regime of the colonial era. Today, the Scheme produces most of the cotton which in turn provides the Sudan with some 65 per cent of the total value of domestic exports, some 17 per cent of Gross Domestic Product, and approximately 20 per cent of the money incomes generated in the Sudan.*

Two factors appear to be particularly important in the explanation of this success: (a) largeness of scale; (b) strong centralized control. Damming the Nile is not a picayune operation. To use such enormous water resources productively (apart from hydroelectricity or industry) very large agricultural irrigation-projects are needed. To use the water for agriculture economically, the irrigation scheme must be regulated and the farming-practices supervised. So far, the analysis is pure Wittfogel: large-scale irrigation generates large-scale economic organization, plus a machinery of close social control.

The 'despotic' centralism which Wittfogel believes is built into large-scale irrigation projects, are not, however, pronounced at all. There is no neat 'fit' between centralized economic bureaucracy and centralized political authority. Here we can only note that the degree of internal manipulation of the Scheme's official rules, aims, and values by the farmers, e.g. rules concerning absentee

* Ali Ahmed Suliman and D. J. Shaw, 'Problems of Income Stabilization in Developing Countries: a case study of the Gezira Scheme', p. 3. See also Arthur Gaitskell, *Gezira*: a study of development in the Sudan; D. J. Shaw, 'Labour Problems in the Gezira Scheme'; and Ahmed Abdel Hamid's excellent *The Agricultural Labour of the Gezira Scheme*.

landownership, the hiring of labour, etc., is considerable; that the normal alignments and processes of politics elsewhere in the country also obtain in this area of the Sudan (though naturally with adaptations to the local situation); and that the Scheme does not appear to be a state within a state.

We are not suggesting that this is a desirable or even replicable model for development, merely observing that it has worked in terms of producing cotton, and that there are principles which can be abstracted from the specific context of this particular structure. It is also singularly shot through with familiar conflicts of class interest: class, ethnic, and others, as well as more specific and local ones: those, for example, which derive from the incorporation into the Scheme of existing farmers in the area, as against those recruited from elsewhere. All of these tensions give promise of plentiful social problems for the future.*

This particular success model, then, brings us back to the central problems of agency and democracy in the mobilization process. We noted that the example of Russia has been of negative value as a supplier of specific organizational models for agricultural modernization (her relevance in the sphere of industry and political organization is another matter.) Only in one very general way can the USSR be held to constitute a model for agrarian societies, as some assert: in that agriculture can only be modernized or rationalized on the basis of a prior, or parallel, developed industry (particularly the tractor/agricultural machinery and chemical fertilizer industries) and urban market. To most theorists and politicians in the underdeveloped world the Soviet model, however, appears rather abstract, since for them industrialization on that scale is plainly not seriously on the agenda. Nor does the prospect of becoming an agrarian appendage of an industrialized society appeal to them. As of now, they are, existentially, agrarian societies with no prospect of establishing machinery, tractor, or chemical industries, and are very often – like India – faced with enormous problems of simply producing enough food despite their agrarianism. Where the possibility of developing industries to supply agriculture exists – as in some Latin American countries or in India – this still remains to be done, quickly and on a vast scale.

* See, for example, Brausch, Cooke, and Shaw, *Bashaqra Area Settlements, 1963,* passim.

Nor, in any case, is it entirely assured that the 'mystique of the tractor' is the answer.

Hence the attractiveness of '*self*-help', to countries wishing to mobilize, but not tyrannize, and the eternal appeal of 'populist' and communitarian solutions that do not depend upon Big Industry or Big Powers. They are also highly sensitive to the dangers of revolution, since although the prospect of revolution is attractive to ideologues, it can mean the death of millions and a disastrous slip back into the kind of situation Algeria finds herself in after her Revolution, with a third of the able-bodied male population from the rural areas unemployed and a quarter in emigration to Europe,* or the disastrous condition of rural Russia after collectivization, when, in the 'muzhik's great Luddite rebellion', the peasantry 'voted with their feet' against Soviet power by killing off 52 per cent of their horses, 45 per cent of their cattle, and nearly two-thirds of their sheep and goats.†

Absence of capital and absence of expertise drive the elite either to exploit the people or to try to enthuse and mobilize them. They call upon them to work hard, and in more rational ways, to dedicate themselves in a spirit of regeneration and self-discipline: laziness, self-aggrandizement, drunkenness, and idleness are castigated.‡

To mobilize on the scale necessary, even in those few countries which dare to conceive of doing so, entails a degree of political resoluteness and an effective machinery of control, at present absent in most backward societies, even in formally single-party and military regimes. Firstly, these machines do not effectively dispose of or monopolize political initiative at village level: they themselves are as often manipulated. Recognizing this, elites sensitive about their own survival, and fearful of the consequences of massive radicalization of the economy and of society generally, hesitate to disturb present uneasy balances. Those committed to liberal values and pluralist institutions, as well as those concerned with to institutionalize 'democratic participation', are also highly likely to be suspicious of the possible wider social consequences of large-scale centralized *étatisme*.

* Jeanne Favret, 'Le Traditionalisme par Excès de Modernité', paper presented to the 6th World Congress of Sociology, p. 12.
† Isaac Deutscher, *Stalin: a political biography*, p. 325.
‡ see Nyerere, op. cit. pp. 12–18.

At a lower level, the problem of agency has already manifested itself. All planning implies more than activation or control of the ruled: it entails the existence of a body of activators particularly at 'field' level: representatives of central government Ministries and planning agencies; settlement managers; agricultural extension workers; teachers and health workers; political agitators and *animateurs*. The difficulties of shortage of personnel at the highest level are well-known: arriving at Independence with only a few score graduates is common enough in Africa (though less so in Latin America or India). But the conventionally-educated product of Indian universities (or British universities) is by no means the stuff of which good Community Development Officers are made; even less do they naturally understand the problems of the soil and the lives of the peasants, without intensive special training.

Planned development thus calls for a supply of trained executors, who are normally simply not available at all, and are substituted for by people with formal educational or traditional administrative skills which are inappropriate to the requirements of the new situation. Plans which depend upon such people will fail, and do. The re-socialization of peasants pushed or pulled into cooperative or collectivistic organizations is similarly a difficult and complex process. These are the social and human problems underlying the failure of so many development schemes. Economists preoccupied with capital-flows, and who see people uni-dimensionally and abstractly as the 'labour factor'; agriculturalists whose expertise lies in their knowledge and handling of plants, animals and soils, rather than people, however technically sophisticated, cannot overcome the cultural and social barriers on which plans founder. Even compulsion is ineffective in agriculture, as Stalin found.

Most Third World governments, therefore, shrink back from large-scale social changes of the kinds effected in the Soviet Union, China, or Cuba. They either resign themselves, in effect (whatever their rhetoric or ostensible ideological pronouncements), to the continuation of their present mixed economies, commonly – as far as agriculture is concerned – 'mixes' of small-scale peasant-farming and plantation-estates, and experiment marginally with diverse kinds of cooperative or State-participant agriculture. More widely, they reconcile themselves to indeterminate and protracted continuation of their uneasy, degenerating position in the world economy.

Gunnar Myrdal has emphasized that without massive redirection of world resources from the richer countries to the backward areas, under international auspices, no serious improvement of the lot of the vast majority of mankind can be expected. The poor countries find themselves living in an era when Europe displays increasingly a narcissistic preoccupation with itself, and the USA, conversely, a somewhat too warm interest in their internal affairs. The USSR strives to stabilize the world power-balance to avoid mutual total destruction in the first place, but also, powerfully, so that she can release resources from military uses in order to satisfy the pent-up 'consumer demand' of a population that has worked, suffered, and waited, in the promise of a new and richer life, for half a century. For the Soviet population and their rulers, the Fiat has come to look more attractive than the rocket, and their own (European-level) consumer-poverty strikes them more immediately than that of the hungry nations. 'Socialism in one country' would indeed come home to roost if ever it appeared to mean '. . . and for no others'. The reconciliation with the USA might thus spell the final phase of the long process in which the USSR has been shedding its world-revolutionary role. The ambiguities are therefore agonizing, for the backward countries equally know that as long as the USSR is locked in a world power-struggle with the USA, rockets will continue to have priority not only over their needs, but over the wants of the Soviet population, whatever sympathy and identification with the interests of the poor countries the USSR might display at Geneva UNCTAD meetings.

Little wonder, then, that, despite severe immediate setbacks, the messages of China and Cuba are still very much on the agenda for the future. No one can be sure that by following these revolutionary examples, positive agricultural modernization will be effectively achieved, but, at least, it is hoped, negatively, existing constraints and present enemies could be eliminated – foreign control, indigenous parasites and tyrants – and at the widest and most general, people would be making active attempts to intervene in the control of their own life-fate, rather than submitting to the perpetuation of the present – and would be sure of some outside support in so doing.

Apart from the major revolutionism, the only other Power seriously acting vis-à-vis the underdeveloped world is the USA, and, on a more modest, though also more constructive level, some of the Western European Powers, notably Britain, France, and Western Germany. Unfortunately, the 'intervention' of the USA increasingly appears as an intervention of Marines and napalm, rather than a serious attempt to contribute positively to the improvement of the quality and meaning of the life led by the majority of the world's population. Whatever the volume of the United States aid programmes, and the excellence of much of the work done under them and under technical assistance programmes, it cannot be said that any serious probability of solving the development problem has resulted from the vast quantities of aid poured into underdeveloped countries.

For all these reasons, the plight of the poor countries, communist or non-communist, but particularly the non-communist Third World countries examined in this book, is an unhappy one and has degenerated rapidly. There is no serious hope that they will be able to modernize as they would wish. The hopes they entertained of the United Nations have faded, as that organization, which they were able to use politically as an instrument in the struggle for independence, has become more and more ineffective in an era when economic development has become the key priority, and where the social space in which to make meaningfully independent political decisions is restricted by very real economic dependence on the aid-market, the commodity market, by fears of destroying 'confidence',* and by fear of damaging existing investments.

At this level, the solidarity of poverty still asserts itself, sometimes quite fiercely, across other barriers. In 1964, from March to June, representatives of 121 countries, including 77 underdeveloped countries, struggled with the problems of world trade and development at the United Nations Conference on Trade and Development (UNCTAD) at Geneva. Some of the underdeveloped countries were, within the limits of that adjective, comparatively well-off. Per capita income in Latin America, for example – using 100 as a world average index number – stands at 75; that of Africa and Asia at 29 (and of Western Europe and the

* see Morgan, D. J., *British Private Investment in East Africa*.

USA at 193 and 620 respectively). But even the richer Latin American countries, like Brazil, are vulnerable to any rapid change in the world-price of such staples as coffee like that which occurred in 1963, and which produced in its train a military coup d'état in response to the mild reforms introduced by President Goulart.

When a country like Brazil experiences as devastating storms what are, for the US economy, mild variations in the economic weather, and becomes subject to violent political stresses and strains as a consequence, the chances of very much poorer countries riding out these depressions are very slight.

But for the great majority of mankind, poverty is not a periodic product of crisis, it is a chronic condition. Even governments with little altruistic concern for the millions over which they rule are interested in avoiding widespread social distress and disorder, since these threaten their own position. Others are more disinterestedly concerned with reform. But none of them, altruistic or self-interested, can be satisfied with the world status quo. Only countries whose populations go to bed well-fed can also afford the luxury of satisfaction with the present.

Hence, at Geneva, on a series of key issues, the developing countries ranged themselves, almost every time, on one side, while the major capitalist Powers either abstained or voted on the other side.

Fifteen 'General Principles' and a further thirteen 'Special Principles' were debated. On one of the Special Principles (iii in the Table below) no action was taken; another (vi) was adopted without dissent. One General Principle (13), and two Special Principles (ii and x) produced no votes against or abstentions. These issues, which did not lead to divisions, were such uncontroversial matters as the problem of land-locked countries (13); the desirability of technical assistance programmes and expanded imports by developed countries from underdeveloped ones (i); new uses for primary products (vi); and extended scientific and technical assistance (x). But on the remaining 23 Principles, which *were* debated and voted upon, the United Kingdom either abstained or voted against the majority on 16 out of 23 occasions; the USA on 20 out of 23. Not only were these two Powers in a minority position fairly consistently; they were also in a very small minority (the normal vote carrying a resolution won the support of 90 or more countries, from a low of 78 votes to a high of 116.) After the Conference, the '75' (later '77') underdeveloped countries issued a joint declaration registering their dissatisfaction with the degree of progress registered in the major fields of economic development, especially as far as the relative prices for primary and manufactured goods were concerned.

Table 9. Voting Patterns of Underdeveloped Countries and of USA and UK at Geneva UNCTAD Conference, 1964

General Principles

	For	Against	Abstained
(1)	113	1 (USA)	2 (UK)
(2)	96	3 (USA)	16 (UK)
(3)	94	4 (UK, USA)	18
(4)	98	1 (USA)	17 (UK)
(5)	97	–	19 (UK, USA)
(6)	114 (UK)	1 (USA)	1
(7)	87	8 (UK, USA)	19
(8)	78	11 (UK, USA)	23
(9)	106	–	10
(10)	115 (UK, USA)	–	1
(11)	92	5 (UK, USA)	19
(12)	83	1 (USA)	30 (UK)
(13)	108	–	–
(14)	90	2 (UK)	2 (USA)
(15)	101 (UK, USA)	–	12

Special Principles

	For	Against	Abstained
(i)	99	2 (USA)	2 (UK)
(ii)	116	–	–
(iii)	No Action Taken		
(iv)	115	–	1 (USA)
(v)	91 (UK)	–	25 (USA)
(vi)	No Dissent		
(vii)	85	13 (UK, USA)	18
(viii)	106	1 (USA)	9 (UK)
(ix)	107	–	9 (UK, USA)
(x)	116 (UK, USA)	–	–
(xi)	93	–	23 (UK, USA)
(xii)	92	7 (UK, USA)	17
(xiii)	111 (UK)	–	5 (USA)

The share of the underdeveloped countries in world exports, as a consequence, which stood at one-third in 1950, had declined to only slightly more than one-fifth in 1962. The resulting picture is very clear: underdeveloped countries are not closing on the advanced countries at all. The gap is widening, and out of this particular alienation of the majority of men from the rich minority will be generated a veritable Pandora's box of endemic human misery, frustration and violence.

If the response of the industrialized world – the USA, Western Europe, Eastern Europe, Australia, South Africa, and Japan – is to ignore the plight of two-thirds of humanity for all practical purposes as a non-problem, to continue profiting from their own dominant position, and to allow those who react against the status quo to be visited with repressive violence, the likelihood of World War IV becomes very high indeed.

It is not inevitable. World War III never happened. As we have seen, the phrase remains a somewhat strained (though useful) figure of speech. 'World War III' was 'eyeball-to-eyeball' confrontation across the world, but never total world war.

It may be that the rehearsals being staged in Viet Nam, the positions now being occupied in preparation for World War IV, may not eventuate in total global war either. The principal actors may draw back, as they did at Cuba, or refrain from further escalation, realizing that they are moving very quickly towards the use, in their repertoire of choices, of the ultimate in escalation, nuclear weapons.

But it would be a bad lapse of memory to forget that the rehearsals staged in Spain *were* followed by the full drama of World War II, and the chances that a Third World growing by 60,000,000 every year will fast get beyond the control of anybody, even the greatest of Powers acting in the most rational of ways, is a sober probability on the basis of present trends. If the major Powers act in less than rational ways, as they are doing, the prospects of containing a world full of revolutionary peasants are nil, as the resistance of such a petty country as Viet Nam to the might of the USA shows. Just as neither side can conceivably 'win' in Viet Nam, and certainly cannot 'win' a nuclear war, so the really serious war – that against world poverty – cannot be won without coordinated redirection of the resources of the developed world. We are a very long way from that, and get further away daily. It is not the war in Viet Nam that we should be engaged in, but the struggle to identify and eliminate the causes of that particular war, and the wider World War IV which it threatens to spark off. This would be a serious human task to set ourselves, for we have as little real need to destroy the world, or to starve its people, as we have to conquer space. We do have an over-riding, cosmic need to solve a very ancient problem: how to make two blades of grass grow where one grew before.

NOTES TO INTRODUCTION

1. Clark, *From Savagery to Civilization*, p. 30.
2. Strachey, *The End of Empire*, p. 19.
3. *Modern Chinese History*, ed. MacNair, pp. 1–11.
4. Waley, *The Opium War Through Chinese Eyes*, p. 33.
5. Turnbull, *Black War*. The results were hardly what had been intended: two natives shot, two captured, for four or five troops killed – cost £35,000. But other measures *were* effective: the last aborigine died in 1876.
6. Roux, *Time Longer than Rope*, p. 31.
7. Benedict, *Race and Racism*, p. 108.
8. *The Travels of Marco Polo*, ed. Mote, pp. 278–96. The 'mile' here is a Chinese mile, i.e. about one-third of an English one.
9. See Bloch, *Feudal Society*, Part II, 'The Environment: Conditions of Life and Mental Climate', pp. 59–120.
10. *The Bernal Díaz Chronicles*, ed. Idell, pp. 148–9.
11. *Encyclopaedia of Southern Africa*, ed. Rosenthal, p. 340.
12. See the bibliography to Chapter 9 in Davidson, *Old Africa Rediscovered*, pp. 275–6, especially Wischoff, *The Zimbabwe Monomatapa Culture in Southeast Africa*.
13. 'Myth in Primitive Psychology', *Magic, Science, and Religion*, p. 146.
14. Davidson, *op. cit.*, p. 86 (my italics).
15. *ibid.*, p. 216.
16. Clissold, *The Seven Cities of Cíbola*, esp. Chapter II: '*Antillia, Seven Cities, and a Fountain*'.
17. Strachey, *op. cit.*, p. 38. As for the general comparability of British and Indian civilization, this writer remarks that 'there was certainly no yawning gap between them' (p.12); 'besides the Delhi of the Moguls the London of 1715 must have seemed in many respects a country town' (p. 16).

NOTES

18. See Kiernan, 'State and Nation: West Europe, Spain, Africa'.
19. Collier, *Indians of the Americas.*
20. Hays, *From Ape to Angel*, p. 257.
21. Camoens, *The Lusiads*, Englished by Burton, Vol. II, Canto X, Stanzas 10, 43,
22. Strachey, *op. cit.*, p. 33 (1959 prices).
23. 'Nuer Socio-Spatial Categories', from Evans-Pritchard, *The Nuer*, p. 114.
24. Malinowski, *Argonauts of the Western Pacific*, and Uberoi, *Politics of the Kula Ring.*
25. Sansom, *The Western World and Japan*, p. 20.
26. Fitzgerald, *China*, pp. 196–201.
27. See Smith's illuminating *European Vision and the South Pacific, 1768–1850.*
28. Smith, *op. cit.*, Plate 138. For contrast, see Plates 79–84, 89–92, 98–101 ff.
29. van Leur, *Indonesian Trade and Society*, p. 325.
30. See Dr Philip's description of the 'Scythian' mode of life of the trek-Boers of the early nineteenth century in Macmillan, *Bantu, Boer, and Briton*, pp. 24–5, and Arendt, *The Origins of Totalitarianism*, pp. 185–207. The barbarism of the Boers, however, differed in one crucial respect from that of the Zulu: it was not merely a simple parallelism of poor technology and unfavourable environment, for 'the Boers lived on their slaves exactly the way natives had lived on . . . nature . . . as though they were just another form of animal life . . . a process which could only end with their own degeneration'.
31. Panikkar, *Asia and Western Dominance*, p. 197.
32. Evans-Pritchard, *The Sanusi of Cyrenaica.*
33. Real democracy they *are* interested in: and democracy will out, even in the most unexpected ways. In 1955, Marshal Pibul Songgram, dictator of Thailand, visited Britain, and was impressed with Speakers' Corner at Hyde Park. On his return, he introduced a Speakers' Corner in Bangkok, and permitted the formation of political parties. This led to such a volume of criticism of his Government that control was clamped on once more. 'A Left-Wing Hyde Park Movement Party was promptly formed in protest' (Rose, *Socialism in Southern Asia*, p. 181.)
34. 'Solde', by Léon-G. Damas, Guianese poet, from 'Pigments', reprinted in *Anthologie de la Nouvelle Poésie Nègre et Malgache de Langue Française*, ed. Senghor, pp. 11–12.
35. *Out of Exile*, p. 146.

NOTES TO CHAPTER ONE

1. For Central Africa, see Gann, *The Birth of a Plural Society.*
2. Thompson and Adloff, *French West Africa*, p. 57.
3. Hamon, 'Introduction à l'Etude des Parties Politiques de l'Afrique Française', *Révue Juridique et Politique d'Outre-Mer*, p. 165.
4. Alleg, *The Question*, p. 45.
5. Hall, *A History of South East Asia*, p. 405.
6. Lévi-Strauss, 'Crowds', *New Left Review*, 15, pp. 4–5.
7. Kuper, *The Uniform of Colour*, pp. 35–6.
8. On the Bantu conception of *muntu*, see Tempels, *Bantu Philosophy*, and Jahn, *Muntu.*
9. Baker, 'Mumiani', *Tanganyika Notes and Records*, No. 21, pp. 108–9.
10. For a few examples of the extremely widespread African belief in European cannibalism, see Kuper, *op. cit.*, pp. 34–5; Shepperson and Price, *Independent African*; pp. 10, 70, 86, 87, and esp. p. 440; and Fraenkel, *Wayaleshi*, who describes how this old belief emerged to terrify Central Africans during the troubles over Federation.
11. Merton, *Social Theory and Social Structure*, p. 427.
12. *Les Damnés de la Terre*, p. 30; *L'An V de la Révolution Algérienne*, p. 34.
13. Smith, *Islam in Modern History*, p. 108.
14. Needham, *Science and Civilization in China.*
15. Radcliffe-Brown, *Structure and Function in Primitive Society*, p. 203.
16. Cecil Rhodes, quoted in Lenin, *Imperialism*, p. 72.
17. See particularly, Robinson and Gallagher, *Africa and the Victorians*, and Semmel, *Imperialism and Social Reform.*
18. *Capital*, Vol. I, pp. 352, 350.
19. Quoted in Emerson, *From Empire to Nation*, p. 243.
20. Hobsbawm, *The Age of Revolution, 1789–1848*, p. 143.
21. See my *The Trumpet Shall Sound.*
22. Fanon, *Les Damnés de la Terre*, pp. 189–235.
23. Fanon, *L'An V de la Révolution Algérienne*, passim.
24. *Prospero and Caliban.*
25. *Slavery.*
26. Srinivas, *Religion and Society Among the Coorgs of South India*, especially pp. 24–32 and 212–22, and the earlier pioneer study by L. S. S. O'Malley, 'The Historical Background', in *Modern India and the West*, ed. O'Maley, pp. 1–43.
27. Marx, 'The British Rule in India', in Marx and Engels, *On Britain* pp. 379–80; Wittfogel, *Oriental Despotism.*
28. e.g. Leach, 'Hydraulic Society in Ceylon', *Past and Present*, 15, pp. 2–26.

29. Noted long ago by Borkenau, in his *World Communism*, p. 296. China's vulnerability to alternative world-views is also evident in the emergence of *Christian* leaders like Chiang Kai-Shek, Chang Hsueh-liang, the 'Young Marshal', or Feng Yu-hsiang, the 'Christian General'.
30. Wertheim, *Indonesian Society in Transition*, pp. 174–5. The style of living of the White colonial official is one of the neglected fields of research, though much casual illustration exists. A perceptive passage like that above suggests that it is a fertile area for examining changes of 'ethic' under changed social conditions: a central problem-area for sociological theory.
31. From Rudyard Kipling's 'The First Sailor', *Humorous Tales*, 1901, quoted in Arendt, *The Origins of Totalitarianism*, p. 210.
32. Levenson, *Confucian China and its Modern Fate*, p. 63.
33. Emerson, *op. cit.*, p. 50.
34. For a fascinating picture of the separate world of the indigenous Indonesian and the Dutch city-dwellers of nineteenth-century Indonesia, see Wertheim, Chapter 7, *op. cit.*

One example of the enforcement of the etiquette of segregation will stand for a thousand such pin-pricks:

'I went to see ... the District Commissioner to explain my predicament ... When I got into the office I said "Good morning". The District Commissioner turned to the head clerk and said "Tell this man in Bemba to say 'Good morning, *sir*' ". Throughout that interview, the D.C. insisted on his head clerk interpreting everything he said into Bemba while I spoke in English. After spending all my school days trying to become proficient in English ... this D.C. wanted to push me back where he thought I ought to be – "just an ordinary native" ' (Kaunda, *Zambia Shall be Free*, pp. 17–18).

That the etiquette might be backed by sanctions severer than mere disapproval is shown in Kaunda's description of a beating-up he received when he defied the colour-bar on Africans eating in White cafés. His friend, Nkumbula, was also later beaten up by the police (pp. 33–4.)
35. Lips, *The Savage Hits Back*, pp. 232–4.
36. Burridge, *Mambu*.
37. African colonial mythology is replete with stories of villagers thrusting forward the village idiot for the new and dubious office of 'chief'. For a more serious study of the creation of 'chiefs' out of traditional rain-makers and similar leaders (of usually ephemeral authority), see Colson, 'The Plateau Tonga of Northern Rhodesia', in *Seven Tribes of British Central Africa*, eds. Colson and Gluckman, pp. 95–6, 102–3, 152, 160, etc. It was for this reason that British Press

comment on the wickedness of Mau Mau's defiance of the 'traditional chiefs' of the Kikuyu was rather beside the point, since they were not traditional chiefs at all.

38. Kahin, *Nationalism and Revolution in Indonesia*, pp. 58, 354.

39. Gluckman, 'The Kingdom of the Zulu of South Africa', *African Political Systems*, eds. Fortes and Evans-Pritchard, p. 37. For a similar arrangement, see Oberg's essay on 'The Kingdom of Ankole in Uganda' in the same volume, p. 132.

40. Cited in Coleman, *Nigeria*, p. 193.

41. Mead, *New Lives for Old*, p. 445.

42. Popper, *The Open Society and Its Enemies* and *The Poverty of Historicism*.

43. Daniel Bell, in rejecting large-scale 'workers' control' and suggesting instead minor instalments only at shop-floor level, remarks; 'These are perhaps small solutions to large problems, what Karl Popper has called "piece-meal technology", but look where the eschatological visions have led!', *The End of Ideology*, p. 390.

44. Mansur, The *Process of Independence* p. 178.

45. Quoted in Emerson, *op. cit.*, p. 42.

46. *ibid.*, pp. 37, 38.

47. de Sauvigny, *Metternich et Son Temps*, pp. 66, 72 (italics in original).

48. Ossowski, 'Social Conditions and Consequences of Social Planning', *Transactions of the Fourth World Congress of Sociology*, Vol. II, pp. 199–222.

49. Goffman, *Asylums*.

50. Wolf, *Sons of the Shaking Earth*, p. 164.

51. Panikkar, *Asia and Western Dominance*, p. 88.

52. Willmott, *The Chinese of Semarang*, Appendix II, pp. 359–60.

53. Panikkar, *loc. cit.*

54. See Hodgkin's characterization of British empiricism, Belgian Platonism, and French Cartesianism, in his analysis of the colonial administrative systems of the respective Powers: *Nationalism in Colonial Africa*, Chapter I.

55. Anderson's articles, 'Portugal and the End of Ultra-Colonialism', *New Left Review*, Nos. 15, 16 and 17, constitute the first rigorous analysis of this type of colonialism, though a large enough descriptive literature exists. Some such labels as 'archaic', however, may be preferable to 'ultra', in view of the associations this latter term has with a mystique of 'last-ditch' ruthlessness per se: the latter can be quite characteristic of advanced imperialisms, e.g. those of France and Holland since 1945.

NOTES TO CHAPTER TWO

1. Salisbury, *From Stone to Steel*. See also Lauriston Sharp's 'Steel Axes for Stone Age Australians,' in Spicer (ed.)
2. See Gluckman, Barnes, and Mitchell, 'The Village Headman in British Central Africa', *Africa*, Vol. 19, No. 2, 1949, pp. 89–106.
3. Dutt, R., *The Economic History of India under Early British Rule*, pp. 296–8.
4. Dutt, R., *The Economic History of India in the Victorian Age*, p. 346.
5. Misra, *The Indian Middle Classes*, p. 197.
6. *ibid.*, p. 375.
7. Dutt, R. P., *India Today*, pp. 223–33.
8. See Wertheim, 'Religious Reform Movements in Southern and South East Asia', *Archives de Sociologie des Réligions*, 12, pp. 53–62.
9. Desai, *The Social Background of Indian Nationalism*, p. 146.
10. Dutt, R. P., *op. cit.*, p. 270.
11. Mansur, *The Process of Independence*, p. 14.
12. Ahmed, *The Intellectual Origins of Egyptian Nationalism*, p. 88.
13. Misra, *op. cit.*, p. 301.
14. *loc. cit.*, p. 303.
15. In Japan, too, a country which narrowly escaped direct colonization, Russian nihilism for a time made inroads amongst militantly modernizing young men. One ballad, sold as a broadsheet in the streets, ran:

> 'Increase the national wealth!
> Increase the people's happiness!
> Nourish the people's strength!
> If this is not done, then,
> Dynamite, BANG!'

(quoted in Sansom, *The Western World and Japan*, p. 429.)
16. Misra, *op. cit.*, p. 394.
17. Chattar Singh Samra, 'Subhas Chandra Bose', in *Leadership and Political Institutions in India*, ed. Park and Tinker, p. 69.
18. Overstreet and Windmiller, *Communism in India*, p. 19.
19. See Toye, *The Springing Tiger*.
20. Hargreaves, *Prelude to the Partition of West Africa*, pp. 348–9.
21. Coleman, *Nigeria*, p. 194.
22. *ibid.*, pp. 193–4.
23. Hunter, *The New Societies of Tropical Africa*, p. 205.

24. Mao Tse-Tung, *On Contradiction*, p. 63.
25. Especially his *The Idea of Nationalism*.
26. See Kiernan, 'State and Nation: West Europe, Spain, Africa'.
27. *The Sociology of Georg Simmel*, ed. Wolff, pp. 67–73.
28. See Hobsbawm, *The Age of Revolution*, Chapter 7.
29. Church, 'Mauritania and her Neighbours', *West Africa*, 2267, 12 November, 1960, p. 1278; and 'Drinks in the Desert', *West Africa*, 2271, 10 December, 1960, p. 1393.
30. Thomson and Adloff, *French West Africa*, p. 173.
31. Kahin, *Nationalism and Revolution in Indonesia*, pp. 47–8.
32. *The Social Psychology of George Herbert Mead*, ed. Strauss, Part V.
33. Stalin, *Marxism and the National and Colonial Question*.
34. Kedourie, *Nationalism*, p. 74.
35. Arendt, *The Origins of Totalitarianism*.
36. On 'primordial' ties, see Shils' 'Primordial, Personal, Sacred and Civil Ties', *British Journal of Sociology*, Vol. VIII, No. 2, June 1957, pp. 130–45.
37. Kedourie, *op. cit.*, p. 101.
38. *The Fear of Freedom*.
39. Merton, *Social Theory and Social Structure*, pp. 19–84.
40. Emerson, *From Empire to Nation*, p. 102.
41. Quoted in Kedourie, *op. cit.*, p. 114.
42. Kedourie, *op. cit.*, p. 79.
43. Emerson, *op. cit.*, p. 107.
44. Of the 8,090 workers on the Kariba Dam project in Northern Rhodesia, only 1,070 were drawn from Northern Rhodesia itself (Hunter, *op. cit.*, p. 200).
45. On the significance of the revolution in communications, see Lerner, *The Passing of Traditional Society*.
46. Métraux, *Voodoo*, p. 323.
47. Notably Herskovits, in *The Myth of the Negro Past*, and other works. This view is also common in writings on jazz (see my article, 'The Spread of Jazz', *Listener*, Vol. LXIX, 14 March, 1963, pp. 456–8.)
48. Shepperson and Price, *Independent African*.
49. See Sundkler, *Bantu Prophets in South Africa*.
50. See the excellent chapter, 'The New Associations', in Hodgkin, *Nationalism in Colonial Africa*.
51. Coleman, *op. cit.*, p. 154.
52. See Legum, *Pan-Africanism*, and Decraene, *La Panafricanisme*.
53. Even at the individual level: Kenneth Kaunda records how he was introduced to Gandhi's writings by an Indian sympathizer of Congress, *Zambia Shall be Free*, pp. 52, 140 ff.
54. See Coulthard, *Race and Colour in Caribbean Literature*.

NOTES

55. *Nations Nègres et Culture.*
56. *Pan-Africanism*, p. 33.

NOTES TO CHAPTER THREE

1. Rose, *Socialism in Southern Asia*, p. 265.
2. Borkenau, *World Communism.*
3. Overstreet and Windmiller, *Communism in India*, pp. 206, 217.
4. *ibid.*, p. 293.
5. Kahin, *Nationalism and Revolution in Indonesia*, pp. 50, 51.
6. Kahin, *ibid.*, p. 160.
7. A little of the deep-rooted ethnic prejudice inherited from earlier times has now been brought directly home to African students expelled from Bulgaria. Ethnic prejudice was evidently the trouble at the popular level: in Government eyes, however, the 'crime' of the African students was strictly a political one: the formation of a Pan-African *nationalist* organization of students instead of adherence to political groupings based on *class* ideologies.
8. Mackenzie Brown, 'Traditional Concepts of Indian Leadership' in *Leadership and Political Institutions in India*, ed. Park and Tinker, p. 14.
9. E.g. W. H. Andrews, the South African Communist leader; see Cope, *Comrade Bill.*
10. Roux, *Time Longer than Rope*, pp. 354-6.
11. Particularly in Burma and India. See Branson's *British Soldier in India.*
12. Mao Tse-Tung, *People's Democratic Dictatorship*, p. 20.
13. Interview with Fernand Gigon, *Texte des Interviews Accordées aux Représentants de la Presse*, p. 107.
14. Interview with Crozier, 'Six Africans in Search of a Personality', *Encounter*, Vol. 16, 1960, p. 40.
15. For a careful examination of the restructuring of politics in a backward part of India along class lines, with the growing-together of conservative elements – formerly sharply divided into pro- and anti-Congress under British rule – in the face of the emergent Communist Party, see Bailey's *Politics and Social Change in Orissa in 1959.*
16. See Feith, *The Wilopo Cabinet.*
17. *Out of Exile*, p. 67.
18. Rose, *op. cit.*, p. 62.
19. Sjahrir, *Indonesian Socialism*, p. 49.
20. *ibid.*, p. 12.
21. Sjahrir, *Out of Exile*, p. 33.
22. *The Birth of Pantjasila*, pp. 13–15.

336

23. 'The Burmese Revolution', cited in Rose, *op. cit.*, p. 118.
24. Ernest Milcent, 'Senegal' in Carter (ed.), *African One-Party States*, p. 91.
25. Rose, *op. cit.*, p. 39.
26. *Indonesian Socialism*, pp. 51–2.
27. Thompson and Adloff, *French West Africa*, pp. 36–7, 96–7, 125–6.
28. Sneevliet's life-history, like that of Ho Chi Minh, must surely be one of the great unwritten Odysseys of our time.
29. Fanon, *L'An V de la Révolution Algérienne*, p. 6.
30. Fall, *Le Viet-Minh*, p. 199.
31. Rose, *op. cit.*, p. 137.
32. *Ibid.*, p. 140.
33. *Loc. cit.*
34. For an early, outstanding example of the power of directed communications in energizing a peasant population, see Snow's classic, *Red Star Over China*, especially on the role of the 'Lenin Clubs' in the Chinese Red Army in the Yenan period (pp. 292–302); the sections on the Communist Youth League (pp. 338–45); and those on propaganda work among Muslims (pp. 327–32, 349–53); also the excellent photographs between pp. 224 and 225. For a more light-hearted but illuminating recent account of the impact of an even more modern communications system on Central African villages, see Fraenkel's *Wayaleshi*. In the urban areas, radio penetration was intense: one survey conducted by Fraenkel in Lusaka showed that 90 per cent of the interviewees had occasional access to a wireless set, and 25 per cent could quote examples of the English programmes (p. 140).
35. Kahin, *op. cit.*, p. 76.
36. Kahin, *op. cit.*, pp. 306 ff.

NOTES TO CHAPTER FOUR

1. 'Elégie pour Aynina Fall', *Nocturnes*.
2. Cited in Mansur, *The Process of Independence*, p. 57.
3. Cited by Emerson, *op. cit.*, p. 70.
4. Quoted in Hughes, *Consciousness and Society*, pp. 71–2.
5. Marcuse, *Soviet Marxism*.
6. *Réflexions sur l'Economie de l'Afrique Noire*, pp. 59–60.
7. These themes have been developed in several of his works: *Contribution à l'Etude du Mouvement Coopératif en Afrique Noire;*

L'Economie Africaine; Réflexions sur l'Economie de l'Afrique Noire; and *Nations Africaines et Solidarité Mondiale* (translated as *The African Nations and World Solidarity*, London, 1962).

8. *Rapport au Congrès Constitutif du PFA*, pp. 64, 46.
9. See, for example, Degraft-Johnson, *African Glory*.
10. *Réflexions* . . ., p. 82.
11. Notably in *Nations Nègres et Culture*.
12. Sékou Touré, *Rapport, Conférence de Planification Economique*, pp. 51–5.
13. E.g. Senghor, *op. cit.*, pp. 64–5.
14. Al-Fāsi, *The Independence Movements in Arab North Africa*, pp. 1–8.
15. Who wrote the celebrated introductory essay, *Orphée Noir*, to the *Anthologie de la Nouvelle Poésie Nègre et Malgache de Langue française* edited by Senghor.
16. *Cahier* . . ., pp. 71–2.
17. 'A New York', *Ethiopiques* (translation from Moore and Beire, pp. 51–3).
18. 'Une Dangéreuse Mystification: La Théorie de la Négritude', *La Nouvelle Critique*, 7 June, 1949, pp. 34–47.
19. In *Nations Nègres et Culture*, Chapter 2.
20. 'Le parti unique en Afrique', p. 7 (my italics).
21. *Past and Future*, pp. 7–8. See also his *Demokrasi Kita*.
22. *Marhaen and Proletarian*, pp. 6–7.
23. Misra, *op. cit.*, p. 229.
24. Misra, *op. cit.*, p. 249. I draw heavily on his chapter on 'Economic Development' here.
25. Misra, *op. cit.*, pp. 251–2.
26. Kahin, *op. cit.*, p. 73.
27. Coleman, *op. cit.*, p. 80, citing P. T. Bauer's *West African Trade* (Cambridge University Press, 1954).
28. *Ibid.*, p. 83.
29. Martin L. Kilson, jr., 'The Rise of Nationalist Organizations and Parties in British West Africa', in *Africa as Seen by American Negroes*, ed. Davis, p. 55.
30. Hunter, *op. cit.*, Chapters 4–6.
31. Hunter, *op. cit.*, p. 135, citing Peter Garlick's *African Traders in Kumasi*, University College of Ghana, 1959.
32. D. McCall, 'Trade and the Role of Wife in a Modern West African Town', in *Social Change in Modern Africa*, ed. Southall.
33. Hunter, *op. cit.*, p. 133.
34. Coleman, *op. cit.*, p. 86.
35. Thompson and Adloff, *op. cit.*, pp. 123–31.
36. *Awo*, pp. 69–70.

NOTES

37. 'The Protestant Sects and the Spirit of Capitalism', from *Max Weber: Essays in Sociology*, ed. Gerth and Mills, pp. 302–22.
38. See Lynd and Lynd, *Middletown*, Sections IV–VI, *passim*.
39. Morroe Berger, 'The Middle Class in the Arab World', in *The Middle East in Transition*, ed. Laqueur, pp. 61–71.
40. See Lockwood, *The Black-Coated Worker* (Conclusion).
41. Mansur, *op. cit.*, p. 13.
42. Kahin, *op. cit.*, pp. 27–8, 65–75.
43. Wertheim, *Indonesian Society* . . ., p. 149.
44. Mansur, *op. cit.*, p. 12.
45. *Congo: Prelude to Independence*, pp. 29–30.
46. Blanchet, *L'Itinéraire des Partis Africains Depuis Bamako*, p. 23. Blanchet also notes that sixty-one of the seventy members of the Ivory Coast Territorial Assembly, and forty out of the sixty members in Niger, were civil servants (p. 22).
47. See Segal, *Political Africa*, *passim*.
48. Mansur, *op. cit.*, p. 32.
49. Rose, *Socialism in Southern Asia*, p. 96.
50. Overstreet and Windmiller, op. cit. pp. 129, 155.
51. Rose, *op. cit.*, p. 39.
52. Clément, 'Patrice Lumumba (Stanleyville 1952–3)', *Présence Africaine*, Vol. XL, pp. 69–70.
53. *Congo, My Country.*
54. Cited in Coleman, *op. cit.*, p. 201.
55. Coleman, *op. cit.*, Table XXIV, pp. 382–3.
56. Smythe and Smythe, *The New Nigerian Elite*, pp. 83, 85.
57. *NEPU 'Sawaba' Manifesto*, and *Manifesto of the Northern Elements Progressive Union for the 1959 Federal Elections*, *passim* (my italics.)
58. *Sawaba Declaration of Principles*, Kano, n.d.
59. Table and footnote from Smythe and Smythe, *op. cit.*, Table XV, p. 81.
60. Table and footnotes from Hunter, *op. cit.*, Table XIII, p. 285.
61. Lipset, *op. cit.*, p. 193.
62. Lipset, *op. cit.*, p. 370.
63. Hunter, *op. cit.*, p. 252.
64. *op. cit.*, p. 245.
65. *op. cit.*, p. 255.
66. Majhemout Diop, in his *Contribution à l'Etude des Problèmes Politiques en Afrique Noire*, uses a Soviet style of analysis in asserting the presence of *objective* class divisions in African societies, even if 'subjective' class consciousness has not yet developed. His picture of the composition of the 'petty bourgeoisie', however, is interesting, starting as it does with intellectuals, and students, and the liberal

339

professions; going on to artisans, employees, and small tradesmen; and concluding with semi- and 'lumpen'-proletarians! When he comes to the bourgeoisie proper, he points out that it is a peculiarly 'bureaucratized', and not a 'compradore' bourgeoisie, consisting as it does of 'some 200 ministers, directors and chefs de cabinets . . . whose material and social situation, in relation to the rest of the population, is relatively the same as that of the "200 Families" in France.' What he is describing, in fact, is a 'new class', a privileged political *élite* – not a classic 'bourgeoisie' (*op. cit.*, p. 245).

67. Fawzi, *The Labour Movement in the Sudan, 1945–1955*, p. 9.
68. *East Africa Royal Commission 1953–1955, Report*, p. 203.
69. From Hodgkin, *op. cit.*, p. 118.
70. Acquah, *Accra Survey*, p. 64.
71. *Tribesmen or Townsmen*, p. 91.
72. See Watson, *Tribal Cohesion in a Money Economy*, and Elkan, *Migrants and Proletarians*.
73. See, for example, *Economic Development and Tribal Change*, ed. Richards.
74. See Epstein, *Politics in an Urban African Community*, and Mitchell, *The Kalela Dance*, Rhodes-Livingstone Paper No. 27.
75. Kuper, Watts, and Davies, *Durban*, p. 54 (Table V), and p. 59.
76. Fawzi, *op. cit.*, p. 10.
77. See Mayer's excellent discussion of the psychology and life-pattern of the Xhosa residents of East London, South Africa, in his *Tribesmen or Townsmen*.
78. *op. cit.*, pp. 133–4.
79. *op. cit.*, pp. 81–9.
80. *Report*, p. 205.
81. See Little, 'The Role of Voluntary Associations in West African Urbanization', *American Anthropologist*, Vol. 59, No. 3, pp. 579–96.
82. Busia, *A Social Survey of Sekondi-Takoradi*, p. 114.
83. Kahin, *op. cit.*, p. 24.
84. From Banton, *West African City; a study of tribal life in Freetown*, p. xiii.
85. Segal, 'The Creeping Tragedy of South Africa', *New Statesman*, Vol. LVII, No. 1459, p. 300.
86. *East Africa Royal Commission Report*, p. 205.
87. Fawzi, *op. cit.*, p. 12.
88. Davidson, *The African Awakening*, pp. 130–2.
89. Mayer, *op. cit.*, p. 215.
90. Senghor, *op. cit.*, p. 77.
91. *East Africa Royal Commission Report*, Appendix IX.
92. Cohn, *The Pursuit of the Millennium*, pp. 28–9.

93. Marris, *Family and Social Change in an African City*, p. 69.
94. Rudé, *The Crowd in the French Revolution*, pp. 18–19.
95. See Thrasher's classic study, *The Gang*, and Allsop's recent book, *The Bootleggers*, particularly pp. 225–7.
96. Coleman, *op. cit.*, p. 143, Table 18, and pp. 332–4, Table 21.
97. See Bello, *My Life, passim*.
98. *Texte des Interviews* . . ., interview given to Mr Kempstone, correspondent of the *Washington Star*; question 42, p. 38.
99. Fanon, *Les Damnés de la Terre*, p. 32.
100. Mannheim, *Ideology and Utopia*, p. 36.
101. *Agrarian Socialism.*
102. Inadequately discussed by Lipset at pp. 119–20, where he underestimates the significance of ideas, here, of the upsurge of egalitarian and left-democratic sentiment in the favourable wartime climate.
103. *op. cit.*, p. 18.
104. See Macpherson's *Democracy in Alberta*. Why prairie radicalism in Saskatchewan turned *Left*, and that in Alberta turned *Right*, is a fascinating question of comparative sociology that Canadian sociologists do not appear to have asked themselves. The answers would appear to lie primarily in the differences in the nature of the economy in the two adjoining Provinces.
105. 'Small Businessmen, Political Tolerance, and Support for McCarthy'. *American Journal of Sociology*, Vol. 64, 1958, pp. 270–81.
106. *op. cit.*, p. 223.
107. *op. cit.*, p. 246.
108. *op. cit.*, p. 225.
109. In the Preface to Venturi, *The Roots of Revolution*, p. xxix.
110. Senghor, *Rapport* . . . *au Congrès Constitutif du PFA*, p. 16.
111. Mamadou Dia, *Réflexions* . . ., p. 88.
112. Mamadou Dia, *L'Economie Africaine* . . ., p. 37.
113. Colson, 'Native Cultural and Social Patterns in Central Africa', in *Africa Today*, ed. Haines.

NOTES TO CHAPTER FIVE

1. *Texte des Interviews* . . ., pp. 108, 107.
2. Debbasch, 'La Tunisie à l'An III de l'Indépendance', *Révue Juridique et Politique d'Outre-Mer*, Vol. XIII, 1959, p. 427.
3. As Talmon argues in his volumes on *The History of Totalitarian Democracy*.

4. *L'Action Politique du Parti Démocratique de Guinée*, Tome V, pp. 56–57 (italics in original).

5. *La Guinée et l'Emancipation Africaine*, p. 188.

6. *La Lutte du Parti Démocratique de Guinée pour l'Emancipation Africaine*, pp. 72–3 (italics in original).

7. 'The Future of African Nationalism', *Tribune*, London, 27 May, 1960.

8. *loc. cit.*,

9. *Observer*, London, 3 June, 1962.

10. *loc. cit.*

11. Myrdal, *Beyond the Welfare State*, p. 99. See also my 'Bureaucracy and Decolonization: Democracy from the Top', in Horowitz, ed., *The New Sociology*.

12. Malcolm, *Sukumaland*, pp. 20–2.

13. Andrzejewski, in his *Military Organization and Society*, has examined the way in which the pyramid of social stratification varies according to the extent to which the masses participate in the prosecution of war (the 'military participation ratio').

14. *The Man on Horseback.*

14a. *The Philosophy of the Revolution*, pp. 11, 13, 17.

15. See Cook, *The Warfare State.*

16. *Op. cit.*, Chapter 2.

17. D. Mackenzie Brown, 'Traditional Concepts of Indian Leadership', in *Leadership and Political Institutions in India*, ed. Park and Tinker, pp. 6–7.

18. *loc. cit.*, p. 7.

19. *Op. cit.*, p. 8.

20. Smith, *Islam in Modern History*, pp. 46–7.

21. According to Carnell, *The Politics of the Developing Areas*, p. 119, this has been argued by S. G. Khan Abbasi and A. de Z. Abbasi in their *The Structure of Islamic Polity*, Part 1: the one-party system in Islam. I have not been able to consult this work.

22. For Europe, cf. Neumann's important distinction between Nazi totalitarianism and earlier 'absolutisms', in *Behemoth*, pp. 275–81.

23. For two useful brief sketches of the British Crown Colony system as a monocentric political system, see Emerson (Harvard political scientist), *op. cit.*, pp. 230–1, and Aaronovitch (Communist Party official), *Crisis in Kenya*, pp. 28–9.

24. Blanksten, 'Fidel Castro and Latin America', *The Revolution in World Politics*, ed. Kaplan, p. 116.

25. Cole, *Studies in Class Structure*, p. 650.

26. In *The New Class.*

27. See Burnham, *The Managerial Revolution*; Berle and Means, *The*

Modern Corporation and Private Property; Berle, *Power Without Property*; Florence, *The Logic of British and American Industry*, and *Ownership, Control, and the Success of Large Companies*; Crosland, *The Conservative Enemy*, Chapter 5; *The Insiders*; Barratt-Brown, 'The Controllers', *Universities and Left Review*, 5, pp. 53–61, and 'Crosland's Enemy', *New Left Review*, 19, pp. 23–31.

28. For the USSR, see Deutscher, *Soviet Trade Unions*.
29. Sékou Touré, 'La Lutte Syndicale', in *La Guinée et l'Emancipation Africaine*, pp. 16, 17, 25, 29 (italics in original).
30. *Ghana Times*, Accra, 11 April, 1960.
31. See Zolberg, 'Politics in the Ivory Coast', *West Africa*, 30 July, 1960, p. 847; 6 August, 1960, p. 88; and 20 August, 1960, p. 939, for an illuminating account of Houphouët-Boigny's methods of maintaining ascendancy over his party, and his skill in diverting opposition by the judicious dispensation of patronage.
32. Debbasch, *op. cit.*, pp. 415–16.
33. Quoted from the 1946 programme of the RDA in Mansur, *op. cit.*, p. 92.
34. Gabriel D'Arboussier (Senegal) 1950.
35. Taieb Mehri (Tunisia) 1956.
36. Sékou Touré (Guinea) 1959.
37. Julius Nyerere (Tanganyika) 1960.
38. Madeira Keita (Mali) 1960.
39. Fischer, 'Quelques Aspects de la Doctrine Politique Guinéenne', *Civilizations*, Vol. IX, pp. 457–74; Wallerstein, 'L'idéologie du Parti Démocratique Guinéenne', *Présence Africaine*, Vol. XL, pp. 44–56.
40. Gigon, *Guinée, Etat-Pilote*, pp. 37–8.
41. Quoted in Segal, *African Profiles*, p. 238.
42. Quoted in Buchanan, 'The Third World – Its Emergence and Contours', *New Left Review*, 18, January–February, 1963, p. 9.
43. Facts in the last two paragraphs drawn from Dumont, *L'Afrique Noire est Mal Partie*.
44. See Newton's excellent discussion of the glamour of the artist 'sprung from the unskilled poor', in *The Jazz Scene*, pp. 205–9.
45. Kahin, *Nationalism and Revolution in Indonesia*, pp. 301–2.
46. Kornhauser, *The Politics of Mass Society*.
47. Mills, *The Power Elite*, p. 304.
48. J. D. Mayne, *A Treatise on Hindu Law and Usage*, ed. N. C. Aiyer, Madras, 1950, p. 44, cited in Bottomore, *Sociology*, p. 238. Bottomore goes on to cite the opinion of K. M. Kapadia that 'the British courts were accepting, for nineteenth-century conditions, the law as it had been expounded in the eleventh and twelfth centuries' (*loc. cit.*).

49. Gluckman, *The Judicial Process Among the Barotse of Northern Rhodesia*.

50. In *Crime and Custom in Savage Society*.

51. Turner, *Schism and Continuity in an African Village Society*.

52. See Dube, *India's Changing Villages*, or almost any of the growing literature on 'Community Development'.

53. 'The African and Democracy', in *Africa Speaks*, ed. Duffy and Manners, pp. 29, 30, 34.

54. See for example, Allan, Gluckman, Peters and Trapnell, *Land Holding and Land Usage Among the Plateau Tonga of Mazabuka District*, esp. Chapter VIII.

55. Lipset, *Political Man, passim*.

56. *Congo: Prelude to Independence*, pp. 85–108; and Biebuyck and Douglas, *Congo: Tribes and Parties*, both give (sometimes contradictory) details of the ethnic composition of the Congolese political parties.

57. Nyerere, 'The Future of African Nationalism', *loc. cit.*

58. Norman D. Palmer and Irene Tinker, 'Decision Making in the Indian Parliament', in *Leadership and Political Institutions in India* ed. Park and Tinker, p. 124.

59. Bottomore, *op. cit.*, p. 142.

60. *Ibid.*, p. 88.

61. *Op. cit.*, p. 159.

62. See Bailey's recent study *Politics and Social Change in Orissa in 1959*.

63. See E. Kathleen Gough's study, 'The Social Structure of a Tanjore Village', in *Village India*, ed. Marriott, pp. 36–52.

64. Lipset, *op. cit.*, pp. 124–6 and Table VI.

65. Hobsbawm, 'The Most Critical Area in the World', *Listener*, No. 1779, 2 May, 1963, pp. 735–7.

66. Sartre, 'Ideology and Revolution', *Studies on the Left*, Vol. 1, No. 3, 1960, pp. 7–16, and Guevara, 'Notes for the Study of the Ideology of the Cuban Revolution', *ibid.* pp. 75–85.

67. *Rebellion in the Backlands (Os Sertões)*.

68. 'The Anatomy of Violence', *New Society*, Vol. I, No. 28, pp. 16–18.

69. Blanksten, *Perón's Argentina*, p. 269.

70. 'Patterns of Rural Rebellion in Morocco', *European Journal of Sociology*, Vol. III, No. 2, pp. 297–311.

71. Kilson, 'The Rise of Nationalist Organizations. . . .' in Davis, *Africa as Seen by American Negroes*, p. 57.

72. See my 'One-Party Democracy', *Listener*, 4 August, 1960, pp. 171–3.

73. Figures from C. C. Wrigley, 'African Farming in Buganda', paper cited in Hunter, *op. cit.*, p. 99.

74. 'The Future of African Nationalism', *loc. cit.*

75. I have not discussed the 'philosophy' of 'personalism', elevated to

the level of received state ideology in Ngo's Viet Nam, as a 'Third World ideology' because (a) it is obscurantist rubbish (b) it is only a sugared rationalization of what is, in reality, a straightforward Right-totalitarian regime (see Donnell, 'National Renovation Campaigns in Viet Nam', *Pacific Affairs*, Vol. XXXII, pp. 73–88.)

76. See Sékou Touré's remarks in *La Planification Economique* . . ., where he rejects the idea of nationalizing key foreign-owned mines, but urges instead the development of the rest of the economy under socialist planning. The same position has been adopted by the Kenya African National Union, which, in a recent policy statement declared 'that there are more urgent tasks for Kenya's scarce capital resources than buying out private owners'.

77. Overstreet and Windmiller, *op. cit.*, p. 533.

78. *Op. cit.*, p. 536 (my italics).

79. See *Fidel Castro Denounces Sectarianism.*

80. In his *Eloge du Colonialisme*, Chapter I.

81. The sub-title of a recent American work, Osanka's *Modern Guerilla Warfare: Fighting Communist Guerillas, 1941–1961*, is illuminating.

82. Brenan, *The Spanish Labyrinth.*

83. See Thomson, *Democracy in France*, Chapter II: 'The Social Bases'.

84. See Christopher Fyfe's letter in *West Africa*, No. 2264, 22 October, 1960, p. 1198.

85. 'Portent at Kissidougou', *West Africa*, No. 2272, 17 December 1960, p. 1429.

86. Neumann, *op. cit.*, p. 383.

87. Mills, *The Sociological Imagination*, p. 46.

NOTES TO CHAPTER SIX

1. *Spearhead*, Vol. 1, No. 4, February 1962, p. 12.

2. *Ghana: the Autobiography of Kwame Nkrumah*, p. 290.

3. See Wertheim, *Indonesian Society in Transition*, p. 333.

4. *Rapport . . . sur la Doctrine et la Programme du PFA*, p. 67.

5. UNESCO, *The Development of Higher Education in Africa.*

6. Tables from Hunter, *op. cit.*, p. 62.

7. See Pierre Chaleur, 'La Guinée apres Trois Ans de l'Indépendence', *Etudes*, pp. 202–15; and Decraene's articles in *Le Monde*, (weekly edition) Nos. 689, 690, and 691, December 1961 and January 1962.

8. *Rapport . . . au Congrès Constitutif du PFA*, p. 47 (my italics).

9. 'The Third World – Its Emergence and Contours', *New Left Review*, No. 18, Jan–Feb, 1963, p. 22.

10. Ly, *Les Masses Africaine et l'actuelle Condition Humaine*. See also Balandier, 'Les Mythes politiques de colonisation et de décolonisation en Afrique', *Cahiers Internationaux de Sociologie*, Vol. XXIII, pp. 85–96.

11. Nyerere, 'Scramble for Africa', *Spearhead*, February 1962, pp. 14–15 (italics in original).

12. Press release, Tanganyika Information Series, 4 February, 1963 (italics in original).

13. *Guardian*, London, 19 April, 1963.

14. Quoted in Fanon, *Les Damnés de la Terre*, p. 51.

15. Touré, *Texte des Interviews . . .*, Question 86, p. 63.

16. Al-Fāsi, *op. cit.*, p. 399 (my italics).

17. Legum, *op. cit.*, Chapter V, 'Africa's Divided Workers'.

18. Legum, *op. cit.*, p. 91.

19. Segal, 'The Free World's Other Face', in *Africa Speaks*, p. 205.

20. Lockwood, *The Black-Coated Worker*, Chapter V.

21. *Studies in Class Structure*, p. 145 (italics in original). See also Gluckman, *Custom and Conflict in Africa*, and Coser, *The Functions of Social Conflict*, for more general analyses of the significance of conflict in social organization.

22. Mills, *The Sociological Imagination*, p. 46.

23. *Chinese Philosophy in Classical Times*, ed. Hughes, p. 23.

24. St John suggests that Mohamed Heikal was, in fact, responsible for much of the writing of *The Philosophy of The Revolution* (*The Boss*, pp. 162–5).

25. St John, *op. cit.*, pp. 160, 209–11. Baulin's chapter on 'Nasser and Neutralism' in his book, *The Arab Role in Africa*, fails to take adequate account of these stimuli from India and Yugoslavia.

26. *Guardian*, London, 11 October, 1961.

26a. Alavi and Khusro, 'Pakistan: the Burden of US Aid,' *New University Thought*, Vol. 2, No. 4, pp. 14–48.

27. President Abboud of the Sudan Republic (a general and a dictator) at the Belgrade Conference.

28. Myrdal, *Beyond the Welfare State*.

29. Bernal, *World Without War*, pp. 243–50, Tables XX and XXI, Maps I and II.

30. See Singleton and Topham, *Workers' Control in Yugoslavia*.

31. Lean, 'An International Newspaper', *Listener*, 2 May, 1963, pp. 737–8.

32. UNESCO, *The Development of Higher Education in Africa*, pp. 15–16.

33. Sigerist, *Socialized Medicine in the Soviet Union*.

34. Abrams, 'The Failure of Social Reform, 1918–1920', *Past and Present*, 24, p. 58.

35. See the chapter 'Joseph's Policy', in Moussa, *The Under-privileged Nations*.

36. See Gellner, 'Time and Theory in Social Anthropology', *Mind*, Vol. LXVII, pp. 182–202.

37. Mannheim, *Ideology and Utopia*.

38. See Hughes' *Consciousness and Society*.

BIBLIOGRAPHY

AARONOVITCH, S. 1947. *Crisis in Kenya* (Lawrence and Wishart, London)

ABRAMS, PHILIP. 1963. 'The Failure of Social Reform, 1918-1920', *Past and Present*, 24, pp. 43-64

ACQUAH, IONE. 1958. *Accra Survey:* a social survey of the capital of Ghana (University of London Press)

ALLEG, HENRI. 1958. *The Question* (John Calder, London)

AHMED, JAMAL MOHAMMED. 1960. *The Intellectual Origins of Egyptian Nationalism* (Oxford University Press)

AL-FĀSI, ALAL. 1954. *The Independence Movements in Arab North Africa* (American Council of Learned Societies, Washington, D.C.)

ALLAN, W., GLUCKMAN, M., PETERS, D. U., and TRAPNELL, C. G. 1948. *Land Holding and Land Usage Among the Plateau Tonga of Mazabuka District*, Rhodes-Livingstone Paper No. 14 (Oxford University Press)

ALLSOP, KENNETH. 1961. *The Bootleggers and their era* (Doubleday, New York)

ANDERSON, PERRY. 1962. 'Portugal and the end of ultra-Colonialism', *New Left Review*, 15, pp. 83-102; 16, pp. 88-122; 17, pp. 85-114

ANDRZEJEWSKI, S. 1954. *Military Organisation and Society* (Routledge and Kegan Paul, London)

ARENDT, HANNAH. 1958. *The Origins of Totalitarianism* (Allen and Unwin, London)

AWOLOWO, CHIEF OBAFEMI. 1960. *Awo:* the Autobiography of Chief Obafemi Awolowo (Cambridge University Press)

BAILEY, F. G. 1963. *Politics and Social Change in Orissa in 1959* (University of California Press)

BAKER, E. C. 1946. 'Mumiani', *Tanganyika Notes and Records*, No. 21. Dar es Salaam

BALANDIER, GEORGES. 1962. 'Les Mythes politiques de colonisation et de décolonisation en Afrique', *Cahiers Internationaux de Sociologie*, Vol. XXIII, pp. 85-96

BANTON, MICHAEL. 1957. *West African City:* a study of tribal life in Freetown (Oxford University Press)

BARRATT-BROWN, MICHAEL. 1958. 'The Controllers', *Universities and Left Review*, 5, pp. 53–61

—, 1963. 'Crosland's Enemy', *New Left Review*, 19, pp. 23–31

BAULIN, JACQUES. 1962. *The Arab Role in Africa* (Penguin Books, Harmondsworth)

BELL, DANIEL. 1960. *The End of Ideology:* on the exhaustion of political ideas in the Fifties (Free Press, Glencoe)

BELLO, ALHAJI, SIR AHMADU. 1962. *My Life* (Cambridge University Press)

BENEDICT, RUTH. 1959. *Race and Racism* (Routledge and Kegan Paul, London)

BERLE, A. A. 1960. *Power Without Property:* a new development in American political economy (Sidgwick and Jackson, London)

BERLE, A. A., and MEANS, G. C. 1933. *The Modern Corporation and Private Property* (Macmillan, New York)

BERNAL, J. D. 1958. *World without War* (Routledge and Kegan Paul, London)

BERTIER DE SAUVIGNY, G. DE. 1959. *Metternich et son Temps* (Hachette, Paris)

BIEBUYCK, DANIEL, and DOUGLAS, MARY. 1961. *Congo: Tribes and Parties*, Royal Anthropological Institute Pamphlets No. 1, London

BLANCHET, ANDRÉ. 1958. *L'Itinéraire des Partis Africains Depuis Bamako* (Plon, Paris)

BLANKSTEN, GEORGE. 1953. *Péron's Argentina* (University of Chicago Press)

BLOCH, MARC. 1961. *Feudal Society* (Routledge and Kegan Paul, London)

BORKENAU, FRANZ. 1962. *World Communism:* a history of the Communist International (University of Michigan Press)

BOTTOMORE, T. B. 1962. *Sociology:* a guide to problems and literature (Allen and Unwin, London)

BRANSON, CLIVE. 1944. *British Soldier in India* (Communist Party, London)

BRENAN, GERALD. 1960. *The Spanish Labyrinth:* an account of the social and political background of the Spanish Civil War (Cambridge University Press)

BUCHANAN, KEITH, 1963. 'The Third World – Its Emergence and Contours', *New Left Review*, 18, pp. 5–23

BURNHAM, JAMES. 1942. *The Managerial Revolution:* or what is happening in the world now (Putnam, London)

BURRIDGE, KENELM. 1960. *Mambu:* a Melanesian millennium (Methuen, London)

BUSIA, K. 1950. *Report on Social Survey of Sekondi-Takoradi* (Crown Agents for the Colonies, London)

CAMOENS, LUIS DE. *The Lusiads,* Englished by Richard Francis Burton (Quaritch, London)

CARNELL, F. (ed.) 1961*. The Politics of the New States:* a selected annotated bibliography with special reference to the Commonwealth (Oxford University Press)

CARTER, GWENDOLEN M. (ed.) 1962. *African One-Party States* (Cornell University Press, Ithaca, New York)

CASTRO, FIDEL. 1962. *Fidel Castro denounces Sectarianism* (Ministry of Foreign Relations, Havana)

CÉSAIRE, AIMÉ. 1956. *Cahier d'un Retour au Pays Natal* (Présence Africaine, Paris)

CHALEUR, PIERRE. 1961. 'La Guinée après Trois Ans de l'Indépendance', *Etudes,* November, pp. 202–215

CHÉVERNY, JULIEN. 1961. *Eloge du Colonialisme:* essais sur les révolutions d'Asie (Juillard, Paris)

CHURCH, R. J. HARRISON. 1960. 'Mauritania and her Neighbours', *West Africa,* 2267, 12 November, p. 1278; 'Drinks in the Desert', *West Africa,* 2271, 10 December, p. 1393.

CLARK, J. G. D. 1946. *From Savagery to Civilization* (Cobbett Press, London)

CLÉMENT, PIERRE. 1962. 'Patrice Lumumba (Stanleyville, 1952–1953)', *Présence Africaine,* Vol. XL pp. 69–70

CLISSOLD, STEPHEN. 1961. *The Seven Cities of Cíbola:* the early Spanish explorations to North America (Eyre and Spottiswoode, London)

COHN, NORMAN. 1957. *The Pursuit of the Millennium:* a history of popular religious and social movements from the eleventh to the sixteenth century (Secker and Warburg, London)

COLE, G. D. H. 1955. *Studies in Class Structure* (Routledge and Kegan Paul, London)

COLEMAN, JAMES S. 1958. *Nigeria:* background to nationalism (University of California Press, Berkeley)

COLLIER, JOHN. 1947. *Indians of the Americas:* the long hope (Mentor, New York)

COLSON, ELIZABETH, and GLUCKMAN, MAX (ed.) 1957. *Seven Tribes of British Central Africa* (Oxford University Press)

COOK, FRED J. 1963. *The Warfare State* (Cape, London)

COPE, R. K. No date. *Comrade Bill:* the life and times of W. H. Andrews, Workers' Leader (Stewart Printing Company, Cape Town)

COSER, LEWIS. 1956. *The Functions of Social Conflict* (Routledge and Kegan Paul, London)

COULTHARD, G. R. 1963. *Race and Colour in Caribbean Literature* (Oxford University Press)

CROSLAND, C. A. R. 1962. *The Conservative Enemy:* a programme of radical reform for the 1960s (Cape, London)

CROZIER, BRIAN. 1961. 'Six Africans in Search of a Personality', *Encounter*, Vol. 16, May, pp. 37–45

DA CUNHA, EUCLIDES. 1944. *Rebellion in the Backlands (Os Sertões)*, (University of Chicago Press)

D'ARBOUSSIER, GABRIEL. 1949. 'Une Dangéreuse Mystification: la Théorie de la Négritude', *La Nouvelle Critique*, 7, pp. 34–47

DAVIDSON, BASIL. 1955. *The African Awakening* (Cape, London)

—, 1959. *Old Africa Rediscovered* (Gollancz, London)

DAVIS, JOHN A. (ed.) 1958. *Africa as seen by American Negroes* (Présence Africaine, Paris)

DEBBASCH, CHARLES. 1959. 'La Tunisie à L'An III de L'Indépendance', *Révue Juridique et Politique d'Outre-Mer*, Vol. XIII

DECRAENE, PHILIPPE. 1961. *Le Panafricanisme* (Presses Universitaires de France)

DEGRAFT-JOHNSON, J. C. 1954. *African Glory:* the story of vanished Negro civilizations (Watts, London)

DESAI, A. R. 1948. *The Social Background of Indian Nationalism* (Oxford University Press, Bombay)

DEUTSCHER, ISAAC. 1950. *Soviet Trade Unions:* their place in Soviet Labour Policy (Royal Institute of International Affairs, London)

DIA, MAMADOU. 1957. *L'Economie Africaine:* études et problèmes nouveaux (Presses Universitaires de France, Paris)

—, 1958. *Contribution à l'etude du Mouvement Coopératif en Afrique Noire* (Présence Africaine, Paris)

—, 1960. *Reflexions sur l'Economie de l'Afrique Noire* (Présence Africaine, Paris)

—, 1960. *Nations Africaines et Solidarité Mondiale* (Presses Universitaires de France, Paris) translated as: 1962: *The African Nations and World Solidarity* (Thames and Hudson, London)

DIOP, CHEIKH ANTA. 1955. *Nations Nègres et Culture* (Editions Africaines, Paris)

DIOP, MAJHEMOUT. 1958. *Contribution à l'Etude des Problèmes Politiques en Afrique Noire* (Présence Africaine, Paris)

DJILAS, MILOVAN. 1957. *The New Class:* an analysis of the Communist system (Thames and Hudson, London)

DOBB, MAURICE. 1947. *Studies in the Development of Capitalism* (Routledge, London)

DONNELL, JOHN C. 1959 'National Renovation Campaigns in Viet Nam', *Pacific Affairs*, Vol. XXXII, pp. 73–88

DUBE, S. C. 1958. *India's Changing Villages:* human factors in community development (Routledge and Kegan Paul, London)

DUFFY, JAMES, and MANNERS, ROBERT A. (ed.) 1961. *Africa Speaks* (Van Nostrand, Princeton)

DUMONT, RENÉ. 1962. *L'Afrique Noire est Mal Partie* (Editions du Seuil, Paris)

DUTT, R. PALME. 1940. *India Today* (Gollancz, London)

DUTT, ROMESH. 1901. *The Economic History of India under Early British Rule* (Kegan Paul, Trench, Trubner, London)

—, 1904. *The Economic History of India in the Victorian Age* (Kegan Paul, Trench, Trubner, London)

ELKAN, W. 1960. *Migrants and Proletarians:* urban labour in the economic development of Uganda (Oxford University Press)

ELKINS, STANLEY M. 1959. *Slavery:* a problem in American institutional and intellectual life (University of Chicago Press)

EMERSON, RUPERT. 1960. *From Empire to Nation:* the rise to self-assertion of Asian and African peoples (Harvard University Press, Cambridge, Mass)

EPSTEIN, A. L. 1958. *Politics in an Urban African Community* (Manchester University Press)

EVANS-PRITCHARD, E. E. 1940. *The Nuer:* a description of the modes of livelihood and political institutions of a Nilotic people (Clarendon Press, Oxford)

—, 1949. *The Sanusi of Cyrenaica* (Clarendon Press, Oxford)

FALL, BERNARD. 1960. *Le Viet-Minh:* La République Démocratique du Viet-Nam, 1945–60 (Colin, Paris)

FANON, FRANTZ. 1962. *L'An V de la Révolution Algérienne* (Maspéro, Paris)

—, 1961. *Les Damnés de la Terre* (Maspéro, Paris)

FAWZI, SAAD EL DIN. 1957. *The Labour Movement in the Sudan, 1945–1955* (Oxford University Press)

FEITH, HERBERT. 1958. *The Wilopo Cabinet, 1952–1953,* a turning point in post-revolutionary Indonesia, Modern Indonesia Project, South-East Asia Program, Department of Far Eastern Studies (Cornell University Press, Ithaca, New York)

FINER, S. E. 1962. *The Man on Horseback:* the role of the military in politics (Pall Mall, London)

FISCHER, GEORGES. 1959. 'Quelques Aspects de la Doctrine Politique Guinéenne', *Civilisations*, Vol. IX, No. 4, pp. 457–74

FITZGERALD, C. P. 1954. *China:* a short cultural history (Cresset, London)

FLORENCE, P. SARGENT. 1933. *The Logic of British and American Industry:* a realistic analysis of economic structure and government (Routledge, London)

—, 1961. *Ownership Control and Success of Large Companies:* an analysis of English industrial structure and policy 1936–1957 (Sweet and Maxwell, London)

FORTES, M., and EVANS-PRITCHARD, E. E. (ed.) 1948. *African Political Systems* (Oxford University Press)

FRAENKEL, PETER. 1959. *Wayaleshi* (Weidenfeld and Nicolson, London)

FROMM, ERICH. 1960. *The Fear of Freedom* (Routledge and Kegan Paul, London)

GANN, L. H. 1958. *The Birth of a Plural Society:* the development of Northern Rhodesia under the British South Africa Company 1894–1914 (Manchester University Press)

GELLNER, ERNEST. 1958. 'Time and Theory in Social Anthropology', *Mind*, Vol. LXVII, No. 266, pp. 186–202

—, 1962. 'Pattern of Rural Rebellion in Morocco: tribes as minorities', *European Journal of Sociology*, Vol. III. No. 2, pp. 297–311

GERTH, H. H., and MILLS, C. WRIGHT (ed.) 1947. *From Max Weber: Essays in Sociology* (Routledge and Kegan Paul, London)

GIGON, FERNAND. 1959. *Guinée, Etat-Pilote* (Plon, Paris)

GLUCKMAN, MAX. 1955. *The Judicial Process amongst the Barotse of Northern Rhodesia* (Manchester University Press)

—, 1955. *Custom and Conflict in Africa* (Blackwell, Oxford)

GLUCKMAN, MAX, BARNES, J. A., and MITCHELL, CLYDE. 1949. 'The Village Headman in British Central Africa', *Africa*, Vol. 19, No. 2, pp. 89–106

GOFFMAN, ERVING. 1961. *Asylums:* essays on the social situation of mental patients and other inmates (Doubleday, New York)

GRANICK, D. 1962. *The Red Executive:* a study of the Organisation Man in Russian industry (Doubleday, New York)

GUEVARA, ERNESTO 'CHE'. 1960. 'Notes for the Study of the Ideology of the Cuban Revolution', *Studies on the Left*, Vol. 1, No. 3, pp. 75–85

HAINES, C. GROVE (ed.) 1955. *Africa Today*, Johns Hopkins Press, Baltimore.

HALL, D. G. E. 1955. *A History of South East Asia* (Macmillan, London)

HAMON, LÉO. 1959. 'Introduction à l'Etude des Partis Politiques de l'Afrique Francaise', *Révue Juridique et Politique d'Outre-Mer*, Vol. 13, pp. 147–96

HARGREAVES, J. D. 1963. *Prelude to the Partition of West Africa* (Macmillan, London)

HATTA, MOHAMMAD. 1960. *Past and Future*, Modern Indonesia Project, South-east Asia Program, Department of Far Eastern Studies (Cornell University, Ithaca, New York)

—, 1960. *Demokrasi Kita* (Pandji Masjarakat, Djakarta)

HAYS, H. R. 1959. *From Ape to Angel:* an informal history of social anthropology (Methuen, London)

HERSKOVITS, M. J. 1941. *The Myth of the Negro Past* (Harper, London)

HOBSBAWM, E. J. 1962. *The Age of Revolution: Europe, 1789–1848* (Weidenfeld and Nicolson, London)

—, 1963. 'The Anatomy of Violence', *New Society*, Vol. 1, No. 28, 11 April.

—, 1963. 'The Most Critical Area in the World', *Listener*, Vol. LXIX, No. 1779, 2 May

HODGKIN, THOMAS. 1956. *Nationalism in Colonial Africa* (Muller, London)

HOROWITZ, IRVING (ed.) 1964. *The New Sociology:* essays in social science and social theory in honor of C. Wright Mills (Oxford University Press, New York)

HUGHES, E. R. (ed. and trans.) 1950. *Chinese Philosophy in Classical Times* (Dent, London)

HUGHES, H. S. 1959. *Consciousness and Society:* the reorientation of European Social Thought 1890–1930 (MacGibbon and Kee, London)

HUNTER, GUY. 1962. *The New Societies of Tropical Africa* (Oxford University Press)

IDELL, ALBERT. (ed.) 1956. *The Bernal Díaz Chronicles:* the true story of the Conquest of Mexico (Doubleday, New York)

ITALIAANDER, ROLF. 1961. *The New Leaders of Africa* (Prentice-Hall, London)

JAHN, JANHEINZ. 1961. *Muntu:* an outline of neo-African culture (Faber, London)

KAHIN, GEORGE MCT. 1952. *Nationalism and Revolution in Indonesia* (Cornell University Press, Ithaca)

KAPLAN, MORTON A. (ed.) 1962. *The Revolution in World Politics* (Wiley, New York)

KAUNDA, KENNETH. 1962. *Zambia Shall be Free:* an autobiography (Heinemann, London)

KEDOURIE, ELIE. 1960. *Nationalism* (Hutchinson, London)

KEITA, MADEIRA. 1960. 'Le Parti Unique en Afrique', *Présence Africaine*, Vol. XXIX, pp. 3–25

KIERNAN, V. G. 'State and Nation: West Europe, Spain, Africa', *Past and Present* (forthcoming)

KOHN, HANS. 1946. *The Idea of Nationalism:* a study in its origins and background (Macmillan, New York)

BIBLIOGRAPHY

KORNHAUSER, WILLIAM. 1960. *The Politics of Mass Society* (Routledge and Kegan Paul, London)

KUPER, HILDA. 1947. *The Uniform of Colour:* a study of white-black relationships in Swaziland (University of Witwatersrand Press, Johannesburg)

KUPER, LEO, WATTS, HILSTAN; and DAVIES, RONALD. 1958. *Durban:* a study in racial ecology (Cape, London)

LAQUEUR, WALTER Z. (ed.) 1958. *The Middle East in Transition:* studies in contemporary history (Routledge and Kegan Paul, London)

LEACH, EDMUND. 1959. 'Hydraulic Society in Ceylon', *Past and Present*, 15, pp. 2–26

LEAN, TANGYE. 1963. 'An International Newspaper', *Listener*, Vol. LXIX, No. 1779, 2 May, p. 737

LEGUM, COLIN. 1962. *Pan-Africanism:* a short political guide (Pall Mall, London)

LENIN, V. I. 1936. 'Imperialism, the highest stage of capitalism', in *Selected Works*, Vol. 5 (Lawrence and Wishart, London)

LERNER, DANIEL. 1962. *The Passing of Traditional Society:* modernising the Middle East (Free Press, Glencoe)

VAN LEUR, J. C. 1955. *Indonesian Trade and Society:* essays in Asian social and economic history (van Hoeve, The Hague)

LEVENSON, JOSEPH, R. 1958. *Confucian China and its Modern Fate:* the problem of intellectual continuity (Routledge and Kegan Paul, London)

LÉVI-STRAUSS, CLAUDE. 1962. 'Crowds', *New Left Review*, 15, pp. 3–6

LIPS, JULIUS E. 1937. *The Savage hits Back*, or the White Man through native eyes (Dickson, London)

LIPSET, S. M. 1950. *Agrarian Socialism:* the Co-operative Commonwealth Federation in Saskatchewan, a study in political sociology (University of California Press, Berkeley)

—, 1963, *Political Man:* the social bases of politics (Heinemann, London)

LITTLE, KENNETH. 1957. 'The Role of Voluntary Associations in West African Urbanization', *American Anthropologist*, Vol. 59, No. 3, pp. 579–96

LOCKWOOD, DAVID. 1958. *The Black-Coated Worker:* a study in class consciousness (Allen and Unwin, London)

LUMUMBA, PATRICE, 1962. *Congo, My Country* (Barrie and Rockliffe, London)

LY, ABDOULAYE. 1950. *Les Masses Africaines et l'actuelle condition humaine* (Présence Africaine, Paris)

LYND, ROBERTS S., and LYND, HELEN MERRELL. 1929. *Middletown:* a study in American culture (Constable, London)

MACMILLAN, W. M. 1929. *Bantu, Boer and Briton:* the making of

BIBLIOGRAPHY

MACNAIR, HARLEY FARNSWORTH (ed.) 1923. *Modern Chinese History*: selected readings (Commercial Press, Shanghai)
MACPHERSON, C. B. 1953. *Democracy in Alberta*: the theory and practice of a quasi-party system (University of Toronto Press)
MALCOLM, D. W. 1953. *Sukumaland*, an African people and their country: a study of land use in Tanganyika (Oxford University Press)
MALINOWSKI, BRONISLAW. 1922. *Argonauts of the Western Pacific*: an account of native enterprise and adventure in the archipelagoes of Melanesian New Guinea (Routledge, London)
—, 1926. *Crime and Custom in Savage Society* (Kegan Paul, Trench, Trubner, London)
—, 1948. *Magic, Science and Religion*, and other essays (Doubleday, New York)
MANNHEIM, KARL. 1948. *Ideology and Utopia*: an introduction to the sociology of knowledge (Routledge and Kegan Paul, London)
MANNONI, O. 1956. *Prospero and Caliban*: a study of the psychology of colonization (Methuen, London)
MANSUR, FATMA. 1962. *The Process of Independence* (Routledge and Kegan Paul, London)
MAO-TSE-TUNG. 1950. *People's Democratic Dictatorship* (Lawrence and Wishart, London)
—, 1956. *On Contradiction* (Foreign Languages Press, Peking)
MARCUSE, HERBERT. 1958. *Soviet Marxism*: a critical analysis (Routledge and Kegan Paul, London)
MARRIOTT, MCKIM (ed.) 1955. *Village India*: studies in the Little Community (American Anthropological Association, Menasha, Wisconsin)
MARRIS, PETER. 1961. *Family and Social Change in an African City*: a study of rehousing in Lagos (Routledge and Kegan Paul, London)
MARX, KARL. 1938. *Capital*: a critical analysis of capitalist production, Vol. I (Allen and Unwin, London)
MARX, KARL, and ENGELS, FREDERICK. 1953. *On Britain* (Foreign Languages Publishing House, Moscow)
MAYER, PHILIP. 1961. *Tribesman or Townsmen*: conservatism and the process of urbanization in a South African city (Oxford University Press)
MEAD, MARGARET. 1956. *New Lives for Old*: cultural transformation, Manus, 1928–1952 (Morrow, New York)
MERTON, ROBERT K. 1957. *Social Theory and Social Structure* (Free Press, Glencoe)
MÉTRAUX, ALFRED. 1959. *Voodoo* (Deutsch, London)

357

MILLS, C. WRIGHT. 1956. *The Power Elite* (Oxford University Press, New York)

—, 1959. *The Sociological Imagination* (Oxford University Press, New York)

MISRA, B. B. 1961. *The Indian Middle Classes:* their growth in modern times (Oxford University Press)

MITCHELL, J. CLYDE. 1956. *The Kalela Dance:* aspects of social relationships among urban Africans in Northern Rhodesia, Rhodes-Livingstone Paper No. 27 (Manchester University Press)

MOTE, F. W. (ed.) 1961. *The Travels of Marco Polo* (Dell, New York)

MOUSSA, P. L. 1963. *The Under-Privileged Nations* (Beacon Press, New York)

MYRDAL, GUNNAR, 1960. *Beyond the Welfare State:* economic planning in the Welfare States and its international implications (Duckworth, London)

NASSER, GAMAL ABDEL. No date. *The Philosophy of the Revolution* (Cairo)

NEEDHAM, JOSEPH. 1954–62. *Science and Civilization in China*, Vols. 1–4 (Cambridge University Press)

NEUMANN, FRANZ. 1942. *Behemoth:* the structure and practice of National Socialism (Gollancz, London)

NEWTON, FRANCIS. 1960. *The Jazz Scene* (Jazz Book Club and Macgibbon and Kee, London)

NKRUMAH, KWAME. 1957. *Ghana: the autobiography of Kwame Nkrumah*, (Nelson, Edinburgh)

NORTHERN ELEMENTS PROGRESSIVE UNION. 1959. *Manifesto of the Northern Elements Progressive Union for the 1959 Federal Elections* (Kano)

—, (no date) *Nepu 'Sawaba' Manifesto* (Kano)

—, (no date) *Sawaba Declaration of Principles* (Kano)

NYERERE, JULIUS. 1962. 'Scramble for Africa', *Spearhead*, Vol. I, No. I, pp. 14–16 (Dar es Salaam)

—, 1962. 'How much power for a leader?' *Observer*, London, 3 June

—, 1960. 'The Future of African Nationalism', *Tribune*, London, 27 May

O'MALLEY, L. S. S. (ed.) 1941. *Modern India and the West:* a study of the interaction of their civilizations (Oxford University Press)

OSANKA, FRANKLIN M. (ed.) 1962. *Modern Guerilla Warfare:* fighting communist guerilla movements, 1941–61 (Free Press of Glencoe, New York)

OSSOWSKI, STANISLAW. 1959. 'Social Conditions and Consequences of Social Planning', *Transactions of the Fourth World Congress of Sociology*, Vol. II. pp. 199–122 (International Sociological Association, London)

OVERSTREET, GENE D., and WINDMILLER, MARSHALL. 1959. *Communism in India* (University of California Press, Berkeley)

PADMORE, GEORGE. 1956. *Pan-Africanism or Communism?* the coming struggle for Africa (Dobson, London)

PANIKKAR, K. M. 1959. *Asia and Western Dominance:* a survey of the Vasco da Gama epoch of Asian history 1498–1945 (Allen and Unwin, London)

PARK, RICHARD L., and TINKER, IRENE (ed.) 1959. *Leadership and Political Institutions in India* (Princeton University Press)

POPPER, KARL R. 1957. *The Poverty of Historicism* (Routledge and Kegan Paul, London)

—, 1962. *The Open Society and Its Enemies* (Routledge and Kegan Paul, London)

RADCLIFFE-BROWN, A. R. 1952. *Structure and Function in Primitive Society:* essays and addresses (Cohen and West, London)

RICHARDS, A. I. (ed.) 1954. *Economic Development and Tribal Change:* a study of migrant labour in Buganda (Heffer, Cambridge)

ROBINSON, R., and GALLAGHER, J. 1961. *Africa and the Victorians* (Macmillan, London)

ROSE, SAUL. 1959. *Socialism in Southern Asia* (Oxford University Press)

ROSENTHAL, ERIC (ed.) 1961. *Encyclopaedia of Southern Africa* (Warne, London)

ROUX, EDWARD. 1948. *Time Larger Than Rope:* a history of the black man's struggle for freedom in South Africa (Gollancz, London)

RUDÉ, GEORGE. 1959. *The Crowd in the French Revolution* (Clarendon Press, Oxford)

ST JOHN, ROBERT. 1961. *The Boss:* the story of Abdel Gamal Nasser (Barker, London)

SALISBURY, R. F. 1962. *From Stone to Steel:* the economic consequences of a technological change (Melbourne University Press)

SANSOM, G. B. 1950. *The Western World and Japan* (Cresset Press, London)

SARTRE, JEAN-PAUL. 1960. 'Ideology and Revolution', *Studies on the Left*, Vol. I, No. 3, pp. 7–16

SEGAL, RONALD (ed.) 1961. *Political Africa* (Stevens, London)

SEGAL, RONALD. 1962. *African Profiles* (Penguin Books, Harmondsworth)

—, 'The Creeping Tragedy of South Africa', *New Statesmen*, Vol. LVII, No. 1459, pp. 294–302

SEMMEL, BERNARD. 1960. *Imperialism and Social Reform:* English social imperial thought 1895–1914 (Allen and Unwin, London)

SENGHOR, L.-S. (ed.) 1948. *Anthologie de la Nouvelle Poésie Nègre et Malgache de Langue Française* (Presses Universitaires de France, Paris)

SENGHOR, L.-S. 1956. *Ethiopiques* (Editions du Seuil, Paris)

—, 1959. *Congrès Constitutif du PFA: Rapport sur la Doctrine et le Program du Parti* (Présence Africaine, Paris)

—, 1961. *Nocturnes* (Editions du Seuil, Paris)

SHEPPERSON, G., and PRICE, T. 1958. *Independent African:* John Chilembwe and the origins, setting and significance of the Nyasaland Native Rising of 1915 (Edinburgh University Press)

SHILS, EDWARD. 1957. 'Primordial, Personal, Sacred and Civil Ties', *British Journal of Sociology*, Vol. VIII, No. 2, pp. 130-145

SIGERIST, HENRY E. 1937. *Socialized Medicine in the Soviet Union* (Gollancz, London)

SINGLETON, FREDERICK, and TOPHAM, ANTHONY. 1963. *Workers' Control in Yugoslavia*, Fabian Research Series, 233, London

SJAHRIR, SOETAN. 1949. *Out of Exile* (Day, New York)

—, 1956. *Indonesian Socialism* (Asian Socialist Publishing House, Rangoon)

SMITH, BERNARD. 1960. *European Vision and the South Pacific, 1768–1850:* a study in the history of art and ideas (Clarendon Press, Oxford)

SMITH, WILFRED CANTWELL. 1957. *Islam in Modern History* (Princeton University Press)

SMYTHE, H. H., and SMYTHE, M. M. 1960. *The New Nigerian Elite*, (Stanford University Press, California)

SNOW, EDGAR. 1937. *Red Star Over China* (Gollancz, London)

SOEKARNO, ACHMED. 1955. *The Birth of Pantjasila:* an outline of the Five Principles of the Indonesian State (Ministry of Information, Djakarta)

—, 1960. *Marhaen and Proletarian*, Modern Indonesia Project, Southeast Asia Program, Department of Far Eastern Studies (Cornell University, Ithaca, New York)

SOUTHALL, A. W. (ed.) 1961. *Social Change in Modern Africa* (Oxford University Press)

SPICER, EDWARD H. (ed.) 1952. *Human Problems in Technological Change:* a casebook (Russell Sage Foundation, New York)

SRINIVAS, M. R. 1952. *Religion and Society Among the Coorgs of South India* (Clarendon Press, Oxford)

STALIN, J. V. 1936. *Marxism and the National and Colonial Question* (Lawrence and Wishart, London)

STRACHEY, JOHN. 1959. *The End of Empire* (Gollancz, London)

STRAUSS, ANSELM (ed.) 1959. *The Social Psychology of George Herbert Mead* (University of Chicago Press)

SUNDKLER, BENGT, G. M. 1948. *Bantu Prophets in South Africa* (Lutterworth Press, London)

TEMPELS, PLACIDE, 1959. *Bantu Philosophy* (Présence Africaine, Paris)

TALMON, J. L. 1952–60. *The History of Totalitarian Democracy* (Secker and Warburg, London)

THOMPSON, VIRGINIA and ADLOFF, RICHARD. 1958. *French West Africa* (Allen and Unwin, London)

THOMSON, DAVID. 1960. *Democracy in France:* the Third and Fourth Republics (Oxford University Press)

THRASHER, FREDERIC M. 1947. *The Gang:* a study of 1,313 gangs in Chicago (Chicago University Press)

TOURÉ, SEKOU. 1958. *La Lutte du Parti Démocratique de Guinée pour l'Emancipation Africaine* (Conakry)

—, 1959. *Texte des Interviews Accordées aux Représentants de la Presse,* (Conakry)

—, 1959. *La Guinée et l'Emancipation Africaine* (Présence Africaine, Paris)

—, 1960. *Rapport d'Orientation du Bureau Politique National,* Conférence Nationale (de planification économique) (Conakry, 1960)

TOYE, H. 1959. *The Springing Tiger* (Cassell, London)

TROW, MARTIN. 1958. 'Small Businessmen, Political Tolerance, and Support for McCarthy', *American Journal of Sociology,* Vol. 64, No. 3, pp. 270–281

TURNBULL, CLIVE. 1948. *Black War:* the extermination of the Tasmanian aborigines (Cheshire, Melbourne)

TURNER, V. W. 1957. *Schism and Continuity in an African Society:* a study of Ndembu village life (Manchester University Press)

UBEROI, J. P. SINGH. 1962. *Politics of the Kula Ring:* an analysis of the findings of Bronislaw Malinowski (Manchester University Press)

UNESCO. 1963. *The Development of Higher Education in Africa* (UNESCO, Paris)

VENTURI, FRANCO. 1960. *The Roots of Revolution:* a history of the populist and socialist movements in nineteenth century Russia (Weidenfeld and Nicolson, London)

WALEY, ARTHUR. 1958. *The Opium War Through Chinese Eyes* (Allen and Unwin, London)

WALLERSTEIN, IMMANUEL. 1962. 'L'Idéologie du Parti Démocratique Guinéenne', *Présence Africaine,* Vol. XL, pp. 44–56

WATSON, W. 1958. *Tribal Cohesion in a Money Economy:* a study of the Mambwe people of Northern Rhodesia (Manchester University Press)

WERTHEIM, W. F. 1959. *Indonesian Society in Transition:* a study of social change (Van Hoeve, The Hague)

—, 1961. 'Religious Reform Movements in Southern and South-East Asia', *Archives de Sociologie des Réligions*, No. 12, pp. 53–62

WILLMOTT, DONALD. 1960. *The Chinese of Semarang:* a changing minority community in Indonesia (Cornell University Press, Ithaca, New York)

WISCHOFF, H. A. 1941. *The Zimbabwe Monomatapa Culture in South-east Africa.* General Series in Anthropology, No. 8 (Banta, Menasha)

WITTFOGEL, KARL. 1957. *Oriental Despotism:* a comparative study of total power (Yale University Press, New Haven)

WOLF, ERIC R. 1959. *Sons of the Shaking Earth* (University of Chicago Press)

WOLFF, K. A. (ed. and trans.) 1950. *The Sociology of Georg Simmel* (Free Press, Glencoe)

WORSLEY, PETER. 1957. *The Trumpet Shall Sound:* a study of 'Cargo' cults in Melanesia (MacGibbon and Kee, London)

—, 1960. 'One Party Democracy', *Listener*, Vol. LXIV, No. 1636, 4 August

—, 1963. 'The Spread of Jazz', *Listener*, Vol. LXIX, No. 1772, 14 March

ZOLBERG, ARISTIDE, R. 1960. 'Politics in the Ivory Coast', *West Africa*, 30 July, p. 847; 6 August, p. 883; 20 August, p. 939

—, 1960. *Congo: Prelude to Independence* (African Research and Publications, London)

—, East Africa Royal Commission 1953–1955, Report, Cmd. 9475 (HMSO, London)

—, 1957. *The Insiders*, Universities and Left Review pamphlet, London.

Additional Bibliography for Chapter Seven

ANDRESKI, STANISLAV. 1966. *Parasitism and Subversion:* the case of Latin America (Weidenfeld and Nicolson, London)

BALDWIN, K. D. S. 1957. *The Niger Agricultural Project:* an experiment in African development (Blackwell, Oxford)

BENDIX, REINHARD. 1963. *Work and Authority in Industry:* ideologies of management in the course of industrialization (Harper, New York)

BRAUSCH, GEORGES, CROOKE, PATRICK and SHAW, JOHN. 1964. *Bashaqra Area Settlements 1963:* a case study in village development in the Gezira scheme (University of Khartoum)

DEUTSCHER, ISAAC. 1949. *Stalin:* a political biography (Oxford University Press, London)

FAVRET, JEANNE. 1966. 'Le Traditionnalisme par Excès de Modernité', paper presented to 6th World Congress of Sociology, Evian

FINER, S. E. 1965. 'The Military in Politics', paper presented to Conference of the Centre for Development Studies, University of Manchester

—, 1967. 'Military and Society in Latin America', *Sociological Review Monograph No. 11, Latin-American Sociological Studies*, pp. 133–151

FITCH, BOB and OPPENHEIMER, MARY. 1966. 'Ghana: End of an Illusion', *Monthly Review*, Vol. 18, No. 3, New York

GAITSKELL, ARTHUR. 1959. *Gezira:* a story of development in the Sudan (Faber and Faber, London)

HAMID, AHMED ABDEL. 1966. *The African Labour of the Gezira Scheme* (Social Development Division, Sudan Gezira Board, Musaad)

HOROWITZ, IRVING LOUIS. 1966. *Three Worlds of Development:* the theory and practice of international stratification (Oxford University Press, New York)

KENYA, REPUBLIC OF. 1965. *African Socialism and its Application to Planning in Kenya* (Government Printer, Nairobi)

MARCUS, JOHN T. 1958. *Neutralism and Nationalism in France* (Bookman Associates, New York)

MARTIN, LAWRENCE W. (ed.) 1962. *Neutralism and Nonalignment* (Praeger, New York)

MAYHEW, CHRISTOPHER. 1967. *Britain's Role Tomorrow* (Hutchinson, London)

MAZRUI, ALI. 1967. *Towards a Pax Africana:* a study of ideology and ambition (Weidenfeld and Nicolson, London)

MONCRIEFF, ANTHONY. (ed.) 1965. *Second Thoughts on Aid:* the theory, problems, practice and future of aid to under-developed countries (B.B.C. Publications, London)

MORGAN, D. J. 1965. *British Private Investment in East Africa* (Overseas Development Institute, London)

MYRDAL, GUNNAR. 1966. 'Paths of Development', *New Left Review*, No. 36, pp. 65–74

ROSZAK, THEODORE. (ed.) (forthcoming.) *Dissent in Social Science* (Pantheon Books, New York)

RUTHENBERG, HANS. 1966. *African Agricultural Production Development Policy in Kenya 1952–1965* (Springer Verlag, Berlin)

SHAW, D. J. 1964. 'Labour Problems in the Gezira Scheme', *ECA-FAO Agricultural Economics Bulletin for Africa*, No. 5, pp. 1–41

SULIMAN, ALI AHMED and SHAW, D. J. 1966. 'Problems of Income Stabilization in Developing Countries: a Case Study of the Gezira

Scheme', *ECA-FAO Agricultural Economics Bulletin for Africa*, No. 8, pp. 37–60

TINKER, HUGH. 1964. 'Broken-backed States', *New Society*, No. 70, pp. 6–7

VITTACHI, TARZIE. 1967. *The Fall of Sukarno* (Mayflower-Dell/Deutsch, London)

WOOD, ALAN. 1950. *The Groundnut Affair* (Bodley Head, London)

—, 1967. *The Arusha Declaration* and *TANU's Policy on Socialism and Self-Reliance*, (Publicity Section, TANU, Dar-Es-Salaam)

INDEX

(The subject matter is analysed under the following headings: Colonialism; Nationalism; Pluralist States; Populism; Society, World; Solidarist States)

365

of a ruling *élite*, 140-9; the *élite* in close touch with the people, 149-50; character of their leadership, 150-1; small labour forces of the backward colonial countries, 151, 152; government employment, 151-3; conditions not conducive to trade unionism, 153-6; urbanization modified by peasant traditions and ethnic ties, 156-62; conclusions on the loose class structure of the new states, 162-4; populism defined, 164-7; the Co-operative Federation of Saskatchewan, 167-9, 171, 177, 184; Social Credit in Alberta, 169-71, 177, 184; McCarthyism, 170; the communitarian ideology, 171-2; Russian populism, 172-3; the ideal of local democracy in a strong state, 173-4; flexibility of practical populism, 175-7; one-party solidarist (*q.v.*) states, 177-209; pluralist (*q.v*) states, 209-22; the possible development to liberalized communism, 222-6; or a humanist internationalism, 257-9

Portugal, 45
Poujadism, 170
Prarthana Samaj, 56
Présence Africaine, 91, 123
Price-Mars, Dr Jean, 89

Rahman, Tungku Abdul, 232
Rassemblement Démocratique Africaine, 197
Renan, on the mass party, 199
Rhodes, Cecil, 28
Rousseau, J.-J., 12
Roy, Ram Mohan, 55, 56, 57
Rwanda, 39-40

Saklatvala, Shapurji, 98
Salah, Ahmed ben, 197

Salim, Hadji, 116
Sanusi, the, 14
Saraswati, Swami Dayanand, 60
Sarekat Islam, 56, 138
Sartre, J.-P., on torture, 23; influence on *négritude*, 124; on the Cuban revolution, 216
Saskatchewan, the Co-operative Commonwealth Association, 167-9, 171, 177, 184
Sen, Keshab Chandra, 55
Senegal, 178
Senghor, Léopold Sédar-, 91, 109, 110; French influence on, 119; on Marxism, 120, 122; on New York, 124-6; on the African Man, 174; on the strength of his party, 178; a possible leader of Africa, 233; on the Sahara tests, 246
Sharma, Isharachandra, 56
Shaw, G. B., 81
Sihanouk, King, strength of his party, 178; on Viet Nam and Korea, 254
Sissako, Fili Dabo, 109
Sjahrir, Soetan, on western civilization, 20; on social democracy in Asia, 103-6, 112
Sneevliet, 94, 111
Social Democracy; failure in Indonesia, 103-8; and in Senegal, 109-10; failure of the French socialist African Deputies, 111; gradualism inadequate, 111-16
Society, World, emergence of; the gulf of mutual ignorance between old civilizations, 1-4, 9-11; and of differing mythologies, 4-6; European superiority in arms and organization, 6-9; the myth of the noble savage exploded, 11-12; final assumption of European 'natural' superiority, 13-15; the end of the European nation-state, 15; colonial resistance becomes revo-

Tonga, the, 38
Touré, Sékou, on Chinese communism, 102; French influence in his thinking, 119; on religion, 123; on social groupings, 127; his prestige, 140; on the peasants of Africa, 162; his Leninism, 179–80; a possible leader of Africa, 233; on the 'haves' and the 'have-nots', 242; on neutralism, 246; on the UN, 256
Trade unions in the new states, 153–6, 194–7
Tsushima, battle of, 18
Tunisia; strength of the one party, 178; position of trade unions, 197
Turkey, achieves her own modernization, 17–18

Uganda, strategic origin of colonization, 45
Union Générale des Travailleurs d'Afrique Noire, 195
United Africa Company, 133–4
United Nations; the influence of the new states, 255–6; the potential for a revived humanist nationalism, 257–9

United States of America; support for reactionary regimes, 185–6; growth of military influence in, 187; influence in Latin America 217

Vargas, Getulio, 215, 217
Veda Samaj, 55
Venezuela, 216
Viet Nam, 222, 254
Vivekananda, Swami, 62
Voltaire, F.-M. A. de, 11

Wahhabism, 56
Welensky, Sir Roy, 265
West Indies, 235
Westerling, 'Turk', 21
William Ponty school, 141
Williams, Sylvester, 89
Wilson, President Woodrow, 18

Youlou, Abbé Fulbert, 245
Yugoslavia; neutralist influence, 253; 'workers' control', 260

Zulu, the, 13, 39